Big Book of Everything for Third Grade

Introduction

The purpose of this book is to provide activities to supplement a third-grade curriculum. The activities are designed to heighten student interest, to provide students with a variety of experiences and to make learning specific skills and concepts exciting for students. By engaging in the stimulating and challenging activities in this book, students encounter fundamental skills which run through all areas of the curriculum, and they learn to use these skills in a wide variety of situations.

This book is organized into seven main chapters—language arts; math; science; ecology; healthy mind, healthy body; social studies and bulletin boards. An introduction at the beginning of each chapter indicates the concepts included in the activities.

Many procedures are presented in this book as a means of introducing concepts. It is hoped that the teacher who uses this book will expand upon its activities and suggestions and incorporate the many strategies of learning presented into other projects and activities outside of this book.

Suggestions for using this book:

As you look through each of the chapters in this book, select activities that correspond with your course of study. Within each chapter are several topics. Within each topic are activities designed to teach students about it. Use the activities as they are presented, modify them or add to them to make them suitable for your group. You can also adapt the activities to topics not included in this book.

The activities presented can be used on a whole-class basis, in cooperative learning groups or individually. Many are also appropriate for centers. To keep track of students' center work, make a chart including students' names down the left side and the activities across the top. You may want to keep just one chart in a central place with all ongoing centers listed on it on which students may record their results after completing each center. Or, you may want one for each center.

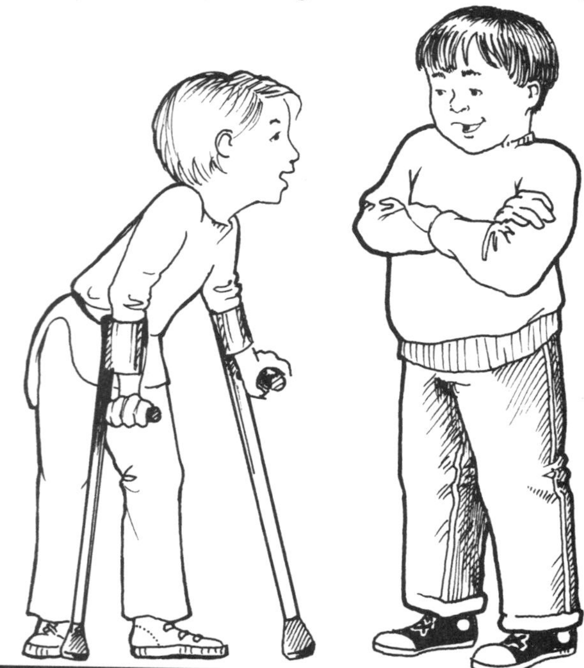

When forming cooperative learning groups, try to place students with different levels of ability and different personalities in each one. This will help all students feel greater self-confidence.

Also included are activities which call for parent involvement. Even when activities do not include them, keep parents informed of what the class is currently studying in all areas and make them feel welcome to drop in for a few minutes almost any time. To do this, send home the letter on page 3 or one similar to it at least four times a year.

____
date

Dear Parents,

We thought you would be interested in knowing what we are primarily studying at this time.

In science, we are mainly learning about ______________________________

In math, ______________________________

In language arts, ______________________________

In social studies, ______________________________

You will be informed if there is anything in particular you can do to help your child. However, if you have anything that you believe would enhance our program at this time, please let me know. Your input and assistance are most appreciated.

There may be times when you will be asked to volunteer to help with a portion of our course of study, but in the meantime, if you would like to see some of the existing activities and projects we are doing, please stop by for a glimpse of the action. So that you won't be disappointed to find us away from the room when you get here, it may be helpful to know the times when we are usually gone from the room.

time ____________ for ____________ time ____________ for ____________

time ____________ for ____________ time ____________ for ____________

time ____________ for ____________ time ____________ for ____________

An appointment for a brief visit is not necessary, but a note saying you're coming would be appreciated.

Sincerely,

____
teacher

Language Arts

Language skills run through all areas of the curriculum. They are with us throughout our lives regardless of what we become. Therefore, they are probably stressed more in school because of the vital role language plays in our lives.

Students learn to speak without ever being taught, but their grammar often needs some correcting, refining and maturing. Taking this into consideration, activities involving specific language skills have been designed for this chapter.

There are three main categories in language—reading, writing and speaking. Attention is given to other topics within each category. Some language concepts included in this book are listed below.

1. **Reading**—story elements, main idea, sequencing, cause and effect, various genres, independent skills, poetry, interpretation, description of characters, following directions
2. **Story Telling**—memorization, oral expression, sequencing
3. **Writing**—poetry, independent skills using dictionary and thesaurus, personal narrative, creative writing, expository text
4. **Grammar**—punctuation, parts of speech
5. **Listening**—following oral directions
6. **Vocabulary**—dictionary and thesaurus usage, word origins

You will find that many of the skills listed above are incorporated into every section of this book as language arts is the foundation for all learning.

Literary Magazine

Writing Genres

Objectives: To introduce students to various genres of writing and to celebrate the creative writing accomplishments of your students

Materials: copies of pages 6-12

Directions: Making a class monthly newsletter is an exciting way to motivate students to write and to encourage parents to celebrate their students' work. This is also a good activity to use to encourage parent involvement.

Discuss with the class the various types of literature. (Some examples are on pages 6-8.) They can be broadly introduced all at once with more detail added over a period of time. Show the students examples of each type of literature and read them to the class. Have the students bring in examples of the different types of literature and present them to the class.

After the students are familiar with the different types of literature, introduce the idea of publishing a class monthly literary magazine. Tell them that each month will be devoted to a specific genre of writing (i.e. October—autobiography, November—biography, December—essay, January—interview, February—reporting, March—fiction, April—poetry, May—students' choice).

Have a brainstorming session with the class to select a name for the magazine. Write all the names on the board. By class vote, narrow the selection down to three names. By secret ballot, select one of these three names.

If you have an art teacher in your school, work together with him/her and the class to develop a layout for the cover of the magazine. Students can also submit their own ideas. Selection should be by class vote. You can use the same cover each month or you can change it each month.

At the beginning of each month, describe, explain and illustrate the writing activity for the month. Give the students an outline (pages 9-11) and have them fill in the outline. Review the outlines with each student in a personal conference time. When the outline is completed to mutual satisfaction, the student will then write the expanded composition.

To encourage parent involvement, send the letter on page 12 home with the students. Send the follow-up letter as the need arises.

The magazine can be distributed throughout the school, on the grade level or just in the class. Be sure to put copies in the school library.

continued on page 6

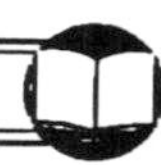

Literary Magazine continued

Writing Genres

Follow-Up: At the end of the year, after the last publication, have a Literary Tea or Author's Tea. Have students fill out the invitation on page 10 to invite parents and/or grandparents, school personnel, local senior citizen groups, etc. Have each student read a selection he/she wrote for any one of the magazines.

The class might want to prepare refreshments themselves (cookies, hot tea/iced tea), or the parents might want to provide refreshments. In any case, the students/authors should serve their guests.

Following are some types of literature you can introduce to students.

Types of Literature

FICTION an invented story; a story invented by the imagination

- **Fairy Tale**—a made-up adventure involving fantastic forces and beings such as fairies, wizards and goblins
  Suggested Reading: *Cinderella, Snow White, Jack and the Beanstalk*
- **Fables**—fiction in which animals speak and act like human beings
  Suggested Reading: *Aesop's Fables*
- **Legend**—story handed down from the past; It may be regarded as "historical," but it is not verifiable. Legends are often retold and illustrated in a variety of ways by authors.
  Suggested Reading: *The Legend of Sleepy Hollow* by Washington Irving
- **Folktale**—an anonymous, timeless and placeless tale circulated orally amongst a people; Folktales are often written down and illustrated in various ways by authors.
  Suggested Reading: *Foolish Rabbit's Big Mistake* by Rafe Martin
- **Myth**—a belief or tradition that has grown up around something or someone; It serves to show a view of people or explain a practice, belief or natural phenomena.
  Myths are also written down and illustrated by authors.
  Suggested Reading: *Classic Myths to Read Aloud* by William F. Russel
- **General Fiction**—any made-up story
  —characters and situations could be real but are not
  —characters and situations are clearly not real
  —first person invented story

NONFICTION a story based on fact

- **Autobiography**—a factual narrative about oneself
  Suggested Reading: *Zlata's Diary* by Zlata Filipovic
- **Biography**—a factual narrative about another person
  Suggested Reading: *Ray Charles* by Sharon Mathis

continued on page 7

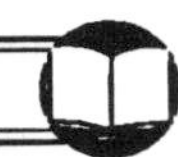

Literary Magazine continued

Writing Genres

NONFICTION continued

- **Essay**—a composition dealing with a subject from the author's point of view; a personal opinion
- **Reporting**—a factual account of an event; a factual description of a person, place or thing; a "how to" report
- **Interview**—a reporting of a conversation with one or more people for the purpose of obtaining information and/or opinion from the person or persons being interviewed
- **Personal Narrative**—a description of some place the author went to, something the author did, something the author has, likes, dislikes, etc.

POETRY Introduce the class to several different types of poetry giving an example of each and explaining the method of composing each type. Following are some examples:

- **Couplet**—a two-line rhyme

  Example: I saw a cloud up in the sky,
  It looked so very, very high.

  Practice composing couplets with the students by presenting one line and having the students give the next line. You could also give two words that rhyme and have the class compose couplets using the two rhyming words. A variation would be to have the students work in pairs. One student could compose the first line, the other providing the second line.

- **Limerick**—a humorous poem that has the rhyme scheme AA, BB, A

  Example: There was a young man from Maine A
  Who liked to stand out in the rain. A
  He got all wet. B
  He's standing there yet. B
  I really don't think he's quite sane. A

  Suggested Reading: *Limericks* by Edward Lear

  Start composing limericks with the class by presenting the first line. The class can then work individually, in small groups or as a whole to finish the limerick.

- **Quatrain**—a four-line poem

  simple rhyme schemes for quatrains: 1) AABB, 2) ABAB

  Example 1: I saw a small boy. A
  He played with his toy. A
  He sat on the floor. B
  He was near the door. B

  This can be converted to the ABAB rhyme scheme.

  Example 2: I saw a small boy. A
  He sat on the floor. B
  He played with his toy. A
  He was near the door. B

  Practice writing quatrains with students using AABB rhyme scheme. To do this, give the students two pairs of rhyming words. Have the students work individually or in pairs using the rhyming words to form a quatrain. Have students convert the quatrain into the second rhyme scheme ABAB. This procedure can also be reversed.

  Suggested Reading: Appropriate selections from *A Child's Garden of Verses* by Robert Louis Stevenson

continued on page 8

Literary Magazine continued

Writing Genres

POETRY continued

- **Haiku**—an unrhymed three-line poem; The first line consists of five syllables, the second consists of seven, and the last line contains five syllables. Often, haiku is written about nature.

  Example: Trees standing proudly
  High above the river's edge
  Oh so beautiful!

- **Diamante**—a five-line poem that is often written about change. Each line contains a specific number of words and parts of speech:

  line one: one word—noun
  line two: two words—adjectives to describe line 1
  line three: three words—verbs, pertaining to line 1
  line four: four words—nouns, with a shift on the third word
  line five: three words—verbs
  line six: two words—two adjectives indicating change
  line seven: one word—a synonym for line one, indicating change

  Example:
  ice
  blue, smooth
  shimmers, glistens, sparkles
  sculpture, skate, glasses, drinks,
  warms, softens, melts
  mushy, messy
  water

  Example:
  skateboard
  narrow, wobbly
  gliding, rolling, riding
  clicking down the bumpy sidewalk
  by wheels

- **Cinquain**—a five-line poem with specific syllabication and parts of speech; The format is as follows:

  line one: noun—two syllables
  line two: adjectives—four syllables
  line three: "ing" words—six syllables
  line four: sentence/phrase—eight syllables
  line five: synonym of line one—two syllables

- **I Am Unique**—To write this poem, students should write five lines telling what they think may make them different, or unique, from a classmate. The format is as follows:

  I am unique because ___________ .
  I am unique because ___________ .
  I am one who ___________ .
  I am one who ___________ .
  I am unique because ___________ .
  I am unique.

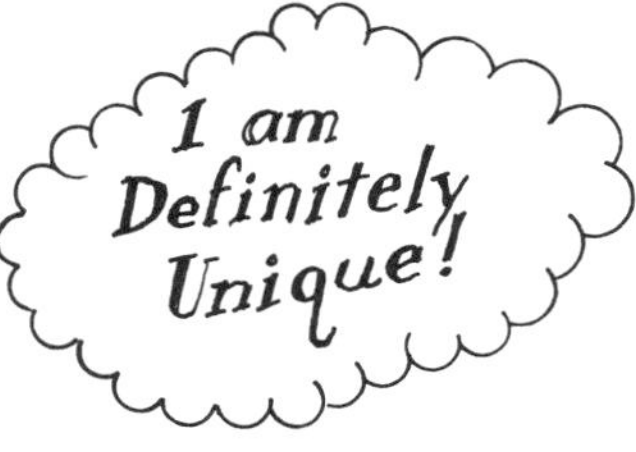

When writing these unique poems, it is helpful to have students brainstorm ten ideas, and then, perhaps after collaboration with classmates, the students could choose the five best ideas.

Example: I am unique because I have three sisters.
I am unique because I enjoy playing the cello.
I am one who loves horses.
I am one who hates carrots.
I am unique because my mom is a writer.
I am unique.

This is a wonderful activity for the beginning of the school year, and parents find it interesting when displayed at "Back to School Night."

continued on page 9

Literary Magazine continued

Writing Genres

AUTOBIOGRAPHY

Paragraphs

1. Factual details about yourself
   a. Name
   b. Age—date of birth
   c. Place of birth
2. Family
   a. Family members
   b. Something you want to relate about your family
3. An exciting or interesting event in your life
   a. Party, trip, vacation, first day of school (suggestions)
   b. How did you feel about it?
4. Opinions
   a. What do you like and/or dislike?
   b. What is something you especially enjoy doing?
   c. Hobbies

BIOGRAPHY

May be of a famous person, a friend or a family member

Paragraphs

1. Identification
   a. Name
   b. Why did you select this person?
2. Factual information
   a. Date of birth
      Date of death (if applicable)
   b. Place of birth
   c. Family information
3. What is this person famous for?
4. Some things to know about this person
   a. An important event
   b. Hobbies, interests
   c. Likes, dislikes

INTERVIEW

(Suggestions—school personnel, family members, etc.)

Paragraphs

1. Identification
   a. Who are you interviewing?
   b. Job or occupation of person you are interviewing
2. Job description
   a. What are things you do in your job?
   b. What do you like about your job?
3. Personal information
   a. What are your hobbies?
   b. What is your favorite book?
   c. What is your favorite TV show?
   d. What is your favorite food?
4. Opinions—What is your opinion about _____?

ESSAY

Paragraphs

1. What is the topic you are writing about?
   (i.e. school lunch time, length of school day, cafeteria food, clubs for students, family trip, family rules, topic of your choice)
2. What is your opinion about your topic?
   a. Positive
   b. Negative
3. Explanation
   a. Why do you feel that way?
4. Changes
   a. Would you make changes?
   b. What changes would you make (if applicable)?
   c. Why?

continued on page 10

Literary Magazine continued

Writing Genres

REPORT—EVENT

Paragraphs

1. Event
   a. What was it?
   b. Where did it take place?
   c. When did it take place?
2. Involvement
   a. Who saw this event?
   b. How were you involved?
3. Description
   a. What happened first?
   b. What happened next?
   c. How did it end?
4. Reaction
   a. What is your emotion about it?
   b. What is your opinion about it?

REPORT —TRIP

Paragraphs

1. Identification
   a. Where did you go?
   b. When did you go? How long?
   c. How did you go?
   d. With whom did you go?
   e. Why did you go?
2. Explanation
   a. What did you do?
   b. What did you see?
3. Opinions
   a. What was the best part of the trip?
   b. Would you recommend it? Why? Why not?

REPORT—"HOW TO"

Paragraphs

1. Identification
   a. What are you giving directions to?
   b. What will be the final outcome?
2. Materials
   a. What materials are needed?
   b. Where can you get the materials?
3. Directions—List and number specific step-by-step directions
4. Usage
   a. Why are you reporting this project?
   b. How can it be used/enjoyed?

You are invited
to a
Literary Tea
to meet
the Authors

Program: Third-grade authors will read from their own writings.

Peruse: The eight issues of our Literary Magazine

Refreshments: ______________

Time: ______________

Place: ______________

Literary Magazine continued

Writing Genres

FICTION

Before you complete this outline, decide if:

____ 1. Your characters and situation could be real but are not.

____ 2. Your characters and situation are clearly not real.

____ 3. You are making up a story about yourself and/or your environment.

Paragraphs

1. Introduction
   a. Who are your characters? (Not more than two)
   b. Describe your characters so that someone reading about them can visualize them.
2. Plot development—beginning
   a. What happened first?
   b. Introduce the situation, problem or conflict.
3. Plot development—middle
   a. What happened next? List the main events.
   b. How did the situation evolve?
4. Plot development—end
   a. How will the story end? (Problem solved?)
   b. What main events will lead to the conclusion?
   c. Will the conclusion be a happy one?

Major Literary Contributor!

This is to certify that

____
name

made a major contribution

to our Literary Magazine with

his/her work on ______________________________

CONGRATULATIONS!

signed______________________ date ______________

Literary Magazine continued

Writing Genres

Dear Parents,

This year, our class is going to publish a Monthly Literary Magazine. We are going to learn about and practice many different kinds of creative writing. We will have eight issues.

We need your help to successfully publish our magazine. Please indicate below in which area(s) you will be able to help and the times you will be available. Please fill out and return to school by ____________________ . Thank you for your cooperation.

Sincerely,

____

- -

_____ I can help with typing (typewriter or word processor)
months ____

_____ I can help with layout
months ____

_____ I can help with copying, collating and stapling
months ____

____

Dear Parents,

Many thanks to all of you who volunteered your time to help us publish our Literary Magazine. We still need some help in the following areas for the months indicated:

Typing/Word Processing ______________________________

Layout ______________________________

Assembly ______________________________

If you can help out in any of the above areas, it would be greatly appreciated.

Sincerely,

____

- -

Yes, I can help in the following areas during the months of ____________________:

_____ Typing/Word Processing

_____ Layout

_____ Assembly

____

Author of the Week

Writing—Bulletin Board

Objectives: To encourage creative writing and to celebrate students' work

Materials: construction paper, stapler, marker, enlarged copy of award (page 15), pictures of students, pins, copies of pages 14-15

Assembly: After you have introduced the various genres of writing to your class, discuss with them the establishment of an Author of the Week. Begin by making a bulletin board. Cover the board with any color of construction paper. In an arch at the top, write the title, **Author of the Week**. On the bottom, attach an enlarged copy of the award (page 15).

Preparation: Use a lottery system to assign each student his/her week. On Monday morning, have the photograph of the Author of the Week mounted on the bulletin board for the students to see as they arrive at school.

In advance, discuss with students the format each author will follow during his/her special week as author. On the first day, have the student present an original piece of writing of any genre including poetry, fiction, report, essay or interview. Prepare a contract (page 15) for the Author of the Week one week in advance. Prepare with the author a list of possible presentations for the remainder of the week. Some ideas include:

1. An autobiography
2. A favorite book to share
3. A funny experience to share with the class
4. A picture he/she drew
5. A list of the author's favorite things such as food, color, game, pet, school subject, sport, hobby, etc.
6. A family photograph
7. A vacation/trip experience

continued on page 14

Author of the Week continued

Send the letter home to parents (below) before initiating the program to make them aware of what is happening in your class. Send home a reminder to parents by having the students fill out the form on page 15 a week or two before he/she is to present.

Directions: On Monday, the Author of the Week sits in the author's "chair" and reads his/her writing to the class and then puts it up on the board. Each day, the author makes another presentation and adds to the bulletin board something representative of the presentation. It may just be a topic heading (i.e. My Trip to Disney World). At the end of the week, give the author the award you attached to the board.

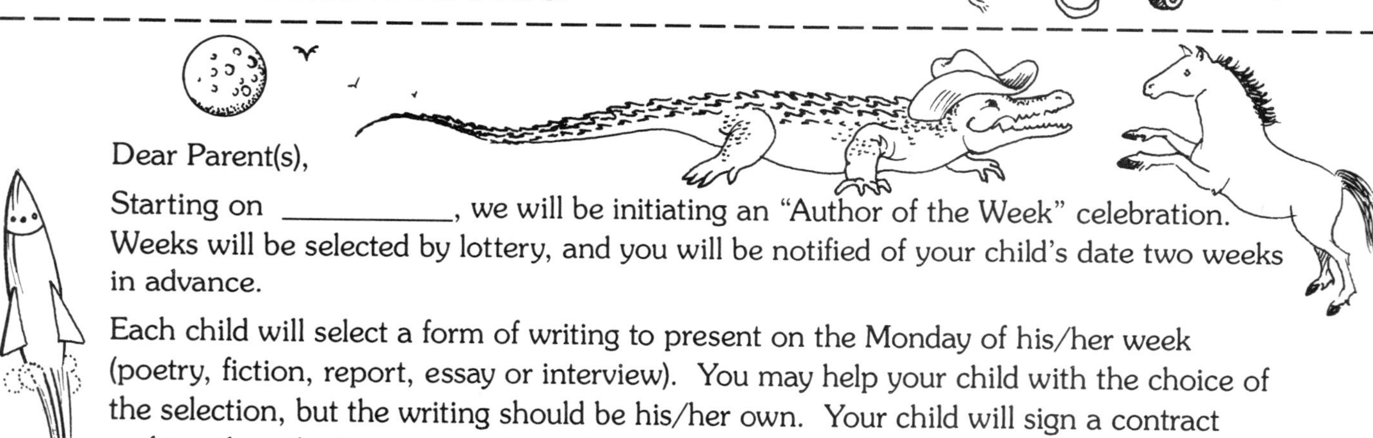

Dear Parent(s),

Starting on __________, we will be initiating an "Author of the Week" celebration. Weeks will be selected by lottery, and you will be notified of your child's date two weeks in advance.

Each child will select a form of writing to present on the Monday of his/her week (poetry, fiction, report, essay or interview). You may help your child with the choice of the selection, but the writing should be his/her own. Your child will sign a contract making the selection one week in advance.

For the remainder of the week, the author will make a presentation each day. Please help your child to make choices or to select something of his/her own choosing. Possible activities include an autobiography, a favorite book or funny experience to share, a picture drawn by the author, a list of the author's favorite things such as food, color, game, sport, hobby, pet, school subject, etc., a family photograph, a vacation/trip experience, etc.

At the end of the week, your child will bring home an "Author of the Week" award. Please share the pride of achievement with your child.

Sincerely,

____

Author of the Week continued

I will select for my presentation the following form of writing:

____________________ .

I will be ready to present it on Monday, ____________________ .
(date)

Signatures,

Student____________________

Teacher____________________

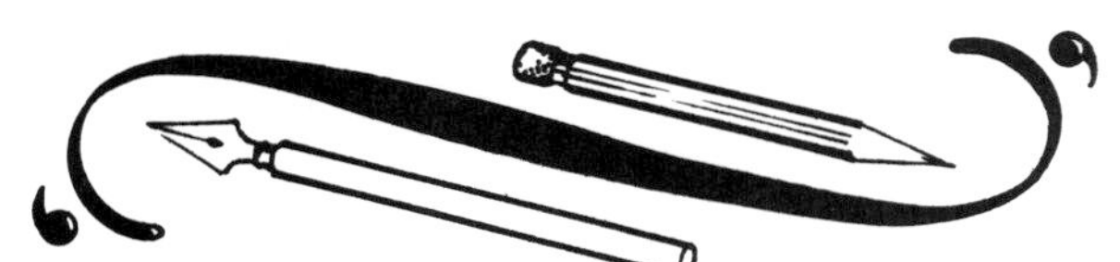

Form for the notification of the date for Author of the Week:

Dear ____________________ ,
(Mom/Dad)

On ____________________ ,
(date)

I will be the Author of the Week.

Love,

____
(child's signature)

Author of the Week Award

Honoring:

____
name

for excellence in writing

____________________ signed

____________________ date

Setting up a Writing Center

Writing Center

Objective: To encourage writing

Materials: writing tools (paper, pencils, markers, tape, stapler, scissors, ruler, dictionary, thesaurus, etc.), folders, pictures students can use for story ideas, copy of the boxes below and on page 17, notebook rings

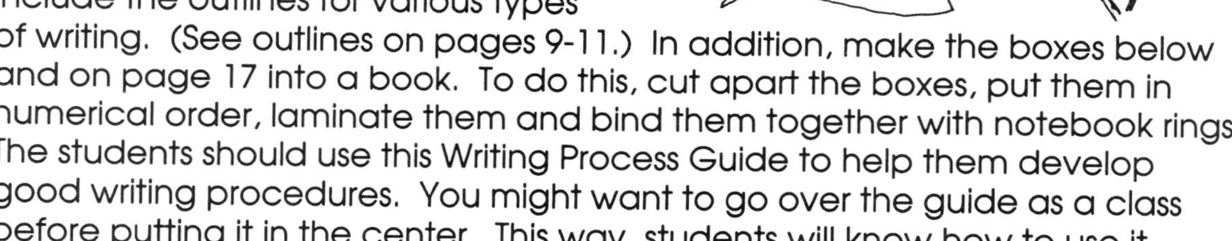

Directions: Find an area in your classroom to use to set up a writing center. It may or may not have a space for students to actually sit down and write, but it should have all the "tools of the trade." Provide students with writing materials. Also, have a folder of pictures students can use as story starters. Change the pictures at regular intervals. In another folder, include the outlines for various types of writing. (See outlines on pages 9-11.) In addition, make the boxes below and on page 17 into a book. To do this, cut apart the boxes, put them in numerical order, laminate them and bind them together with notebook rings. The students should use this Writing Process Guide to help them develop good writing procedures. You might want to go over the guide as a class before putting it in the center. This way, students will know how to use it.

Pre-Writing

- What am I going to write about?
- Who might read it?
- What thoughts and feelings do I have about it?

1

Writing

These are my main thoughts and feelings—written clearly—in the most sensible order.

2

continued on page 17

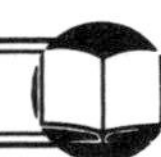

Setting up a Writing Center continued

Revising

- Should I add anything?
- Should I take anything out?
- Should I rearrange anything?
- Do my words and sentences say exactly what I mean?

3

Editing

- Are my tenses and usage correct?
- Have I checked:
  —Punctuation?
  —Capitalization?
  —Spelling?
- Is my handwriting neat and legible?

4

Sharing, Publishing and Extending

- Who else would enjoy my writing?
- What is the best way of sharing it?
- Does it give me any ideas for something else I might write?

5

Proofreading Marks

insert a period

take out

capitalize

change spelling

new paragraph

lower-case

insert comma

take out and close up

6

Book Report Alternatives

Creative Writing/Art

Objective: To allow students to reflect upon and share books by means of creative and enriching projects

Materials: chart paper, list of activities below

Directions: Below is a list of possible activities students may wish to do upon the completion of a book. The activities may accompany or replace the traditional written report. Display the choices on a chart and keep it out all year.

Book Follow-Up Projects

- an interview with a character in a book
- a list of things a character may say
- a favorite scene illustrated
- a commercial selling the book
- a critique of the book
- a front page newspaper article about an event in the book
- a journal entry written from the author's point of view
- a letter written to a character
- a letter written to the author
- a mobile depicting a character(s)
- a diorama
- a book jacket
- a new ending

- a poem about the book or a character
- a comic strip involving characters from the book
- a phone conversation between two characters
- a slogan for an event in the book and a poster
- a Venn diagram comparing and contrasting items, characters, settings, etc.
- a play written about a scene in the book
- a puppet show
- a game show incorporating new information gained from the book
- a list of things not known before the book was read

Independent Literature Response

Critical Thinking

Objective: To respond to literature that is read individually

Materials: one copy of the form below for each student

Directions: After students have completed a short story or book, you can keep in contact with what they are reading and get an idea of how well they are comprehending it with the use of the literature response form below.

LITERATURE RESPONSE

Name____________________________ Date ____________________

Title of book: ____

Author: ____

Why did you choose this book? ________________________________

____

____

Was it a good choice? Why or why not? ________________________

____

The best part of the story was _______________________________

____

If you could change or rewrite one part of the story, it would be ____

____

Write one sentence from the book that you feel is well written. _____

____

What do you like about this sentence? _________________________

____

Which character in the story do you feel you got to know best? ____

____

Write two things you know about this character.

1. ____
2. ____

Tic-Tac-Read

Reading

Objective: To encourage students to select and read a book from a variety of genres

Materials: a copy of a Tic-Tac-Read matrix pattern per student, construction paper, container, glue, scissors, slips of paper, colored markers

Directions: Tic-Tac-Read is a fun game whose objective is to persuade students to select books to read from a wide variety of literary genres. Too often, students who read one mystery book and enjoy it will then focus all their time on reading these kinds of stories. Indeed, every reader has a favorite genre. However, students do need to base their opinions on experience. Tic-Tac-Read will expose them to a wider variety of books in a gamelike fashion.

western	nonfiction	sports
biography	science fiction	fantasy
mystery	poetry	student's choice

To begin, make and distribute a 9-square matrix to students. Have them cut out the matrix and glue it to a piece of construction paper. The students might also decorate their new gameboard if they like. Prior to the lesson, prepare small slips of paper with the categories of literary genres written on them. Select nine topics, one for each box of the gameboard, such as biography, mystery, poetry, fantasy, nonfiction, sports, science fiction, western and students' choice. Explain to students that they are going to be able to fill in the boxes on the gameboard in any order they choose. However, they should only write one genre in each box. Call out the names of the book topics until all spaces are filled in. Put the slips of paper in a container. Now, students are ready for Tic-Tac-Read! When the students have joined three boxes in a row, reward them with a special treat! When students have filled in the whole gameboard, reward them with something extra special!

Rules for Tic-Tac-Read

1. Select a slip of paper from the topic box and show your teacher.
2. Read a book that fits into this category. The book must be at least 50 pages long, and it also must be approved by your teacher.
3. When you have completed the book, select a project from the list. (See "Book Report Alternatives" on page 18.) Use the project to tell others what the book was about.
4. Share your project with your teacher. Projects might also be shared with your classmates.
5. Mark your space on the Tic-Tac-Read chart and pick again.

Reading Record

Reading/ Sequencing

Objectives: To supply students with a format to record what they are reading on a daily basis and to hold students more accountable for reading at home; to inform parents what and how much their child is reading

Materials: a copy of the Reading Record Sheet and parent letter (page 22) for each student

Directions: The Reading Record Sheet requires the student to read five nights during the week. He/she is allowed two evenings "off." The student is to complete all required information and have it signed by a parent. The summary portion should be completed the night before the record is due.

The parent letter informs them of the process. It would be a good idea to introduce the reading record format at the "Back to School Night."

After several weeks, in order to provide variety and to keep the assignment "fresh," the summary requirement could be changed. Instead, ask students to write a character sketch or a critique of the portion of the book read. Or, they could name one thing they have learned from the book, etc. (Note: One record sheet is used for a two-week period.)

Class Story Chain

Objective: To develop sequencing and comprehension

Materials: paper, pencil, chart paper, marker

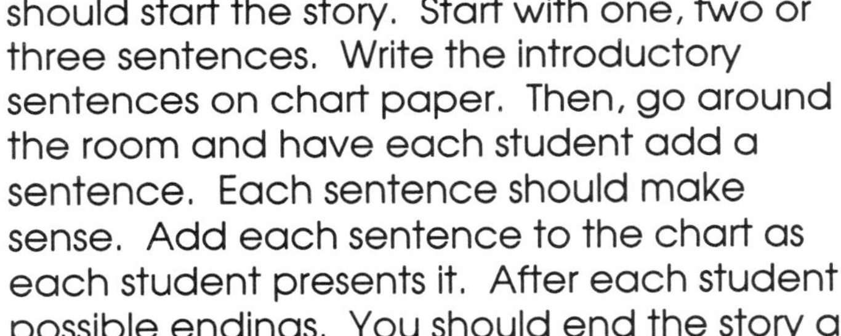

Directions: Discuss with the class the idea of writing a cooperative class story. Select a topic. You should start the story. Start with one, two or three sentences. Write the introductory sentences on chart paper. Then, go around the room and have each student add a sentence. Each sentence should make sense. Add each sentence to the chart as each student presents it. After each student has added a sentence, discuss possible endings. You should end the story and write it on the chart. As a class, choose a title for the story. Discuss the story by asking students questions such as, "Does it make sense? Does it follow in sequence? Should any sentences be moved?" The next day, discuss with the class a new chain story. Again, you should choose the topic and start the story. Write the topic on the board. However, write the introductory sentences on a sheet of paper. Pass it to one of the students. As each student writes a sentence, he/she will pass it on to another student. This story may take a day or more to complete. The last student can end the story, or it can come back to you to end. Read the final story and discuss it with the class.

Extension: Have one student pick the subject and start the story.

Dear Parent(s),

Attached you will find a copy of a Reading Record Sheet. Please have your child read five evenings per week for approximately 20 minutes each night. After reading each night, your child should record what he/she has read and the page numbers. At the end of the seven-day period, your child should summarize what he/she has read and ask you for your signature. You can help your child by:

1. providing a quiet place/time for your child to read
2. reading with your child (either the same material, or material of your own)
3. asking your child questions about what he/she has read
4. reading his/her summary

Thank you for your cooperation.

Sincerely,

____

Reading Record

Name ____________________________

title of book ____________________

author ____________________

date ______ pages read ________

date ______ pages read ________

date ______ pages read ________

date ______ pages read ________

date ______ pages read ________

summary ____________________

____

____

x __________________________

parent signature

title of book ____________________

author ____________________

date ______ pages read ________

date ______ pages read ________

date ______ pages read ________

date ______ pages read ________

date ______ pages read ________

summary ____________________

____

____

x __________________________

parent signature

Story Chain

Creative Writing

Objective: To encourage creative writing and cooperation

Materials: paper, pencils, copies of the outlines (below)

Directions: Divide the class into groups of three. Try to arrange good working groups—ones in which the three students work well together and plan together. The assignment for the groups is to write a story. One student writes the beginning, one the middle and one the end. Present the groups with possible choices of titles such as, "Best Friends," "A Day at the Circus," "The Funniest Thing," etc. The groups, however, should be able to select their own title if they so desire. Each group can select the title cooperatively, or the person writing the beginning can choose the title and then pass it on after the introduction.

To help students, give them the following outlines. Be sure to give Student #1 only the Introduction Outline. Student #2 gets only the Middle Outline and Student #3 gets only the End of the Story Outline. This is to avoid confusion in the group.

Introduction Outline

A. Who is the story about? (Limit it to two characters.)
   1. Describe each character.

B. Where does the story take place?
   1. Describe the setting.

C. What are the characters doing when we meet them?

D. What are the characters going to do?

Middle Outline

A. Develop the plot
   1. What action takes place?

B. Statement of the problem—
   Suggestions:
   1. One day, . . .
   2. Suddenly, . . .
   3. They didn't realize it, but . . .
   4. When they arrived, . . .

End of Story Outline

A. Solution to the problem
   1. What finally happened?

B. Closure
   1. A satisfactory conclusion

Going Bananas Over Books!

Reading

Objective: To motivate students to read

Materials: brown, green and yellow construction paper; markers; thumbtacks or push pins; a copy of the parent letter for each student (page 25); scissors; monkey pattern (below); banana pattern (page 25)

Directions: Using the brown and green construction paper, create a palm tree to fit your bulletin board. (The trunk of the tree can extend below the board to the floor.) Using the yellow construction paper and the banana pattern, draw and cut out 100 bananas. Use thumbtacks to hang the bananas around the border of the board. Each time a student completes a book, he/she is to remove a banana from the board. On his/her banana, have the student write the following information: 1) the title of the book, 2) the author of the book, 3) his/her rating of the book (on a scale of one to ten), 4) his/her name. Then, the student places the banana on the palm tree. When 100 books have been read, reward the class with a banana split ice cream party.

Extension: Reinforce the concept of tenths and hundredths by marking the trunk into ten sections. The first section at the bottom of the tree should represent .10. Label the sections .10, .20, .30, etc. Make a monkey using the pattern. As students place bananas on the tree, move the monkey up the trunk of the tree to correspond with the number of books read.

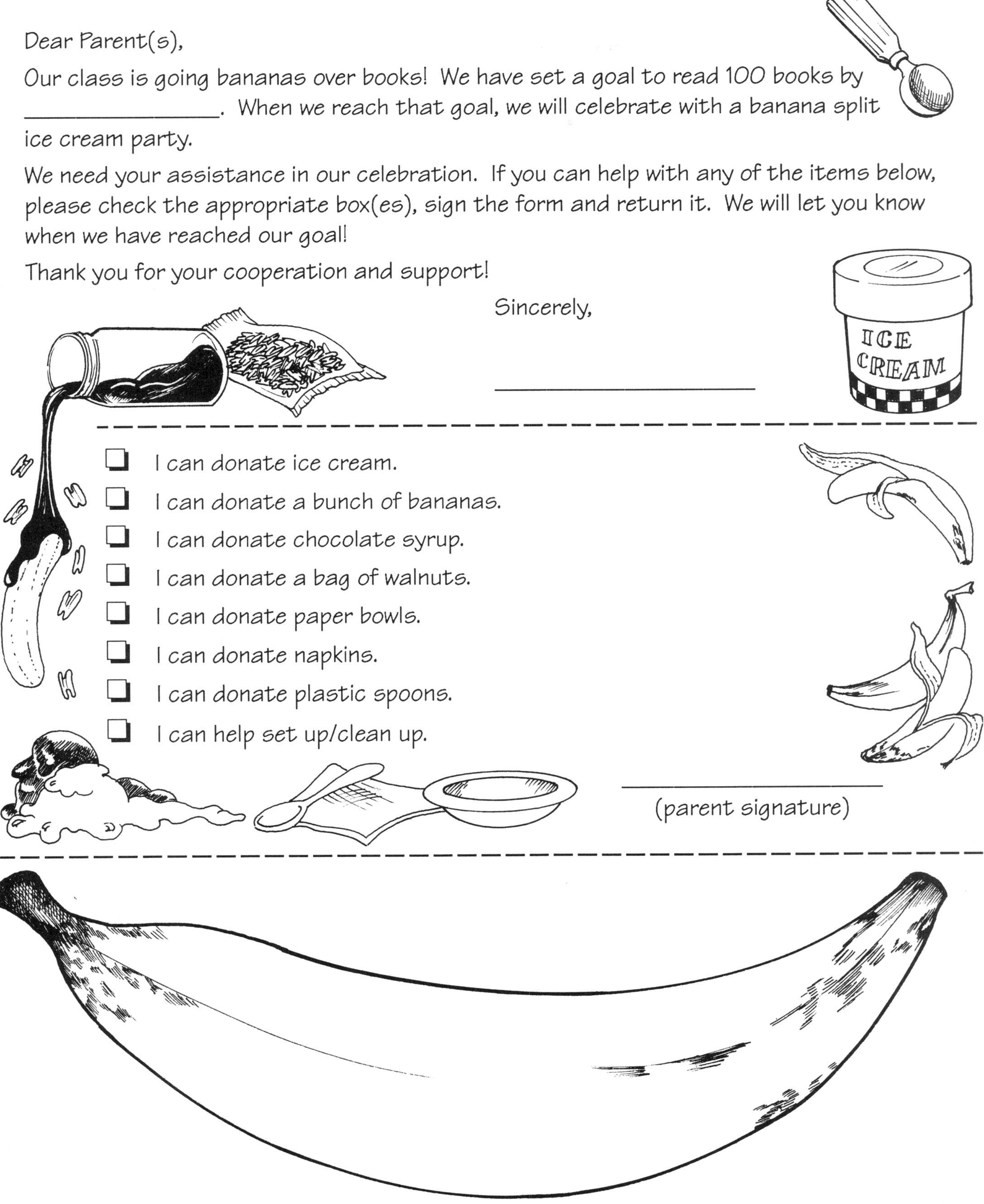

Dear Parent(s),

Our class is going bananas over books! We have set a goal to read 100 books by ________________. When we reach that goal, we will celebrate with a banana split ice cream party.

We need your assistance in our celebration. If you can help with any of the items below, please check the appropriate box(es), sign the form and return it. We will let you know when we have reached our goal!

Thank you for your cooperation and support!

Sincerely,

____

- ☐ I can donate ice cream.
- ☐ I can donate a bunch of bananas.
- ☐ I can donate chocolate syrup.
- ☐ I can donate a bag of walnuts.
- ☐ I can donate paper bowls.
- ☐ I can donate napkins.
- ☐ I can donate plastic spoons.
- ☐ I can help set up/clean up.

____
(parent signature)

Independent Reading With the Basal Reader

Reading

Objective: To use the basal reader to promote independent reading

Materials: basal reader for each student, a copy of the worksheet below (or similar) for each student

Directions: Basal readers are still accessible in many classrooms, and they contain some good stories. You can have students choose, or you can assign, a story from the basal appropriate for the students' independent reading level. Before students read, work with the new vocabulary. On the worksheet, next to the category "words to know," the students should record the new words and their definitions. The students could be assigned the story and worksheet as a long-term reading assignment. (The first time through, students may need your help on how to fill out the worksheet.)

Name ______________________ Date ______________

Story Organizer

title of book: ______________________________

title of story: ______________________________

words to know: ______________________________

____

____

characters: ______________________________

____

problem: ______________________________

____

solution: ______________________________

____

How well did you understand this story?

1	2	3	4	5
I did not understand it.				I understood it very well.

How well did you enjoy this story?

1	2	3	4	5
I did not enjoy it.				I enjoyed it very much.

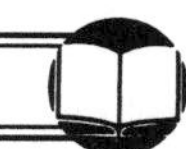

Nursery Rhyme Newscast

Creative Writing

Objective: To enhance reading comprehension

Directions: Read the following news items to the students and have them figure out from the clues given which nursery rhymes they represent. Have the students indicate which clues were important in helping them make their decision.

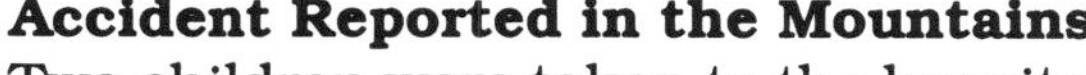

Lost!
Lost—three pairs of mittens, size small. Owners are very sad and are crying. If you find them, please return them to the rightful owners and you will receive a reward of a slice of pie. (The Three Little Kittens)

Accident Reported in the Mountains
Two children were taken to the hospital after a bad fall down a hill. One, a boy, hurt his head rather badly. (Jack and Jill)

Theft!
Theft reported in the Royal Household from the Royal Kitchen—fresh baked goods stolen; Thief returned stolen goods and vowed to repent. (The Queen of Hearts)

Animal Escapes
A white animal was found wandering about school. The children were not able to do their schoolwork since they were playing and laughing with the animal. (Mary Had a Little Lamb)

Provide a list of other nursery rhymes for the students and have them write their own news items to read to the class. The students will then use the clues to figure out the rhymes described. If the students cannot identify the rhymes, more clues should be added.

Follow-up: The same activities can be used for Fairy Tale News. It would be a good idea to incorporate vocabulary expansion as part of these activities. Several words such as *transparent, trauma* and *claustrophobia* may need to be defined for students regarding the news items below. Read the examples.

Wedding Announcement
A young, beautiful woman marries a handsome prince. The bride's attendants are seven small men. (Snow White)

Lost Children Found Safe
Two children, a boy and a girl, lost in the woods, suffered a trauma from an encounter with a woman living in a house made of candy. Both children escaped without injury. However, the girl still suffers from claustrophobia. (Hansel and Gretel)

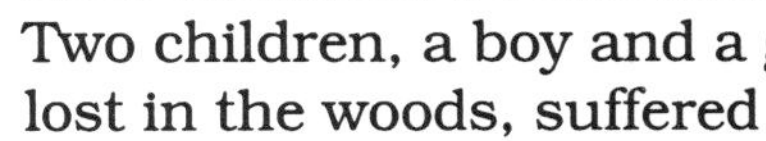

Wedding Announcement
A handsome prince marries a beautiful young woman who likes to wear transparent shoes. (Cinderella)

Hunters to the Rescue
A girl is saved from a wolf dressed in woman's clothing by hunters. (Little Red Riding Hood)

Story Specifics

Vocabulary Development

Objectives: To encourage creative writing and to expand descriptive vocabulary

Directions: Follow the directions below to help students with creative writing using pictures or posters as inspiration.

Action Story

Present a picture or poster to the class indicating considerable action. Discuss the picture with the class. Ask students the following questions:

1. What is happening in the picture? (Have students describe the action.)
2. Who is involved? (Students should describe the characters.)
3. What do you think happened before the scene in the picture?
4. What do you think will happen after the scene in the picture?

Reassure the students that there are no right or wrong answers to questions 3 and 4. An answer that makes sense is acceptable.

After several ideas are set forth, the students can write individual stories. Or, you can divide the class into groups of two to four students, and each group can come up with a story.

After all the stories are read, the class can select the best ideas and write a class story.

Emotion Story

Present a picture or poster to the class that shows very little action but which has a person with a facial expression that indicates considerable emotion. Ask students the following questions.

1. How does this person look? (Have students describe his/her facial expression.)
2. What on his/her face or in the picture indicates that emotion?
3. Why do you think he/she feels that way?
4. Have you ever felt that way?
5. What may happen to change his/her expression (feeling)?

When writing about this type of picture, students can follow the same format as above writing individual, group and/or class stories.

Can You Picture That?

Art/ Sequencing

Objective: To demonstrate how illustrations support the various elements in the text

Materials: drawing paper, markers, student stories, picture books

Directions: Students will gain a greater recognition of the powerful impact illustrations can have upon a story with this activity. To begin the activity, share several picture books with the students. Try to select stories whose illustrations are drawn in a variety of different ways (i.e. pen and ink, watercolor, bold colors or muted tones, real photographs or drawings).

Discuss with the students how the illustrator's choice of medium affects the reader. Then, turn their attention to the subjects in the pictures. Ask students to identify the setting, characters, plot, problem and/or solution of the story as they are depicted in the illustrations. Encourage students to share their opinions by answering the following questions: "Did the illustrator draw scenes that helped you understand the story better? Did the illustrations "suit" or "fit" the story? How might the illustrator have illustrated the story differently?" Once you have discussed these questions, have students illustrate these elements in their own pre-written stories.

Extension: To heighten student sensitivity to these elements, have students exchange stories and illustrate someone else's writing. The young authors will be amazed to see how others interpret their characters, setting, plot and solution in pictures.

Use the Funnies

Objective: To practice story sequencing

Materials: newspaper comic strips, index cards, pen, scissors, glue

Directions: Cut a comic strip into individual frames. Glue each frame to an index card and laminate them for reuse. Number the backs in correct sequence. Shuffle the cards and have students try to put them in the correct order.

Now, That's Funny!

Creative Writing/ Art

Objective: To write dialogue for characters in a comic strip

Materials: newspaper comic strips, writer's correction fluid or self-adhesive dialogue balloons, wipeable markers, construction paper, glue

Directions: Glue complete comic strips to pieces of construction paper. Block out words in the dialogue using writer's correction fluid or the self-adhesive dialogue balloons often used to add comments to photos in photo albums. This creates a sequence of picture events. Laminate and allow students to use a wipeable marker to create dialogues to go along with the pictures in the frames.

Oh, I Get It!

Objective: To evaluate and describe humor in various comic strip situations

Materials: newspaper comic strips

Directions: This is a fun activity that promotes and encourages students to express their opinion and to share their ideas in a group situation. A day before the actual lesson, distribute a complete comic strip to each student. Ask the students to try to explain why the comic is funny. To help guide the students, ask them questions such as: "Is it the dialogue? Is it the pictures? How do the two work together?" Tell them to be ready to share their opinions tomorrow. The next day, gather students together in small, cooperative groups and have them share their comic strips, explain their meaning and enjoy the laughter!

Cartoonist Corner

Objective: To use dialogue and illustrations to tell a short, humorous story

Materials: drawing paper, colored pencils, markers

Directions: Students will enjoy creating comic strip characters of their own and writing humorous adventures for them. Tell the students that they are going to become cartoonists. Ask them to design a character(s) that they could create a strip for. Then, through a series of illustrations and dialogue, have the students write a short story for the characters. Encourage the students to think carefully about what each frame of the strip will show and guide them in selecting dialogue that is humorous.

Adjective/Verb Cloze Story Starters

Grammar

Objectives: To use adjectives and verbs (separately) and to complete cloze story starters

Materials: one copy of the cloze story starter(s) below for each student

Directions: Each of the cloze paragraphs below isolates one part of speech, either adjectives or verbs. Instruct students to read the entire story starter before filling in any of the blanks. After students have filled in the blank spaces, compare the stories the students created, highlighting the difference that the choice of words can make. Make a list of the words students chose and discuss the similarities and differences between them. Label the list with the corresponding parts of speech. Students can then write endings to the stories.

Cloze Story Starter—Adjectives

The _________ truck roared down the _________ road. It had to reach the _________ store before morning. Besides the full moon, it's _________ headlights were the only lights in the area. On either side of the road were miles and miles of _________ desert. Nicky, the driver of the truck, was tired and anxious to unload his _________ truck. Suddenly, the truck's engine stopped roaring and began to hiss. What could be the matter? The truck came to a complete stop.

Cloze Story Starter—Verbs

William and Kenny _________ together almost every day. They love to _________ and _________, and on rainy days, they _________ inside. One day, they decided to have a race. They _________ some friends to join them. They _________ banners, _________ a starting and finish line, and _________ some prizes for the winners of the race. William and Kenny and several of their friends lined up at the starting line. "On your mark, get set, go!" _________ William's older brother.

continued on page 32

More Adjective/Verb Cloze Story Starters

Cloze Story Starter—Adjectives

I have a friend who is very __________ . We do a lot of __________ things together. The __________ thing we did was during our summer vacation. It was a __________ day, and we took a __________ walk to a __________ park. In the park, there was a zoo. We visited the __________ giraffes, the __________ elephants and the __________ monkeys. We watched the __________ sea lions swim. Our favorites were the __________ penguins. We watched them for a __________ time.

Cloze Story Starters—Adjectives

Missy and Scott had been at the _________ beach all day. They had gone swimming in the __________ ocean, built __________ sand castles in the __________ sand, collected __________ shells, and eaten ____________ ice cream. It had been a __________ day, but it was almost time to leave. They decided to walk down the __________ beach just one more time before going home.

As they walked along the __________ shore, Scott spotted something on the __________sand. He ran ahead to investigate the ___________ object. When he got up close, he realized that it was just a __________ bottle. __________ Scott looked away. Then, Missy began to shout. She picked up the __________ bottle and to their surprise . . .

continued on page 33

More Adjective/Verb Cloze Story Starters

Cloze Story Starter—Verbs

On a beautiful Monday morning, I __________ to school with my sister. Suddenly, we __________ a big truck __________ up the street. We __________ beautiful music coming from the truck. On top of the truck, we __________ these clowns who were __________ . We __________ to the clowns, "Why are you __________ ? Where are you __________ ?" The clowns __________ back to us, "The circus __________ to town to see us." We __________ so excited. We __________ for a long time, and we __________ late for school.

Cloze Story Starter—Verbs

Allison always loved to __________ her grandmother's house. There __________ so many wonderful things to do there. When Allison would __________ her grandmother, they would __________ delicious desserts to eat or __________ interesting books about animals. Most of all, Allison liked to __________ in the basement. It __________ cool down there, and she always found something fun to __________ with.

One day when she __________ in the basement, she __________ an old storage chest. It was __________ of wood and __________ big metal hinges. The trunk __________ covered with dust. When Allison __________ the dust off, she could __________ that it __________ very old. She carefully __________ the lid and __________ inside. What she __________ made her eyes grow bigger and bigger. The trunk __________ all kinds of . . .

Imagination Walk

Creative Writing

Objective: To encourage students in the art of creative writing

Materials: *And To Think That I Saw It On Mulberry Street* by Dr. Seuss, notebooks, pencils

Directions: After reading *And To Think That I Saw It On Mulberry Street* to the class, discuss the story with them. Ask students questions such as: "What did Marco actually see? What did he "invent" in his mind? What did Marco make up?"

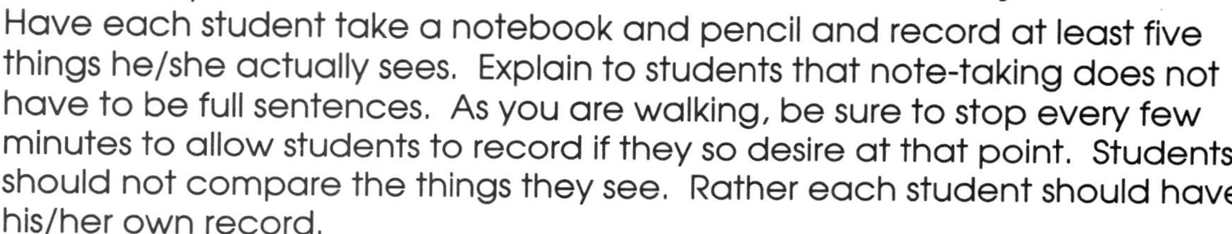

Then, take the class on a walk either around the block, down the street, or if this is not possible, in the school. Have each student take a notebook and pencil and record at least five things he/she actually sees. Explain to students that note-taking does not have to be full sentences. As you are walking, be sure to stop every few minutes to allow students to record if they so desire at that point. Students should not compare the things they see. Rather each student should have his/her own record.

When you return to the classroom, have each student write what he/she actually saw, and next to it, his/her own imaginative elaboration (i.e. house—a castle with sentries, a moat and flags flying from the turrets; fire engine—a dragon racing down the street making roaring and frightful sounds). Review the lists either in private conferences with each student or with the whole class.

After reviewing the list, have each student write two paragraphs: 1) To think that I saw it on ______ Street (or in school), 2) What I really saw. This compilation can also be laminated, bound and made into a class book.

Pen Pals

Objective: To introduce the students to the art of writing a friendly letter

Materials: writing paper, pens, envelopes, stamps

Directions: Contact a school in a neighboring community and arrange with a third-grade teacher in that school to exchange pen pal letters. Try to match up the students so that each student has at least one pen pal. If there is not an even match of students, some students may volunteer to have more than one pen pal.

Discuss with your class the difference between an introductory letter and a letter that he/she might write to a grandparent, a cousin or an old friend. In an introductory letter, each student should follow the outline on page 35 to tell a little bit about himself/herself.

continued on page 35

Pen Pal continued

Creative Writing

Outline

1. Name
2. Age
3. Class
4. Information about family
5. Information about school/class
6. Something you like (i.e. sport, hobby, subject, etc.)

Have students write an introductory letter to their new pen pal. When students are finished, mail all the letters at the same time. When return letters arrive, have students begin writing subsequent letters to their pen pals.

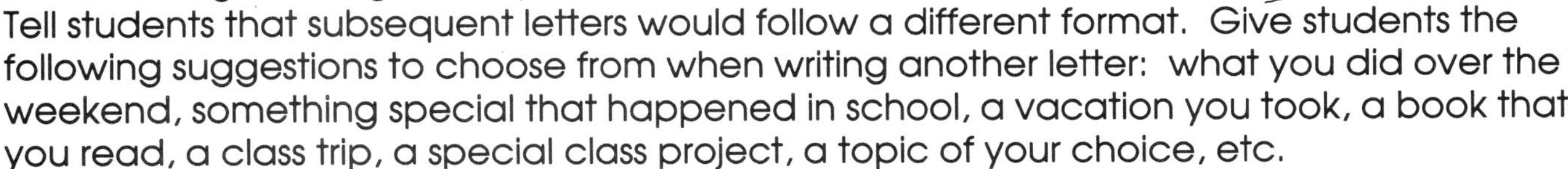

Tell students that subsequent letters would follow a different format. Give students the following suggestions to choose from when writing another letter: what you did over the weekend, something special that happened in school, a vacation you took, a book that you read, a class trip, a special class project, a topic of your choice, etc.

At the end of the year, arrange for a visit to the "Pen Pal School" to meet the pen pals. This trip can also be to a mutual visiting place such as a park so that the pen pals can meet each other.

Story Starters

Objective: To stimulate creative writing

Materials: 12" x 18" sheets of construction paper, crayons or markers, tape, ruled story paper, 6" x 9" sheets of colored construction paper, stapler

Directions: Give each student a 12" x 18" sheet of construction paper. Have students fold it in half. Then, they staple the ruled story paper inside. On the outside of the folded paper, just across the top, have students tape a 6" x 9" sheet of colored construction paper so that it can be flipped up to create a flap. Tell students to draw a picture under the flap. Tell them that they are not to share their idea with anyone. Some suggestions include: a forest, a beach, a house, a monster, an animal, a person doing something, a rocket ship, a clown, etc.

When the pictures are completed, collect all the booklets. Later in the day, pass out the booklets making sure that no one gets his/her own picture. Have each student write a story using the cover illustration as a story starter. Have the student put an appropriate title on the cover. The flaps can then be removed. Have the students share their stories with the class.

Under Construction!

Editing/Writing

Objective: To emphasize the importance and value of the editing and revising process in writing

Materials: students' rough drafts of written work; construction paper; marker; pins or stapler; decorative pictures of construction site vehicles, cones, etc.

Assembly: Line a bulletin board with construction paper. Write the title, **Under Construction**, at the top. Hang decorative pictures of construction site vehicles, cones, etc. around the board.

Directions: With the class, discuss what the revision process should entail. Perhaps you would like to create a chart or poster of "revision rules." For Example: 1) When revising, use a different color pen, marker or pencil. 2) Use the revision symbols. 3) Always revise with a dictionary and thesaurus at hand. 4) Ask a friend for his/her opinion on parts of the story you are unsure of. 5) Reread your story to be sure it has a beginning, middle and an end. (See "Setting up a Writing Center" page 16.) Hang the work of students who are taking the time to do a good job revising and editing on the bulletin board. Students can share some of the reasons why they made revisions with the rest of the class.

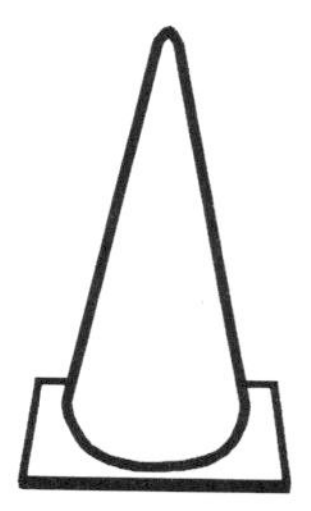

Sentence Celebration

Objectives: To share and applaud student writing, to reinforce writing skills and to model sentence structure

Materials: well-written sentences from students' work (or literature)

Directions: This activity can be implemented on a daily or weekly basis. It allows you to highlight a student, often the less-able student who may not have developed the ability to write a story yet. All the activity entails is choosing a well-written sentence from a piece of a student's work, (or literature) writing it on the board, talking about why it is a good sentence, and applauding the author. A sentence may be chosen because it employs a new vocabulary word, because it is punctuated correctly, because it contains a descriptive adjective, because it makes use of onomatopoeia, because the student is using a writing skill you have introduced recently, etc. You will find that students will strive to write better sentences, and the activity only takes a minute.

Writing/Art

Soaring Stories

Objective: To use context clues to write a sequence of story parts

Materials: writing paper, pencils

Directions: Your students will "buckle their seat belts" and listen to instructions when they hear that they are going to write stories and make paper airplanes, too. Tell students to pretend that you are the air traffic controller. (This would be a great time to review the job responsibilities of the airport control tower personnel.) Tell students that they must listen carefully to all instructions to avoid any accidents. Now, you're ready to "taxi" to the runway.

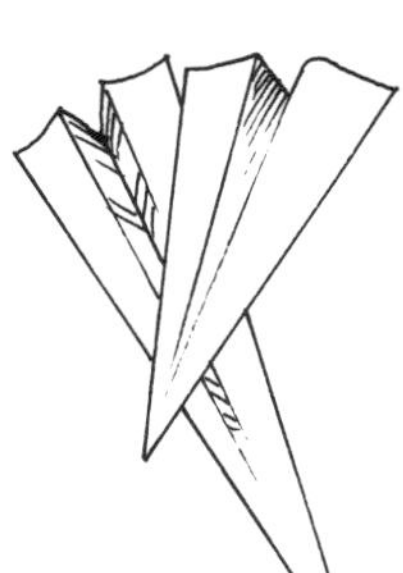

Direct students to have paper and pencils ready. Tell them that when you give them a "signal," they are to write down the best opening paragraph for a story that they can think of. Allow time for the students to brainstorm ideas. Then, give them the signal to write. At this time, each student writes down one paragraph. After they have had sufficient time to write their sentences, have students fold their papers to make paper airplanes. Again, with a signal, instruct students to fly their airplanes across the room. Request that students do not touch the planes until all have landed. Then, each student is to pick up the plane that is closest to his/her desk. After the "go" signal is given again, the students should unfold the airplanes, read the paragraph and then add a second paragraph. Continue this procedure until students have had time to develop their stories.

Then, ground all flights and share the stories.

Extension: Begin similarly, except have students play musical chairs to exchange stories. Play students' favorite music while they circle the desks in their group. When the music stops, the students must sit down at the nearest desk and add a paragraph to that story. Continue in the same manner until the stories are developed and then share!

Picture That!

Objective: To illustrate scenarios in such a way as to respond to a question

Materials: copies of pages 38-39, pencils, crayons or colored pencils, writing paper

Directions: Cut apart the different scenarios on pages 38-39. Put them on a table and have each student select one (or more). Ask students to think creatively about the question and then draw a picture to answer it. When the students have completed their illustrations, have them write stories to go along with their pictures.

continued on page 38

Picture That! continued

What do you see on the computer screen?

What do you see through the camera lens?

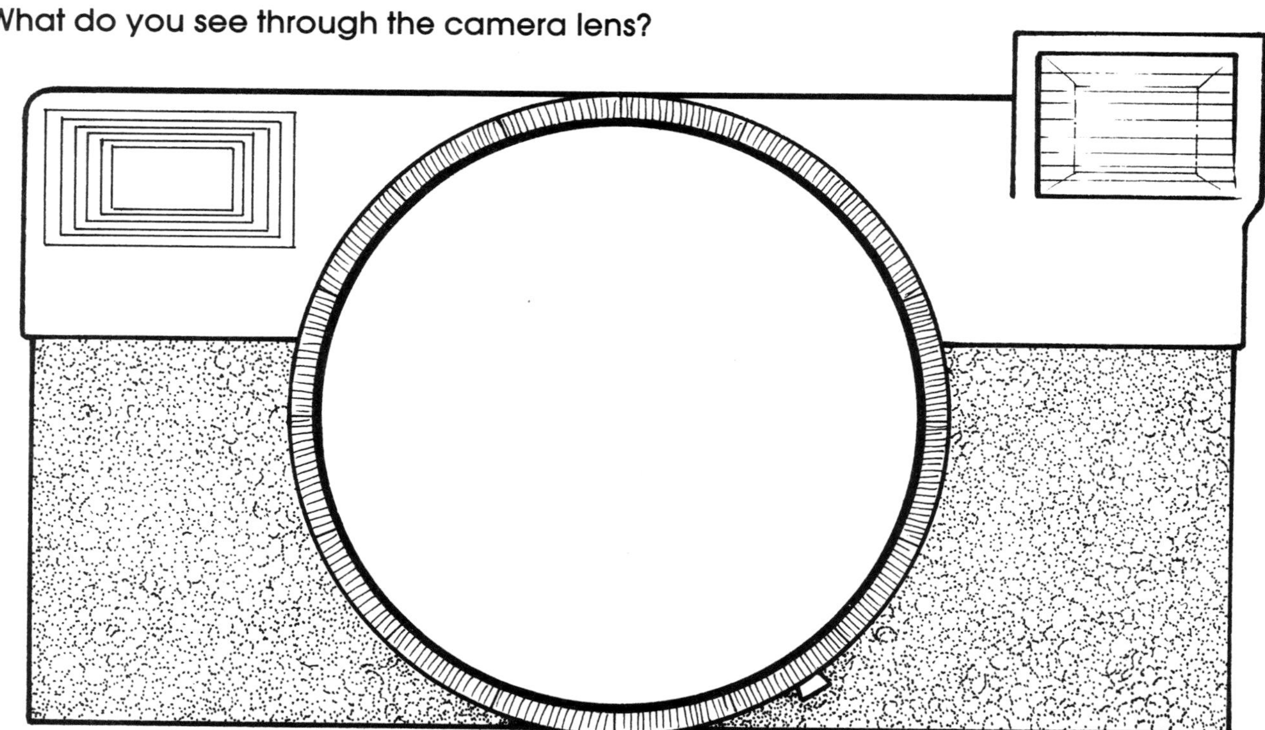

Picture That! continued

The Stories of a House

Writing/ Classifying

Objective: To write a story with a focus on setting

Materials: two copies of the house pattern (page 41) for each student, pencils, crayons

Directions: Tell students that the house pattern is story paper. The students are to write a story that takes place within the house, and it can begin on any one of the floors. If the story begins in the basement, the students should write the beginning sentences in the basement. When the setting changes to another floor of the house, tell students that the "moving sentence(s)" should be written on the staircase. For example, the following sentence would be written on the stairs from the basement to the first floor: "When the water in the basement reached my knees, I decided to go upstairs to dry off." Tell students that the house could be their own, a historical site, a haunted house, their grandmother's house, etc.

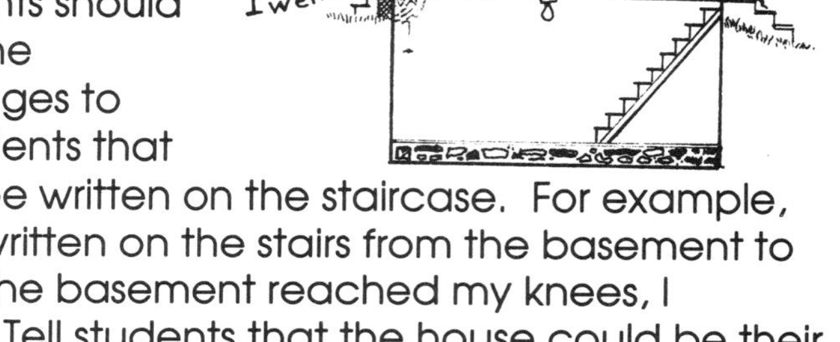

After the first copy is written, revised and edited, provide students with a second house pattern to use for a final copy. The students can add character to the house by coloring it.

Mystery Box

Objectives: To promote classification skills, to write and order clues and to promote listening and speaking skills

Materials: a sturdy box (or bag) labeled **Mystery Box**, index cards, pencils

Directions: Each day, one student is responsible for bringing in one item small enough (and interesting enough) to fit in the Mystery Box. On an index card, this student writes five clues to describe the object, with no more than one clue for each attribute. (For example, if clue one is, "It is the color of my shoes," clue two may not describe color. It must describe shape, smell, texture, etc.)

After each clue, the clue-giver can choose four classmates to guess the contents of the box. If a student repeats an answer already given by another student, that student may not guess again for that day. The same holds true if a person guesses without being called upon.

You might want to model the game the first week and begin anytime thereafter. A curriculum-related object in the mystery box can make an excellent introduction to a lesson.

House Pattern

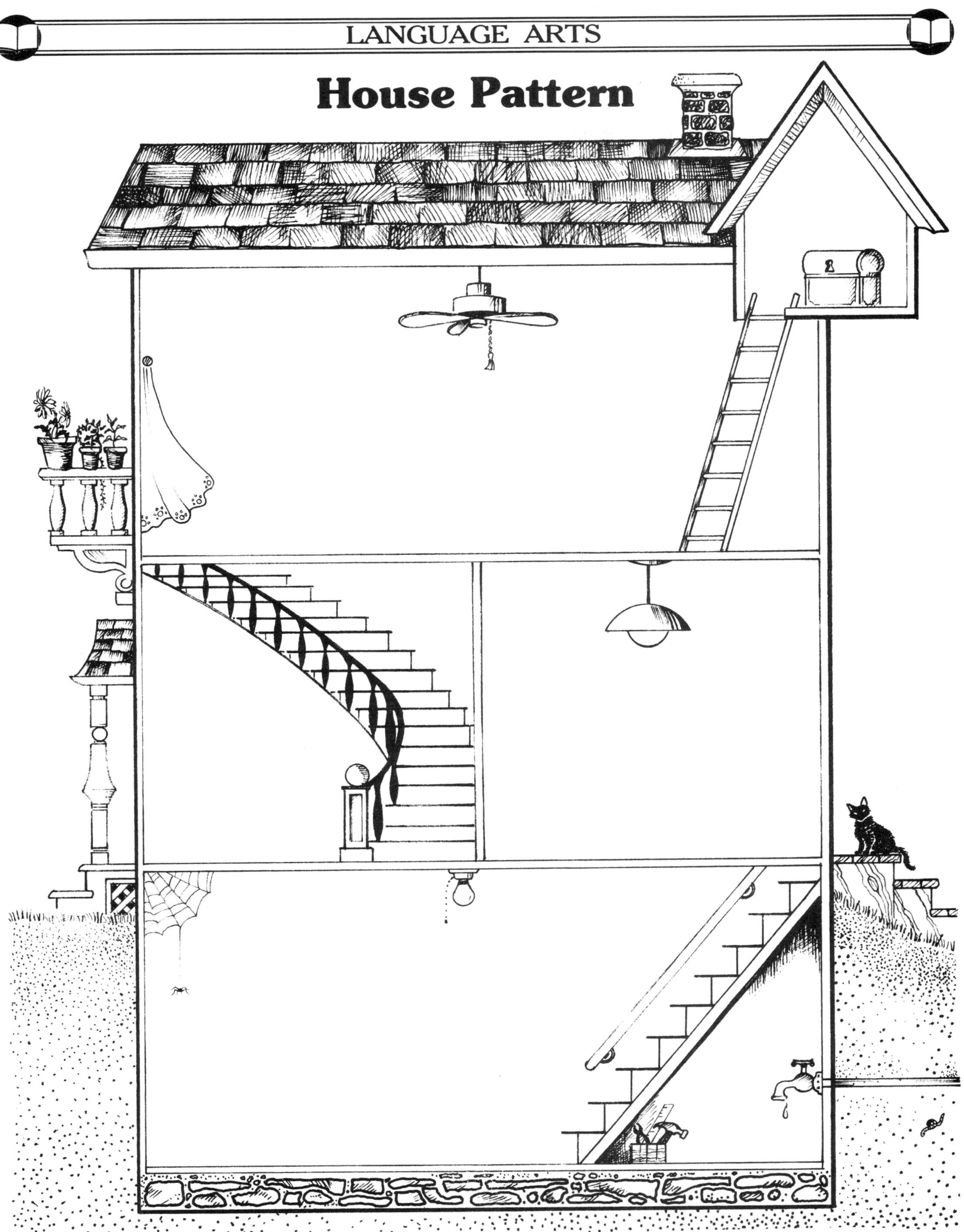

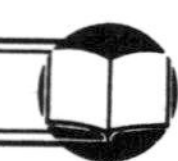

My Parents Can Write, Too!

Creative Writing

Objectives: To reinforce elements of a story; to emphasize the importance of the revision process; to create a parent/student/teacher writing connection

Materials: a copy of the parent letter below for each student, pencils, writing paper

Directions: Students will particularly enjoy this assignment because they will have the opportunity to assign their parents homework.

Review the elements of a story with students (setting, time, characters, problem, solutions, beginning, middle, end, etc.). Tell students that they will write a rough copy of the beginning and middle of a story. When this part of the story is written and revised, they will give their parents homework! Their parents will write the end, or the solution, to the story.

Send the rough copies home to parents accompanied by the letter below. (If desired, students could write their own letters.) When filling in the due date, it would be a good idea to allow them several nights to complete their assignments.

As stories are returned, final editing and revising should take place by the students. Students should then create a title. The final copy should include the names of both authors. A copy of the polished product should be sent home to the co-author as it makes a beautiful keepsake.

Extension: This makes an adorable bulletin board. Hang up parent/student stories with pictures of both authors. Students could illustrate a scene or character from their story.

Dear ________________,

Today, my homework assignment is to assign YOU homework! I have written the beginning and middle of a story. I have included the setting, characters and problem. Your job is to write the solution, or the ending. The story I am giving you is a first draft. When your homework is done, I will add a title and revise and edit the story to create a polished final copy.

Your homework is due on ________________. Thank you and good luck!

Love,

____

Advice Column

Letter Writing/ Sequencing

Objective: To practice letter writing skills

Materials: paper, pencil

Directions: Set up a weekly advice newspaper column. One student will be the author of the column. Select four or five students to write in for advice about a problem—real or imaginary. Tell students that each letter should have a heading and a greeting and should end with a closing and a signature. The problem letters should be submitted on Monday, and answers should be printed on the following Monday. Alternate problem-presenters and advice-givers.

Sample problems:

Mix and Match Story Parts

Objectives: To randomly select story parts and then compose a story using them; to distinguish and develop story parts

Materials: index cards, markers, 4 paper bags, writing paper, pencils

Directions: This "mixed-up" game is an exciting way for students to practice the skills of distinguishing and developing story parts. Prior to the lesson, prepare a variety of selections for each story part on index cards (character, setting, problem, solution). A fun way to do this is to have the students brainstorm two or three ideas for each story part and write them on index cards. Some suggestions are: Characters—master chef, bus driver, dog, caterpillar, surgeon, teacher; Problem—lost key, ran out of gas, missed the bus, forgot birthday, burned dinner; Setting—back yard, swimming pool, an amusement park, cafeteria, supermarket, school; Solution—rescued by friend, found some money, a surprise party, an ice cream cone, summer arrived.

continued on page 44

Mix and Match Story Parts continued

After the categories have been determined, label the four bags with the story part categories. Then, put the index cards into their proper bag. Have students select a card from each bag. If there are not enough cards for each student to select and keep, have them write down their choices and then return the cards to the bag. Once all the students have chosen from all four story parts, they are ready to write the details to "match" the parts together. The stories may be silly, but they are bound to be quite creative.

Wandering Words

Vocabulary Development

Objective: To use writing resources and build vocabulary by means of construction stories

Materials: 12" x 18" sheets of construction paper; old, age-appropriate magazine articles; lined writing paper; pencils; glue or tape; scissors

Directions: Here's another great way to use old periodicals and to help boost creative writing and vocabulary skills at the same time.

Give each student a sheet of construction paper. Ask students to fold their paper in half to form a booklet. Then, distribute magazine articles to students and have them secure the articles to the left side of the construction paper with glue or tape. On the right side, students should secure a lined piece of writing paper. Next, tell them that they are going to read their articles twice. The first time, they should read the story silently all the way through. The second time, they should skim the paragraphs and choose any words they feel might be interesting to use in a story of their own. Have the students indicate their choices by underlining them in the article. Tell the students they may choose any words they like for any reason, and they should try to incorporate these words into a creative composition of their own. Have students write these stories on the lined paper. When the stories are complete, invite students to share the list of words that "wandered" into their stories. Enjoy the finished products.

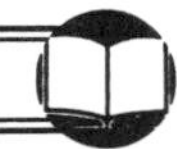

Alphabet Soup

Art/Spelling/ Poetry

Objective: To draw a large bowl of soup on construction paper and glue letters "inside" to make alphabet soup

Materials: construction paper, glue, markers, crayons, alphabet pasta or cereal, small paper cups

Directions: Begin this series of activities by motivating students with this fun and easy art project. First, distribute construction paper to the students. Have them draw a large bowl of soup on the paper. Encourage them to add details such as a tablecloth, spoon, crackers and a napkin. When the drawings are complete, give students a small cup full of dry alphabet pasta or cereal. Then, have students glue the letters in the center of the "soup." Voilà! Alphabet soup!

Alphabet Soup Words

Objectives: To create words from a random set of letters, to arrange them in alphabetical order and to determine the number of syllables in each word

Materials: alphabet soup drawings (above), paper, pencils

Directions: Using the letters that are in the soup bowls, have students form as many words as possible. When they have created at least 15-20 words, ask the students to arrange the words in alphabetical order. Go over the rules for alphabetizing as needed. After the students have alphabetized the words, have them divide the words into syllables. Demonstrate syllabication as necessary.

Acrostic Poems

Objectives: To write an acrostic poem

Materials: alphabet soup words (above), colored glue, drawing paper, pencils

Directions: Students will enjoy selecting one word from their alphabet soup words and creating an acrostic poem from the letters. This activity becomes even more fun when the students use colored glue to outline the letters of the word going down the left side of the drawing paper. This adds a tactile aspect to the activity. To write an acrostic poem, the students write adjectives or short statements that describe the word beginning with one of the letters in the word.

Green
Rug for the Earth
Ant - playground
Scratchy
Sod

Categorizing

Categories

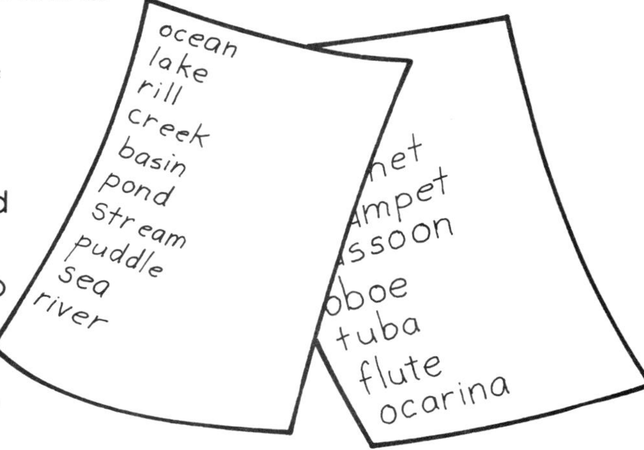

Objective: To reinforce students' abilities to recognize and identify categories of related words

Materials: writing or spelling journals, paper, pencils, timepiece with second hand

Directions: List-making is a basic skill that is used daily to help us get organized and to help us think as well. Categorizing these lists stimulates creative and critical thinking and problem solving. This activity begins with the creation of a variety of lists. These lists can be generated as five-minute time fillers, instant homework assignments or lesson lead-ins. The lists should be titled and kept in a common section of a journal or notebook. Other ways the words generated on the lists could be grouped should also be discussed, as should words that appear on more than one list. The following categories for generating lists are just a few suggestions: pets, fruits and vegetables, girls' names, boys' names, types of jobs, colors, items in a kitchen, things in a classroom, things in a mall, things that make sounds, zoo or farm animals, nouns, verbs, adjectives, adverbs, musical instruments, cities, transportation, clothing, snacks, countries, insects, etc.

You might also choose a category that is related to a classroom theme or favorite student-suggested catalog. After 12-15 lists have been generated, "Categories" can be played.

To introduce Categories, you will be the caller and the students will be the guessers. Ask one student to be the timekeeper. He/she will watch the clock and call "time's up" after one minute. When the timekeeper says, "begin," start to name things from a particular list. Continue naming items from the list until a student can recognize and name the title of the category in which those items belong. When they think they know the category, students should raise their hands. Quickly call on a student. If he/she gives the correct answer, move on to a new category. If he/she is incorrect, keep naming items, repeating as necessary until the students guess correctly or time runs out.

Once the students get the hang of it, they can break up into cooperative groups to play the game. In teams of four or five, the students will face off against opposing teams. Team A does the calling and timekeeping while Team B guesses and vice versa. Teams may also appoint a scorekeeper to record the number of correct guesses each team makes in one minute.

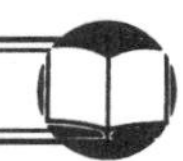

My Favorite Words

Vocabulary Development

Objective: To encourage students to examine and reflect on the meaning of words in their everyday lives

Materials: 12" x 18" sheets of construction paper, newspapers and magazines, scissors, glue sticks, crayons, markers

Directions: To tune your students into looking at words in a new way, teach them to be collectors of words. First, distribute a piece of construction paper to each student. Allow students to decorate a fancy frame around the border of the paper. Then, direct students to look through magazines and newspapers and cut out words they like. Instruct them to keep in mind the reasons why they chose specific words. For example, students may select the word *sassafras* because they like the way it sounds, *Popsicles* because they are the student's favorite summer treat, or *popcorn* because they like the letter p. Students should then glue the words they selected in the center of the frame and sign their name to the collage. Have students share their words and what these words mean to them.

Extension: Have students use their favorite words in a creative writing story. Encourage students to look up any words that they do not know in the dictionary. Enjoy learning about your students in a way that increases their awareness of themselves and the words that have meaning to them.

Word Books for Word Collectors

Objective: To complete a book of unusual, fascinating, theme-specific words

Materials: construction paper, blank paper, paper fasteners or book rings, markers

Directions: This activity is designed to help you create a theme-specific vocabulary book that is readily available to your students. As you read aloud to students or brainstorm ideas on a specific theme, ask students to be on the lookout for new and unusual words. Then, list these words on blank paper. At the end of the theme, decorate a cover to identify the category of words. (A shape related to the theme is a nice touch, too.) Make a booklet by fastening the pages and the cover together. Store the booklet with the dictionaries or in the writing center for easy access.

"Shape" Words

Vocabulary Development/Writing

Objective: To reinforce meanings of words

Materials: drawing paper, colored markers, crayons

Directions: Let students be creative in drawing pictures to relate words and their meanings. Have students choose a word and then manipulate the size and shape of the actual letters of the word so that they look like what the word means or like the object that the word names.

Words in "Action"

Objective: To reinforce verbs and their meanings

Materials: chart paper, alphabet stencils, construction paper, colored markers, crayons

Directions: Have students brainstorm a list of "action words" (i.e. hop, gallop, crawl, run, skip, etc.). List their responses on chart paper. Then, have students select a verb and stencil the letters that spell that word on a piece of colored construction paper. Direct students to outline the letters using a black marker and then add characteristic features to make their word "come alive." Students should add background details to show the word doing the action related to its meaning.

Chalk Talk!

Objective: To write speech balloons and quotation marks

Materials: poster or large picture of children, animals or inanimate objects; chalk

Directions: Mount the poster/picture on the board. Direct the students to think about what the people/animals/inanimate objects might be saying/thinking. For example, you may hang up a picture of an overstuffed dresser with clothes hanging out of the drawers. The dresser may be thinking, "I'm stuffed!" and the clothes could be thinking, "I'm squashed! I want to get into the laundry basket!" During center time, or when students have a free moment, they may write their ideas on the board in a speech balloon. (You may want to have students initial their balloons.) If desired, award a prize to the funniest, the most creative, etc.

Palindromes

Objective: To list words that read the same backward and forward

Materials: paper, pencils

Directions: Brainstorm words with students that read the same backward and forward (i.e. did, pop, mom, etc.). To add excitement to this word style, make the brainstorming a game by putting the students into cooperative learning groups and setting a time limit. Then, have groups share their lists. If you like, award points to unique words that the students have listed.

Homophones

Objectives: To practice using homophones correctly and to identify them in sentences

Materials: paper, pencils, chart paper, marker

Directions: Homophones are words that are pronounced alike but are different in meaning and spelling. Over several days, brainstorm a list of homophones with your students on chart paper. When the list is complete, hang it in the writing workshop or game center. Then, teach your students a fun way to practice using these new words correctly by playing the "Teakettle" game. Explain that two players are needed, and each one must have a pencil and paper. The first player says a sentence in which two homophones are replaced by the word *teakettle*. For example: "I teakettle an ocean liner sailing on the deep blue teakettle. (see, sea) He teakettle a hamburger and teakettle French fries for dinner last night." (ate, eight) The second player could guess the homophones aloud or list them on paper and check them at the end of the game.

HARE WITH HAIR

HOMOPHONES

hear, here	read, red	stair, stare	mail, male	kernel, colonel
ant, aunt	tea, tee	eye, I	peace, piece	not, knot
eight, ate	wear, where	threw, through	hoarse, horse	steel, steal
hair, hare	blew, blue	maid, made	tail, tale	peal, peel
knew, new	no, know	roll, role	nose, knows	write, right
to, two	flower, flour	pare, pair	deer, dear	pause, paws
weight, wait	poll, pole	patience, patients	weak, week	doe, dough
plain, plane	see, sea	heard, herd	bury, berry	pale, pail
by, bye	bear, bare		knight, night	you, ewe

Rebus Riddles

Vocabulary Development/ Grammar

Objective: To relate words to symbols and word meanings

Materials: drawing paper, pencil, marker, crayons

Directions: Rebus drawings include representations of words or the letters or syllables of words that are created through the use of pictures of objects or symbols. Share some examples of rebuses with the class. Point out the way in which the symbol or picture's name resembles the actual intended word, letter or syllable in that word. Then, have students write some riddles and draw the answers using rebuses. Students will enjoy exchanging papers and solving each other's riddles while relating the pictures, symbols and meanings to words.

IF U

–B T+ ,

U R (This color) t

Variation: To practice creating compound words, have students draw a pair of pictures which, when put together, make a compound word. Display several of the students' rebus drawings on the chalkboard each day. Have students guess the compound word that is being represented by the rebus drawings. Provide a manila envelope for students to put guesses in until it's time to reveal the answer.

Illustrating Similes

Objective: To create descriptive phrases using the words "like" or "as" (similes) and illustrate them to create a class book

Materials: construction paper, markers, crayons

SOFT AS A MARSHMALLOW

Directions: Discuss what a simile is with students and why/how they can improve their writing. Next, have students brainstorm familiar similes such as "as green as grass," "as big as a house" and then create new ones. When a list of similes has been created on the board, explain to students that they will each choose one and illustrate it. The illustrations should include the object or person (the noun) that is being described with the simile written across the top of the paper. For example, if the students chose the simile "as sweet as candy," they may want to draw sugar and candy.

Extension: This activity makes an interesting class book. If you choose to create a book, you may want to monitor the student choices to ensure variation.

Antonym and Synonym Wheels

Objectives: To build student knowledge of antonyms and/or synonyms and to create an antonym and/or synonym wheel

Materials: markers, scissors, paper fasteners, wheel patterns (pages 52-53), paper

Directions: The word wheels that are created in this lesson vary slightly when the object is for the students to list synonyms rather than antonyms. However, the general construction of the wheel itself is the same for both.

Begin by distributing the appropriate word wheel pattern to students. Instruct them to carefully cut out both parts of the wheel pattern. When they are finished cutting, they should place the smaller wheel in the center on top of the larger wheel. The sides with sections should be facing up. Have the students place a paper fastener in the center of the two wheels to secure the two parts together. The top and bottom circles should be able to turn independently of each other.

When the students have completed the wheel construction, turn their attention to the definitions of an antonym or synonym, depending on the lesson. Share some examples of the topic and encourage the students to do so as well. List the examples on the board. If the topic is antonyms, some examples might be: hot—cold, tall—short, fat—thin.

Tell students that they are going to list ten words and the antonyms of those words on a sheet of paper. Encourage students to choose words related to a classroom theme or perhaps even their weekly spelling words. When they are satisfied with their selections, they are going to write the first word in each group in a space on the inner wheel. Then, they are going to write the opposite of those words in the spaces on the outer wheel. When all the students have finished, they can exchange "Word Wheels" and turn them until they have found the antonym pairs for each word on the inner circle. Request that the students write down the word matches they make. This fun activity gives students an opportunity to build their vocabulary and to share ideas with each other.

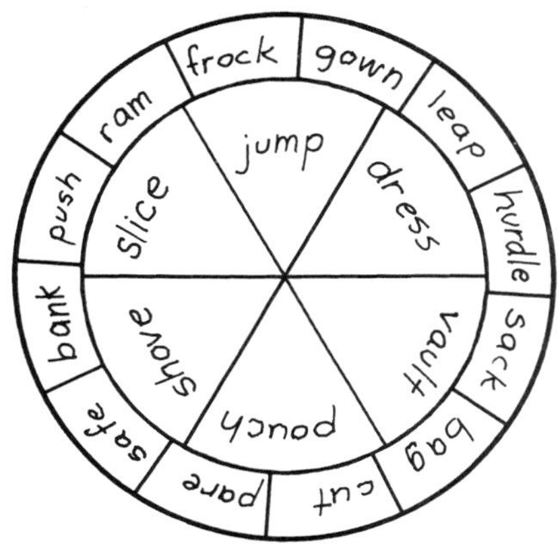

The synonym wheel varies in that students will select six words and then brainstorm two synonyms for each word. The first six words are written on the inner circle and the six pairs of synonyms are listed on the outer wheel, each pair being written side by side in the spaces that are linked together in the outer wheel. Students should then exchange wheels and match the inner wheel words with its synonyms.

By using the word wheels, students have the opportunity to increase their vocabulary.

Antonym Wheel Patterns

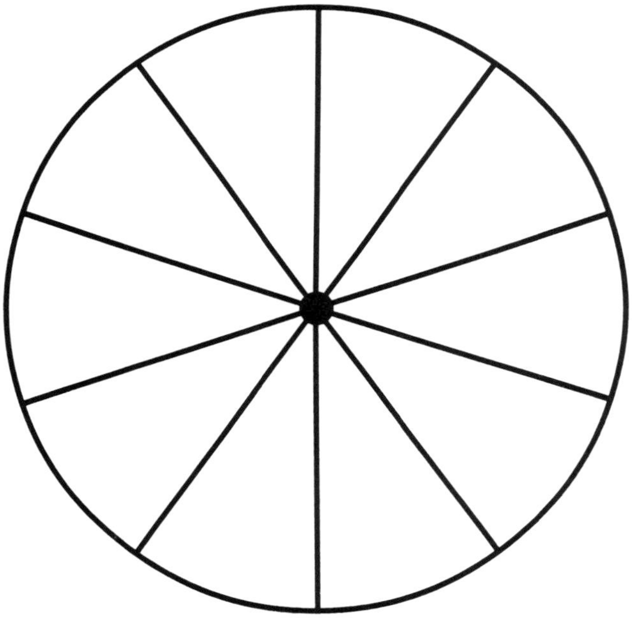

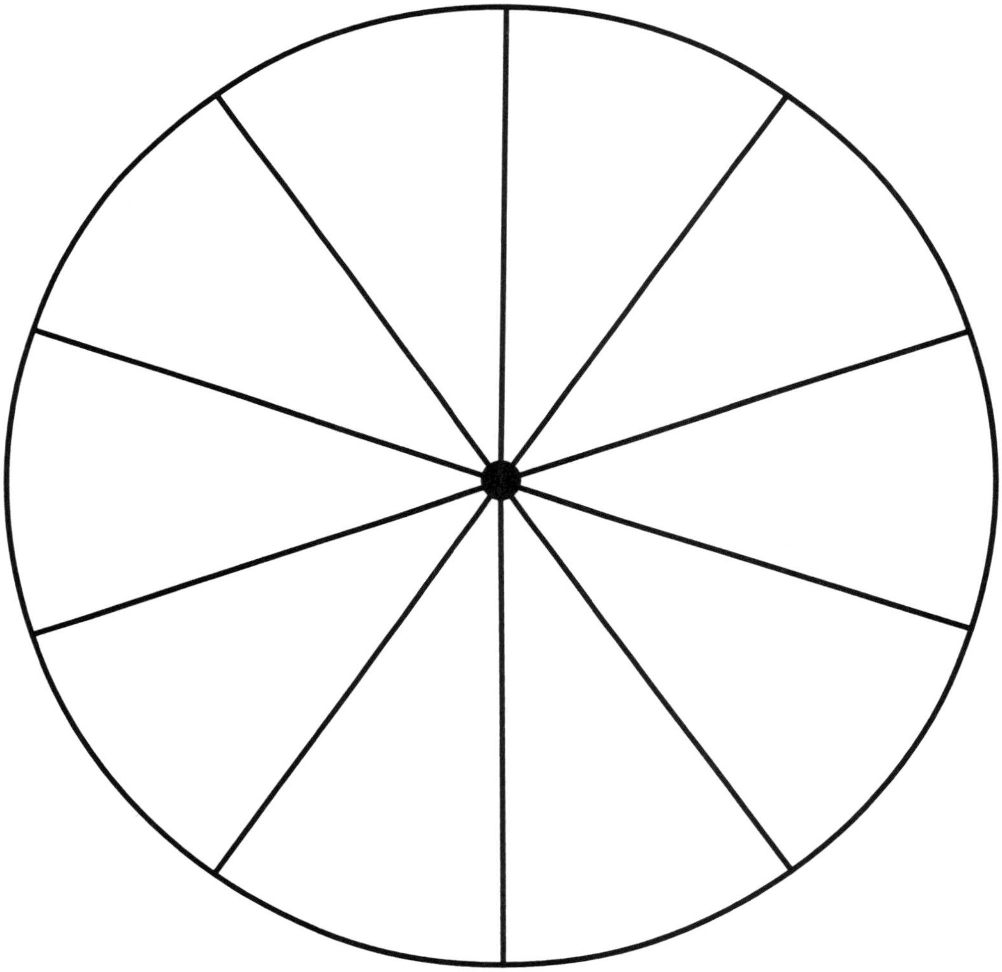

Synonym Wheel Patterns

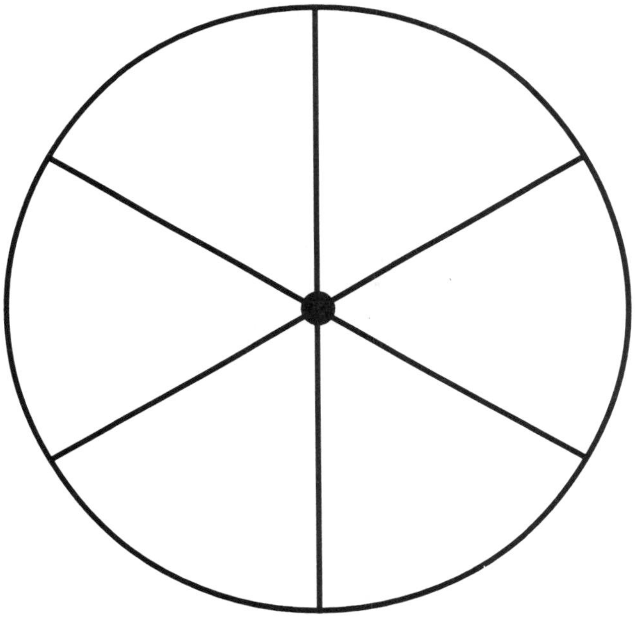

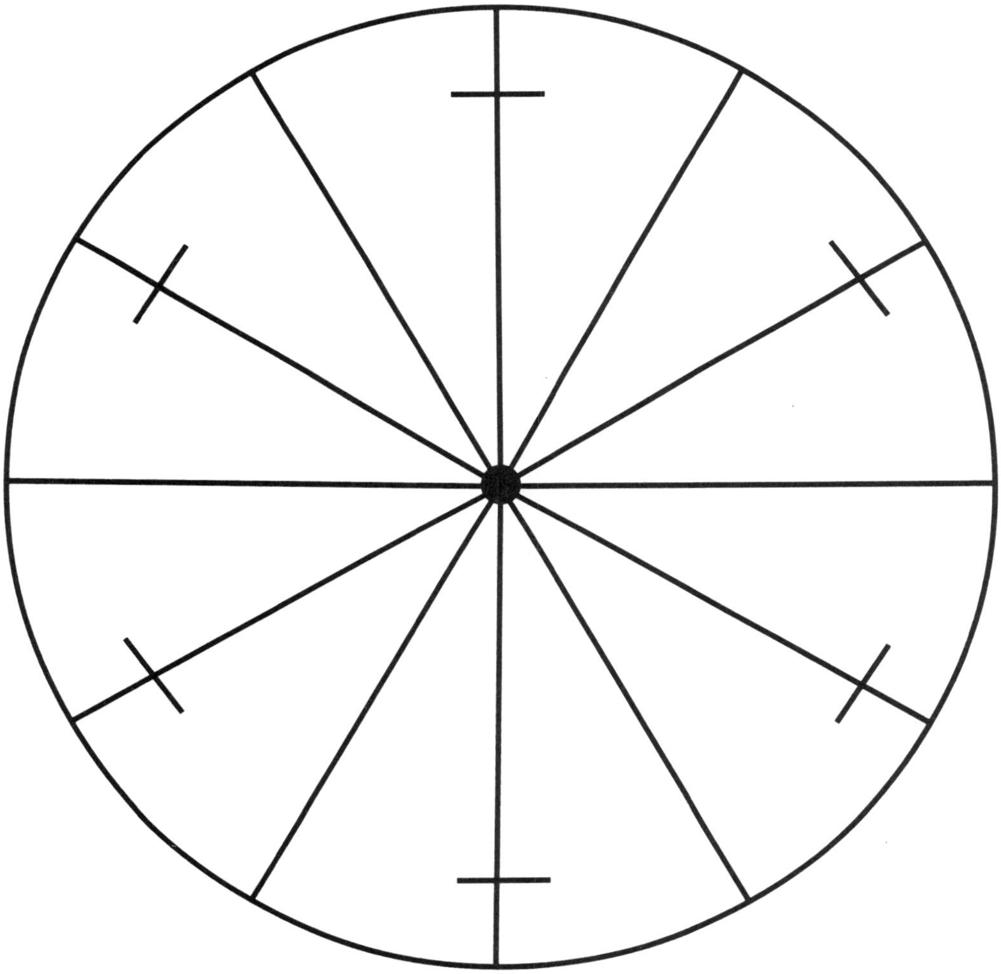

Tic-Tac-Contractions

Grammar/Vocabulary Development

Objective: To identify and write contractions

Materials: paper, pencils, bingo markers

I'm	he's	won't
it's	who's	can't
don't	she's	let's

Directions: Your students will enjoy working with contractions as they play this version of Tic-Tac-Toe. Explain to students that a contraction is a short way of saying or writing two or more words and that an apostrophe takes the place of letters that are dropped. Together, brainstorm all sorts of contractions and the words that are represented in the shortened form. Write the list on the board. Make sure you have a large list.

Once the students have grasped the concept, they are ready to play the game. Have the students divide a piece of paper into nine squares (a Tic-Tac-Toe board). Ask them to choose nine contractions and write them in any of the nine boxes, one word to a box. Then, call out words whose contractions are included on the list. Students must identify the contractions of those words and then mark the contraction if they have listed it on their board. The first player to have three correctly identified contractions in a row wins.

I'm	**aren't**	**wouldn't**	**I'd**	**let's**	**he's**
couldn't	**weren't**	**shouldn't**	**haven't**	**she's**	**won't**
wasn't	**who's**	**can't**	**it's**	**isn't**	**he'd**

Adjectives Take Shape

Objective: To build descriptive vocabulary

Materials: paper (writing journals), pencils, mural paper, markers

Directions: This activity is designed to increase your students' knowledge of adjectives and to give students practice using descriptive language in story writing. The benefits are even greater when you use this lesson to create an interactive bulletin board to brighten the room and really make those "adjectives take shape."

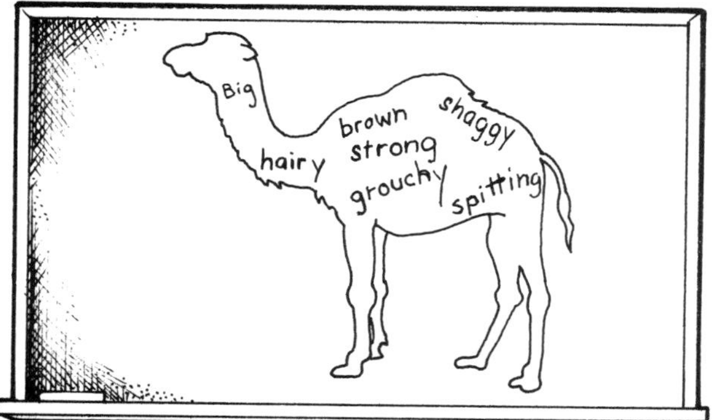

To begin, draw and label the outline of an object on a bulletin board covered with mural paper. Throughout the day, have students brainstorm words describing the object. Record students' ideas in the outline of the object. Toward the end of the day or as a homework assignment, have the students copy the adjectives in their writing journals and then create stories or poems about the object using the descriptive words.

What's That Sound?

Objectives: To introduce students to onomatopoeia and to enhance listening skills

Materials: a prerecorded tape of household, school and outdoor sounds (i.e. a bird chirping, the sound of the lunchroom, a baby crying, a car starting, a bell ringing, the sound of chalk on a chalkboard, footsteps, a sneeze, a ball bouncing, etc.); tape recorder; paper; pencils

Directions: Tape ten sounds found in the world around you. When taping, leave space, or "dead air," between recordings to give students the opportunity to respond. When you are ready to begin the lesson, have students number their papers from one to ten. Tell students that they are going to hear some sounds and that they should try to write a word to describe the sound they hear. Play the tape. (You may want to provide an example such as buzz—the sound a bee makes.) Instruct them not to talk and not to share ideas.

PUTTPUTTPUTTPUTTPUTTPUTTPUTT

Next, play the tape again. As students listen to the sounds, ask for volunteers to share the word they provided or the sound. Play the tape a third time. This time, the students should try to identify the sound. Again, play the tape and discuss the sound sources. Explain to students that onomatopoeic words are used to imitate sounds. Discuss why authors use it. For homework, have students listen for sounds at home and write words for those sounds.

Chart Thesaurus

Objectives: To create a class chart and journal page consisting of words to describe the attributes; to classify words; to expand vocabulary; to encourage more descriptive writing

Materials: chart paper, markers, a small object, blindfold, paper

Directions: Prepare a chart with the following words written across the top: Size, Color, Texture, Smell, Taste. Ask students how they may describe an object so that someone else may know what it is like (shape, size, color, etc.). Ask students if they could possibly include smell and taste to describe an object. Next, blindfold a volunteer, and ask the rest of the students to close their eyes. Place an object in the hands of the blindfolded student, and ask him/her to describe it using as many of the attributes as possible. On the chart paper, write down the words the blindfolded student supplied under the appropriate categories. Remove the object from the student's hands and conceal it.

continued on page 56

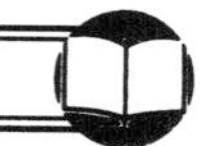

Chart Thesaurus continued

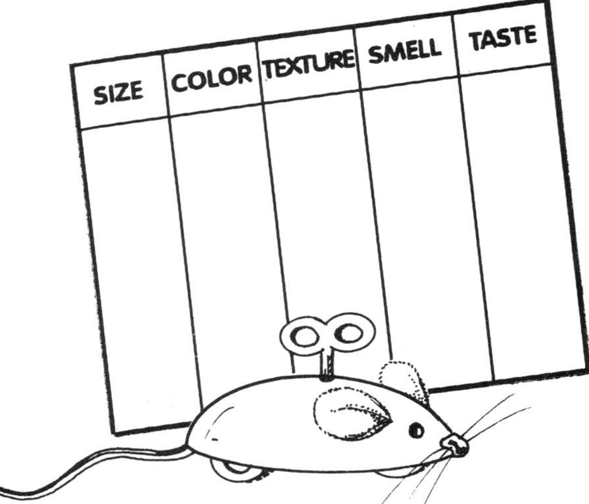

Remove the blindfold and ask all students to open their eyes. Using the words written on the chart, ask the students to try to identify the object. If they cannot, add words under the appropriate categories, one by one, until students solve the mystery.

Tell students to make a chart on a piece of paper with the same headings that are on your chart. Ask students to write down as many words as possible to fit under each category. Encourage them, however, to use words they wouldn't normally use. For example, in the size category, discourage words such as *big* and *small*. Encourage *tremendous* and *tiny*. Before students begin, tell them that you will be asking them for their favorite word to place on the class chart. In order to give students enough time, you may want to give them this assignment for homework. The assignment could be completed with or without the help of a thesaurus. Tell students that you want at least ten words for each category.

The next day, ask students to chose their favorite word from their chart to place on the class chart. As each student supplies his/her word, ask the rest of the students to identify the category it belongs in (i.e. if the word supplied is sticky, the class should identify the category "Texture"). As words are shared, students may add any words desired to their personal charts.

When the class chart is complete, hang it near your writing center where students can refer to it. The individual charts can be stapled into students' journals. Students will be amazed at the sound of their own writing when they employ words from the chart.

Extension: Supply students with the following paragraph. Using their charts, ask them to replace or add as many words as they can to make the paragraph detailed and illustrative.

Daniel decided to make doughnuts. What a disaster! The bowl he chose was too small, and the spoon was too big. When he began to stir the dough, the flour poured out all over the table. When the dough was made, it was icky. Daniel had a tough time following the recipe. When the doughnuts were baking, the smell filled the house. When they were done, Daniel ate one. He thought they tasted good!

Student/Class Thesaurus

Vocabulary Development/ Grammar

Objectives: To create a personal and class thesaurus

Materials: notebooks or student-made booklets, a classroom notebook or booklet

Directions: After students have become familiar with the makeup and purpose of a thesaurus, they can create one of their own. Begin by having students title their notebook or booklet, **My Thesaurus**. Next, students should write a letter of the alphabet (in order) at the top of each page. Throughout the school year as the students submit work to you, you may want to circle words and mark them with a "T." This would indicate to the student that a more elaborate word would improve his/her writing, and that the student should enter this word into his/her thesaurus.

A second way to implement the thesaurus is to have students enter theme words or words that may pertain to a particular writing assignment. For example, if the students will be writing about their pets, it will help them to have synonyms for words such as *cute*, *love*, *happy*, *play*, *furry*, etc.

A third way to use the thesaurus is to have students enter commonly used words such as *nice*, *big*, *a lot*, *very*, etc.

The class thesaurus should include any words that the entire class entered into their personal thesaurus. Plus, individual students could choose to enter a word that they feel would be helpful to their classmates. These individual entries could be made on a daily or weekly basis depending on time and interest.

Noun/Verb Word Booklets

Objectives: To create booklets illustrating words that act as both a noun and a verb

Materials: 11" x 18" sheets of white construction paper, crayons, word list (page 58), dictionaries

Directions: Using a dictionary, have students compile a list of words, each of which can be a noun and a verb depending on how it is used in a sentence. (Discuss characteristics of nouns and verbs with the students.) Have students choose a word from the list or assign one to each student. Give each student a sheet of white construction paper and have him/her fold it in half to create a booklet. The students should write their noun/verb word on the cover and decorate it. Instruct students to open the booklet. On the top left side, the students should write **noun**, and on the top right side, they should write **verb.** At the bottom of the noun page, students should write a sentence using the assigned word as a noun.

continued on page 58

Noun/Verb Word Booklet continued

They should do the same on the right side, using the same word as a verb. Next, they should illustrate their sentences. Share them with the class, and put them in your writing center.

Extension: Instead of using the dictionary, students could flip through magazines for ideas. Instead of illustrating the sentences, students could cut magazine pictures to accompany their sentences.

noun/verb list

sail	mold	sun	shade	cover	dock
check	bite	match	tick	soil	sand
call	change	buckle	milk	toast	spray
garden	kick	garnish	salt	dot	sign
flour	play	harness	number	field	
sample	float	run	map	cruise	
storm	screen	flood	flip	dress	

Holiday Nouns and Verbs

Writing

Objectives: To match a list of nouns and verbs to construct sentences, paragraphs and stories

Materials: chart paper, marker, paper, pencils

Directions: Review the definition of nouns and verbs with the students. Then, have students make a list of all the nouns they can think of associated with a particular holiday. Have students make a list of creative verbs to go along with them. For example, if the holiday is St. Patrick's Day, the lists might include: Nouns—leprechaun, clover, gold, rainbow, pot; Verbs—skipped, disappeared, whistled, searched, tricked. Then, have the students work independently to pair the nouns and verbs and add other words to create "holiday" sentences. To extend the activity, the students might also arrange the sentences into paragraphs to create a story or team up with a classmate to combine their sentences into one story.

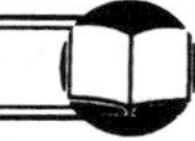

Writing

Alliteration Tongue Twisters

Objective: To introduce a writing "device" to heighten interest in a story or poem

Directions: Explain to students that alliteration is the repetition of initial consonant sounds in two or more neighboring words (i.e. wild and woolly, threatening throngs, ghastly ghosts). To help students get started writing alliteration tongue twisters, say a word and call on a student to give an alliterative answer. After all the students have had a turn, tell them to write a sentence using two alliterative words. If this is too difficult, you may want to divide students into pairs. Have students share their sentences.

Write one of the following tongue twisters on the board.

She sells seashells by the seashore.

Peter Piper picked a peck of pickled peppers. A peck of pickled peppers, Peter Piper picked. If Peter Piper picked a peck of pickled peppers, where's the peck of pickled peppers Peter Piper picked?

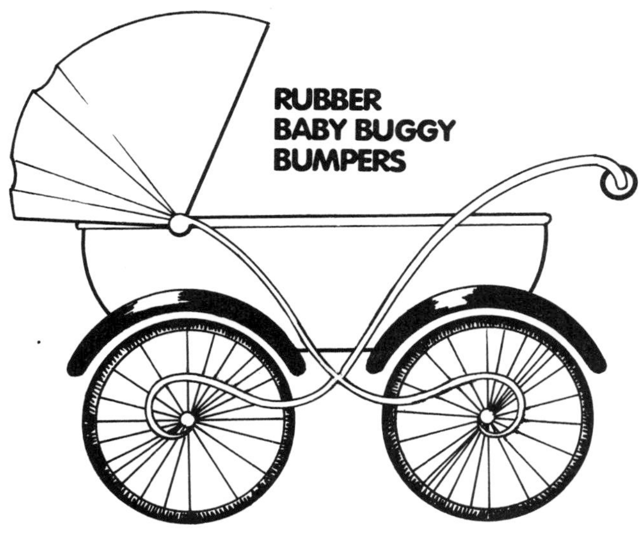

Say them out loud. Then, have the students repeat them. Explain what a tongue twister is. Then, attempt to write a tongue twister with the class. Pick a letter or blend that you are going to use. (For example: L—Long legged loons looked like large lilies.) Divide students into cooperative learning groups. Have each group write its own alliterative tongue twister. After the groups have selected a letter or a blend, they may want to use a dictionary to help them. When the tongue twisters are completed, have the groups share them with each other.

Suggested Reading: *The Bells* by Edgar Allen Poe

Prefix Posters

Word Recognition

Objectives: To learn the meanings of prefixes and to became familiar with words containing prefixes

Materials: large sheets of construction paper, crayons, markers, dictionaries, paper, pencils

Directions: To the right is a list of prefixes and their meanings. After discussing what prefixes are and where they're located, share the list of prefixes and their meanings. Students should then choose one of the prefixes and, with the help of a dictionary, create a list of words that begin with their prefix. Next, each student will create a prefix poster. It should include the prefix along with the definition at the top. The remainder of the poster should include an illustration of one of the prefix words. The completed prefix list could be stapled to the bottom of the poster.

prefix	meaning
re	again
sub	under
pre	before
un	not
com	together
dis	apart
in	not
mis	bad
multi	many
tri	three
bi	two
octo	eight

Prefix Flip Book

Objective: To create a class flip book to reinforce prefixes/root words

Materials: 2 index cards for each student, 4 book rings, hole punch, piece of cardboard

Directions: After students have become familiar with the concept of prefixes and root words, students should then choose a word containing a prefix. Give each student two index cards. On one, students write the prefix of their word, and on the other card they write the root word. Collect each set of cards. Punch two holes at the top of each index card so that you may later attach them with book rings. To create a cover, label one index card **Prefixes** and a second card **Root Words**. Punch two holes at the top of these two cards as well.

SUBTERRANEAN

To assemble the book, place the cardboard piece on the table. Lay the pile of prefix cards on top of the cardboard to the left, and the root word cards on the right side of the cardboard. Use the book rings to fasten the index cards to the cardboard.

To use the book, set it in your writing/reading center. Independently or in pairs, students can flip the prefixes and the root words over to try and create words. Students should record the words they were able to form. When everyone has had a chance to work with the flip book, create a chart of all the words found.

Yesterday, Today and Tomorrow
Getting Words to Agree

Grammar/ Spelling

Objective: To examine verb agreement

Materials: index cards, chart paper, paper, pencils, markers, box

Directions: Prepare for this lesson by writing verbs on index cards. (See list to the right.) You will need one verb card for every two students. Place the cards in a box.

go	sit	ride	drive
sell	teach	can	fall
send	steal	run	see
shake	wake	buy	take
catch	hold	tell	dive

On chart paper, create four columns. Label the columns: **verb, yesterday, today, tomorrow**.

I sat.....

I will sit.....

I am sitting.....

When you are ready to begin the lesson, pair students and have each pair pick a verb card from the box. Students must use the same verb in three sentences, using the word "yesterday" in the first sentence, "today" in the second and "tomorrow" in the third. When the sentences are complete, have the pairs exchange papers. Students can then check the work they have received and share it with the class by placing the verb card on the chart and writing the sentences in the appropriate columns. Discuss how each verb form changes under the yesterday column and how each verb needs a helper under the tomorrow column.

Spelling Rules

Objective: To introduce students to some mnemonic devices to help them with the anomalies of spelling and pronunciation

Materials: construction paper, crayons, markers

Directions: Discuss with the students some of the spelling rules listed below.

1. ***I* before *e* except after *c* or when sounded like *a* as in *neighbor* or *weigh***
2. ***U* always follows *q*.**
3. **When two vowels go walking, the first one does the talking (i.e. road, lied).**
4. **When adding *ing* to words that end in *e*, drop the *e* and then add the *ing* (i.e. take—taking, have—having).**
5. **When making a plural word from words that end in *y*, change the *y* to *i* and add *es* (ie. bunny—bunnies, pony—ponies). The exception is words that end in *ey*. You just add *s* (i.e. monkey—monkeys).**

Read the stories on page 62 to illustrate rule #1 and #2. This will help students remember the rules. Invite the students to write their own stories illustrating any one of the five rules. When the stories are complete, encourage students to present them to the class in a creative manner.

continued on page 62

Spelling Rules continued

The Alphabet council was having its regular monthly meeting. All 26 members were in attendance. The Grand Hoo Ha was presiding. All the members had received their sounds, and there were no big problems to be discussed. The good friends i and e were sitting together, i in front of e as usual.

The meeting was adjourned and all the letters left. I and e left together, i walking in front as usual. E was pretty happy about this arrangement. After all, if there was a hole in the ground, i would be the one to fall in.

After several months, e began to realize that there were no holes for i to fall into. E was also beginning to think that it should be first sometimes, too. I and e began to have big arguments. They finally decided to bring the problem before the Grand Hoo Ha.

The Grand Hoo Ha thought about it for several months, and it was decided that a special meeting of the Alphabet Council should be called. All 26 letters arrived and e set forth the problem. It just wasn't fair for i to always be first when they were together. E wanted a turn to be first, too. The letters considered the problem. They agreed with e also, but they had no solution. Finally c said, "I'll help out. After all, I already share a sound with k and s so I know how to cooperate. When I'm with e and i, I'll go first, e will follow me and i will be behind us."

This seemed like a good solution. Everyone thanked c, and they all went home. E was satisfied, but after a while, e realized that c was not around all that much, and e wasn't getting so many chances to be first. At the next meeting of the Alphabet Council, e discussed the problem. Finally, a said, "I have so many different sounds, both long and short, I'll share a sound with you. When i and e are together and they sound like a, e will go first."

Finally, everyone was satisfied. The Grand Hoo Ha wrote down the new plan.

I before e except after c or when sounded like a as in neighbor or weigh

---

One day q brought a problem to the Alphabet Council. Q was very conceited. It was all curved with a cute little curly tail—nothing sharp anywhere. It really resented being followed by that strange creature u. U had two sharp points sticking up in the air and q thought that that was quite unattractive. The Grand Hoo Ha listened to the complaint and gave a ruling immediately. Q with only curves, was apt to be rolling around all the time. Q definitely needed u to follow it around to stop it from rolling to the wrong places. U with its two strong arms was just the protection q needed. Henceforth u would always follow q.

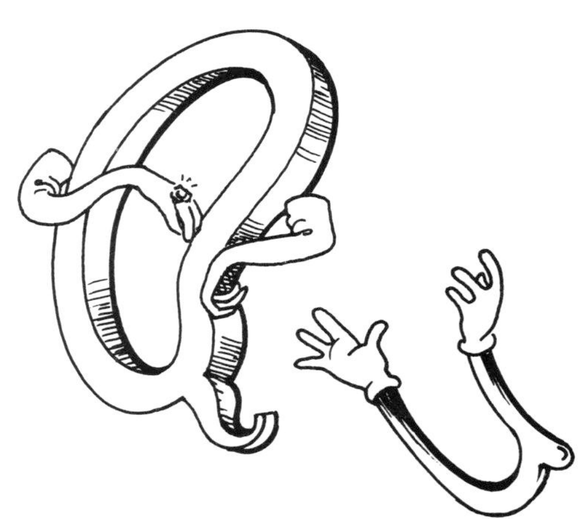

Grammar

Word Values

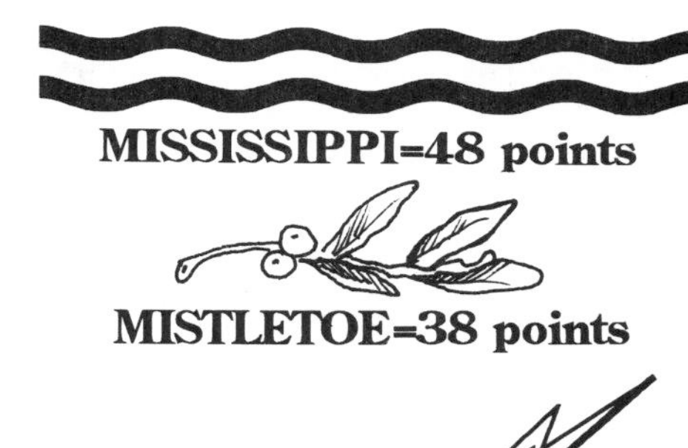

Objectives: To recognize vowels, consonants and syllables and to practice computation skills

Materials: paper, pencils, calculators (optional)

Directions: This activity encourages students to examine spelling words more closely and increases students' computational skills at the same time. To begin, have students select at least five words. The words might be drawn from the students' weekly spelling list, or they may be theme-specific words such as "holiday" words, science terms or new reading vocabulary. Explain that there are rules for this game which require the students to know what vowels, consonants and syllables are. Go over these definitions as needed and practice identifying these word parts together. Then, present students with the following list of word part values: Syllables are worth 2 points, vowels are worth 3 points, consonants are worth 4 points. The second rule that the students will need to follow is to add the syllable value to the vowel value. Then, take their answer and add it to the consonant value. For example: Microscope—3 syllables = 2 + 2 + 2 = 6; 4 vowels = 3 + 3 + 3 + 3 = 12; 6 consonants = 4 + 4 + 4 + 4 + 4 + 4 = 24; 6 + 12 + 24 = 42. At your discretion, have students work with a partner and use a calculator to solve the point value. When all students have completed their answers, have them add up all the values. Then, ask students to share their highest value word and lowest value word. Encourage them to share their reasons to invoke answers such as, "This word had many consonants which also has the highest individual value of all the word parts."

Conjunctions

Objective: To learn to use conjunctions

Materials: paper, pencils

Directions: Explain to the class that conjunctions are words used to connect words and/or sentences together. Tell students that the conjunctions most often used are *and, or, so, because, but, however, therefore*. Give students some examples of sentences using conjunctions such as: "I like baseball and soccer. Which do you want, an ice cream cone or an ice cream soda? I was sick, so I stayed home. I started to read, however, I was too tired."

Divide students into pairs. Assign a conjunction to each pair. Give a topic to the class to write sentences about. One student in each pair writes a sentence. The second student writes an appropriate second sentence to be joined to the first sentence by using the assigned conjunction. The combined sentence should make sense.

Conjunctions Can Count

Grammar/ Writing

Objective: To make sensible sentences using conjunctions

Materials: construction paper, stapler, markers, index cards, push pins

Directions: Assign a topic to the class. Divide the class into six groups. Have each group write a sentence related to the topic on a large piece of construction paper to make a sentence strip. Post all the sentence strips on a bulletin board in random fashion. At the top of the board, write the topic. On index cards, write conjunctions and put them at the bottom of the board. You or the students could also make pictures to relate to the topic to display on the bulletin board.

Assign a group of students each day to rearrange the sentence strips using the conjunctions so that there is a "story" that makes sense. Each week, change the topic and write new sentences.

Let's Join Together

Objective: To join student-generated, group-written sentences using conjunctions to create a paragraph

Materials: scrap paper, sentence strip paper (or adding machine tape), pencils, tape

Directions: Supply students with one writing topic (i.e. The Snowy Day, I Missed the Bus!). Organize the class into cooperative learning groups of two to three students. Each group should write one sentence about the topic on scrap paper. The group should edit and revise its sentence and write it on the sentence strip paper (or horizontally on the adding machine tape). As each sentence is completed, students should tape their strip to the board. When everyone has finished, examine the sentences to see which sentences can be combined using conjunctions (and, so, but, because, etc.).

continued on page 65

Let's Join Together continued

I wanted to try some different sports this summer. I found out I don't like golf **because** golf is hard to learn. Rollerblading is exciting **but** you have to wear a helmet (**and** that messes up my hair). Now I take tennis lessons. I am good at tennis, **so** I like to play tennis. I was in a tournament **and** I came in first place!

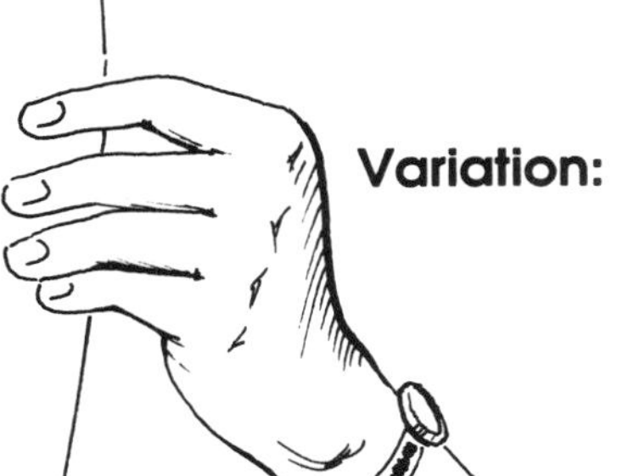

Next, students could use some or all of the sentences from the board to write a story. Students should focus on using compound sentences and conjunctions.

Variation: This makes an interesting lesson when students are asked to react to literature, discussing their feelings and thoughts.

Grammar

Pop-Up Punctuation

Objective: To review and reinforce the correct use of final punctuation

Materials: variety of sentences (below), 3" x 8" sheets of construction paper, crayons, markers

Directions: Learning to use correct final punctuation marks becomes more memorable and fun when it is turned into a whole body experience. Assign students one of the following punctuation marks: a **.**, a **?**, an **!**. Direct them to draw their assigned punctuation mark on construction paper using markers or crayons. Then, read a variety of sentences out loud. (See examples below.) Students whose punctuation mark is appropriate for the sentences should quickly stand and hold up their punctuation sign. Identify and compare declarative, interrogative and exclamatory sentences.

1. Tim and I visited Mr. Day, a beekeeper, last week.
2. We saw some bees squeeze through a tiny hole.
3. Mr. Day said, "Don't move too quickly!"
4. One bee landed on a flower.
5. I asked, "What is the most important bee?"
6. "The queen bee, of course!" exclaimed Mr. Day.
7. "How fast do a bee's wings beat?" I asked.
8. Mr. Day replied, "About 250 times a second."
9. The beekeeper knows many facts about bees.
10. "Wow! What a great visit!" we chimed.

Punctuation Has a Purpose!

Grammar

Objectives: To emphasize the importance and purpose of punctuation and to enhance punctuation awareness

Materials: a prepared tape recording of an excerpt, student writing or the short story below; a written copy for each student of the recorded materials (without any punctuation); a transparency of the recorded material (without punctuation)

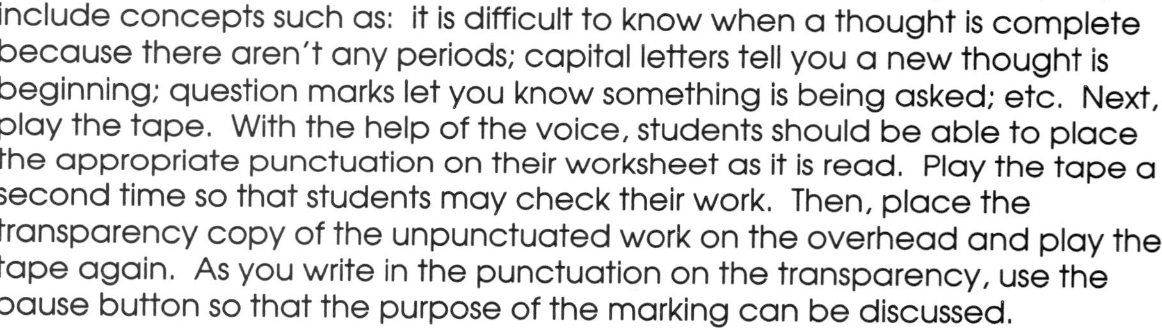

Directions: Before this lesson, tape record an excerpt, student writing or the short story below. The recorded material must also be written out, excluding the punctuation and a copy must be made for each student. To begin the lesson, distribute copies of the unpunctuated material and ask the students to read it. After they have expressed their frustrations, ask them to state why it was so difficult to read. Discussion should include concepts such as: it is difficult to know when a thought is complete because there aren't any periods; capital letters tell you a new thought is beginning; question marks let you know something is being asked; etc. Next, play the tape. With the help of the voice, students should be able to place the appropriate punctuation on their worksheet as it is read. Play the tape a second time so that students may check their work. Then, place the transparency copy of the unpunctuated work on the overhead and play the tape again. As you write in the punctuation on the transparency, use the pause button so that the purpose of the marking can be discussed.

Note: You may want to begin this type of lesson omitting periods only or quotation marks only depending upon the ability of your students and the time of year.

George and Maria sat next to each other in the lunch room last Tuesday that day George had forgotten his lunch at home what am i going to do i am so hungry cried George dont worry responded Maria my dad gave me a huge lunch I ate all my snack earlier and Im really not that hungry do you like cheese sandwiches yes thank you so much Maria that is very kind youre a good friend sniffled George

Dial a Word

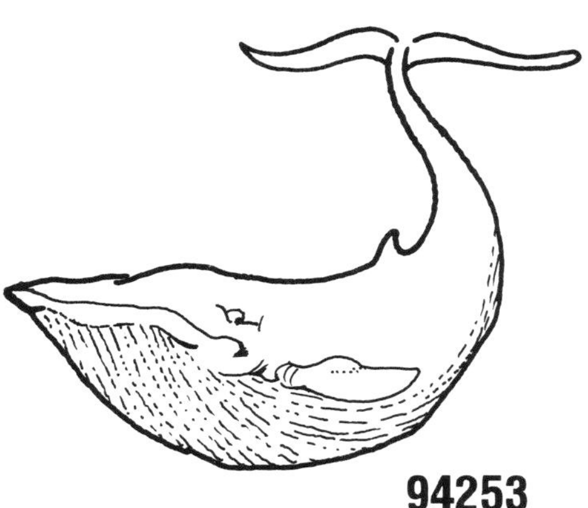

Objectives: To reinforce spelling and vocabulary skills and to develop problem-solving skills

Materials: phone button pattern (below), 8 1/2" x 11" sheets of colored construction paper, lined writing paper, pencil, scissors, glue

Directions: Distribute a copy of the phone button pattern to each student. Have students cut out the pattern and glue it to a sheet of construction paper. When these telephones are complete, have students take a closer look at the symbols on the buttons and let them share their observations. Be sure they notice that some numbers also have a letter value assigned to them. (Point out that the letters Q and Z are omitted.) Keeping that relationship in mind, tell students that they are going to have a variety of tasks to complete. First, have the students practice working with the "button values" by writing the letters of their name on a piece of paper. Then, ask them to refer to the phone buttons, and write down which number is on the same button as each letter in their name (i.e. Chris 2 + 4 + 7 + 4 + 7). Tell them that this could be the "code" for their name. Next, have the students add those numbers to find the value of their name. (Calculators may be used if you so choose.)

Post a coded word on the board. Have the students figure out the word from the number values. Provide a clue or a riddle to help them determine the letters. For example, "What is a method of transportation used on the water?" 2 + 6 + 2 + 8 = ? The students will need time to experiment with different letter arrangements. Additional clues might be given a such as, "The answer has only one syllable and a vowel blend in the middle." If this seems too difficult for the students, allow them to work in pairs.

When the students seem comfortable with these activities, have the students select a list of words to convert into "code" and find the value of and/or write questions for the number values. This is a great activity to use to strengthen problem-solving computational skills.

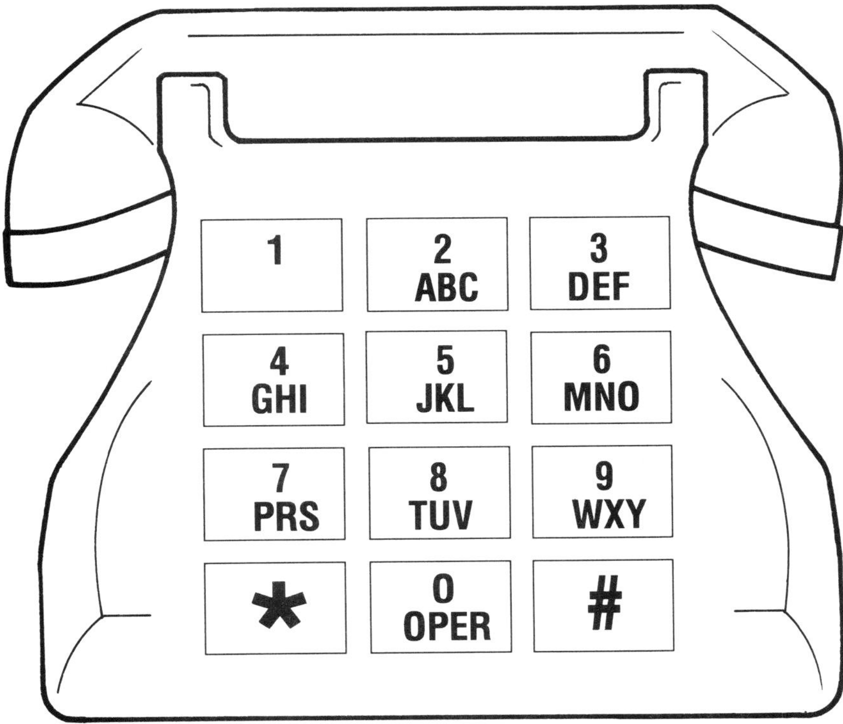

Which Came First?

Objective: To reinforce main idea and sequencing skills

Materials: copies of a story from a reading book, scissors, index cards, glue

Directions: For a great cooperative group activity and a great way to reuse old basal readers, copy several stories from an old textbook. Cut apart the paragraphs of each story and glue each paragraph to an index card. (Keep stories separate.) Give one group of cards to each cooperative learning group. Direct each group to divide the cards among themselves. Then, students are to read the paragraphs on each index card and decide the main idea. The groups should then read their paragraphs aloud to each other and share what they think the main idea of each paragraph is. To conclude the activity, have the groups arrange the cards in the proper sequence. For fun, students may draw an illustration to accompany their stories.

Cause or Effect

Objectives: To reinforce sequencing and to promote logical thinking

Materials: construction paper, scissors, stapler, push pins, sentence strips (page 69), 2 boxes

Directions: Cover a bulletin board with construction paper. Label the board as shown. Prepare a group of sentence strips. You can either enlarge the ones on page 69 or make up your own. Laminate them and put them in a box near the bulletin board. Also prepare a batch of blank sentence strips and put them in another box near the bulletin board.

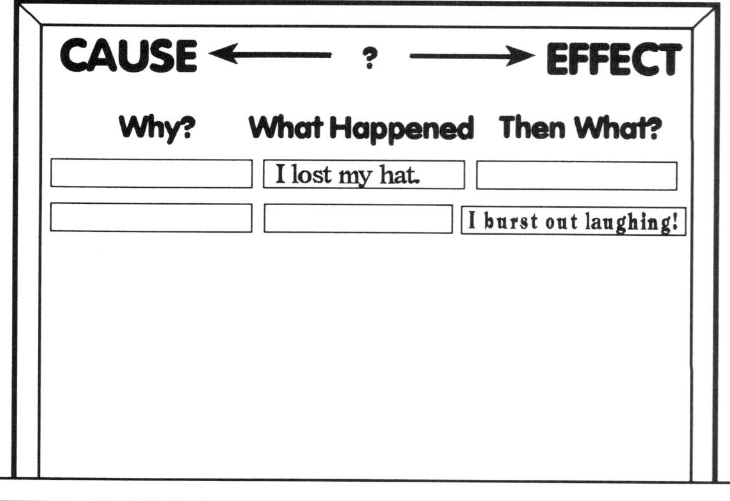

Have the students take turns selecting a sentence strip and putting it in the appropriate place on the bulletin board. On a blank strip, they will write either the cause or effect or both and post it in the appropriate place on the bulletin board. Change the sentence strips regularly or leave the sentence strips and have the students change the cause and/or effect strips.

Cause and Effect Sentence Strips

Ouch! He bit me!

I was so scared!

I burst out laughing.

I lost my hat.

There was a big clap of thunder.

My homework was gone!

My sister borrowed my sweater.

My brother fell off his bike.

Cause and Effect

Sequencing/ Predicting

Objectives: To reinforce sequencing and to promote logical thinking

Materials: paper, pencils

Directions: Tell the students that you're going to read a sentence. While you are reading it, tell them you want them to think of something that could cause that statement to occur. Read one of the following sentences and call on various students to give you a "cause" response.

1. The shoe fell to the floor.
2. The television set went off.
3. The dog ran out of the house.
4. The car stopped.
5. The students laughed.

For more fun, follow the same format, but now tell the students that you want them to think of the effect that your statement would have.

1. The lights went out.
2. It started to snow.
3. The alarm went off.
4. The telephone rang.
5. The fire alarm sounded.

Follow the same procedure by dividing the class into pairs. Have one student write the sentence, and the other one will write either the cause or effect or both. Have the pairs change roles. When the sentences are complete, have the pairs share their sentences with the class.

You Name It!

Objectives: To make predictions about a story based on the information given in the title; to practice writing titles for stories; to compare and select the most appropriate title for a magazine article; to write stories to go along with a title

Materials: empty cereal boxes, wrapping paper, short articles from students' magazines, index cards, tape, scissors, glue, marker, construction paper

Directions: To help students make predictions when they read, introduce them first to the information that often springs from a good title. Titles that are intriguing and that speak to our curiosity tend to be more popular among readers of all ages. Of course, the title must also give the reader a hint as to what the story is going to be about.

To prepare for this investigation of titles, collect several empty cereal boxes. Cover all sides with decorative wrapping paper except the bottom. This will enable you to open the box later. Cut a rectangular slit in the top of the box a bit larger than the width of an index card.

continued on page 71

You Name It! continued

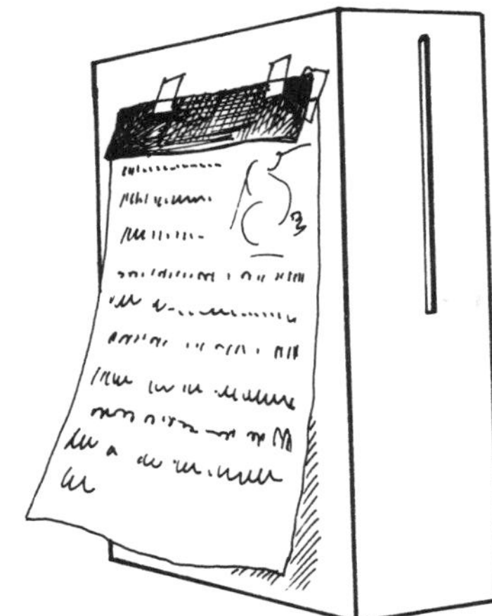

Then, choose several one-page articles that relate to a classroom theme or topic. Selections might be drawn from age-appropriate student publications such as *Ranger Rick*, *Scholastic News* or *Highlights* magazines. Secure each article to the face of a covered cereal box with tape or glue and cover the original title with a piece of construction paper. Now, you are ready to begin.

Share a few books or articles that have appropriate, "catchy" titles with your students such as *Ira Sleeps Over* or *The Grouchy Ladybug*. Talk about why these titles might capture a reader's attention. Select a short story, tell students the title and ask students to make predictions as to what they think the story might be about. Have them base their predictions on the information suggested in the title. Then, read the story aloud to the students. When you are finished, have students check their predictions and discuss whether or not they feel the title "fits" the story. Tell students that they are now ready to use their "naming" skills in the writing center.

Display the covered cereal boxes and explain to the students that they are to read one or more of the articles attached to each box. After completing their reading, the students should think of a good title for the article and write their suggestions on an index card. Tell students to be sure to initial their ideas. Then, they should drop the card into the slot in the box. When all the students have had the opportunity to visit the center, gather the students together and select volunteers to read the articles aloud. After each article is read, open the box and share the students' titles. Display all the suggestions and discuss the "fit" of each title to the story. Then, reveal the original title of the article and compare it to the students' suggested titles.

Extensions: You may also choose to have students select a title from a box and write a story to "fit" the title.

This activity may also be used to further reporting skills. Have students record the "5 W's"—Who, What, Where, When, Why from the article. Have students describe what happened in the article as if they were news reporters. Be sure students include only the facts—no opinions!

Setting the Stage

Creative Writing

Objectives: To reinforce map skills; to sharpen recognition of story setting elements; to write an original story and create a map for the setting using details from the story

Materials: 12" x 18" sheets of construction paper, markers, crayons, *Solomon's Secret* by Saviour Pirotta, paper, pencils

Directions: In this creative approach to map drawing, students will also be practicing reading and writing skills and developing the setting of a story. To begin the activity, discuss how important it is for the author to set the scene of a story for the reader by using descriptive words and specific details. The story *Solomon's Secret* is about a young boy's trip through a very special garden. This is a great story to use to model the activity. Point out details that describe the setting as you read. Then, create a map together of Solomon's adventure. The students should now be ready to write and map their own stories. Have students begin to write a creative story and guide them in clearly describing the setting. If a variety of sites are involved in the plot, ask students to try to identify the relationships of the sites to one another in as much detail as possible. When the stories are complete, distribute construction paper to students. Have them draw maps of their books' settings using their written descriptions to direct them. Stories with less specific settings will be more challenging to map.

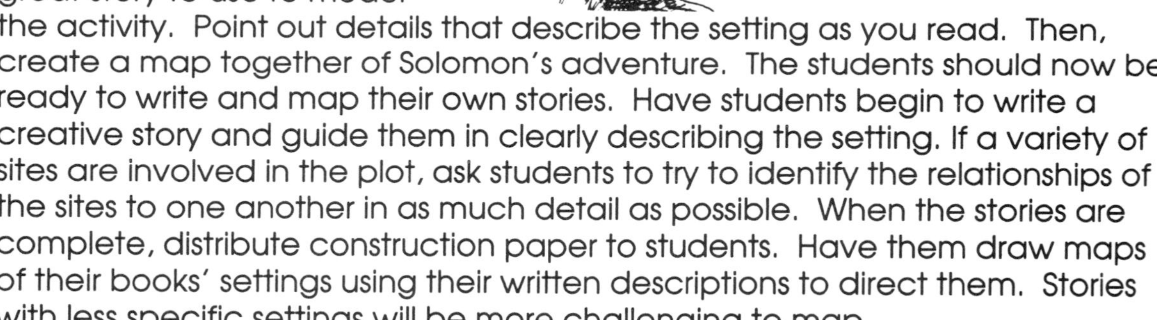

Follow-up Game:

Post up to five of the students' completed setting maps on the board and number them. Then, have the authors (and cartographers) read their stories. Ask the audience to listen carefully and write down their guesses as to which map belongs to which story. After all five stories have been read, have students share their choices and ask them to explain why each map belongs to a particular story. Then, reveal the actual answers and have students check their predictions.

Story Elements Flip Book

Writing

Objective: To reinforce elements of a story in a creative fashion

Materials: white drawing paper, scissors, crayons

Directions: Instead of writing out the elements of a specific story, students can draw them! Instruct students to fold a white sheet of paper the long way. Next, they turn the paper so that the fold is away from them. Students then divide the top sheet into four equal sections and cut the three dividing lines (on the top portion only). Have students label the top four sections: **main characters**, **setting**, **problem**, **solution**. Under each section, students draw an appropriate picture. (Students may want to use symbols to represent the problem and solution.)

Character Cube

Objective: To create a character cube which will describe a character from a novel using pictures, sketches and short statements

Materials: cardboard boxes, colored paper, drawing paper, markers, crayons, scissors, glue

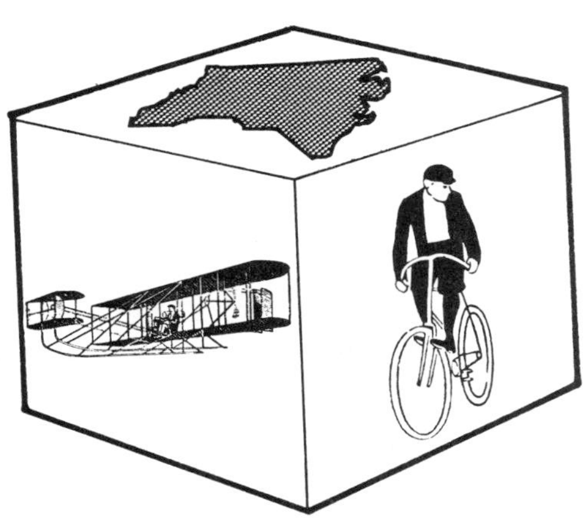

Directions: This activity can be used during or after the reading of a novel to help students understand how an author develops the characters in a story. Instruct students to bring a cardboard box to class and cover the box using colored paper. Students should then choose a character from the book. On the board, list the various characteristics that they will need to include on their cubes (i.e. physical features, personality, feelings, attitudes, actions). The students may use adjectives, pictures, sketches, short statements or any other creative method to describe the character they select.

Extension: If the novel is being read by the whole class or a small group, add a little mystery by having each student keep his/her character a secret. When all the cubes have been completed, unveil the cubes and have students try to guess the subject of the cube merely by examining the pictures, adjectives and sketches on the box and remembering what they have learned about the characters in the novel.

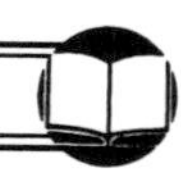

Character Riddles

Descriptive Writing

Objectives: To recognize student awareness of character attributes; to create a series of riddles describing the attributes of a character from a story

Materials: writing paper, pencils, shoe box, index cards, marker

Directions: This activity works best with students who are familiar with the same story characters. Participants in this activity might be those students who have completed the same book, or you may choose characters from common picture books that all students will undoubtedly be familiar with. Some suggestions include: *Little Red Riding Hood, Big Bad Wolf, The Very Hungry Caterpillar, Paddington Bear, Sleeping Beauty, Amelia Bedelia, Clifford, Curious George, Jack and the Giant, Goldilocks, The Ugly Duckling.*

Ahead of time, prepare a shoe box filled with the names of various characters written on index cards. (There may be more than one card with the same character if you do not have enough names to equal the number of students.) Have students discretely select a card from the box and create a character sketch of that subject. (See pattern to the right.) Encourage students to list as many attributes of each character as they can think of. Try to have the books available for the students to refer to as needed. When the students' sketches are complete, they are then ready to create their character riddles.

CHARACTER SKETCH

What does your character look like?

What are some feelings that your character expresses?

What are some examples of things your character might say?

How does your character behave or act?

Tell students to write five to six riddles that describe their character's attributes. Students should begin with uncommon attributes first and continue ending with the most recognizable attribute. (For example: Who wears a hat and an apron? Who is polite and hardworking? Who sees things differently than most people? Who mixes up directions but always means well? Who enjoys her job and works for Mr. and Mrs. Rogers? Answer: Amelia Bedelia)

When students have finished their riddles, have them share them with the class. They will have a great time seeing how quickly they can recognize the characters, and this activity will heighten their awareness of character descriptions in the future.

Extension: The attribute riddles work well with any topic to strengthen students' attention to detail and their ability to identify attributes of things.

Association

Timely Characters

Objective: To make a list of characters associated with a particular holiday

Materials: paper, pencils, drawing paper, crayons, markers

Directions: This is a short holiday activity that will enhance the study of characters and character descriptions. To begin, students will make a list of characters commonly associated with a holiday. For example, if the holiday is Halloween, the students might write wicked witch, Dracula, ghost, spider, black cat.

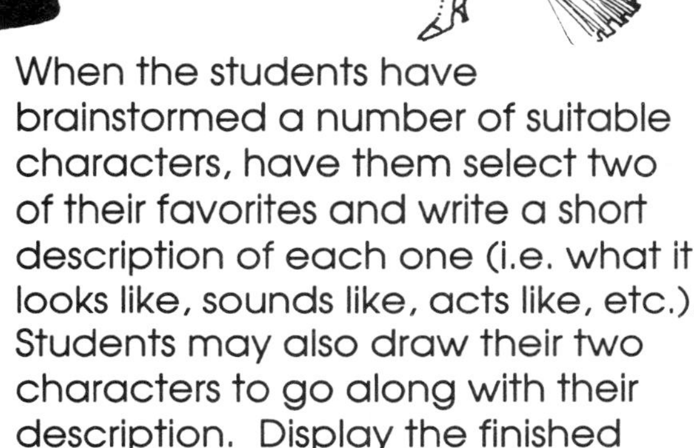

When the students have brainstormed a number of suitable characters, have them select two of their favorites and write a short description of each one (i.e. what it looks like, sounds like, acts like, etc.). Students may also draw their two characters to go along with their description. Display the finished descriptions around the room.

Timely Objects

Objectives: To make a list of objects associated with a particular holiday and to write a riddle for each object

Materials: paper, pencils, crayons, markers

Directions: Have students brainstorm a list of objects associated with a particular holiday. Then, have students select two of the scariest, funniest, best tasting, etc. objects and write a riddle about them. Have students share their riddles and enjoy the holiday fun!

Daily Journal Ideas

Creative Writing

Objective: To practice writing skills

Materials: journals, pencils

Directions: Have students keep a daily journal. They can either write whatever they want in it, or you can give them some of the topics below to write about.

---

1. Write your feelings about a story or book that you have read in school.
2. Summarize the day's activities.
3. Write a new word with its definition. Use it in a sentence.
4. Write an alliterative sentence.
5. Write an opinion about today's lunch. Support your opinion.
6. Write two similes. Use them in sentences.
7. Write something about your pen pal or pretend pen pal.
8. Write your feelings about a book or story you have read at home.
9. Describe a good friend. What do you like about him/her?
10. List five places you would like to visit.
11. Predict what you will do when you get home from school.
12. Comment on your prediction of the day before. How was it accurate? How was it not accurate?
13. Write a couplet.
14. Write a reaction to an assembly (when applicable).
15. Write a thank-you note to the cafeteria/custodial staff.
16. Conduct a class interview.
17. Read a news article. Discuss it. Summarize it.
18. Place an object on your desk. Write five words to describe it.
19. Write a haiku poem.
20. Write an opinion about a new movie.
21. Write a restaurant review.
22. Imagine you woke up one day with wings. What would you do first?
23. One day, it started to rain, but it wasn't water!! Describe what fell.
24. You are about to put your fork into your meatball, when it rolls away. What happens next?
25. You forgot your homework. What are you going to do?
26. Your mom tells you to clean your room. Your friend calls you to play. What do you do?
27. Draw an inanimate object. Give it human characteristics.
28. You are packing a suitcase. What are you putting in it? Why?
29. You're having a birthday party. What are you serving?
30. Write a postcard to your friend in another class.

Math

The activities in this chapter are designed to make math meaningful to students as they explore, understand and apply concepts by experimenting with manipulatives, testing with the abstract, and creating visuals and models.

Third-grade students should be given the opportunity to develop number sense and to understand the relationship between numbers. They should also be guided to see how math directly relates to their own lives.

Critical thinking skills, decision-making processes and proficiency in addition and subtraction are a focus at this level. Many of the activities in this chapter can be incorporated into and also relate to other disciplines.

The concepts included in this chapter are listed below.

1. **Computation**
2. **Fractions and Mixed Numbers**
3. **Measurement**
4. **Time**
5. **Money**
6. **Geometry**
7. **Problem Solving**
8. **Graphing**
9. **Pattern and Number Sense**
10. **Decimals**
11. **Comparing and Ordering Numbers**
12. **Technology**

Math Journals

Writing

A math journal allows students the opportunity to think about what they have learned—reinforcing new concepts, sorting out problems the students may be experiencing, realizing difficulties and successes, and applying concepts to new authentic situations. It can be used for specific units in math or throughout the year as you see fit.

Objectives: To evaluate students' learning and to promote writing in the content area

Materials: several sheets of paper assembled to create a journal

Directions: Below is a list of possible journal ideas. The first set of questions (below) could be applied to almost any area of math. The second set of questions (page 79) deals with specific topics. These questions may help you better understand the function of the math journal.

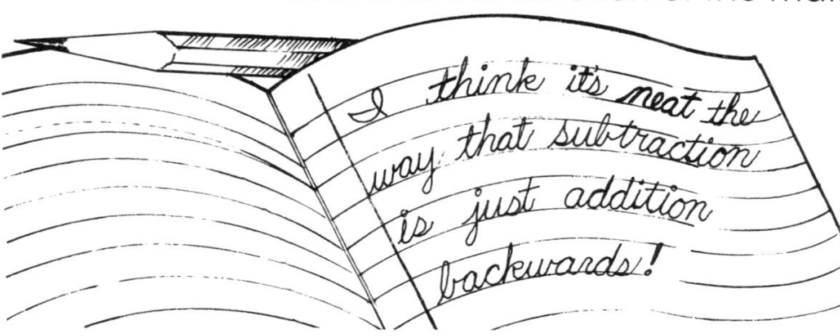

Use the journals also to quickly assess a student's comprehension of a new skill or concept. You may roam the room as students are writing, and/or collect several journals each day to read. To place emphasis on the importance of the journals, respond to what your students have written.

General Questions That Can Be Applied to Almost Any Unit

1. How did you feel about . . .?
2. What was the hardest part about . . .?
3. Explain the word _________ .
4. Imagine you were to teach _________ to a younger student. What would you say?
5. What should you do if you feel you can't solve _________ ?
6. Tell me about your greatest success in class today/this week.
7. When might you need to know how to _________ ?
8. I felt that the homework this week/last night was _________ because _________ .
9. I would like to learn more about _________ .
10. Name the steps involved in solving _________ .
11. Before you can _________ , you must first know how to _________ .
12. Choose the most important piece of work that tells about _________ . Explain why you chose this work.

continued on page 79

Math Journals continued

Topic Specific Questions

1. What does a numerator/denominator tell you?
2. What is the meaning of *sum*?
3. What operation does the word *if* indicate?
4. What do the zeros in the number *100* mean?
5. Create a Venn diagram to show similarities and differences between decimal numbers and fractions.
6. Is it possible to have/hold less than one?
7. Name a time or place that you would use or need a number like 0.05.
8. If you had your choice, which system would you rather use, degrees Celsius or degrees Fahrenheit? Why?
9. Do you have a favorite time of the day? If so, what is it and why?
10. If you could make your room any shape you'd like, what shape would it be? How many angles would it have?
11. If you had to live in a climate where the temperature was the same every day, what temperature would you choose?
12. You have divided __________ , and you have a remainder. What will you do with it?

Math Picture Dictionary

Measurement

Objective: To create a class math dictionary of new and important vocabulary

Materials: 15 sheets of paper stapled or fastened with book rings

Directions: Title the first page of the dictionary and label the second page **Word Entries**. On this page, students will write their name and the word you want them to record in the dictionary (i.e. John—product). This page can be used to help you determine who has had a turn to record a word and which words have been entered in the dictionary. Label the remainder of the booklet with a letter of the alphabet at the top of each page. Explain to students that as math words arise that they feel are new or important, they can enter each word under its corresponding letter. (You could also assign students to enter a particular word.) The student making the entry should supply a definition and a picture, diagram or example. When the entry is complete, the student who entered it should share it with the class.

Jared- **NUMERATOR**- A number on the top part of a fraction. It tells you how many in a group have something in common. Example: 3 shoes out of six are missing shoelaces =**3/6**

A Measurement of Our Own

Objective: To better understand standard units of measurement by creating new units of measurement

Materials: metric and standard rulers, pencils, paper, scissors, one copy of the form below per student

Directions: After examining the rulers, inform students that they will create their own unit of measurement and a new system of measurement. Brainstorm ideas on what and how students should base their new unit. (For example, they may use the length of their finger, the length of a juice box, the length of their backpack, etc. as a base.) Students should create a ruler using their new unit of measurement. Depending on students' ability and time, you may or may not want them to break the standard unit into smaller units. When the rulers are complete, have students fill out the form below.

A Measurement of Our Own

Name ____________________

Answer the questions below.

1. Why did you choose this unit of measurement? ____________________

   ____

2. What is the name of your unit of measurement? ____________________
3. What would your unit of measurement be best suited for measuring? long distances? __________ microscopic organisms? __________ Why? __________

   ____

4. Would you rather use your new unit of measurement versus the standard unit? __________ Why or why not? ____________________

   ____

5. Measure an object using your new ruler. What did it measure? __________ ____
   If you were to tell someone in your class that the object you measured was long, do you think that person would be able to picture its length? __________
   Why or why not? ____________________

   ____

6. Why do you think everyone in the entire country uses the exact same unit of measurement? ____________________

   ____

How Does Your School Measure Up?

Measurement

Objective: To estimate and measure various areas and items around the school in inches and/or centimeters

Materials: paper, ruler with centimeters and inches, pencils, tape measure or string

Directions: Take students on a measuring journey through school. To begin, brainstorm a list of various destinations around school. Then, list five items found in each room on the board. For example:

Library	Art Room	Cafeteria	Music Room
encyclopedia	easel	tray	music stand
shelf	paintbrush	table	piano
card catalog	construction paper	lunch bag	staff
almanac	ball of clay	food item	speaker
bookmark	drawing utensil	utensil	baton

Have students copy the items found in the rooms on the left-hand side of a piece of paper. Students should draw a vertical line down the right side of the words and draw another line to create two columns. Have students label one column **Estimate** and the other **Actual**. (See sample chart below.) During free time, have students examine the items from the list and jot down estimations of their measurements. (Predetermine the unit of measurement that students will use and if they should measure length, width or both.) After all the estimations have been recorded, have the students actually measure the items. (A tape measure or string may be used to measure the size or circumference of any oddly shaped objects.) To organize the measuring, you may elect to have students measure all the items independently or assign specific groups of students to measure the items in specific rooms. Check with the special area teachers to establish a convenient time for the students to take the measurements. Then, have the students share and compare their estimations with the actual measurements.

Item	Estimate	Actual

Variation: Have the students estimate and measure the items one room at a time. The repeated experiences should improve their ability to make reasonable estimates.

Will It Fit?

Capacity

Objective: To estimate liquid amounts in different sizes of containers

Materials: a one-cup measuring cup, water, several jars of various sizes and shapes (i.e. olive jars, baby food jars, peanut butter jars, water glasses, baby bottles, etc.) You may also want to include tall, thin containers and short, fat containers.

Directions: Fill the one-cup measuring cup with water. Have the students estimate which of the various containers will hold the one cup of liquid and which containers will not. Ask students which containers will need more than one cup of liquid to be filled and how much more.

Extension 1: Showing two containers, have the students estimate which container will hold more liquid or if they will hold the same amount. (For example: Will the olive jar hold more, less or the same amount of liquid as the baby food jar?)

Divide the containers into pairs. Label each pair and number the containers in the group (i.e. Pair A—1 and 2, Pair B—1 and 2). Have each student enter the pairs' letters and numbers on a sheet of paper. For each pair, the students estimate which container will hold more liquid or if they will hold an equal amount. The students then record their estimates. After all the estimates have been recorded, let students conduct the experiments to check their estimates. It would be a good idea to conduct the experiments over a basin.

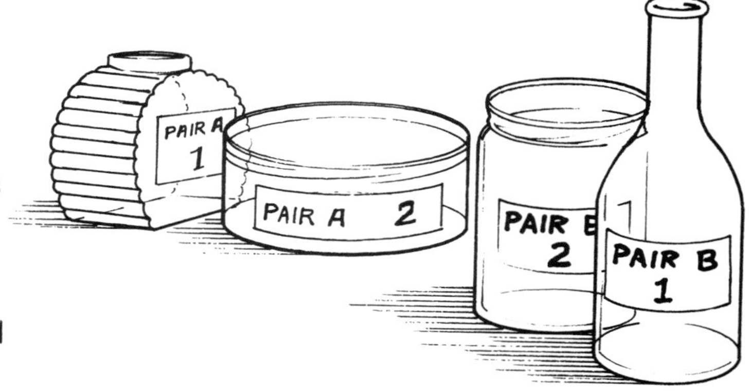

Extension 2: Using two 9" x 12" sheets of construction paper, make two cylinders. Roll one the long way and one the short way. Tape them together to keep them secure. Fill one cylinder with popcorn. Have the students estimate if the popcorn will fit into the other cylinder. Ask students if there will be too much popcorn, too little or if it will fit exactly the same and why.

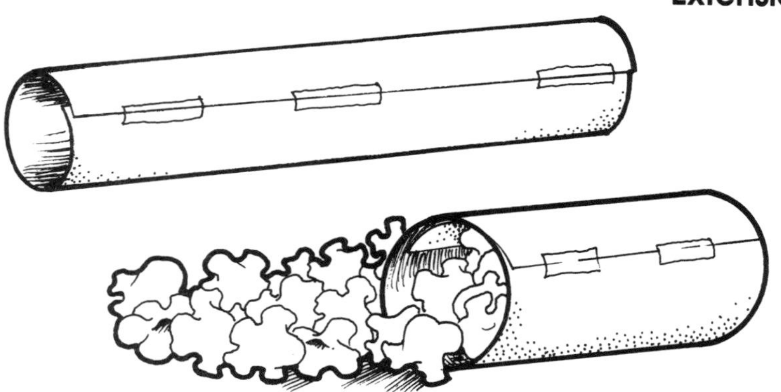

Geometry

Look at the World From a Different Angle

Objective: To recognize right, acute, obtuse and straight angles and perpendicular lines

Materials: drawing paper, rulers, pencils

Directions: The students first need to create a matrix upon which they will record their observations. To do this, distribute the drawing paper to the students. Instruct them to hold the paper horizontally and draw five columns. The columns should be labeled as shown.

right	acute	obtuse	straight	perpendicular

When all the students have constructed a neat matrix, explain to them that they are going to make some observations in the classroom. Divide the students into four groups. Direct each group's attention to its own corner or wall of the room. Let the students move so that they have a clear view of their assigned section. Then, have the students silently look for objects that illustrate each category on the chart. Ask the students to draw a sketch of each object and label it. Encourage the students to find as many objects for each category as possible. After 5-10 minutes, have the students in each group compare their charts. Ask if there were any objects they missed. Next, have each group share its observations with the class. You will be amazed at how this will heighten your students' awareness of their surroundings.

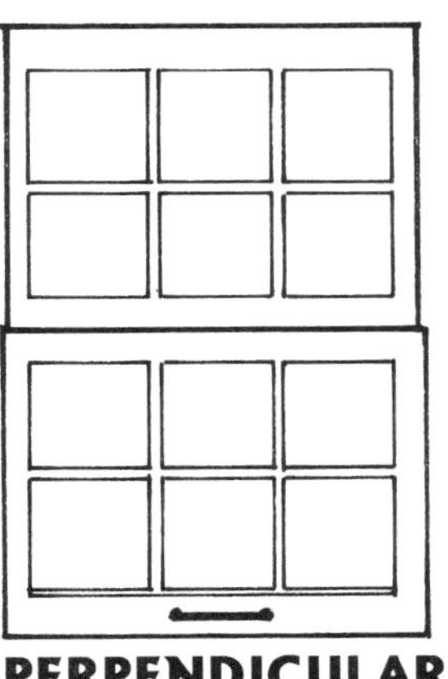
PERPENDICULAR

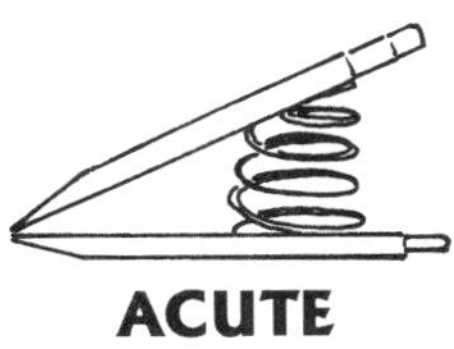
ACUTE

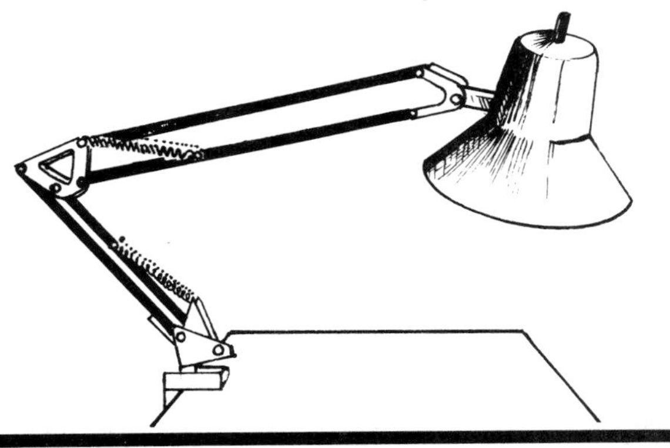

Extensions: To challenge your students, ask them to look around the classroom and find one object that illustrates all five geometric categories. Have them sketch the object and label the various types of angles, lines or shapes that it possesses.

Change the label on the matrix to highlight other geometric shapes.

Geometric Art

Geometry

Objectives: To become familiar with geometric figures and to use them creatively

Materials: 12" x 18" sheets of white construction paper, geometric shapes of assorted colors (one of each color for each student), glue, crayons

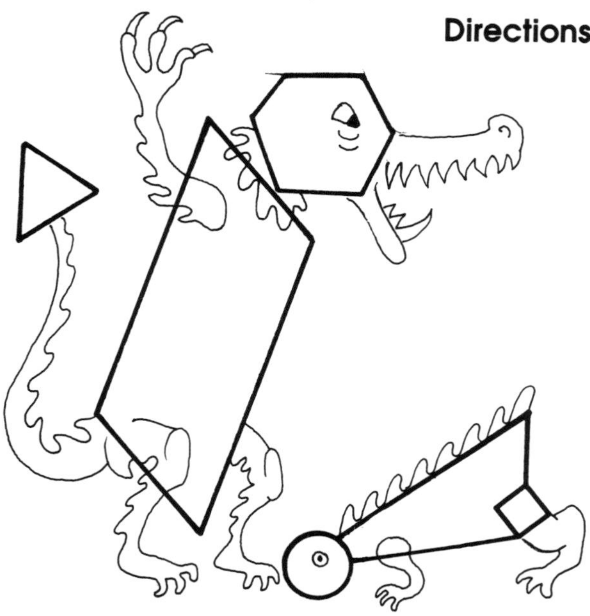

Directions: Give each student a sheet of the white construction paper. Next, hold up a sample of each of the shapes you would like to reinforce. Supply each student with a set of the shapes. Instruct them to glue each shape anywhere on their paper as you call out its name. For example, if you call "hexagon," the students must pick out the hexagon from their pile of shapes and glue it on their paper. When all the shapes have been called and glued, tell the students that they will use their crayons to create a picture using the shapes that have already been placed. Students can create a house, city, flower garden, robot, . . . the possibilities are endless! When all the creations are completed, ask volunteers to share with the class what they created.

Geometry Match-Ups

Objective: To reinforce the concept of geometric shapes

Materials: shapes (page 85), paper or cloth bag, oaktag, scissors

Directions: On oaktag, trace and cut out two of each of the polygons on page 85. Put all ten shapes in a bag. Have a student draw one shape from the bag without looking. After the shape has been selected, have another student name the shape and tell how many sides and angles are in the polygon. This student then puts his/her hand in the bag and, without looking, tries to "feel" for the same shape. Continue the game until all students have had a chance.

Extension: Have the first student pull out a shape and without showing it to the class, tell how many sides and angles it has. He/she should name the shape. The second student then puts his/her hand in the bag and tries to match the shape from the description. The students then compare to see if they have matching shapes.

Shapes

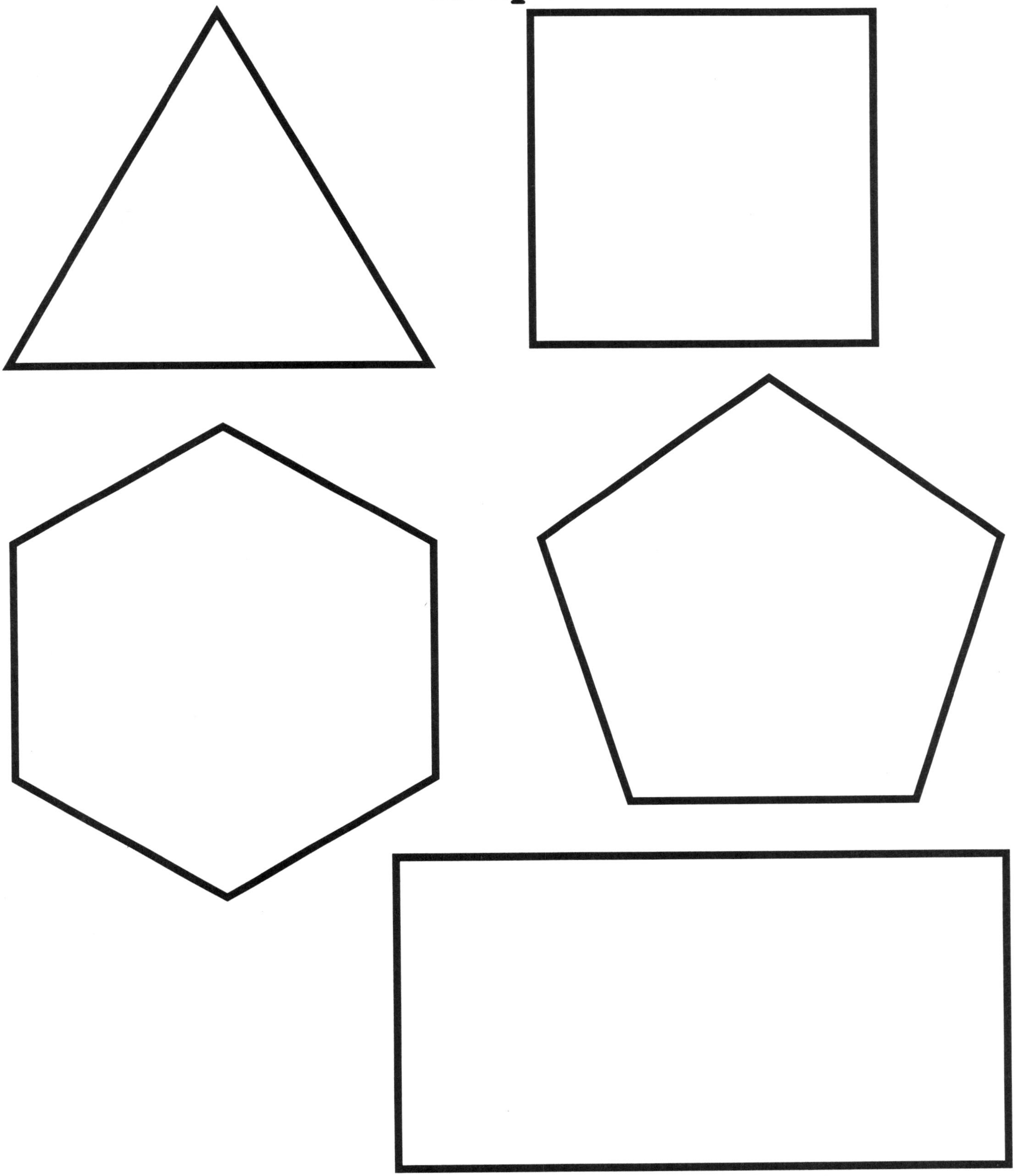

Triangle Puzzle

Geometry

Objective: To predict the relationship of shapes to each other

Materials: colored construction paper, scissors, glue, one envelope per student, one copy of the gameboard per student (pages 87-88)

Directions: Using the triangle pattern, cut out 37 triangles per student using the same color of construction paper. If you want, glue the gameboard to oaktag for added strength.

Discuss with the students the attributes of the triangles that each student has. Ask students how they are the same. (They are the same size, color and shape and have the same number of sides and angles). Ask students how they are different. (They are not different in any way.)

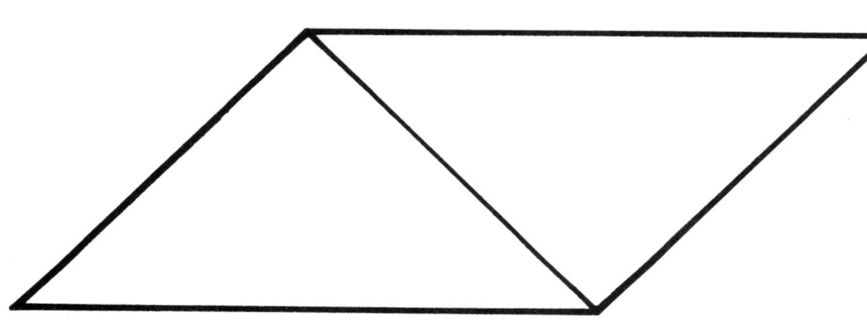

Next, have students arrange the triangles to make the shapes on the gameboard. Tell students that they have the exact number of triangles needed and that the triangles may not be folded or cut in any way. Have students describe the new shapes they make and let them take their puzzle home in an envelope to use with their siblings and/or parents.

A Native American Wall Hanging

Objective: To understand congruence

Materials: pencils, crayons, markers, one copy of the Native American wall hanging pattern (page 89) per student

Directions: Have students draw two congruent figures of any shape to create a new shape. Students can use triangles, squares, rectangles, pentagons, hexagons, octagons, semicircles, quarter-circles or trapezoids to make their shape. Each student should use his/her shape to create a wall hanging design using the pattern on page 89. Instruct students to connect their two congruent figures at one side. Have them color each part of the congruent pair a different color. Display students' wall hangings on a bulletin board.

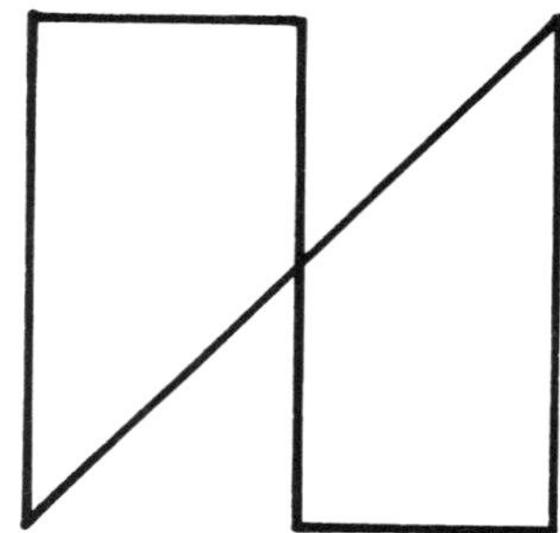

Gameboard

Gameboard

Wall Hanging Pattern

Geometric Drop Art

Objectives: To reinforce geometric shapes and to use them to create a work of art

Materials: geometric shapes cut from oaktag (approximately 4"-6" in height), 11" x 18" sheets of white construction paper (one piece for every 3 students), pencils, erasers, crayons or markers

Directions: The process of this activity is gamelike. Group students in threes. Provide each group with a set of geometric shapes, an eraser and one sheet of 11" x 18" construction paper. Instruct students to lay the paper down on the floor. Assign each student in each group a number—one through three. Direct Student Number One to choose a shape. Student Number Two should then name the shape that Student Number One chose. Next, Student Number Three should hold this shape above the paper on the floor and gently drop it onto the paper. Student Number One should then trace the shape exactly where it landed. This process is repeated beginning with Student Number Two. (Student Number Two chooses the shape, student Number Three names it, Student Number One drops it, and Student Number Two traces it.) Next, a new step is added! Student Number Three must erase the lines, if any, that the second shape covered on the first shape. For example, if the second shape, a rectangle, landed on the corner of a hexagon, then that hexagonal corner should be erased so that the rectangle actually appears to be "on top." (See illustration.)

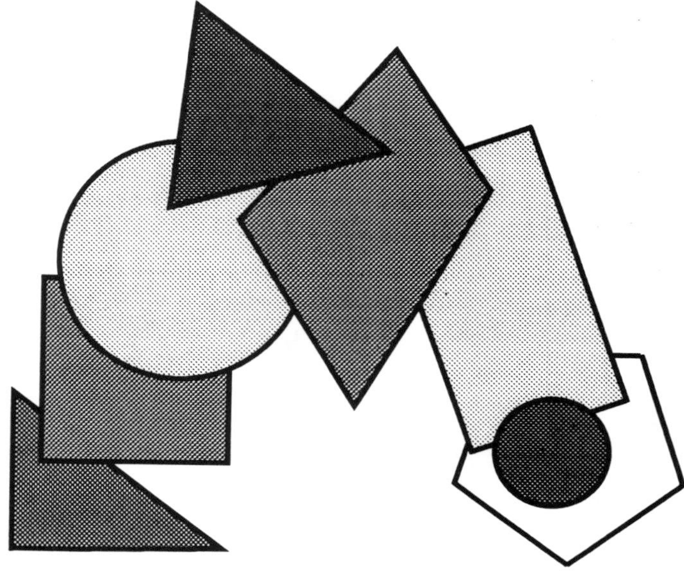

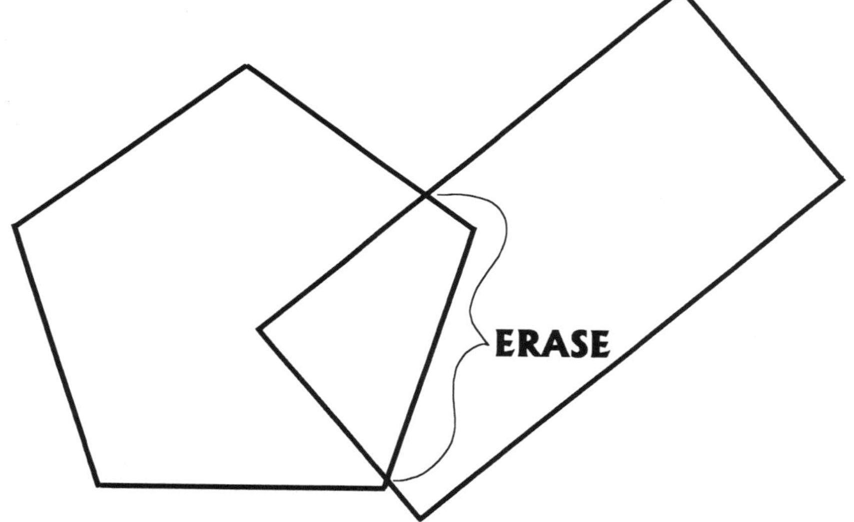

Once students have caught on to the process, they may work on their own. For the final challenge, students should color the visible parts of each shape one color. Students can continue to take turns with each student coloring one shape at a time. (Note: You may want to complete this activity in two sessions.)

Who's New in the Zoo?

Geometry—Bulletin Board

Objectives: To recognize geometric plane figures and to introduce geometric concepts

Materials: construction paper, scissors, crayons, markers, glue, index cards, pencils, rulers, stapler

Directions: Tell the students that they are going to create a New Zoo. That is, they are going to create and name all new animals. They may use circles, squares, rectangles, triangles, trapezoids, pentagons, hexagons and octagons.

Have each student draw and cut out as many shapes as he/she needs to create a new animal. Students can use rulers to make sure lines are straight. Circles may be traced using jar covers, coins, etc. Have students glue the shapes together to form the animals. Staple the animals to the bulletin board. Have each student give his/her New Zoo Animal a name. Students can write the name on an index card along with the shapes used to create the animal. The animal name should indicate some special feature (i.e. triangle toad, round-nosed runners, rectangle-tailed tootsie, etc.).

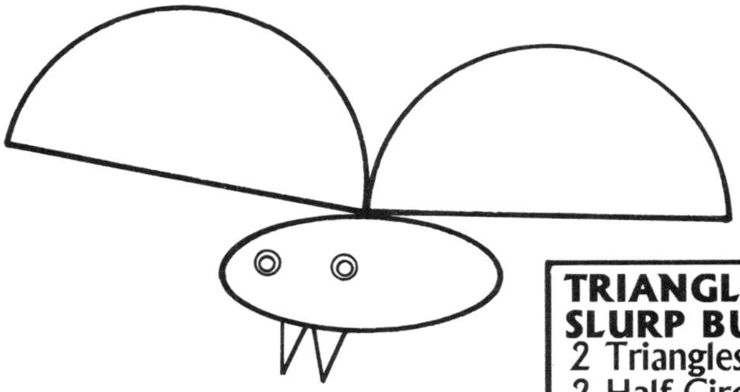

TRIANGLE FANGED SLURP BUG
2 Triangles
2 Half-Circles
4 Circles
1 Oval

TRAPEZOID-BILLED YOIT
3 Trapezoids
2 Circles
4 Triangles
1 Hexagon

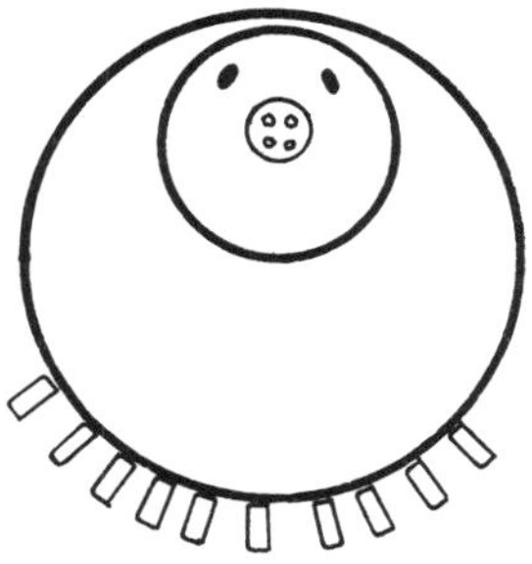

ROUND NOSED RUNNER
7 Circles
10 Rectangles
2 Ovals

Block Blueprints

Building/ Estimation

Objective: To create and read blueprints

Materials: blocks of any type—Lego™, Duplo™, wood blocks, etc. (All students do not need to use the same type of block.), large sheets of graph paper or construction paper, rulers, pencils

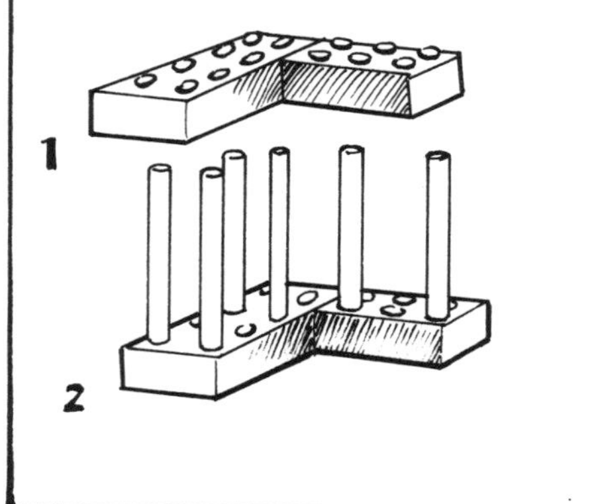

Directions: Discuss what a blueprint is and what it is used for. Explain to students that they will design a blueprint of a building they will create. Direct students to build a structure from the blocks they have in front of them. When the structures are complete, discuss with the students the steps they will need to take to make the blueprint (i.e. create a scale, work from the bottom up, etc.). When the blueprints are complete, collect them and randomly pass them back out so that another student can read the blueprint to construct the building!

Guesstimation

Objectives: To develop number sense and to develop estimation skills

Materials: two containers of different sizes but preferably the same shape (i.e. a quart milk container and a 1/2 gallon milk container, or a baby food jar and a large glass bottle), small objects to fill the container (i.e. macaroni, beans, marbles)

Directions: Fill the smaller container with the small objects. Ask a helper to count how many pieces it takes to fill the container. Tell the students the number of objects in the small container. Then, have them "guesstimate" the number of objects it would take to fill the larger container. When all "guesstimates" have been secretly recorded and collected, distribute piles of the small object (or similar) to each student. Ask them to count out 20 objects. Circulate around the room, allowing students to drop one pile of 20 objects in the larger container. Count the number of "twenties" that are deposited. Circulate around the room until the container is full. Calculate the number of objects in the container, and then check "guesstimates" recorded earlier to see who had the closest "guesstimate!"

Let's Take a Trip!

Money

Objectives: To use mathematical functions including addition, subtraction, multiplication and division to work with money and percentages; to break down a problem into its components

Materials: one sheet of graph paper per student, one copy of page 94 per student, pencils

Directions: Students are to plan an automobile trip to figure out approximately how much the trip will cost. The students have to calculate distances between locations and calculate the amount of gasoline needed based upon miles per gallon of the car. They then calculate the cost of the gasoline. Hotel and food costs and entertainment expenses must also be estimated.

Using graph paper, have each student plot out his/her trip starting and ending at "point A." (The trip should have five points of travel, including point A.) Each square on the graph paper will represent 10 miles. Using 10 miles to the square as the base, the students can calculate the mileage between points.

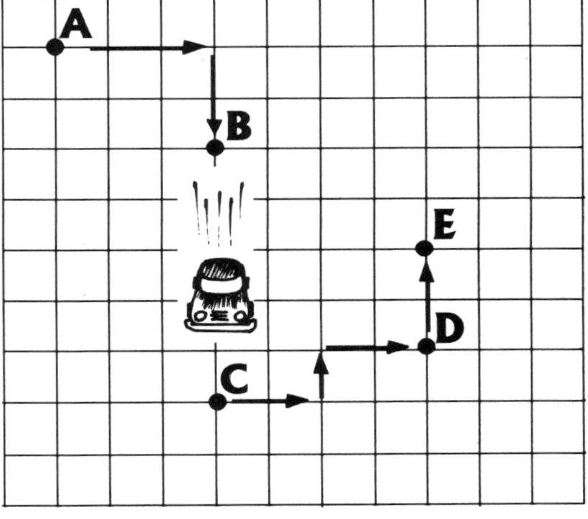

Give each student a copy of the chart on page 94 to use for keeping track of his/her calculations. At this time, it would be a good idea to indicate to the class how to break down a problem into its components. Point out each individual problem step-by-step and then show them how to bring it all together at the end.

When students have completed page 94, ask them some of the questions below.

1. If two people go on this trip, how will the cost change? (Gas will be the same. Hotel will probably be the same. Food and entertainment will probably double.)
2. If a family of four goes on the trip, how will the cost change? (Gas will still remain the same. The hotel may or may not double depending upon whether the family uses two rooms or if they all stay in one room. Food and entertainment will quadruple.)
3. How may the cost of gas change? (There may be a detour. The itinerary may change.)
4. What else could change the cost of the trip? (Unexpected expenses such as auto repairs, illness, etc. may have to be incurred.)
5. Why is this just an estimate? (Price of the gas, hotel and food may vary. Price of admissions may change.)

Extension: Have students use newspapers, travel brochures and menus to help estimate costs of food, gas, hotels, entertainment, etc.

Calculation/Expense Chart

Distance to travel

miles from Point A to Point B __________

miles from Point B to Point C __________

miles from Point C to Point D __________

miles from Point D to Point E __________

miles from Point E to Point A __________

total miles to travel __________

Car gets 22 miles per gallon of gas.

total gas needed __________

Gas costs $1.19 $^9/_{10}$ per gallon.

total amount needed for gas __________

You will stay at a hotel/motel for four nights at $79.00 per night.

There is a 6% tax per night on the hotel room.

total cost per night __________

total cost for four nights __________

Estimated food cost per day (5 days)

breakfast—$2.50

lunch—$4.75

dinner—$9.25

total per day __________

total for 5 days __________

Estimated entertainment expenses

admission to movies __________

admission to museums __________

admission to theme parks __________

admission to sports events __________

Add up all the entries to get a total estimate for the cost of the trip.

Total estimated cost of the trip	__________

Class Store

Money

Objectives: To reinforce the values of different denominations of money and to reinforce making change

Materials: one copy of the letter to parents (page 97) per student, boxes, paint, paintbrushes, markers, crayons, construction paper, scissors, one set of paper money per student (page 96), one copy of each chart on page 97 per student

Directions: Send home a copy of the letter on page 97 with each student. Use the materials listed above to set up an area in your classroom as a class store. In order to stock the store, discuss with the students some things they might bring from home. Stress the idea of inexpensive items that they might want to "exchange" for something else (since they will be "buying" someone else's donation). There might also be some things in your classroom that you might want to add to help stock the store.

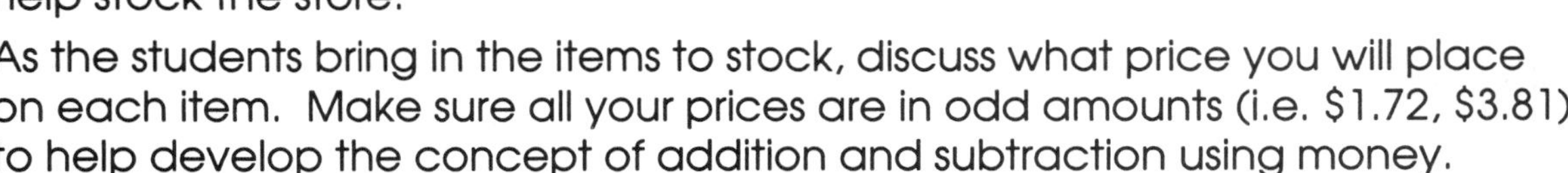

As the students bring in the items to stock, discuss what price you will place on each item. Make sure all your prices are in odd amounts (i.e. $1.72, $3.81) to help develop the concept of addition and subtraction using money.

When the store is completely stocked with at least two items per student, give each student $5.00 in play money in the following denominations: 2 one dollar bills, 2 half dollars, 4 quarters, 5 dimes, 8 nickels and 10 pennies. (See page 96.) Give each student a copy of the "Total Money To Spend" chart (page 97). Have students fill in the money values on it to find out how much they have to spend. Then, give each student a blank chart (page 97) to use to figure out how much money he/she has left after making a purchase.

Now, the store is ready to open for business. Invite one or two students to be the cashiers. Make sure you provide enough money in the "cash register" so that proper change may be made.

continued on page 96

Class Store continued

Invite two or three students to shop at a time. Make sure they fill out their blank chart after their purchases. (Students should label the chart **First Purchase**.) Have the students check to make sure that the change they received plus the cost of the purchase adds up to $5.00. Change cashiers frequently. After everyone has made one purchase, let them make a second purchase if they have money left over. Give these students another blank chart to fill out and have them label it **Second Purchase**. You can continue in this way until most of the money is spent and/or most of the stock is depleted.

continued on page 97

Class Store continued

TOTAL MONEY TO SPEND		
Number	Money	Value Amount
2	dollar bills	
2	half dollars	
4	quarters	
5	dimes	
8	nickels	
10	pennies	
Total Money to Spend		

Number	Money	Value Amount
	dollar bills	
	half dollars	
	quarters	
	dimes	
	nickels	
	pennies	
Total Money Left		
Cost of Purchase +		
Amount Started With =		

Date ____________________

Dear Parents,

We are establishing a class store. The purpose of this project is to help students learn the value of money, to help them learn to add and subtract money, to make change and to check if they have received the correct change. We will be working with play money. However, we need real things to buy and sell, and we need your help. Please send to school two or three items that we can "sell" in our store. These should be inexpensive items that you have at home (i.e. a magazine, a paperback book, pencils, pens, a small toy, etc.). The items should not be new. However, they should be of interest to a third grader so that they will be salable in our store. Your child will be able to keep whatever he/she has purchased with the play money in the store.

Please send these items by ____________________ so that we can open for business on ____________________ . Thank you for your cooperation.

Sincerely,

On Sale!

Money

Objective: To practice adding and subtracting money values

Materials: sale sections from the newspaper, construction paper, scissors, glue, pencils, calculators

Directions: Give each student a piece of construction paper and the sale section from the newspaper. Have the students cut out and glue a predetermined number of prices onto their paper. Then, let them have some "sale day" fun by doing the following activities.

1. Have the students write the prices rounded off to the nearest dollar.
2. Students add the three lowest prices or the three highest prices together.
3. Ask students to choose a price and then write down the various combinations of dollars and coins that could be used to create that amount.
4. "Give" students $10 and have them buy (subtract) a selection of sale items from that amount.
5. Have students "buy" multiples of items and compute the cost using multiplication.
6. Students can order the prices from smallest to greatest.

7. Pair up the students and have them pose a variety of money and change situations to each other (i.e. I if buy item one and item two, and I give you $5.00, how much change will I receive?).
8. Have students estimate the total cost of the sale items glued onto the paper and then tally the prices. Have them check their predictions.
9. Have the students write several word problems incorporating the prices on their construction paper. Let them exchange papers with a neighbor.
10. Teach students how to calculate sales tax. Allow students to use calculators to determine the sales tax on a variety of transactions.

Let's Go Shopping!

Money

Objective: To add and subtract using money

Materials: scrap paper, pencils, one copy of page 101 per student

Directions: Give each student a copy of page 101. Tell the students that they are to make-believe that they have received $25.00 for a birthday present. They are to spend some of it and save some of it using the "Shopping Map." However, they owe a sister/brother $3.52. So, after they fill in the amounts they spend/save on the map during their shopping/saving spree, they should end up with $3.52 to pay off the debt. Provide scrap paper for the students so that they can figure as they go along.

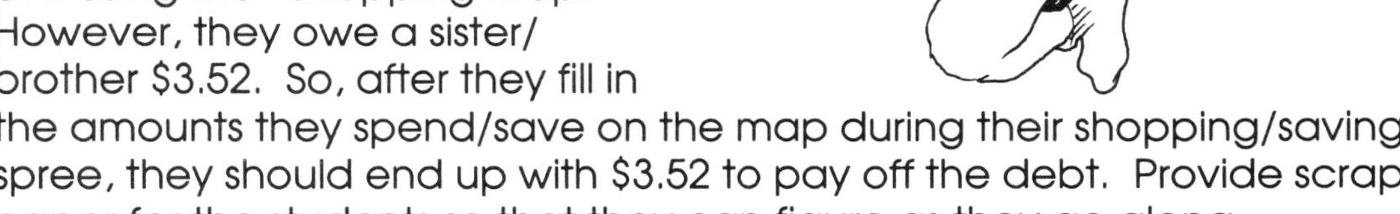

What's for Lunch?

Objectives: To solve problems using operations with money and to read a menu board

Materials: an overhead transparency of the menu below or a copy for each group of students, lunch scenarios (page 100), paper, pencils

Directions: Explain to students that they will use the menu to solve problems. Divide students into teams of three or four. Explain to students that the teams will be given a scenario and a problem to solve. All students in the group must work toward an answer and all students must agree on an answer. The team to come up with the correct answer first earns a point. The team with the highest score at the end of the five scenarios wins.

Lunch Menu

salad $2.25
hot dog $1.10
grilled cheese $1.00
pizza .... $.90

DESSERT
pudding .... $.90
ice cream .... $.85

BEVERAGES
milk .... $.50
orange juice .... $.60
soda .... $.75

continued on page 100

What's for Lunch? continued

Money

Scenarios

1. Craig, Thomas and Laura stopped on their long trip for lunch. Craig had had a late breakfast and only wanted some milk to drink. Thomas was feeling a little carsick, so he simply wanted a soda. Laura was starving! They spent a total of $4.25. What was for lunch?

   (Craig—milk $.50, Thomas—soda $.75. This leaves Laura $3.00 to spend on her lunch. She could have had a salad and a soda; or a grilled cheese, hot dog and a slice of pizza; or a grilled cheese, hot dog and pudding.)

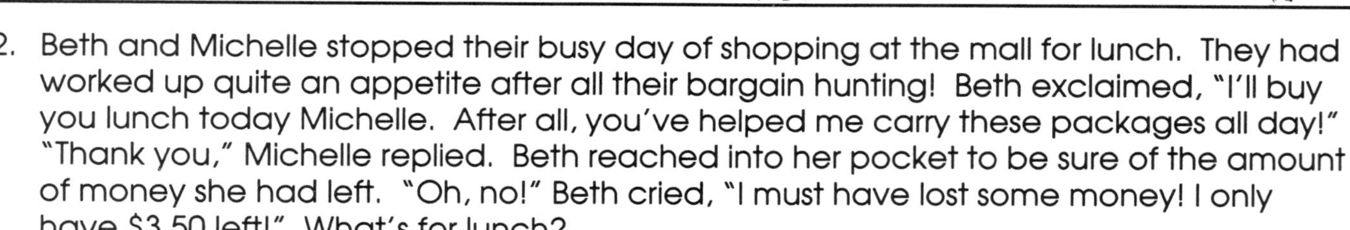

2. Beth and Michelle stopped their busy day of shopping at the mall for lunch. They had worked up quite an appetite after all their bargain hunting! Beth exclaimed, "I'll buy you lunch today Michelle. After all, you've helped me carry these packages all day!" "Thank you," Michelle replied. Beth reached into her pocket to be sure of the amount of money she had left. "Oh, no!" Beth cried, "I must have lost some money! I only have $3.50 left!" What's for lunch?

   (Two grilled cheese sandwiches and two sodas)

3. Diane spent $1.60 on lunch. She was too full to eat or buy dessert. What was for lunch?

   (Either she had a hot dog and milk, or a grilled cheese and orange juice.)

4. The twins had a little too much pizza for dinner last night, and certainly did not want it today. They each had the same meal, including pudding for dessert. They spent $5.50. What was for lunch?

   (Pudding for the two of them is $1.80, leaving $3.70 for the rest of the meal. Their lunches were identical, meaning they each spent $1.85 and ate a hot dog and had a soda.)

5. Sue is a vegetarian, and she's allergic to milk. Bob ate two slices of pizza and a soda. Together, their lunch cost them $5.40. What was for lunch?

   (Bob's lunch cost $2.55, leaving Sue $2.85 to spend on her lunch—salad and orange juice.)

Shopping Map

$25

HOBBY

Spends

MOVIES

Spends

SNACKS

Spends

Spends

ZOO

Spends

NEWS

Spends

BANK

Deposits

$3.52
to pay off debt

Money on the Ladder

Money

Objectives: To add money amounts mentally and to use a ruler

Materials: 12" x 18" sheets of white construction paper, rulers, crayons, pennies (one penny per player), pencils

Directions: Each student will create a gameboard. To do this, give each student a sheet of white construction paper, a ruler and a pencil to draw a large ladder. The length of the ladder should measure approximately 17" and the rungs should be placed one inch apart. Next, in each rung of the ladder, students should draw coins and their value. Students should draw more than one coin per rung. (You may want to tell students which coins to draw in each rung.) Students may color their drawings if they want. When the ladders are completed, laminate them if possible.

To play the game, divide students into pairs. Place one gameboard on the floor or table top. Player One takes his/her turn by placing a penny at the bottom of the paper and flicking it with his/her thumb and forefinger. The penny should land on a drawn coin. (If it does not, Player One does not receive points. Or if desired, the player may "shoot" again.) Player One must then remember that coin value while Player Two takes his/her turn and repeats the process. Player One then receives a second turn. This time, however, Player One must add the new coin value to what he/she acquired from the first turn. This procedure is repeated until one player makes a mental addition error and is "caught" by another player. His/her score returns to zero and the players must start all over!

Money in the Bag!

Objective: To solve problems by adding and subtracting money amounts

Materials: play money, copy of the money questions (page 103), a paper bag for each group of students, index cards, marker

Directions: The object of this game is to earn money as a group by answering money problems correctly. Use the list of questions on page 103 or prepare a list of questions involving the addition and/or subtraction of money. Before you play the game, use the index cards to create "money cards." Place monetary values on one side of each card (i.e. $1.35). Place the play money on a table to create the "bank." Group students into threes and supply each group with a money bag (paper bag). Students can write a dollar sign on the bag. Students are now ready to play "Money in the Bag!"

continued on page 103

Money in the Bag! continued

Money

Explain to students that you will read them a question. They are to work on the question and answer it as a group. After each question is read and the answer is discussed, a student will be chosen to turn a "money card" over. The group of students who answers the question correctly will earn the amount of money indicated on the money card. If the group has answered correctly, it should go to the bank to collect the amount indicated on the card, and then put its money in the bag. When the questions are completed, students should add the total amount of money in their group's bag. The group with the most "money in the bag," wins!

Money in the Bag Questions

1. Justin just finished mowing his neighbor's lawn. His neighbor paid him $5.00. Then, Justin decided to visit his friend down the street. On the way, Justin lost three quarters. How much money did he have now? ($4.25)
2. Using five dimes, two quarters and two nickels, how many different coin combinations can you come up with to equal $1.00? (1. five dimes, two quarters, 2. four dimes, two nickels, two quarters)
3. Alexa is going shopping. She has three dollars. She needs to buy bread, ($1.10), milk ($1.50) and she would like a candy bar ($.50). Does she have enough money for the candy bar? (no)

4. (Note: Write the items below and their prices on the board prior to asking this question.)
   video game—$69.00
   tape recorder—$42.00
   tape (audio)—$11.00
   tape (video)—$15.00
   Imagine that your group is at the electronic store. You have $75.00. What item(s) will you buy? How much money will you have left? What will you save it for? (Answers will vary. Be sure to check each group's answers.)
5. Schyler, Brandon and Daniel went to the movies. Each ticket cost $4.50. They all had popcorn for 75 cents each. How much did they spend? ($15.75)

Party Plans? You'll Need a Budget!

Money

Objective: To estimate the cost of hosting a party using problem-solving strategies

Materials: chart paper, marker, paper, pencils

Directions: This is a great activity that can be used with the "Thanksgiving Celebration" (page 254) or for planning any special classroom event. To begin, tell the students that you are having a party and that their help is needed to determine how much the party will cost. Then, have students work in cooperative groups to make a list of information they think will be needed to plan a great party. For example: "What kinds of food or snacks do we want to serve? How much do we want to spend? How will we raise the money?"

After the groups have discussed the possible solutions, gather the whole class together and allow the groups to present their ideas. Compare the suggested solutions. Guide the students to reach a consensus and list these ideas on chart paper. Decide what should be done first and then get busy!

A Legend of Estimation

Objectives: To develop reasoning skills, to create word problems and to practice estimating decimal sums and differences

Materials: sentences (See examples below.), chart paper, marker, lined writing paper, pencils, calculators

Directions: This activity requires students to use their estimating skills to solve word problems involving money. First, create a chart of sample sentences that the students will use to construct the word problems. For example:

First Sentence:

Sue saved $5.36.
Robert has $16.73.
Stephanie bought a CD for $12.95.
The Davis family saved $482.25 for their vacation.
Mrs. Smith has $341.98 in her savings account.

Legend of Estimation continued

Second Sentence:
Scott spent $2.95 for lunch.
Jessie saved $18.79.
Andrea purchased a pencil for $.36 and a binder for $3.45.
Mr. Smith has $214.82 in his savings account.
John has $20.43 in his wallet.

Third Sentence:
What is the estimated difference between their purchases?
What is the estimated sum of the purchases?
What is the estimated sum of their savings?
What is the estimated difference between their savings?
About how much money do they have left?

Pair up students. Direct students to choose one sentence from each category. (Tell students to be careful because the sentences must make sense together.) The students should write down the sentences in the correct order. The students can then exchange papers with their partner and solve the word problem by estimating their answer to the nearest dollar. Finally, distribute calculators and have students check each other's answers.

Extension: To create multiplication word problems using this format, the students need only to change sentences. For example:

First Sentence:
Kyle has 3 boxes of match box cars.
Natalie bought 5 cases of canned peaches.

Second sentence:
Each box contains 12.
There were 7 in each case.

Third Sentence:
How many were in all?

Diorama Drama

Word Problems

Objectives: To review all problem-solving strategies, to write and solve word problems and to illustrate word problems

Materials: shoe boxes; scissors; glue; crayons; tissue paper; clay; pipe cleaners; Legos™, plastic toy figures, etc.

Directions: The final result of this activity is a game. Groups of students will solve word problems that other groups of students have written and depicted in the form of a diorama. It is a pleasure to watch students eagerly move from word problem to word problem with such eagerness and then solve them.

Begin by reviewing with students the strategies on page 107 to solve word problems. Write the list on the board. Divide students into cooperative learning groups. Each group should choose a strategy listed, and then write a word problem to fit the strategy. (You may or may not want students to label their questions with the strategy.) The students writing the word problem should also solve it, and then have it approved by you. The questions and answers should be kept a secret.

Next, each group should create a diorama using the materials listed above to depict its word problem. For example, if one group writes a word problem that requires drawing a picture, the students may create a diorama of the character(s) involved in the problem accompanied by the setting. (See example below.) When the questions, answers and dioramas are completed, you are ready to play.

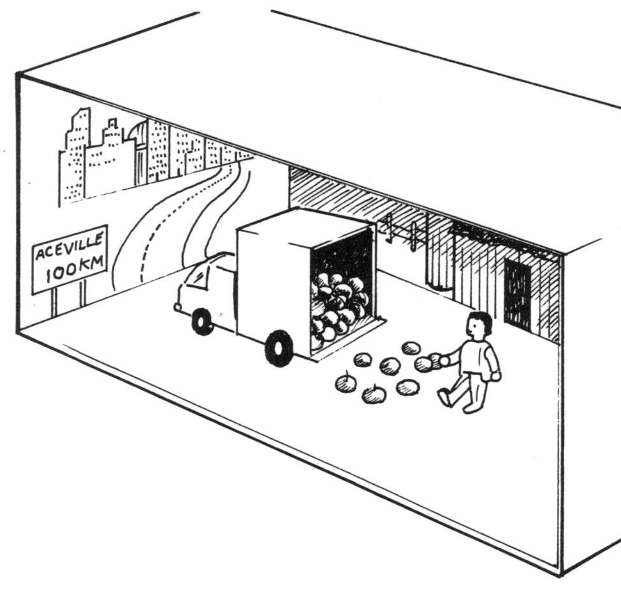

To set up the game, students in the cooperative groups move their desks together to create a table. Each group should place its diorama and question on its table. Assign and label each set of desks with one number. Explain to students that they will move from table to table in a clockwise fashion to solve each other's word problems. Assign one student to become the recorder. Students will have no more than five minutes to solve each problem. When time is up, they must stop working and move to the next table to solve the problem located there. If students do not finish a word problem, they may complete it if they finish another problem quickly, but they may not go back to the table where the problem is set up.

continued on page 107

Diorama Drama continued

When all students are back in their original position, review each problem. The team who solved the most problems correctly wins!

Problem-Solving Strategies

Choosing the Operation
Identifying Extra Information
Checking for a Reasonable Answer
Drawing a Picture
Two-Step Problems
Identifying Missing Information
Finding a Pattern
Guess, Test and Revise
Making a Table
Making an Organized List

Create a Math Book!

Objectives: To encourage mathematical thinking

Materials: paper, pencils

Directions: Give each student a sheet of paper and have him/her create a math story problem involving addition, subtraction, multiplication or division or a combination of these functions. When students have completed their story problem, give each student another sheet of paper on which to figure out the solution. Each student should sign both papers.

Collect the problem and the solution papers. Assemble the pages of problems to create a *Math Story Problem* book. Keep the solution pages separate.

Over a period of two weeks, each student should solve all of the problems in the book. Designate a solution day at which time all solutions should have been reached. On Solution Day, take out the solution papers and have each student present the solution to the problem he/she made up. The rest of the class will check it against their own solution. Ask students if the presenter was correct and if their answers were correct. If not, have students make the necessary adjustments.

At Home With Math

Word Problems

Objectives: To recognize the significance of math in everyday life and to create and solve word problems

Materials: chart paper, markers, pencils, small notepads, paper

Directions: Ask each student to bring in a small notepad, one that they can easily carry and have on hand. Then, for several days, have the students observe how they and their families use math every day and record these activities in their notepads. Encourage whole family participation and remind students to look very carefully for math even in the simplest tasks. Explain that math is "hiding" around every corner.

After several days, gather the students together and allow them to share their findings. Record their observations on a chart. For example, the students' ideas might include: Time—get up, get ready, go to bed, read, chores, piano lessons, TV programs; Weather—temperature highs and lows; Money—lunch, snacks, games, books, field trips, allowance, gifts, savings, checkbooks; Gas—amount, cost; Speed Limit—miles per hour, time; Food—how much, cost, servings; Scores—report card, tests, teams, etc. Model for the students how to create word problems from their lists. For example:

"I get up at 6:45 a.m. It takes me 25 minutes to get ready for school and 25 minutes to get to school. What time do I arrive at school?"

"My two brothers and I needed money for lunch. Lunch costs $2.45 for each of them and $1.85 for myself. How much money will we need all together?"

Have each student write a set number of problems. The students may create the problems using realistic family situations. Have students exchange papers with their classmates. The activity is sure to heighten student awareness and understanding of the significance of mathematics in their lives.

Every Problem's Different!

Word Problems

Objective: To create and solve word problems involving the division of a three-digit number by a two-digit number

Materials: 3" x 5" index cards, pencils, calculators, dice, paper

Directions: Distribute an index card to each student. Ask students to write a word problem in which they must divide a three-digit number by a two-digit number in order to solve the problem. For example: "Over the summer, our class ate __ __ __ ice pops. There are __ __ students in our class. How many ice pops did each student eat?" The students should leave blanks where the numbers should go. Then, collect the cards. Place them in the Math Corner along with several calculators and sets of dice. Students may visit the center in their free time.

To play, students do the following:

1. Choose an index card and read the problem on the card.
2. Roll the dice to fill in the five blank spaces in the problem with five digits.
3. Write the problem on the back of the index card (i.e. 258 ÷ 43 = ____).
4. Find the quotient using paper and pencil and check the answer using a calculator. Students then write the answer on the back of the card.

Students will enjoy seeing the problems that others have created and solved as well as making some of their own.

Graham Cracker Denominator Determinator

Objective: To understand how a denominator is determined

Materials: one graham cracker (or similar) per student, scrap paper, pencils

Directions: Distribute one cracker to each student. Ask students to observe the lines on the cracker. How many lines do they see? Direct students to break their crackers into as many or as few pieces as desired. Students should then record the number of pieces on their scrap paper. Explain to students that the number of pieces into which an object is broken is how the denominator obtains its numerical value.

continued on page 110

Graham Cracker...continued

Group students and have them tell each other the number of pieces they have broken their crackers into. Stress the fact that they all have one cracker, despite the number of pieces they have. Students should then be instructed to write the number of pieces as a denominator.

Extension: To introduce or reinforce how the numerator is determined, allow students to eat part of their crackers. Stop them from eating after about one minute. Ask them to show what pieces they have left. Explain to them that when there is only a part of something, the part you want to describe is the numerator. Therefore, the number of pieces they have left is the numerator. Direct students to write two fractions—a fraction to show what is left and a fraction to show what was eaten.

Possible Practice in Pairs

Objectives: To practice creating fractions and to interpret numerical symbols into visual, tangible models

Materials: Popsicle sticks (approximately 13 for every two students), construction paper, one marker for every two students

Directions: Pair up students. Supply each pair with a piece of construction paper and a Popsicle stick. The construction paper will serve as a work mat. (A work mat helps the visuals stand out, as it provides a solid background. It also helps you easily decipher if the students have created the correct model.) Next, ask one student from each pair to color its Popsicle stick using a marker. Explain to students that this stick will act as the line that separates the numerator from the denominator. Place the remaining Popsicle sticks on a supply table. Have the second student from each pair count out 12 Popsicle sticks from the supply table. When this is done, explain to students that they will be creating fractions using the Popsicle sticks. To begin, have the pairs place the colored Popsicle stick horizontally in the center of their work mat. Next, write a fraction on the board. Students should then place the number of Popsicle sticks the numerator indicates on the top, and the number of Popsicle sticks the denominator indicates on the bottom. When students are comfortable with this, make the activity more challenging by calling out a value for the denominator, not necessarily in order. The students can create the fraction and then write the appropriate numerical symbols.

Creating and Working With Fraction Bars

Objectives: To create fraction bars, to use them to find equivalent fractions and to compare fractions **Fractions**

Materials: crayons, markers, one 3" x 8" strip of oaktag for each student, one 3" pre-cut circle of any light colored paper for every two students, rulers, pencils, index cards

Directions:

Creating the Fraction Bars

Distribute an oaktag strip to each student. Tell students that they are to create a visual to depict a fraction. Begin by asking students to measure the strip of paper. Next, they should divide it into equal sections. They may divide the strip into as many sections as they would like. (Model these steps on the board.) Direct students to trace over the sections they have created using a marker or crayon. (It is best if all students use the same color.) Next, students should use a different color to color in a fraction of the strip. Be sure to tell them not to color over the section markings. When each student has created his/her fraction, distribute the index cards and instruct students to neatly record the numerical symbols to correspond with their fraction bar on it. Students should write their names on the back of their card and strip.

Finding Equivalent Fractions

With fraction bars in hand, line up students around the perimeter of the room. Hold one student's fraction bar up for all to see. Ask the class to take a look at it and then to compare the shaded portion to their own bar. Ask students who feel that the shaded portion of their bar is the same, or nearly the same as the one you are holding, to all go to a certain area of the room. Once those students have moved, hold up another student's bar and continue with the same procedure. When all students are part of a group, instruct them to find someone else in their group who has colored the exact same amount of space on their bar as they have. When they have found that person(s), direct them to sit down together on the floor. Last, share results. Grouped students can hold up their fraction bars and supply the class with the corresponding numerators and denominators.

continued on page 112

Creating and Working...continued

Comparing Fractions

Again, with fraction bars in hand, randomly pair students. Direct them to see whose fraction is larger and whose is smaller by placing one fraction bar over another and comparing the portion that has been shaded in. (Stress the fact that the bars are all the same size.) Give each student one of the 3" circles. Have students create a math "sentence" comparing the fraction bars using <, > or = (i.e. place the fraction bars next to each other and have the students put the circle in between them with <, > or = on it). Display the paired fraction bars, the circles and the index cards to create a meaningful display!

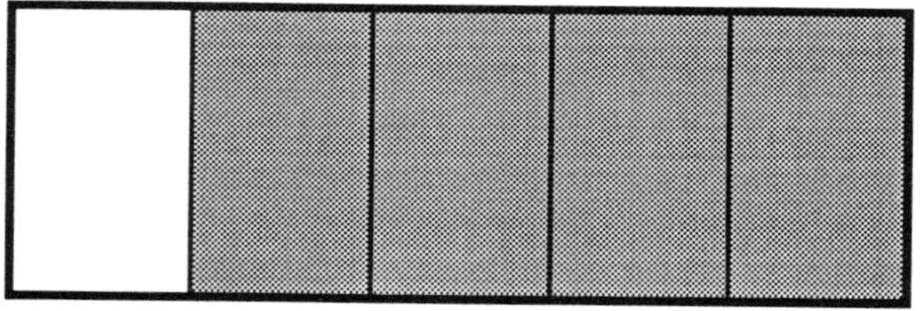  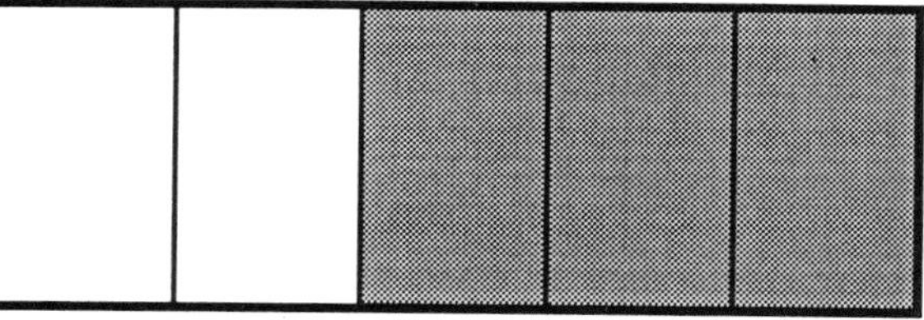

Let's Play Cards!

Fractions

Objective: To determine fraction values in terms of greater, lesser or equal

Materials: 132 index cards, marker

Preparation: Write 66 different fractions on index cards (one per card). Make two cards for each fraction (132 fraction cards in all).

Create a deck of cards making sure there are two cards for each fraction. Choose the fraction cards for the deck depending upon the abilities of the players.

Directions: This is a card game for two players similar to the card game "war." Deal out the cards so that each player gets half of the deck. Both players turn over their top card simultaneously. Whoever has the fraction of a greater value takes both cards. Both players turn over the next card and continue playing in this manner. If both players turn over cards of equivalent value, there is a war. Both players put out three more cards face down. Then, they choose a fourth card which they put down face up. The one with the fraction of greater value takes all the cards in play from the "war." Students continue playing until one player has won all the cards. If you set a time limit for the game, the one with the most cards wins the game.

Fractional Frogs

Fractions

Objective: To use fractions to complete an art project

Materials: 12" x 18" sheet of dark green paper for each student, 9" x 12" sheet of light green paper for each student, 4" x 4" square of black paper for each student, 4" x 4" square of white paper for each student, scissors, glue, pencils, crayons

Directions: Explain to students that they will be creating frogs and that they will be using fractions to help determine the size of each part of the frog. This activity involves completing one body part at a time, with everyone working at the same time. When one part is complete, the students will stop and listen for the next direction to create the next piece of their fractional frog.

When students are ready to begin, distribute the dark green paper. Instruct students to use $^1/_3$ of the dark green paper to create the frog's body. (Students can draw and cut out a circle or oval.) If students are having difficulty determining $^1/_3$, stop to model how they can fold the paper into the number the denominator indicates (3), and use only the amount of space the numerator indicates (1). Next, tell students to create the frog's head using only $^1/_2$ of the remaining dark green paper. Students glue the head to the body. To create the back legs, instruct students to use $^1/_3$ of the light green paper for each leg. An easy way to create a frog leg is to draw a large 2, add frog toes and close the figure.

Students draw the second leg the same way, but should flip it over before gluing it on. Next, students should use $^1/_2$ of the remaining light green paper to create the front legs. When all legs are secured, instruct students to use $^1/_2$ of the white paper to create the white of the eyes, and $^1/_4$ of the black paper to create each eye. Students can use a crayon to create a mouth. Use the remaining scraps to create a background for a bulletin board. The green paper can be a used to create swamp grass and lily pads, and the black paper can be used to create bulletin board letters.

Extension: Before using the scraps, ask students to determine what fraction of each sheet of paper is left! ($^1/_3$ dark green, $^1/_6$ light green, $^1/_2$ white, $^1/_2$ black)

Fraction Wheels

Fractions

Objective: To help students visualize and understand equivalent fractions

Materials: one thin, white paper plate or circle cut from oaktag per student; rulers; crayons; markers; scissors; pencils

Directions: Pair up students. Explain to students that each of them will depict a fraction using a circle. The partners in each pair must create a different fraction, and the fraction's denominator must be a multiple of the fraction's denominator, or a factor of the partner's denominator. (For example, if one student chooses to divide his/her circle into fourths, then his/her partner could divide his/her circle into eighths, because eight is a multiple of four; or, the partner could divide his/her circle in two, because two is a factor of four.) As a class, create lists of multiples and factors.

Before students begin dividing their circle, check each pair of students to be sure they have followed the directions and understand the concept. Next, students should work with a pencil and ruler to divide the circle into the number of pieces they have chosen. They should label each section of the circle with the appropriate fraction. Each fractional piece of the circle should be colored a different color. Students are now ready to create their fraction wheels!

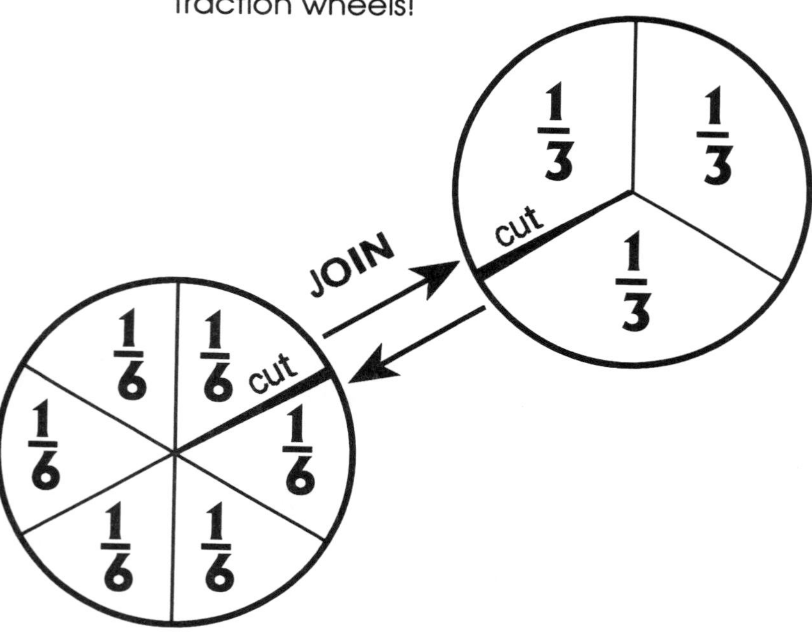

Direct students to cut along one of the division lines that they have drawn in order to divide the circle. Next, one student in each pair should fit his/her fraction circle with his/her partner's circle by joining the two at the radius line they cut. (See diagram.) When students manipulate the circle, they should be able to visualize and name equivalent fractions. Have students share their fractional circles with the rest of the class.

Pie Graph Surveys

Pie Graphs

Objectives: To create a table for a survey, to conduct a survey using the table and to create a pie graph depicting the results of the survey

Materials: one blank pie graph per student (See Step Three on page 116.), paper, pencils, markers, scissors

Directions:

Step One: Conducting a Survey

FAVORITE DESSERTS

Ice Cream ✔ ✔ ✔
Pecan Pie ✔
Apple Pie ✔ ✔
Chocolate Cake ✔ ✔ ✔
Candy Bar ✔ ✔
Milkshake ✔ ✔ ✔ ✔ ✔

Explain to students what the purpose of a survey is. Tell them that they will be conducting one themselves. Brainstorm possible topics with students (i.e. favorite television show, food, career choice, etc.). Once every student has chosen a survey topic, you are ready to create the survey table. Have students begin by creating a title for their survey and writing it across the top of their page. Next, the students should come up with several choices for their survey. For example, if the title of the survey is "Favorite Subject," the students should then choose some popular subjects and write them vertically along the left margin of the paper. Explain to students that next, they will survey sixteen people. (Sixteen is an easy number to work with to section off the pie graph in Step Three.) You may want to discuss the sample population and perhaps set restrictions. Will students test a homogeneous group? only students in their class? the first sixteen people they see on the playground? teachers?

Step Two: Creating Fractions

Chocolate Cake ✔ ✔ ✔ **means three children out of sixteen picked the cake as their favorite dessert = 3/16**

When all the tables are complete, it is time to convert the results into fractions. Discuss with students what the denominator will be for each choice and why (16, because that is the number of people who make up the whole survey). Next, discuss how to determine the numerator. (The number of people who chose an item is the numerator. For example, if four people chose math as their favorite subject, the fraction would then be $^{4}/_{16}$.) When all tallied results have been converted into fractions, you are ready to create the pie graph. Depending on the ability level of your students, you may or may not want students to reduce fractions.

continued on page 116

Pie Graph Surveys continued

Step Three: Creating the Pie Graph

Before students begin this step, draw a circle, divide it into sixteen sections and make a copy for each student. Distribute the circles and discuss how students will show their results, or fractions, on the pie graph. Instruct students to shade in the number of sections that each numerator indicates, using a different color for each numerator, or topic. Students should write the fraction and the corresponding choice in the shaded areas. Students can then cut the circles out, mount them, create a title and share them with the class.

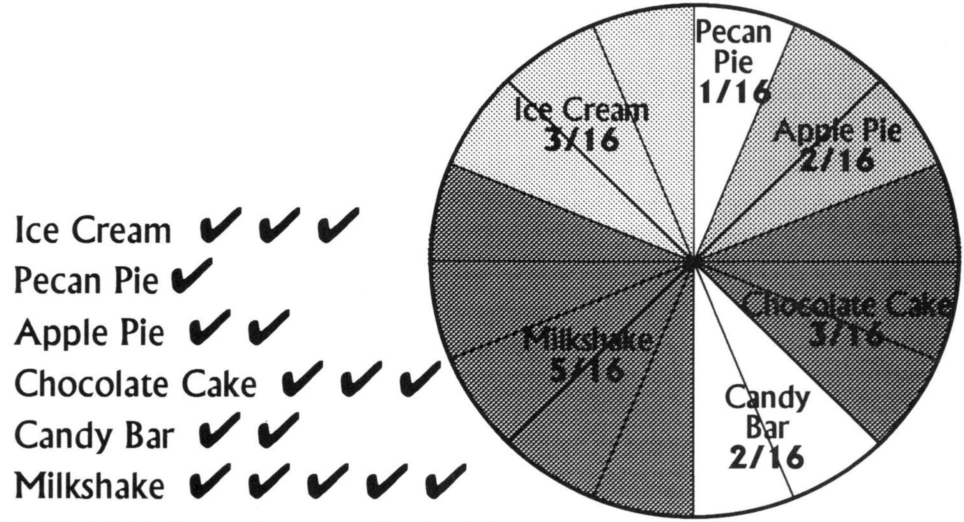

Pictographs Speak a Thousand Words

Objectives: To complete a pictograph and then to tell a story about it **Graphs**

Materials: drawing paper, markers, rulers, lined paper, pencils

Directions: This is a lesson which uses pictographs in a backward way. To begin, distribute drawing paper and have each student create a pictograph minus the title, labels and symbol key. Then, collect, shuffle and redistribute the pictographs to the students. (No one should have his/her own.) Have students decide on data that fits the pictograph, adding a title, column headings and a key to create a graphic representation of their topic. Then, have the students write a paragraph or story that explains their pictograph.

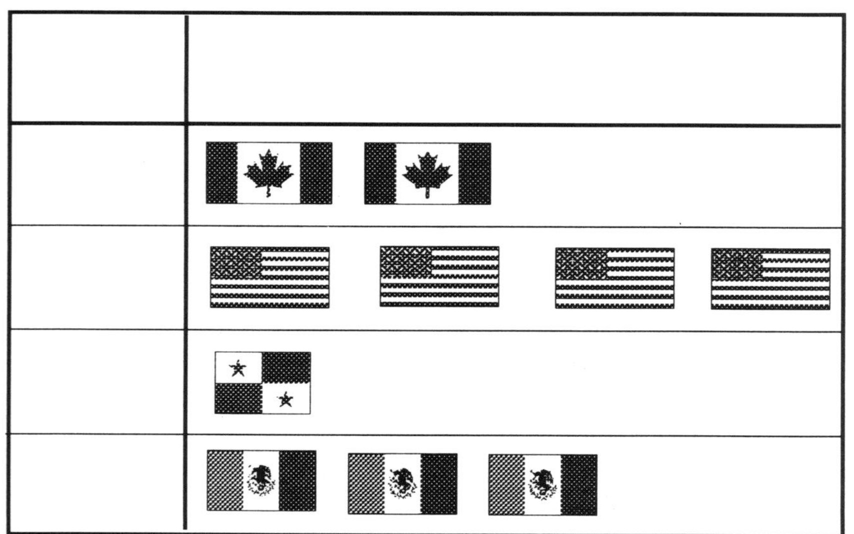

Dueling Decimals

Decimals

Objectives: To reinforce place value and to order decimals

Materials: one number spinner per pair of students (preferably spinners that include the numeral zero), copies of place value cards (directions below), scissors

Directions: This makes a terrific math center activity! Before you are ready to play, create a place value card for each student. (See the example shown.) You can easily fit several cards on a sheet of paper, run them off and then cut them apart. To play "Dueling Decimals," pair up students and supply each pair with a spinner. Give each student a place value card. Player Number One should spin the spinner. The number that comes up should be recorded under the thousandth's place column on the player's place value card. Player Number Two repeats the process. Player Number One then spins again, this time placing the number under the hundredth's place column on his/her place value card. The process is repeated until both players have a complete decimal number. Students should then compare the two numbers. The player with the larger number earns a point. Students have now completed the first round and should continue for four more rounds. The student with the most points after the fifth round wins "Dueling Decimals!"

Extension: Ask students to add their five decimal numbers. Within the pairs, ask students to compare the sums. Is the winner of the game also the player with a higher sum? Why? Next, have students compare decimal sums with the entire class. Who is the player with the highest and lowest sum? Name them the "Dynamic Dueling Decimal Players of the Day!"

Number Research—Did You Know. . .?

Objective: To become more familiar with place value

Materials: encyclopedias, *Guinness Book of World Records*, nonfiction books and magazines, white construction paper, colored markers or crayons

Directions: Create a bulletin board of numbers by having students research to find out one or two interesting facts that involve numbers. For example, did you ever wonder how many mosquitoes a bat may eat in an evening, or how many miles away the sun is, or how many bones there are in our bodies?

continued on page 118

Number Research...continued

Place Value

Begin by having students brainstorm possible questions to research. Then, have students formulate at least two questions of their own. Next, have students take a trip to the library in search of answers. When students are ready, have them write the question and answer on white construction paper, illustrate it and share it. Display students' papers.

Extension: When you are ready to take down the display, assemble the pages into your own class *Book of Numbers!*

Place Value Riddles

Objective: To reinforce students' place value skills

Materials: lined writing paper, pencils, scrap paper

Directions: To begin, write five similar numerals on the board such as:

305 3005 35 3050 3500

Ask students to copy the numbers on a piece of scrap paper. Then, provide students with three clues, one at a time. Example:

1. I have a 5 in the one's place.
2. I am greater than 300.
3. I have a 0 in the hundred's place.

Tell the students to make an X on all the numbers that do not go with the clue. Students should continue to eliminate the numbers that do not fit. After you have given all the clues for each riddle, there should be only one number left. Try several of these riddles to model the process for students. When students have grasped the concept, have them fold their writing paper in half three times to create eight boxes. Direct them to create eight of these place value riddles. List the following terms on the board for students to refer to when writing their clues:

one's, ten's, hundred's, thousand's places
greater than
less than
have a __ somewhere

Have the students exchange papers and solve each other's riddles.

What's The Difference?

Computation Skills

Objective: To practice computation skills

Materials: copies of the flower below, pencils

Directions: Pair up students and distribute several copies of the flower to each pair. Instruct one of the players to name a number. Both students should write the number in the center of the flower. Then, at your signal, tell the students to race to see who can be the first to fill in all the petals with problems whose differences are the same as the number in the center. All the petals must be filled in for the puzzle to be complete. Team members then exchange and correct the papers. If all the subtraction problems are correct, the student who finished first receives one point. If not, the second player receives one point (provided all those answers are correct). The loser names the next center number. The first player to have a total of five points is the winner.

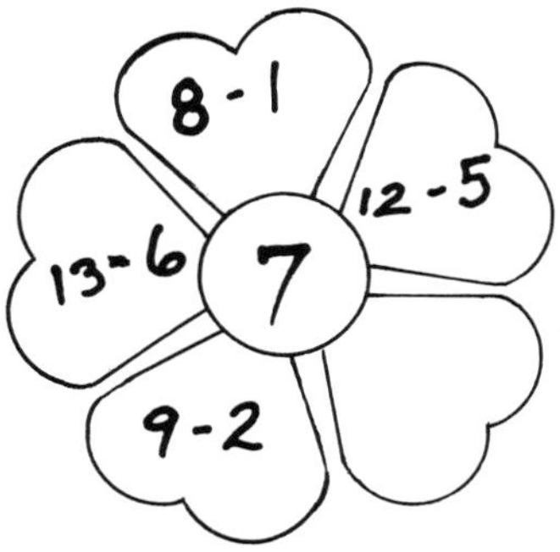

8 - 1
12 - 5
13 - 6
7
9 - 2

Hello or 07734

Computation Skills

Objective: To develop number sense and proficiency in using a calculator

Materials: paper, pencils, calculators, overhead projector calculator (if available)

Directions: Your students will delight in experimenting with calculators while they create letters, words and sentences. Give a calculator to each student. Ask students to look at the digit buttons very carefully. Keeping the calculator turned off and flat on their desk, have students try to determine if any of the numbers appear to form letters when holding the calculator upside down. The students then turn on their calculators and experiment to discover which numbers form letters. On a piece of paper, ask students to write down each number and the letter it forms . Guide students to come up with the following list:

0 = o 1 = L or I 3 = E 4 = h 5 = S 7 = L 8 = B

Ask students how many vowels/consonants they discovered. Then, ask them to create words using the letters they discovered, such as Boss, less, shell, Bell, she, etc. When they have created a list, have the students write the numbers that form those letters (i.e. Boss = 8055).

Allow time for the students to experiment and discover that the last letter of the word must be punched into the calculator first when forming the word (i.e. Boss = 5508 when keying in numbers).

Challenge your students to then use the new words in sentences. To do this, students must replace the word with its number equivalent. (Remind students to write the numbers down in the order they should be keyed in on the calculator.) Example:

345 gave me 5537 ice cream than you have.

A 77345 is found on the beach.

Then, have students exchange papers and complete each other's sentences using a calculator.

Palindrome Summations

Computation Skills

Objectives: To practice computation skills and to increase number sense

Materials: writing paper, pencils

Directions: Explain to students that a number palindrome is similar to a word palindrome in that it reads the same backward or forward. For example:

75457

1689861

Challenge students to create number palindromes using addition. To do this, have students choose any number:

652

Then, they reverse that number's digits:

256

and add the two numbers together:

652 + 256 = 908

If the sum is not a palindrome, instruct the students to reverse the digits in that sum and add as they did in the first step:

908 + 809 = 1717

Have the students continue in this manner until the sum is a palindrome.

1717 + 7171 = 8888

The example required three steps to produce a palindrome. Allow students to share the number of steps it took for them to create a numerical palindrome. Who had the fewest steps? the greatest?

Rat Race Relay

Objective: To drill addition and/or subtraction facts while running a relay race

Materials: flash cards with addition and/or subtraction facts on them, gym or outdoor area

Directions: Students will be more than willing to practice their addition and subtraction skills in order to prepare for the "Rat Race Relay." Divide your class into relay teams. Each member of the relay team is a "rat." (However, you will need two volunteers from each team to play the part of the "cat," which is explained on page 122.)

continued on page 122

Rat Race Relay continued

Computation Skills

Review the procedures of a relay race. Split up each team, lining half of the students from each team on opposite sides. The rat's job is to run a relay, like any other relay race. However, each rat must carry an addition/ subtraction fact card to the team member, or rat, on the opposite side of the gym. When they reach the rat, the runner must ask the awaiting rat the addition/subtraction fact that they are holding (i.e. 8 + 9). The receiving rat must answer correctly before running with a new card to the team member on the other side of the gym. Two team members will play the role of the cat. The cats' role is to hold another team accountable for answering correctly before running.

When you are ready to begin, issue a flash card to each team player. The cats should then take their places at the head of the team lines. The first team to have answered all facts correctly and to all sit down wins! Repeat the relay so that the cats have the opportunity to become rats and vice versa.

Using Number Concepts

Objectives: To add whole numbers and to use logical thinking

Materials: 3" x 5" index cards, paper, pencils

Directions: Give each student a set of cards marked 1 through 9. Make enough answer cards 11 through 15 so that each student will get one. Then, pose the following to the students:

1. Using only two cards, list all the ways you can make the sum of _____ . (Students fill in their answer card number in the blank.)
2. How many ways did you find _____ ?
3. How did you know you found all the ways?

Extension: Repeat this exercise using three cards to make the sum.

What's My Number?

Logical Thinking

Objective: To reinforce logical thinking

Materials: one copy of the clue card per student (below), pencils, one copy of the score card per student (below)

Directions: In this guessing game, a student will think of a number and then give a series of clues to help the rest of the class guess the right number. This can be done as a whole class activity, or it can be played in teams of two, three or four students with a point score system. Students can use the score card below to keep score. One score card per team is used. After all the teams have completed their score cards, determine which team has the highest score.

10 points for an identification at clue #1
9 points for an identification at clue #2
8 points for an identification at clue #3
7 points for an identification at clue #4
6 points for an identification at clue #5
5 points for an identification at clue #6
4 points for an identification at clue #7
3 points for an identification at clue #8 (if necessary)
2 points for an identification at clue #9 (if necessary)
1 point for an identification at clue #10 (if necessary)

Using a copy of the clue card below, have each student think of a number between 11 and 99. Then, they fill out the sentences on the card. Have each student present his/her clues to the class. See how many clues it takes for students to figure out the number. If the number has not been identified after all seven clues, have students repeat clues #6 and #7 narrowing the span of greater and less than.

Extension: Make a bar graph indicating the scores of each team.

My number is ______ .

1. It is a _____ -digit number.
2. The sum of its digits is _____ .
3. It can or cannot be divided by two _____ .
4. It can or cannot be divided by three _____ .
5. It can be divided by _____ .
6. It is greater than ______ .
7. It is less than _____ .

On clues #6 and #7, do no more than 10 in either direction.

What's My Number?

Team ________________

Clue Number	Clue Value	Earned Points
1	(10)	
2	(9)	
3	(8)	
4	(7)	
5	(6)	
6	(5)	
7	(4)	
8	(3)	
9	(2)	
10	(1)	
Total points earned		

Fact Snacks

Multiplication and Division

Objective: To create sets or arrays to demonstrate the relationship between multiplication and addition

Materials: small snack food (popcorn, pretzels, candy corn, M&M's), paper plates

Directions: Provide each student with a paper plate and a couple of snacks to use as manipulatives. Have the students arrange the snacks into sets, such as five sets of five with two left over or nine sets of three.

Ask the students to add the sets together. Explain the related multiplication facts to them. When the activity is complete, allow the students to enjoy the tasty fact snacks.

Dominoes in Motion

Multiplication

Objective: To practice basic multiplication facts

Materials: dominoes, paper, pencils

Directions: Begin this exciting "drill and practice" activity by arranging the students' desks in a circle. Each student should also have a sheet of paper and a pencil ready. Then, pass out a domino to each student. Instruct the students to hold the domino horizontally and create a multiplication problem from the numbers/dots on the domino. Example:

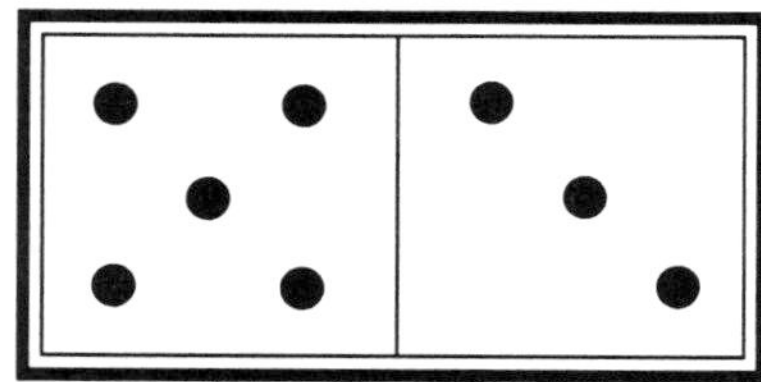 = 5 x 3 = 15

After creating and solving their problem, have the students pass their domino to the person on their right. Continue this activity until each student's original domino returns to him/her. Finally, have the students exchange and correct each other's papers.

Extension: Repeat the activity challenging students to improve their scores and to beat their time. Have students keep track of their own progress by creating line graphs.

Crazy Eights

Multiplication

Objective: To multiply two- and three-digit numbers by a one-digit number

Materials: deck of cards, paper, pencils, calculators

Directions: Students will enjoy this multiplication card game where the eights are wild! First, draw a diagram of three boxes to represent a multiplication problem involving a two-digit number times a single-digit number.

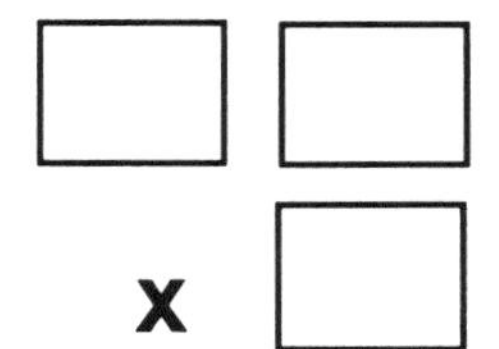

Demonstrate the game by choosing a card from a deck of cards with the face cards and the tens removed. Write that number in one of the boxes. Repeat this two or more times. After a number is written, it may not be changed. Then, students solve the problem. Now, the crazy eights become important. Have the students check the product using their calculators. Then, award points using the following rules.

1. If the product is incorrect, the score is zero.
2. If the product is correct, the score is five points.
3. Bonus—If the product contains a crazy eight, the following bonus points are scored:
   1 point—one's place, 2 points—ten's place,
   3 points—hundred's place.

Continue the game by calling the cards aloud and having the students solve the problems independently.

Cartographer's Count

Division

Objectives: To use a calculator to compute the number of miles traveled in a journey and to estimate quotients

Materials: one U.S. road map per pair of students, calculators, paper, pencils, reference books, library books, index cards

continued on page 126

Cartographer's Count continued

Division

Directions: Your students will love this activity that combines social studies map reading skills with mathematical reasoning. Best of all, it's realistic—a quality that always draws student interest. To begin, pair up students and distribute a United States road map to each team. Ask the students to select a city located on the east coast and a city located on the west coast.

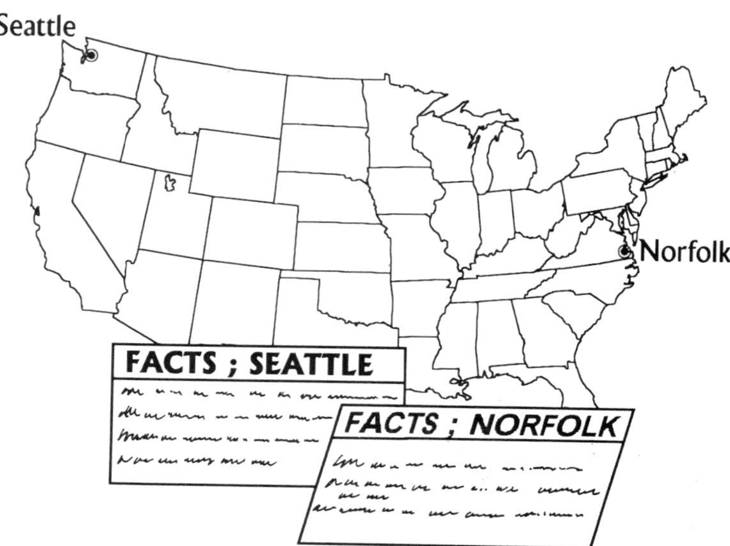

When they have done this, send the students to the library or have them use encyclopedias and other sources to research some basic facts about the two cities such as population, climate, physical features or tourist attractions. Have the students list these "Facts of Interest" on the index cards.

With the research completed, the students are ready to plan a cross-country route from one city to the other. Demonstrate how to use the map's mileage gauge to determine the number of miles they will "travel." (For example, students might measure the mileage from New York City to Louisville to Kansas City to Denver to Salt Lake City and then finally to San Francisco.) Encourage students to check their calculations several times before determining the mileage of the trip.

Extensions: Have the "racing teams" determine the amount of gas needed to make the cross-country journey. To do this, the students will use the total miles traveled and divide this number by the number of miles per gallon of gas that their vehicle can travel. (Either tell the students how many miles per gallon their car can travel or have them choose an amount.) Have each team estimate the number of gallons of gas that will be needed. Students may then use a calculator to find out exactly how many gallons of gas they will need. Higher estimates—the extra gas slowed you down! Lower estimates—you ran out of gas!

Use an average price for a gallon of gasoline and have students multiply to find out how much money will be spent on gas for the cross-country trip.

Dial a Word Revisited

Mental Math

Objective: To give students practice in doing mental math computations

Materials: Dial-a-Word value box (page 67), list of spelling or thematic words, paper, pencils

Directions: Turn around the objective for Dial-a-Word to focus on computation this time. Distribute copies of the Dial-a-Word value box. Then, provide students with a list of words related to a specific classroom theme or perhaps the spelling word for the week. Have students determine the "value" of the words by using the value box to find out how much each letter is worth. For an added challenge, have the students mentally add the numbers to find the total value of the words and then write their answers on a piece of paper.

SPIDERS = 7743377
7 + 7 + 4 + 3 + 3 + 7 + 7
= **38**

Extensions: Give students a specific value sum and ask them to find a word whose letter values add up to that sum.

Give the students two words and ask them to determine which has the highest or lowest value. Students might first make predictions and then calculate the answers. Encourage the students to explain the reasons for their predictions.

Have students determine the value of each word when the sum value is multiplied by the value of one of the following: the sum of the vowels only; the value of the first or last letter; the sum of the consonants only.

Math Charts

Objective: To reinforce math concepts

Materials: copy of the chart (page 128), pencils

Directions: On the chart, fill in multiples of any number you are wanting the students to learn. Make enough copies of the chart so that each student gets one. Then, instruct students to color all the squares that are multiples of the chosen number.

continued on page 128

Math Charts continued

ComputationSkills

When students are finished, discuss with them other charts that can be made with other directions. Have the students make suggestions. Some examples:

1. Double numbers when the digits differ by 1
2. Odd numbers/even numbers
3. Addition/subtraction problems that have the same answer
4. Equivalent fractions
5. Multiplication/division problems that have the same answer

Extension: Give each student a chart. Have him/her decide what directions he/she is going to give. Have students write them on the paper. Then, each student should make up an appropriate number chart to fit his/her directions.

When each student has completed his/her chart, have the class exchange papers. Each student will follow the directions on the paper he/she has received. When students have finished, papers are to be returned to be checked by the originator.

Today's Temperature

Objective: To become familiar with the thermometer

Materials: an indoor thermometer and an outdoor thermometer (Fahrenheit as well as Celsius, if available), poster paper and marker to use to post the temperature outside your classroom

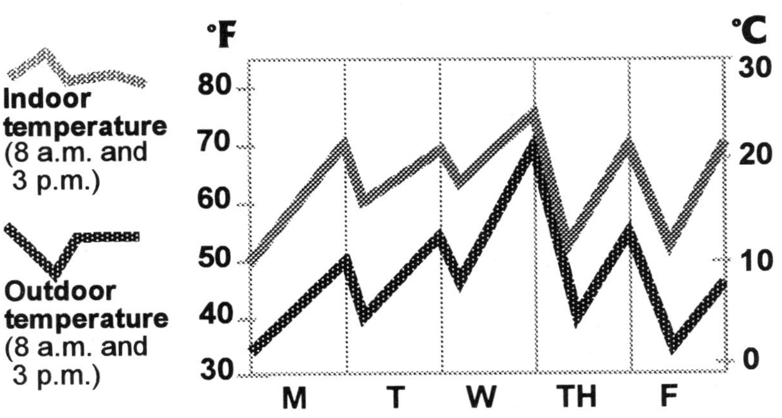

Directions: Have students record indoor and outdoor temperatures in degrees Celsius and Fahrenheit. Students can share their findings with the rest of the school by posting the daily temperatures on poster paper outside your classroom or in the main hall for the school. If desired, use an almanac or newspaper to share record high and low temperatures for each day.

Extension: Create ongoing line graphs to show temperature differences. Each day, ask individual students to plot the temperatures. Display them near the daily temperature recordings your class has posted.

Weather Wizards

Objectives: To reinforce concepts of time and temperature, to read and interpret the weather page and to make predictions

Materials: the weather page from the newspaper for two or more consecutive days (preferably the two days prior to this activity), one copy of the wizard wand for each student (page 130), paper, pencils

Directions: Students need authentic experiences with temperature and time, which is exactly what this activity provides! Give a copy of the weather page to each pair of students. Instruct students to examine the pages for the following information: time of sunrise and sunset for each day, low temperature for each day, high temperature for each day, high and low tides (if applicable).

Weather Wizards continued

After reviewing the information (to be sure students are interpreting the page correctly), instruct students to compare daily high and low temperatures, sunrises, etc. by calculating the differences between days. Next, students should use the information to predict tomorrow's weather. Students should record their predictions on the "weather wizard wand," cut them out and decorate them. Hang them on the wall or board. Ask volunteers to share and explain their numerical choices. When the day for which the predictions were made has passed, compare predictions with actual times and temperatures. Students whose predictions came the closest can be named the "The Weather Wizards of the Week!" This activity can be repeated for several weeks.

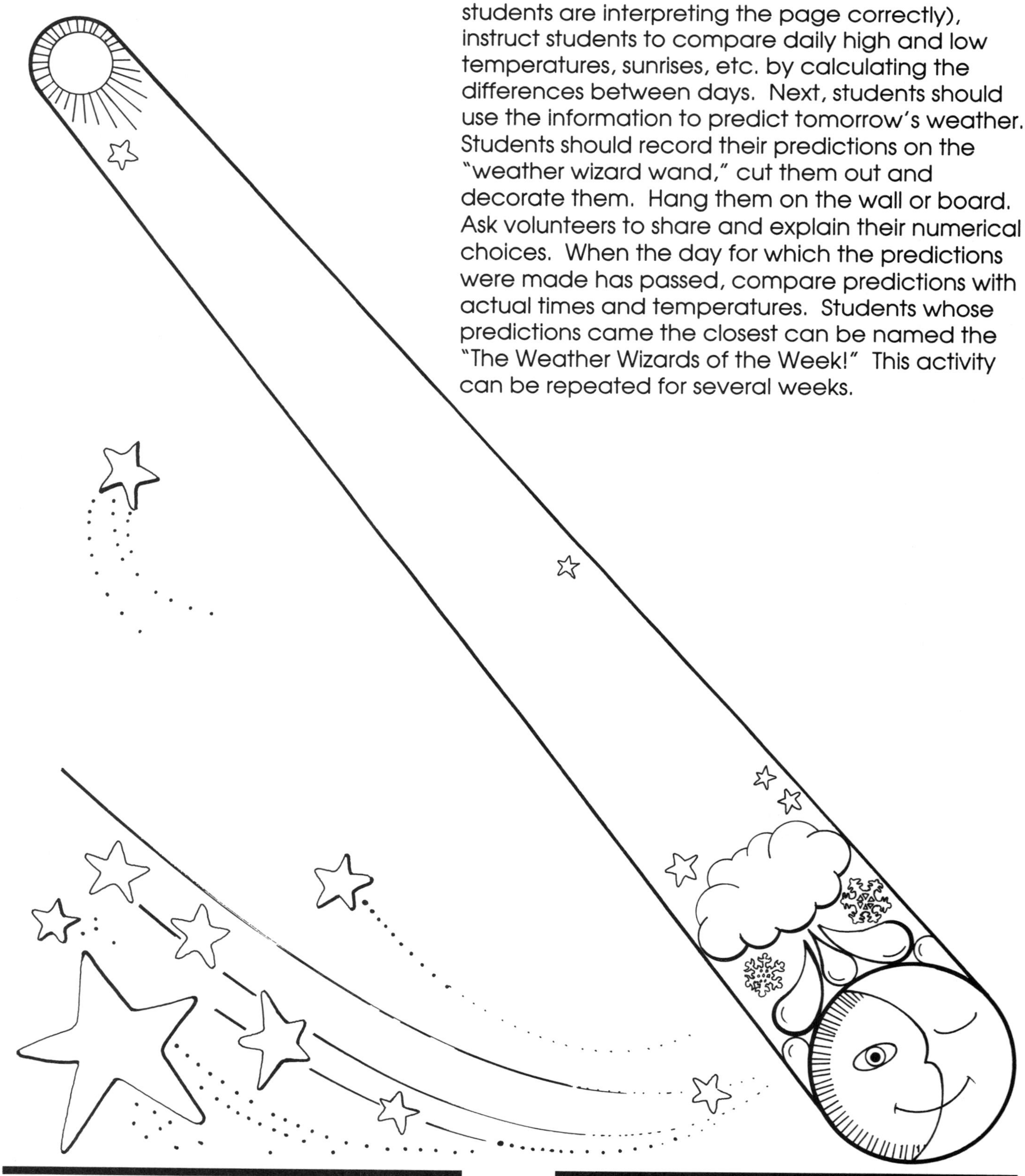

Science

The objective for the study of science in the third grade is to have the students increase their understanding of basic science concepts in the biological sciences, the physical sciences and the Earth-space sciences. The students will investigate the interrelationships among living and nonliving things in the environment. They will become interested in the natural world while they develop skills in observing, collecting, classifying, comparing, measuring, drawing conclusions and reporting.

The activities in this chapter have been designed keeping the above goals in mind. They include the following concepts:

1. using the scientific method
2. recording data from observations
3. understanding concepts of light reflections and shadows
4. understanding the relationships between variation and sound
5. experimenting with buoyancy
6. investigating the properties of magnets
7. creating simple circuits and applying them
8. identifying and using simple machines
9. investigating the behavior, characteristics and habitats of birds, insects and animals
10. understanding the concept of metamorphosis

The Scientific Process—Writing and the Experiment

Scientific Process

Objective: To introduce and/or reinforce the method of the scientific process

Materials: outline (below)

Directions: Help students become familiar with the method and terminology that goes along with conducting a scientific experiment by introducing the students to the simple outline below. This outline guides students through the experiment process. It will conform to any experiment.

Discuss the vocabulary on the outline with students. Then, demonstrate an experiment discussing the outline as you proceed with the experiment. You can help students do this by completing and discussing one section at a time. Brainstorm appropriate vocabulary and sentence frames students can include in their write-ups. Don't forget connecting words such as "the next step . . .," "I think that . . .," etc. When you feel students are ready, have them perform experiments in small groups, in pairs and on their own completing a write-up for each.

TITLE: (Allow students to create one.)

PROBLEM:	What are you trying to find out? What are you trying to solve?
MATERIALS:	These will vary with each experiment.
PROCEDURE:	What steps will you take? What will you do first? next? last?
VARIABLE:	What, if any, is the one thing that may change when/if the experiment is repeated?
OBSERVATIONS:	What did you see? hear? feel? smell? What happened?
CONCLUSIONS:	What is the answer to the "problem?" Why do you think what happened, happened?

A Model of Metamorphosis— The Monarch Butterfly

Butterflies— Observation

Objectives: To understand the concept that all living things produce other living things like themselves and to understand that some living things do not necessarily resemble their parents when they are born

Materials: butterfly raising kit or larva (caterpillar), twig, grass, jar with lid (Poke holes in lid.), observation diaries (paper bound together), books and other references about butterflies, copies of "Research Form" (page 134)

Background: Insects pass through many changes in their life cycles. This is called metamorphosis. To watch a caterpillar experience metamorphosis as it changes into an adult butterfly is very exciting for students as well as adults. The Butterfly Garden is a live butterfly raising kit which gives students the opportunity to watch metamorphosis firsthand. These kits are available from Insect Lore, P.O. Box 1535, Shafter, California 93263. Perhaps your PTA would be willing to fund this activity.

Directions: If you are working with the butterfly raising kit, have each student in the class keep an observation diary. Entries should be kept daily noting changes that occur as the larva changes into the chrysalis and then into the adult butterfly.

Tell the students to record the color, shape, size, texture, etc. of each stage. Have students write down any questions they might have regarding the process. Have students describe the emergent adult (butterfly). Point out the symmetry of the wing design. Explain to students that the butterfly has a slender body, jointed legs and two antennae on its head.

Using reference books, the observation notebooks, film strips and science encyclopedias, have the students research to answer the questions on the "Research Form" on page 134. When they have completed this, they should write up a report on metamorphosis using complete sentences and in paragraph form. Have them illustrate their reports and present them to the class.

Research Form

1. What kind of animal is a butterfly? ____________________
2. Describe the larva. ____________________
3. How was the chrysalis formed? ____________________
4. How long did it take for the butterfly to emerge? ____________________
5. What did the butterfly look like? ____________________
6. Does the butterfly make any sounds? ____________________
7. What do a butterfly's wings look like when it lands? ____________________
8. How is a moth different from a butterfly? ____________________
9. How is a moth the same as a butterfly? ____________________
10. What other animals change in appearance as they grow into the adult stage? ____________________

Let's Make a Butterfly!

Butterflies—Art

Objective: To show the coloration and symmetry of a monarch butterfly

Materials: 9" x 12" sheets of construction paper, glue, paint, paintbrushes, scissors, pencils, pipe cleaners, copies of the butterfly pattern (page 136)

Directions: Show students how to fold a piece of construction paper in half so that it measures 9" x 6". With a straight end on the fold, have students trace around the butterfly pattern and cut it out. The students can then use the paint to duplicate the design and coloration on the monarch's wing. Tell students to paint on one wing only as they will fold the butterfly closed (on the fold) while the paint is still wet to ensure duplication on the other wing. Students should glue a pipe cleaner to the head for the antennae. Attach the butterflies to a bird bulletin board to create an attractive spring theme. The students can also design their own flowers to make a more colorful welcome to spring.

Caterpillar Camouflage

Insects—Experiment

Objectives: To reinforce the concept that animals and insects have many ways to protect themselves from predators and to introduce camouflage as a means of protection for animals/insects

Materials: about 50 pieces of yarn—half of which are green

Directions: Tell the students that they are going to be hungry predator birds. They're out looking for nice juicy caterpillars (yarn pieces) to eat. Scatter the "caterpillars" on a grassy area around school. In a period of two or three minutes, see how many caterpillars the "birds" can find. Check to see if students found more plain (not green) or more camouflaged (green) caterpillars. Ask students if they think color is important in the selection of food by predators.

Butterfly Pattern

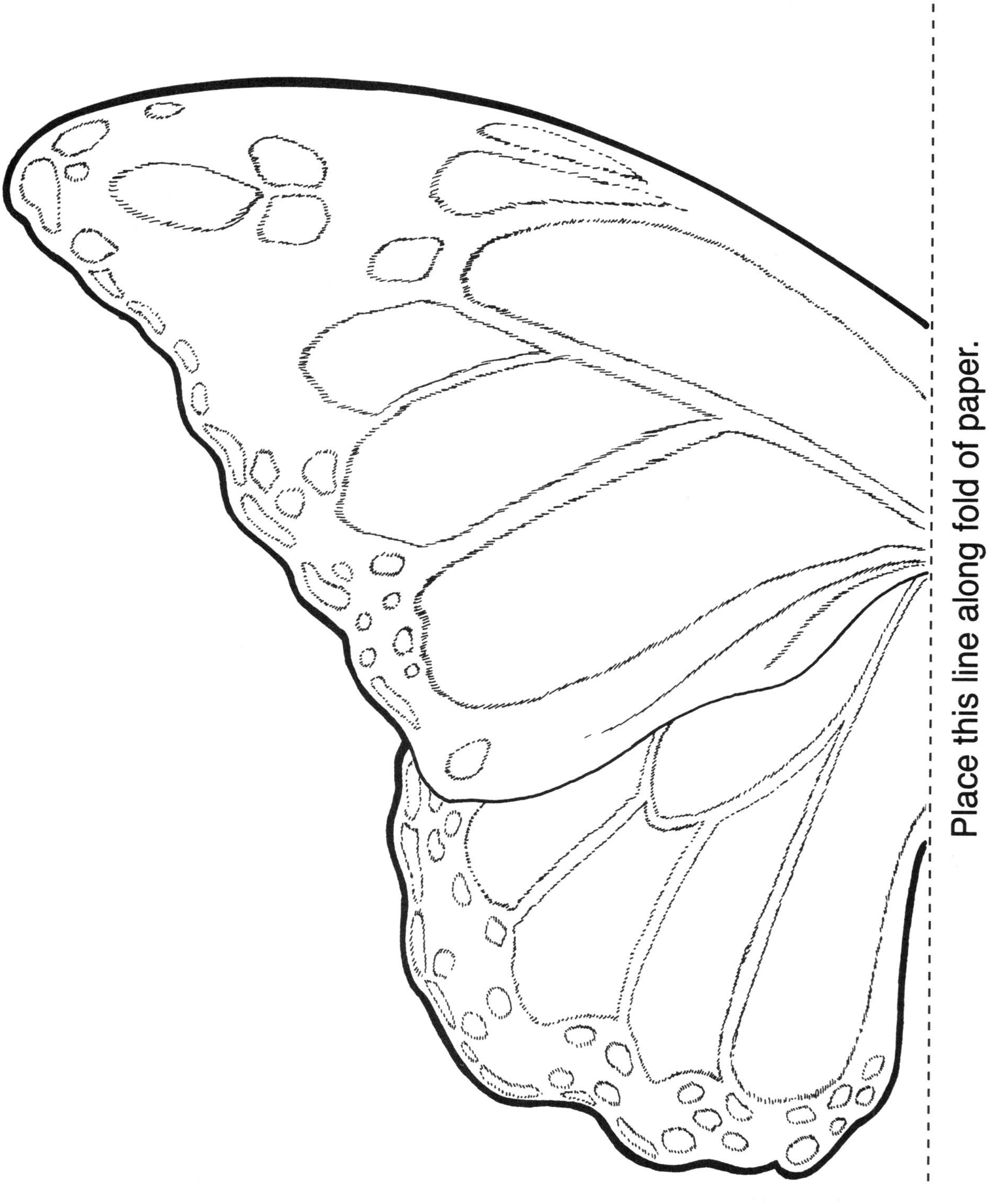

Place this line along fold of paper.

Ant Antics

Ants—Observation

Objective: To observe that ants live in families and care for their eggs

Materials: clear glass jar with lid, dirt, ant hill, trowel, dark construction paper, tape, cotton ball, chart paper, marker, scissors, book *Ant Cities* by Arthur Dorros

Directions: Read *Ant Cities* to your students. On chart paper, write some fun facts about ants described in the book such as:

1. Ants are insects.
2. Ants use their antennae or feelers to find food. They smell and touch with their antennae.
3. Ants live together in groups called ant cities.
4. In every "city," there are three kinds of ants—the queen(s), the workers and the males. Each kind has a specific job to do.
5. The queen's job is to lay the eggs.
6. The ant city has lots of rooms and tunnels.
7. Ants are very strong. Some can lift things that weigh 50 times as much as they do.
8. Ants are like people working together and helping each other to build a community.

Now, students are ready to observe the ants firsthand. To begin, fill a large glass jar about half full with dirt. Tape dark construction paper around the jar. Then, take a nature walk with your students to find an ant hill. Take time to observe the ants coming and going to the hill with food. Carefully dig up the ant hill, including the surrounding dirt and place it all in the jar. (This will encourage the ants to go underground.) Place a wet piece of cotton on the dirt and keep it damp to provide moisture for the ants. The ants may also be fed by adding crumbs of cookies or bread to the jar twice weekly. Finally, poke holes in the lid and secure.

To observe the ants, remove the dark paper. Students will be able to see tunnels that are close to the sides of the jar. Enjoy watching your own ant city but be sure to only keep it for about a month. Then, let students return their friends to their natural environment.

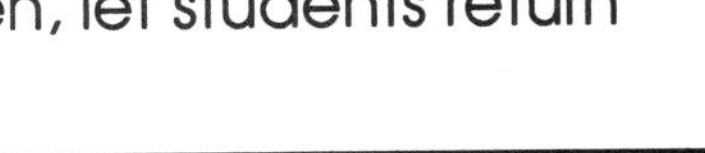

Ants in Your Pants!

Ants—Art

Objective: To create an ant city using fingerprints

Materials: ink pad, construction paper, pen, crayons

Directions: Explain to students that ants are busy insects, always moving, always working hard. They live together in colonies, and every ant has a job to do to help the others. So, tell students that when they cannot sit still and are wiggly and eager to get going, people sometimes ask, "Are there ants in your pants?"

As a culminating activity in a study of ants, have your students create an ant city. Begin by having them draw a series of underground tunnels on a piece of construction paper. To create ants in their tunnels, have the students press their finger tips onto an ink pad and then press their inky prints onto the paper. When the ink dries, students can use a pen to draw legs and antennae on the ants.

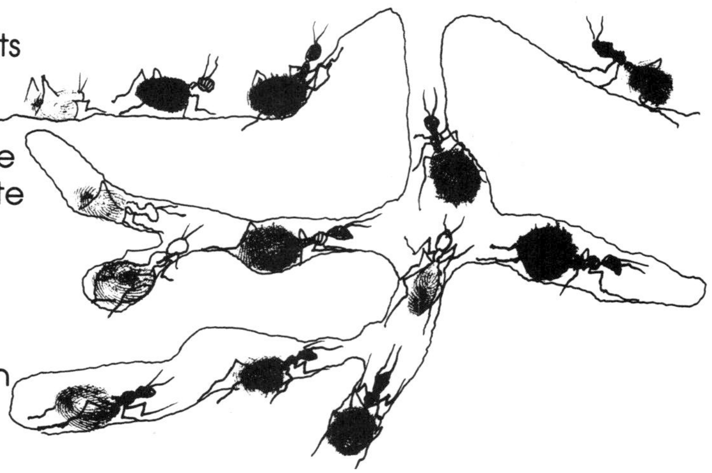

As an added touch, have the students create a story about their busy ant communities. A story starter could be as follows:

My teacher asked me, "Are there ants in your pants?" I truthfully had to answer, "Yes ma'am, there are." I began to explain that . . .

Getting the Message Across— Bee Style

Bees— Creative Dramatics

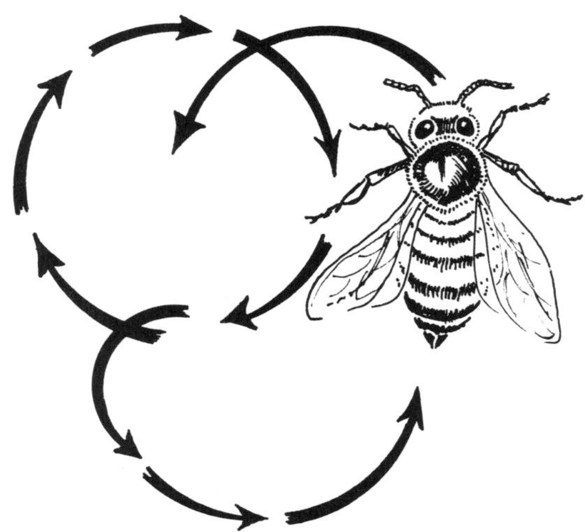

Objective: To recreate the way in which worker bees communicate the location of food using body language

Materials: "food" source

Directions: Explain to students that bees in a hive have many jobs to do. The work is divided into several kinds, and bees specialize by doing one particular job. One of the most important jobs is finding food. When one of the bees finds food, it communicates the location to other bees by using special body movements.

continued on page 139

Getting the Message Across—Bee Style continued

To introduce students to a fun kinesthetic activity which simulates the communication patterns of bees, divide students into cooperative learning groups of three or four. Provide each group with an object to represent a food source. Instruct one member of the group to hide the food. Then, using only body language, the "hider" must communicate to the other group members where the "food" is located. They then try to find the food source. Repeat the activity until all the food finders have had a chance to hide and communicate the information to the group.

Extension: Have the groups try to develop some standard body movements which would indicate something to the group or class (i.e. one foot in front of the other—indicates straight path; tip one's head—indicates a direction, etc.).

The Hive Is the Place to Be!

Bees—Math

Objectives: To explore the relationship of shapes and to relate the study to the efficient storage of a beehive

Materials: round objects to trace around (coin, soda pop cap, lid), pencils, drawing paper

Directions: Explain to students that a beehive is divided into efficient hexagonal storage shapes called cells. These cells are massed together to form honeycomb. Ask students why circles or squares are not utilized by bees. Have them try the following activity to explore the reasons why a six-sided shape is the most functional for bees.

Have students make a circle by tracing around a circular shape. Have them mark the circle with an X. Tell them that this will be the center circle. Ask students to predict how many circles of the same size will fit around the center circle (six). Then, have them draw the circles to test their predictions.

continued on page 140

The Hive Is the Place to Be! continued

Extend the exercise by having the students predict how the number might change if all of the circles (including the center one) were larger or smaller than the first example. (Six is still the answer.)

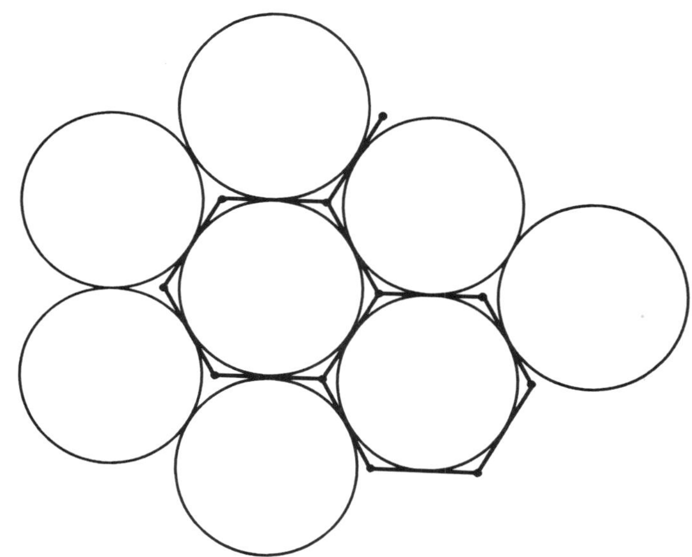

To create a honeycomb pattern, have the students continue making circles as instructed above. Then, by putting a dot in the center of the triangle-shaped spaces that are formed between the circles and connecting these dots with lines, the student can create the hexagonal clusters of a real honeycomb.

Guide the students in a discussion of the relationship of the hexagonal shapes to the bees' bodies. Lead students to the conclusion that circles would be good shapes for bees' bodies, but they do not fit together well. Squares fit together well, but the space would be wasted since bees have rounded bodies. Therefore, the six-sided shapes are perfect for a beehive.

Extension: The class can create a honeycomb of bee facts for an attractive bulletin board. Provide nonfiction books about bees and an assortment of hexagons cut out of colored construction paper. On the hexagon shapes, have the students record new and interesting facts about bees as they are learned. Post these on a bulletin with the title **Honeycomb of Bee Facts!**

You Can Judge a Critter by Its Cover!

Animals—Analyzing

Objective: To classify fish, mammals and birds by examining their exterior (scales, hair or feathers)

Materials: chart paper, markers, magazines, scissors, glue or tape

Directions: Several days before this lesson, ask students to collect pictures of animals. Time permitting, allow students to search through magazines in school as well. When each student has at least two pictures, divide students into cooperative learning groups and ask them to examine the exterior of their "critters." Each group should write down two or more observations regarding the outside of the animals they have photos of. (For example, the birds are colorful; the puppies are furry; the snakes don't look that slimy, etc.) Have the groups share their observations.

Next, ask students to categorize their pictures into three groups by looking at what is on the "outside" of their animals. Ask students to be prepared to tell how they decided to group the pictures and why. When each group has shared, discuss the three "coverings" on the animals—scales, feathers and hair. On chart paper, create three columns. Title one **Fish**, one **Birds** and one **Mammals**. Work clockwise around the room having each group bring up one of its pictures to glue under the specific category you call. (Example, would one person from each group bring up a picture of a critter with scales?) As students bring up their pictures, discuss the similarities of the animals and glue them under the proper category. When the supply of pictures has been exhausted, make generalizations about the coverings of critters. (For example, If a critter has feathers, it is a bird.) You CAN judge a critter by its cover!

Bird Watching Is Fun!

Birds—Observation

Objective: To encourage students to become more aware of the variety of birds living in a particular area

Materials: a picnic lunch or snack for each student, small note pads, pencils, several bird identification books from the library, binoculars (optional), copies of the "Bird Identification Chart" for each student (page 144)

Directions: To begin a unit on birds, introduce the class to a variety of bird identification books. (*The Bird Book*, by Neil and Karen Dawe is easy to read and answers many questions about birds. It also identifies markings and habits of specific birds as well.) Allow time for the students to become familiar with the books. Have them locate the names of birds they already know. Encourage the students to share any information they might have on birds or bird watching. Explain to students that they are about to discover a new hobby that will teach them about birds and their fascinating behaviors. Then, set a date for your first bird watching adventure.

In preparation for your outing, have students bring a picnic lunch or snack to school. They will also need a pencil and note pad to jot down the names or descriptions of birds they observe. Also, if any of the students have junior binoculars, you might ask them to bring them to school (with a note granting permission from their parents) on the day of the outing.

You will undoubtedly be able to observe many species of birds in your school yard. To ensure this, have the class create several simple feeders to attract some feathery friends to the area. (See "Feathered Friend Feeders" on page 145.)

Finally, instruct students on how to identify a bird. Tell students that birds are very alert and often move before we have time to get a good long look at them. Share with them the list of key features on page 143 that they should observe when trying to identify a new bird.

Give each student a copy of the "Bird Identification Chart" on page 144 and have fun bird watching.

continued on page 143

Bird Watching Is Fun! continued

Size—Tell students to compare the size with an object or animal that they are familiar with.

Shape—Is the tail long or short? What is the shape of its bill? Is it fat or thin? Is its head smooth or crested?

Color—Students should look at feathers, legs, eyes, bill.

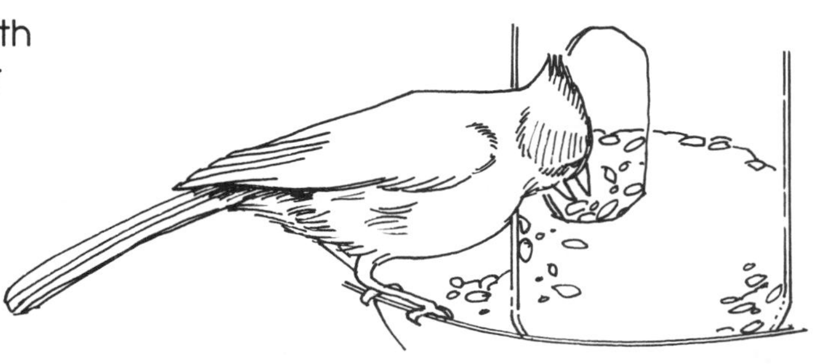

Habit—Does the bird walk or fly? Is it hanging around in the trees or on the ground?

Flight—Tell students to watch the path that the bird flies in. Is it a wavy path or does it fly in a straight line?

Voice—Tell students that each species of birds has a unique song. Tell them to try to remember the songs as they are hard to describe on paper.

Birds

As the Crows Flies

Objective: To draw a map and to write a story about it

Materials: drawing paper, crayons, pencils

Directions: Explain to students that people often use the expression "as the crow flies" to describe how to get from one place to another in the most direct route. The most direct route usually entails flying from one spot to another in a direct line, thus avoiding turns.

Have students draw a map showing how to get from their house to school "as the crow flies." Students should include any buildings/features they would fly over if they took this route. Have students write a story pretending they are birds and can fly to school. Students should include real landmarks in their story.

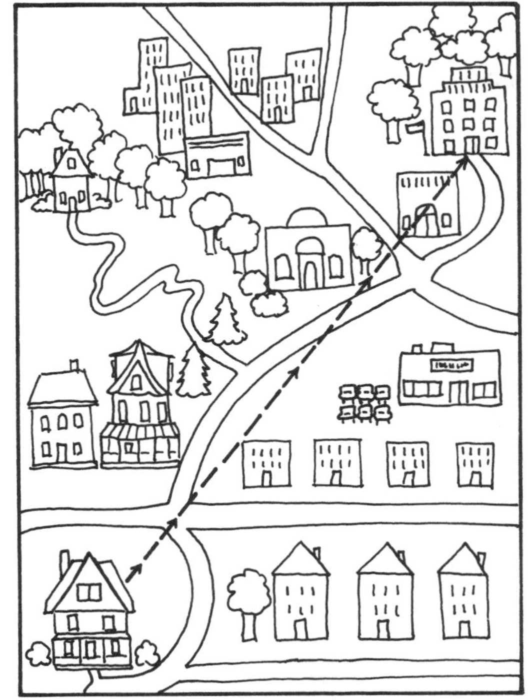

Bird Identification Chart

Sketch of Bird/ Name of Bird	Size: Compared to an object you are familiar with	Shape: tail, bill, body (fat or thin)	Color: feathers, head, tail, wings, feet	Habits: walks?, hops?, in trees?, on ground?, eats?	Flight: Is path wavy or straight?

Feathered Friend Feeders

Birds—Art

Objective: To create a bird feeder

Materials: grapefruit halves, cereal, peanuts, birdseed, string or yarn, stale bread, peanut butter, plastic knives, cookie cutter shapes

Directions: To create two very simple kinds of bird feeders, follow the directions below.

Note: Birds may become dependent on the feeder for their food supply. Students should continue feeding the birds during the winter months when food may be scarce.

1. Grazing Grapefruits

Give each student an empty grapefruit half. (Clean these beforehand and share the fruit with the class if you like.) Poke three holes in the grapefruit and thread three pieces of string through the holes. Tie them together so the grapefruit will be balanced when it hangs. Fill the grapefruit halves with nuts, cereal or birdseed. Hang the bird feeders on a tree branch.

2. Cookie Cutter Café

Give each student a slice of stale bread. Have the students cut out a shape for the bread using a cookie cutter. Then, have students spread one side of the bread with peanut butter and sprinkle nuts or seeds onto the peanut butter until the bread is well coated. Next, students carefully poke a small hole through the center of the bread and thread a piece of yarn through it. Students can hang the bird feeders in a tree to create a yummy café for their feathered friends.

Circling Whirly Birds

Birds—Art

Objective: To create a paper bird mobile

Materials: 1 1/2" wide by about 8" long strips of construction paper (8 per student), scissors, markers, glue, drinking straws, yarn

Directions: Bring the beauty of the birds indoors by creating these whirly bird mobiles.

Each student will need eight strips of construction paper to create two birds. Instruct the students to bring the ends of four of the strips together and glue them to create four loops.

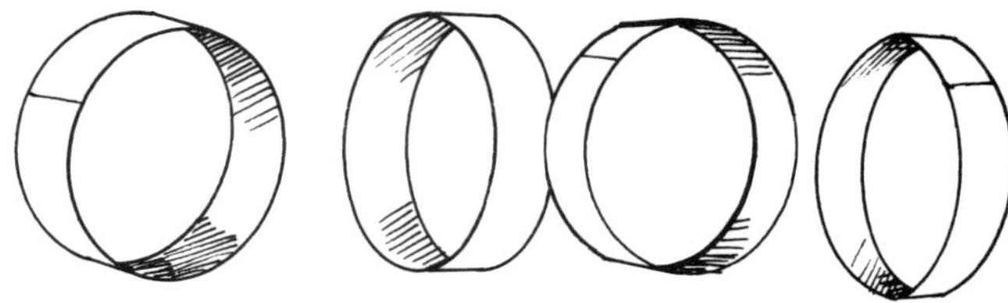

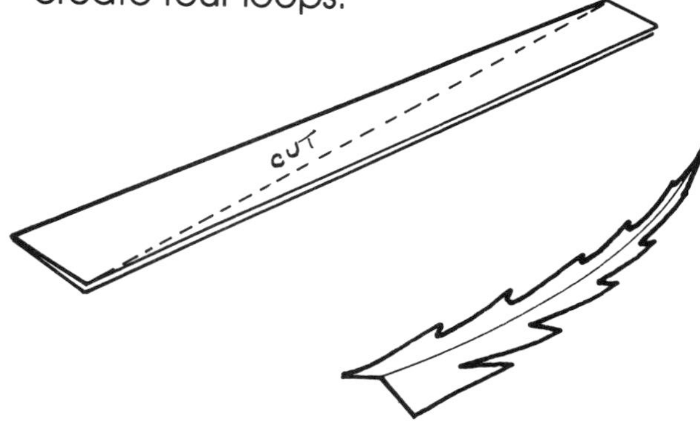

Students fold the fifth and sixth strips in half lengthwise and cut from the bottom corner of one side to the top corner of the opposite side. This will create a triangle shape to be used for the tail. Cuts can be made in these triangular shapes to give the "tail" a feathery look.

Finally, have students cut angles in the last two strips to form the wings. Students can also use markers to add details to the birds.

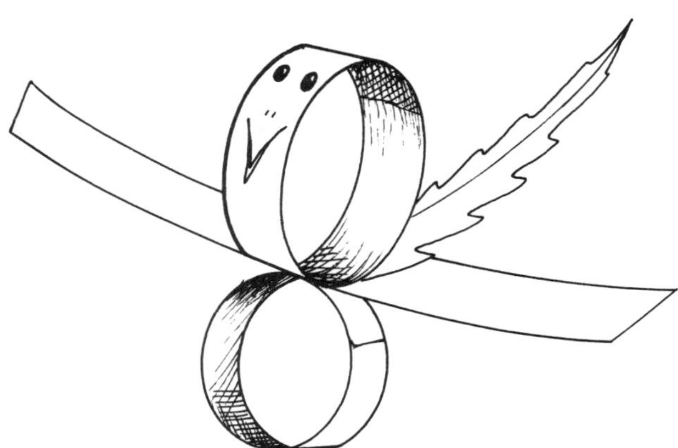

To assemble one bird, have students glue the wings to the top of one of the loops. Then, they glue the wide end of the tail on top of the wings. Finally, have students glue the last loop to the body. Add a beak and an eye. Students do the same thing for the second bird.

Have students tie a piece of yarn through each bird head loop. Then, they can tie each of the birds to opposite ends of a drinking straw. Suspend the mobiles from the ceiling by tying one more piece of string in the center of the straw. Open a window and let a gentle breeze whirl these birds to life.

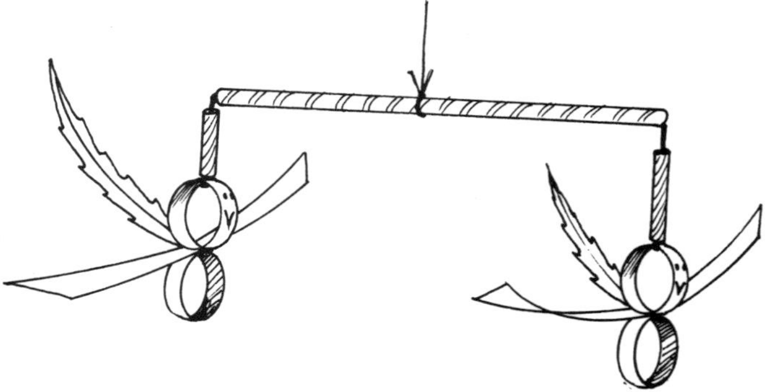

Bird Book

Birds—Research

Objectives: To research and gather information about specific birds and to create bird cards that can be compiled into a book

Materials: one copy of the bird card pattern per student (page 148), nonfiction books about birds, markers, 12" x 18" sheets of construction paper, white drawing paper, glue, hole punch, yarn, scissors

Directions: Have students begin this activity by selecting a bird to research. Using nonfiction books about birds, guide the students in researching their bird. Encourage them to discover what the bird looks like, where it lives (habitat), what it eats, and an interesting fact about it. After they have recorded their research notes, give each student a copy of page 148 and have the students revise and rewrite the information on it. When the students have completed their cards, give each one a sheet of construction paper. Then, have students glue the bird card pattern to the right side of the construction paper.

Using the information that the students have gathered about the appearance of their bird, have them draw a sketch of their bird on a piece of drawing paper. Remind students to include important identification markings and to add color. Tell students to glue the drawing to the left side of the construction paper. When all of the students have completed their bird cards and drawings, have each student stand and introduce his/her bird to the class.

Have the students finish the project by working together to place the bird cards into alphabetical order according to the birds' names. Punch a hole in the top left corner of the construction paper pages. Use yarn to tie them together to make a class book. Add a fun title like **Mrs. Smith's Class Is for the Birds!**

Extension: Put all the names of the birds that were researched into a word search or crossword puzzle.

Bird Card Pattern

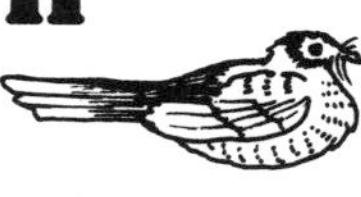

____
name of bird

Characteristics: ______________________________

Habitat: ______________________________

Food: ______________________________

Bird Bills

Birds—Experiment

Objectives: To experiment with a variety of beak types and to identify the kind of food a bird with each type of beak might eat

Materials: five sets, each containing the following materials, to use to set up five stations: tweezers, pliers (regular and needle nose), salad tongs, fish tank net, 2" pieces of string, eyedropper; The following materials are also needed: sunflower seeds, regular birdseed, gummy fish, small paper cups, shallow pan of water, small square of indoor/outdoor carpet, food coloring.

Directions: Explain to students that different kinds of birds like different kinds of foods. A bird's beak sometimes gives a hint about what it likes to eat. To help guide students to an understanding of this fact, create the following manipulative activity.

Put the sets of materials listed above on tables (one set per table). Then, place a different "food" source at each table according to the following directions:

1. Float several gummy fish in a shallow pan of water. (fish in water)
2. Place some water in a small paper cup. Add a drop of food coloring to it. (nectar or sap)
3. Sprinkle some birdseed onto a third table. (nuts and seeds)
4. Lay a piece of string on a small square of indoor/outdoor carpet. (worms in the grass)
5. Line the bottom of a small paper cup with shelled sunflower seeds. (insects in trees)

Divide the class into five cooperative learning groups. Tell them to imagine that the tools located at the center are the beaks of different birds. Have each group of students experiment with the various tools to determine which tool is best for gathering the "food" at each station. Rotate the groups so that all the students have the opportunity to experiment with each type of food.

When all the students have visited each station, gather the students together and discuss their findings. In general, they should have determined that the fish net offered the greatest chance for scooping up the "fish," the long, slender eyedropper worked best for drinking "nectar," regular pliers or tweezers gathered the most "nuts and seeds,"

continued on page 150

Bird Bills continued

Birds—Experiment

the tweezers worked best at grabbing the "worm" from the grass, and the needle nose pliers were successful in catching the "insects" in the tree.

Help the students realize that the beaks of birds are variously adapted for procuring different foods. They should also know that beaks are also important for nest building, preening feathers and protection.

If the students have already begun to research different species of birds, invite them to describe the beaks of some birds and their diets. Here are some examples:

Seed-eating: short thick bill for crunching seeds—grosbeak or finch 	**Insect-eating:** slender, pointed beak for picking up insects—warbler, swallow 	**Probing:** long slender bill for probing in mud or flowers for food—hummingbird, flamingo 
Preying: strong, sharp hooked beak for tearing flesh of prey—owl, hawk 	**Straining:** broad, flat bill for straining food from mud—duck, goose 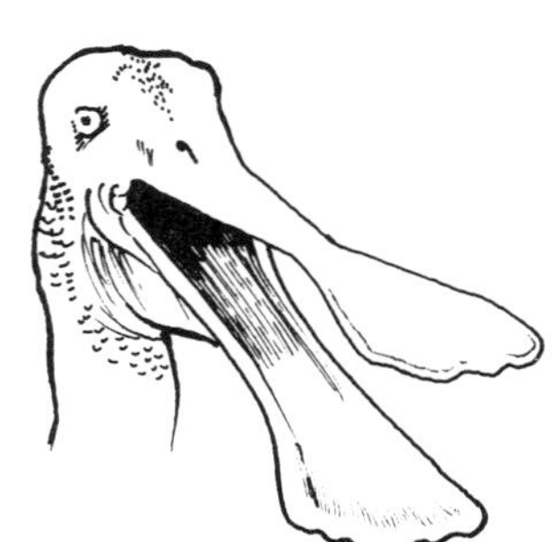	**Fish-eating:** long, sharp bill for spearing or with a pouch—heron, pelican 

Extension: Various species of birds have also developed adaptations of their feet, wings and tails. Encourage your students to read and research these other wonderful examples of nature's amazing ingenuity in solving the problems of survival.

Home Sweet Nest

Birds—Observation

Objective: To examine the various kinds of bird nests, including where they are located, how they are built and what materials are used

Materials: examples of a variety of bird nests (real or pictures), dry grass, string, roots, yarn, leaves, bits of paper, twigs, mud, straw, wood chips

Directions: Explain to students that not all birds build nests, but most of them do. Nests hold eggs and protect baby birds. Many birds build nests in trees. But some are found in bushes, in barns and on the ground. Nests can also be found on ledges and in holes.

Have the students research and observe how and where various birds build their nests. Provide an abundance of pictures that show birds building or roosting in their nests. Encourage students to note where each nest is located and what each bird uses to build its nest. For example, some birds, like eagles, build big strong nests that are used year after year. Other birds build new nests every year. Observe, too, that nests come in many different sizes.

After students have studied a variety of nests, have them gather grass, twigs, roots, etc. to try and make a bird nest of their own. Students can pretend the nest is their home. They can write a story telling what kind of bird they are, what they eat, what they do all day, who their friends are, etc. The stories can involve real or pretend birds.

State Birds of North America

Birds—Research

Objectives: To identify state birds and to study the living habits of a particular kind of bird

Materials: encyclopedias or nonfiction books that contain information on the birds of each state, mural paper, markers

Directions: Tell students that each of the 50 states has a state bird. Have each student take a closer look at one of these birds to learn about its living habits. While students complete their research, create the chart on page 152 on mural paper.

continued on page 152

State Birds of North America continued

State	Picture of Bird	Description: color, size, etc.	Special Fact
Environment: temperature, geography, etc.	Nest	Eggs: size, number, etc.	Food

As each student completes his/her research, have him/her fill in the information in the appropriate categories on the chart. Encourage the students to sketch and color a picture of their bird. Be sure to have a map of North America handy for quick geographical references.

Save the Birds!

Birds— Letter Writing

Objectives: To recognize projects and groups that work to protect wildlife, such as birds, and the wild places in which the animals live and to write a business letter requesting information

Materials: *The Puffins Are Back* by Gail Gibbons, writing paper, pens

Directions: Have students read the book *The Puffins Are Back*. The story details the Audubon Society's project to restore the puffin population to the shores of Maine. Gibbons explains in simple fashion the efforts of the environmentalist group to raise, tag, observe and care for a new family of puffins in the hopes that they will return to the rocky shores from their winter migration. After sharing the successful story, your students will want to learn more about how they can help protect birds and other wildlife.

Have students write business letters to the National Audubon Society requesting information about the various wildlife protection projects that they are currently involved in. (950 3rd Avenue, New York, NY 10022) Don't forget to mention the puffin project and your own classroom bird study.

The Arctic Environment

Arctic—Research

Objective: To learn about plant and animal life in the Arctic region

Materials: books, magazines, film strips, etc. about the Arctic; copies of the outlines below; markers; paper

Directions: Divide the class into groups. Each group should choose a different aspect of the Arctic about which to prepare a report. Encourage the students to use the different resources listed above for their information.

Give groups a copy of the appropriate outline below and have them research and answer the questions it contains. Tell students to add any questions if they like. After the outline is completed, have the students put the information into report form using complete sentences and paragraphs. Tell each group to illustrate its report.

When all the reports are completed, assemble them into a resource book about the Arctic region.

Extension: Try this activity with other environments (i.e. desert, jungle, rainforest, etc.).

"Plants in the Arctic" Outline

1. What plant life would you see in the tundra in the summer?
2. Is there a plant that can live in the Arctic without soil? Is it useful?
3. How are animals dependent upon the plant life?
4. How do the people use the plants?

"Animals in the Arctic" Outline

1. What animals are found in the Arctic?
2. What animals are the people dependent upon?
3. How do the people use all the different parts of the caribou?
4. How do the people hunt for animals? Are there any special rules and customs that they should know about?

We're All Connected!

Analyzing Information

Objective: To show the interdependence among living things

Materials: index cards, one ball of twine per group of students

Directions: Divide the class into two, three or four groups depending upon the size of the class. Have each student in each group write down the name of a living thing on an index card (i.e. crow, worm, bee, fox, cat, robin, corn, flower, person, tree, etc.). Each card should be different within the group. Tell each group to form a circle. Tell students that they will take on the identity of the living thing written on their card. Have students prominently display their cards so that everyone in the group can see what is written on them. Select one student in each circle to start the "web." He/she will tell one way that the living thing on his/her card is dependent upon one of the other living things in the group. This student will hold on to the end of the twine and will then pass the twine onto the student holding the card of that living thing. This student will do the same passing the twine on to the living thing that he/she is dependent upon. The game will continue in this manner with each student holding the twine as it is passed on forming a web.

When the activity is over, there will be a trail of string connecting the students and showing the interdependency of living things.

Name That Vegetable

Vegetables—Research/Art

Objectives: To introduce students to a variety of vegetables and to research basic facts about vegetables

Materials: a variety of fresh vegetables, nonfiction books about vegetables, clay, tongue depressors, one copy of the garden marker per student (page 155), glue, scissors

Directions: This is a great theme to begin in the spring when a larger variety of vegetables are available. Visit your local produce department and purchase several types of common vegetables as well as some that students might not be familiar with. Arrange these on a table for the students to examine. Gather the students around and ask for volunteers to name each vegetable that they know. When all the vegetables have been identified, have the students move into cooperative learning groups.

continued on page 155

Name That Vegetable continued

Divide and distribute the produce among the groups. Using the nonfiction books, tell the groups to do research to find background information about the vegetables they were given such as where and how they are grown, what part of the plant is edible, how they are prepared, etc. Give each student a copy of the garden marker below. Encourage students to summarize their facts to fit on it. Then, have them record the information on the marker and draw and color a picture of their vegetable. Each label should be cut out and glued to a tongue depressor. Students then wrap a small piece of clay around the bottom of the stick to create a base. Finally, have the students place all the identified and labeled produce back on the table for display. Allow time for the students in each group to come forward and share the background information they researched.

Extensions: The leading vegetable producing states are California, Idaho, Washington, Wisconsin and Oregon. Have students locate these states on a map. Ask students which vegetables on the display table came from these states. Ask them what other areas the produce came from. See if they know which produce comes from your state.

Assign a particular vegetable to each student. Have them visit the local market, locate, purchase and bring one to class.

Vegetable Verification

Vegetables—Classification

Objective: To identify food items that are considered vegetables

Materials: variety of fresh produce, chart paper, markers

Directions: A vegetable can be defined as a food coming from a part of a certain plant. Vegetables can also be grouped according to the part of the plant that is eaten. Using the vegetables from the display table created in the "Name That Vegetable" activity (page 154), have the students rearrange the vegetables into two groups—vegetables that grow above the ground and vegetables that grow below the ground. Record these on chart paper. Some will be obvious and easy to categorize, and others may not. Encourage students to research and use their "garden marker" information to classify the remaining vegetables. As an added challenge, have the students organize the produce further by dividing them into eight groups according to what part of the plant is edible. (See eight groups below.) Discuss how the vegetables are cared for and harvested.

Extension: Have the students take turns putting a vegetable secretly in a box. Then, have the remainder of the class ask questions whose answers are yes or no to try to identify the item in the box. Encourage the students to pose questions based upon what they have learned about the following: the areas where their vegetable is grown, why it is grown, what part of the plant is edible, how it is prepared.

Eight Groups of Edible Parts of Plants

stems	flowers	seeds	roots
asparagus kohlrabi	cauliflower broccoli	peas lima beans	carrots beets radishes rutabagas turnips sweet potatoes
leaves	**bulbs**	**tubers**	**fruits**
spinach cabbage chard cress endive kale lettuce	onions leeks garlic	potatoes	eggplant cucumber okra peppers pumpkins squash tomatoes

Super Sprouters

Vegetables—Experiment

Objectives: To observe how vegetables sprout and to compare the growth of roots and leaves

Materials: carrot(s), sweet potato(es), toothpicks, clear jar(s), small container(s) (i.e. butter dish), water

Note: The amount of materials depends on whether you make this a class project or one that groups of students will do.

Directions: Help the students cut the carrot one inch from the top and place the top in a small container such as a butter dish. Have the students add a small amount of water to the dish.

Then, demonstrate how to push several toothpicks into the top section of a sweet potato so that it will be suspended when put into a small jar. Have the students add enough water so that the bottom of the potato is submerged.

Encourage the students to make predictions as to which vegetable will sprout first and how many days it will take before roots and leaves appear. Have students observe and record the results.

How Does Your Garden Grow?

Objectives: To experience the four steps of vegetable production—planting, caring for, harvesting and packaging and to observe the growth of vegetables

Materials: radish seeds, milk cartons, soil, sandwich bags

Directions: To guide the students through the experience of planting, caring for, harvesting and packaging vegetables, have the students plant a small garden of radishes. To begin, ask the students to save their milk cartons from the lunchroom. Wash and clean these thoroughly and fill them three-fourths full with soil. Guide the students in planting radish seeds according to the package directions. (Radishes are great for this activity as they are fast-growing vegetables, and the students will be able to harvest them within 20-30 days.) Demonstrate how to water and care for the seedlings. When they are ready, allow the students to harvest, or pull, their "crop", wash them and package them in sandwich bags. Then, "ship" them home with the students.

continued on page 158

How Does Your Garden Grow? continued

Extension: Throughout the care and growth of vegetable production, discuss with the students the various ways in which vegetables are packaged. Have samples of fresh, frozen, canned and dried vegetables available for the students to examine. Discuss where each should be stored.

Dissecting a Seed

Plants—Observing

Objective: To observe and describe seed coats, cotyledons, embryos, roots, stems and leaves of plants as they germinate

Materials: dried lima beans, a quart of water, magnifying glasses, paper towels

Directions: A day prior to beginning the experiment, soak the lima beans in the water. They will swell as they absorb some of the water.

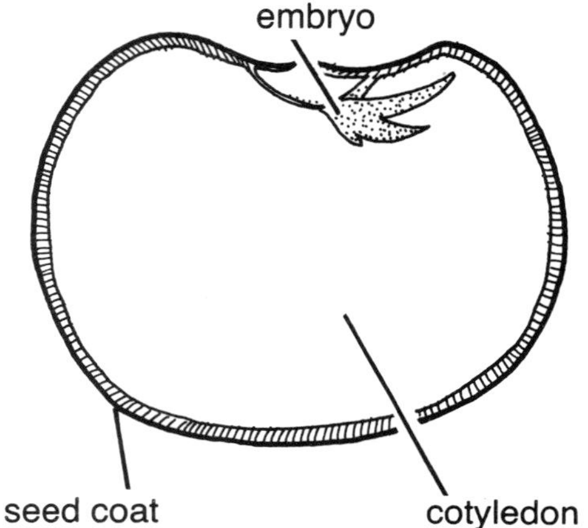

When you are ready to begin, distribute a paper towel and a lima bean to each student. First, identify the seed coat of the bean. (This is the outer protective skin or coating of the seed.) Have the students then carefully scrub the seed between their forefinger and thumb. The seed coat should be soft enough to crack and peel open. The large oval part of the seed is the cotyledon. Tell the students that this is the part of the seed that contains stored food used by the embryo for its initial growth (before it breaks out of the seed coat and can obtain nutrients from soil and water). The students should also be able to see the rudimentary plant contained in the seed. This is the embryo, or baby plant. Allow time for the students to observe and explore these seed parts using a magnifying glass.

Extensions: Have students compare green beans, wax beans and lima beans. Ask them how they are similar and different.

Sprout some lima beans following the directions in the activity "Sprouting Seeds Without Soil" (page 160). Observe how the baby plant breaks out of the seed coat and how it falls away.

Plants Need...

Plants—Experiment

Objective: To observe that plants need light, air, water, soil and proper temperature in order to grow

Materials: six growing plants (identical if possible), two clear plastic bags, large jar, water, rubber band, science notebooks

Directions: Explain to the students that plants need food just like our bodies do. To demonstrate what plants need in order to live and thrive, select six healthy plants. (Try to find six that are identical as this will make it easier for students to make observations and draw conclusions.) Allow time for the students to examine the plants, perhaps measuring their height, number of leaves, color, etc. Then, vary the conditions as follows:

Plant 1—Put in an unlighted area. Water regularly.

Plant 2—Do not water. Set in sunlight.

Plant 3—Remove plant from the pot. Put a plastic bag around the roots and soil. Secure the bag with a rubber band. Then, submerge the entire plant in a large jar filled with water so that no parts come in contact with air.

Plant 4—Place the plant in an area of extreme temperature (i.e. on the heater, outside the window).

Plant 5—Take the plant out of the pot. Wash the soil away from the roots. Place the roots in a container of water.

Plant 6—Control Plant—Give this plant normal care with regular watering, exposure to light, etc.

Discuss with students the importance of having a control group when conducting an experiment. Have the students observe each plant for one week and record any changes that occur in their notebook. After one week, identify with the students what was deprived from each plant and discuss the observable results. You will generally find that:

Plant 1 will turn yellow.
Plant 2 will shrivel and die.
Plant 3 will rot.
Plant 4 will wilt or have stunted growth.
Plant 5 will eventually die due to lack of nutrients.
Plant 6 will live and show growth.

Students should be able to conclude that plants need light, air, water, soil and the proper temperature in order to thrive.

Plants

Sprouting Seeds Without Soil

Objective: To observe and describe the germination of a seed

Materials: bean and pea seeds, paper towels, clear plastic sealable bags (quart size), water, stapler, household bleach (optional), strainer, one copy of the "Seed Growth Chart" per student (page 161)

Directions: This activity will allow your students to actually see how a seed germinates and begins to grow. They will marvel at the wonder of nature as roots, sprouting from the top of the seed, will turn and grow downward, and stems, sprouting from below, will knowingly grow upward. Motivation runs high and the best part is that germination will occur within just a few days.

Preparing the Seeds:

1. To help prevent mold in the germination bags, dip the seeds in a solution of diluted bleach ($^1/_4$ cup of chlorine bleach to one gallon of water).
2. Put the seeds in a strainer and dip them in the solution for 15 seconds.
3. Without rinsing, place the seeds in the germination bags. (See below.) Have students wash their hands after handling the seeds.

Assembling the Germination Bags:

1. Place the paper towel in the clear bag, folding as necessary so that it will lay flat.

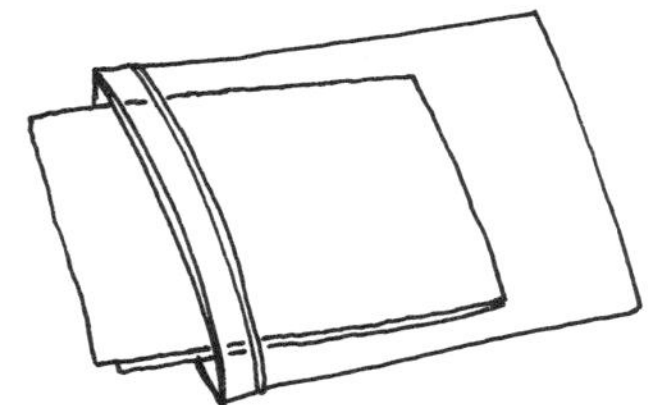

2. Staple across approximately 4 cm from the bottom of the bag.

3. Position the seeds above the staples.
4. Add 3 tablespoons of water to the bag.

5. Close the bag and hang it from the side of the students' desks. (It is better not to hang these in direct sunlight.)

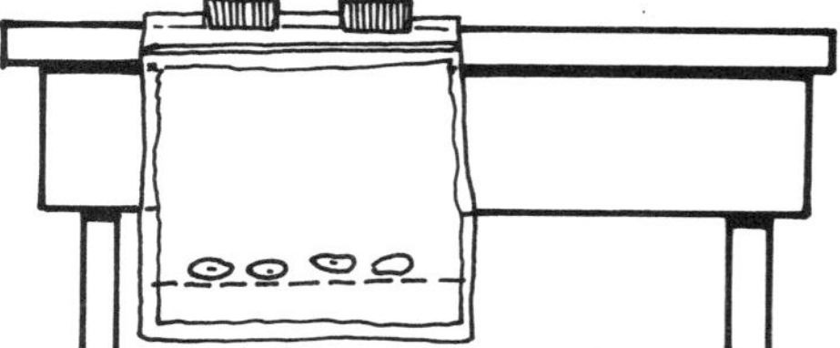

As the seeds germinate, students should observe and record seed growth each day on their "Seed Growth Chart."

Note: Do not plant the seeds. After completing your observations, dispose of the entire germination bag.

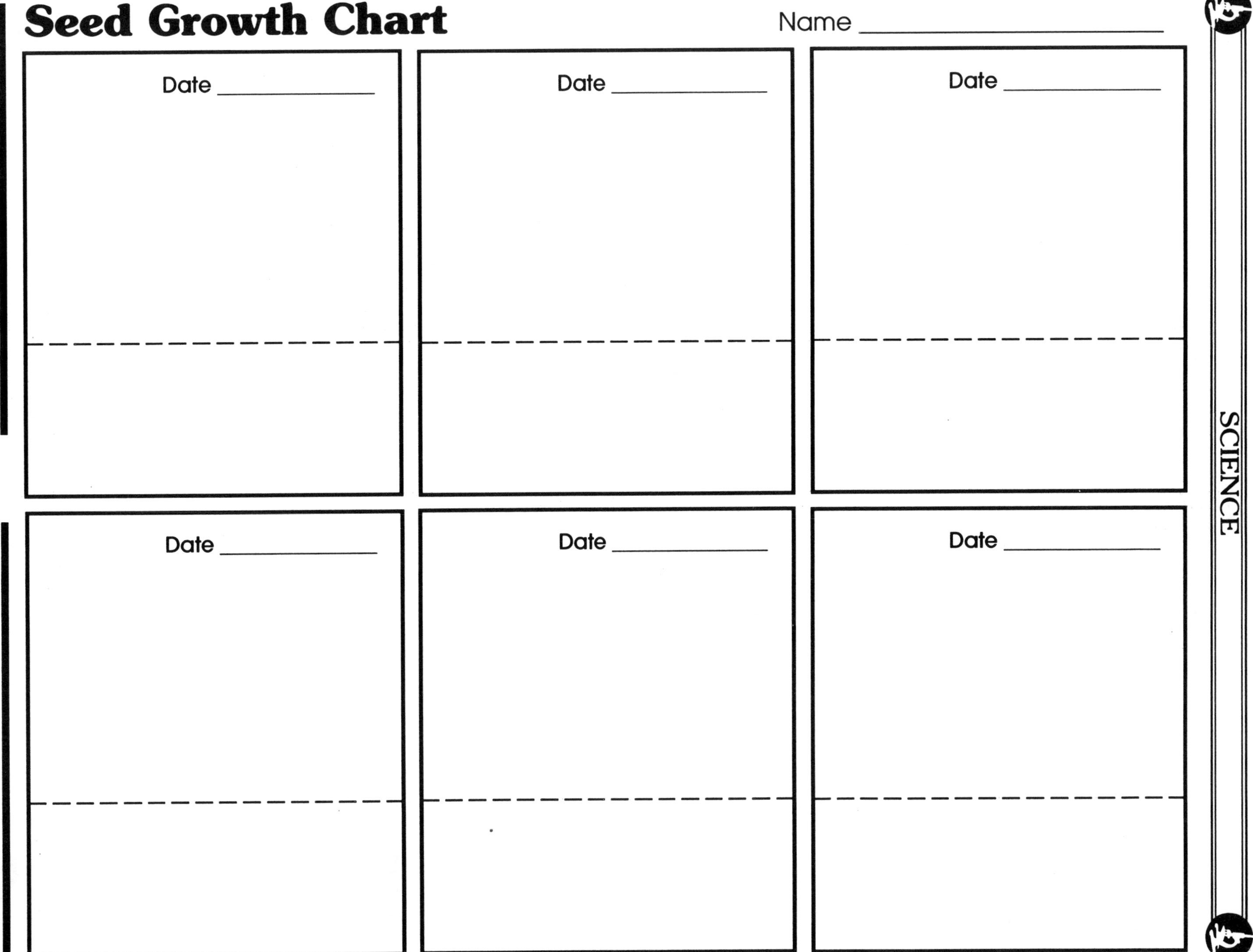
Seed Growth Chart
Name
Date
Date
Date
Date
Date
Date

Partying With Plants

Plants—Games/ Cooking

Below are some more suggestions for adding excitement to a unit on plants.

Games

1. Steal the Fruit or Vegetable

Directions: Divide the class into two teams. Line up the students across from each other. In between the two teams, place several different kinds of fruits and vegetables. Then, assign each student on each team a number so that each team has the same numbers beginning with one. Call out the name of a fruit or vegetable and a number such as broccoli—7. The two players with that number run to the fruits and vegetables in the center. The one who gets the fruit or vegetable first and returns back to his/her team with it scores a point for the team.

2. Veggie Relay Races

Directions: Form teams and establish start and finish lines. Include any other rules you want. Then, have the students conduct races like rolling potatoes with their nose, carrying radishes on a spoon, passing peppers under their chins, etc. Let the students invent same games as well.

3. Steaming Squash

Directions: Have the students sit in a circle. Choose one student to be the leader. Students begin passing the squash around the circle until the leader calls out "OUCH!" The student holding the steaming squash is out. Continue until all students have been eliminated.

Cooking

1. Tasting Party

Directions: Slice up a variety of raw vegetables. Have the students sample them and discuss how best to classify each one. For example, they can classify them according to taste, texture, color, good taste, etc.

2. Friendship Soup

Directions: Have each student choose one vegetable from the group that was studied and bring it to school. Help the students wash and chop up their vegetable. Place the vegetables in a large crock pot with eight cups of water and eight bouillon cubes. Let the soup cook for about 30 minutes. Add salt and pepper to taste and enjoy.

Rain in the Classroom

Weather—Experiment

Objective: To demonstrate rain

Materials: hot plate, frying pan, water, ice cubes, saucepan

Directions: You can make it rain in the classroom! Before beginning this activity, hold a serious safety discussion with your students. Tell them that you will be working with a hot plate and will be heating water. Explain that everyone must remain in their seats so that no one is hurt.

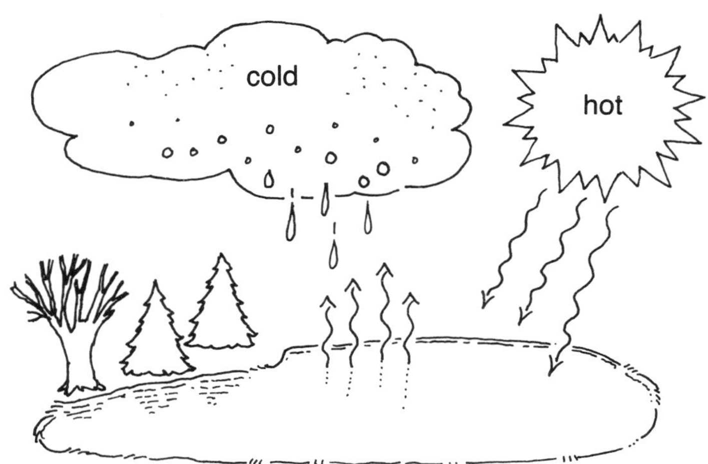

Fill the frying pan with water. Place it on the hot plate. With students seated a good distance away, turn the hot plate on. Ask students to imagine that the frying pan is a lake. Place ice cubes in the saucepan. Explain to students that high above the Earth, the air is cold. Ask them to imagine that the saucepan is cool air, high above Earth. Hold the saucepan above the frying pan. As the water in the frying pan heats up, ask students to observe the steam. Ask them in which direction it is moving. (up) Next, ask them to observe the condensation on the bottom of the saucepan. Finally, have them observe the heavy droplets of condensation, or rain, falling back into the "lake."

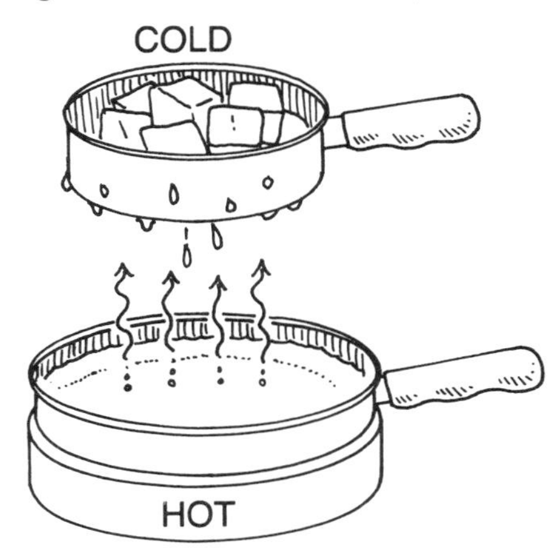

To sum up the experiment, explain to students that the sun's heat sucks up water from the land, lakes, rivers and oceans. The air containing this moisture cools. As it cools, droplets of liquid form. These fall to Earth as rain.

Cloud Coverage

Weather—Art

Objective: To become familiar with the three major types of clouds

Materials: cotton balls, dryer lint or gray flannel, glue, 11" x 18" sheets of oaktag (one per student), pencils, crayons, markers, white paint, paintbrushes, glitter, book *Cloudy With a Chance of Meatballs* by Judi Barrett, fiction and nonfiction books about clouds, stapler

Directions: This activity should be completed over a period of a week or so. Through fiction and nonfiction books, introduce students to the three major types of clouds—cirrus, cumulus and stratus.

continued on page 164

Cloud Coverage continued

To begin the project, use a pencil to divide the oaktag into six sections. (You can do this for the students, or the division of the paper can become a lesson in itself!) Students will use the three top sections to simulate the three major types of clouds by following the directions below.

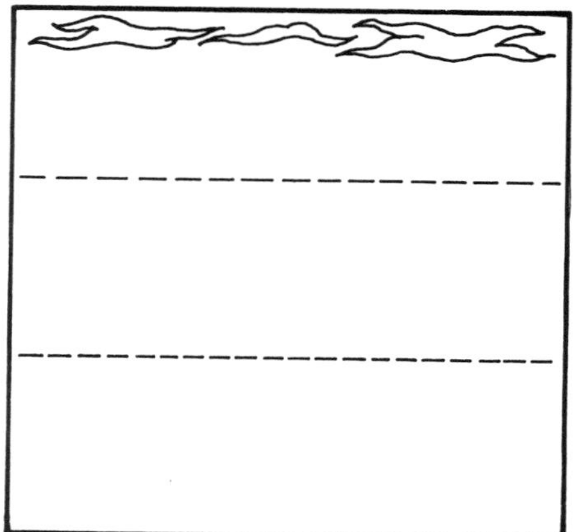

1. **Cirrus Clouds**—high, white clouds with a feathery appearance
   To create this type of cloud, students should paint white streaks at the very top of their paper and sprinkle glitter sparingly while the paint is still wet to represent the ice that may be present in these high clouds.

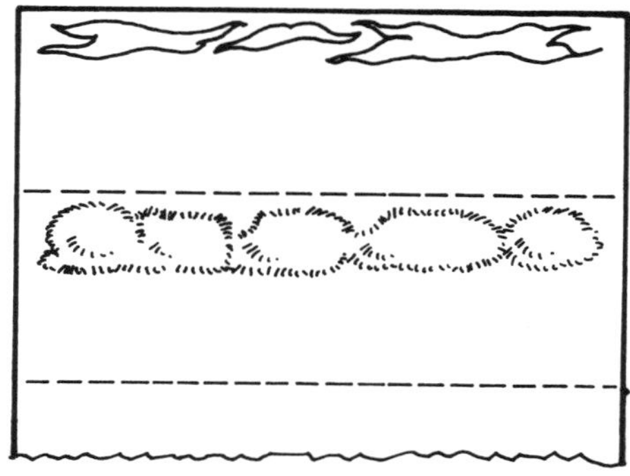

2. **Cumulus Clouds**—puffy, white low clouds with flat bottoms
   In the second top box, have students glue cotton balls of various sizes approximately 1/3 of the way down the paper.

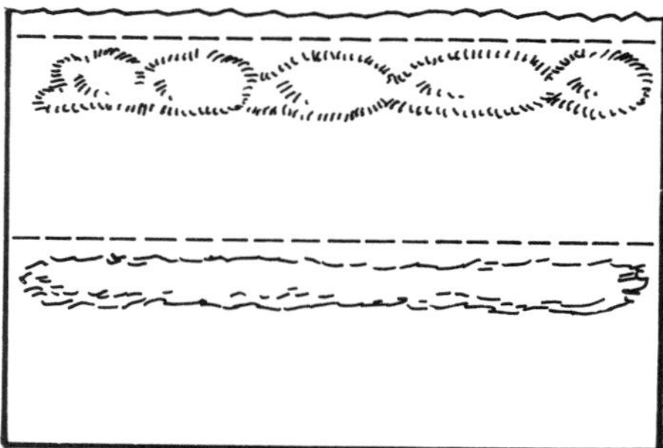

3. **Stratus Clouds**—wide, often gray, low clouds that can drip snow flurries and drizzle
   Tell students to glue dryer lint or gray flannel across the top of the third top box covering the length of the box.

After each of the three major cloud types is completed, ask students to draw pictures in the box underneath each cloud. The pictures should show activities the students could do if they were to observe that particular type of cloud on any given day.

At some point in the week, read *Cloudy With a Chance of Meatballs.* Then, ask students to imagine that it rained something other than water or food. Ask them questions similar to: "What would come out of the clouds? What would this type of cloud look like? What would your umbrella look like? What would you do on a 'rainy' day?" Have students write their own story answering these questions. When the final draft is completed, staple it to the bottom of their cloud charts. Sing or listen to "If All the Raindrops!"

Windy Weather

Weather—Experiments

Objectives: To reinforce that wind is moving air and to discuss the good and bad effects of wind

Directions: Most students will know of the dangerous aspects of wind—hurricanes, tornadoes, property damage, trees down, electric wires and telephone wires down, windstorms at sea, etc. Brainstorm with the students some of the helpful aspects of wind such as to create energy as in windmills, to cool you off on a hot day, to move sailboats (Columbus, the Pilgrims sailing to this country), drying wet areas, transporting seeds, etc.

Let students try some of the following activities to help them learn some of the helpful aspects of wind.

Sailboat Race

Objective: To create wind

Materials: toy boats; large tub of water; feather, piece of cardboard, tissue paper, folded paper fan, piece of material, block of wood, etc.

Directions: Put two toy boats in a large tub of water. Give one student a feather with which to create wind. Give another student a piece of cardboard to use. Let the students try to "sail" the boats. Ask students which boat they think will win the race. Why? Let students try some of the other materials to try to create wind and "sail" the boats.

Dry That Spot

Objective: To see that wind can be channeled to do work

Materials: sponge or paper towel, water, piece of cardboard

Directions: Using a sponge or paper towel, put two equal sized wet spots on the chalkboard. Let one dry by itself and let a student fan the other one using a piece of cardboard. Ask students which one will dry faster. Why? Discuss with students the other ways wind can be used to do work. Let students illustrate one of them.

continued on page 166

Windy Weather continued

Weather—Experiments

Sow the Seeds

Objective: To learn how wind disperses seeds

Materials: white, seeded dandelions; drawing paper; crayons

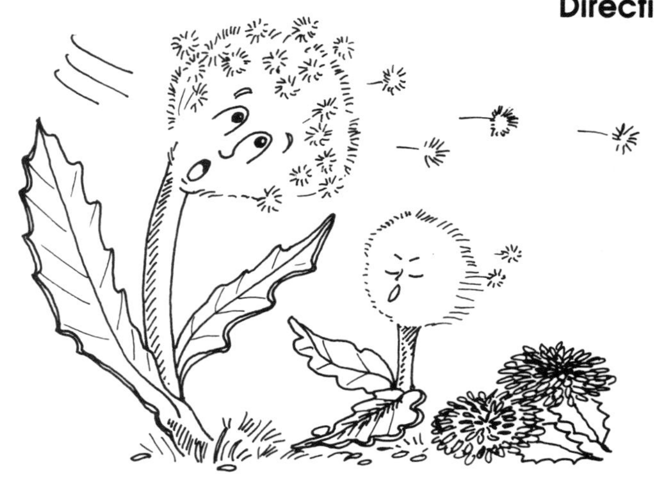

Directions: When a dandelion has turned to seed (from yellow to white), let students blow it or wave it and watch the seeds scatter. Discuss with students what is happening and why it is happening. Tell them how important it is for seeds to disperse. Discuss with students other ways seeds are dispersed (animals, dropped from the plant itself, etc.). Have students draw pictures of as many ways as they can think of showing how seeds are dispersed.

Watch That Wind!

Objective: To depict how wind can be helpful and harmful

Materials: paper, crayons, markers

Directions: Divide a bulletin board in half. Label one side **Destructive Wind Forces** and the other side **Helpful Wind Forces**. Have students draw illustrations with appropriate captions to enter on one or both sides of the bulletin board.

Wind and Weather

Weather—Experiment/Art

Objectives: To determine if wind direction is a prediction of weather and to construct a weather vane

Materials: pencil with an eraser; drinking straw; straight pin; small, round wooden bead; construction paper; scissors; tail pattern (below); tape; red paint; paintbrushes

Preparation: Prepare a classroom chart similar to the one to the right for students to use to record dates. Make a copy for each student.

Wind Weather Chart

Month ____________________

Wind Direction	Weather
Day 1	Day 1
Day 2	Day 2
Day 3	Day 3
Day 4	Day 4
Day 5	Day 5

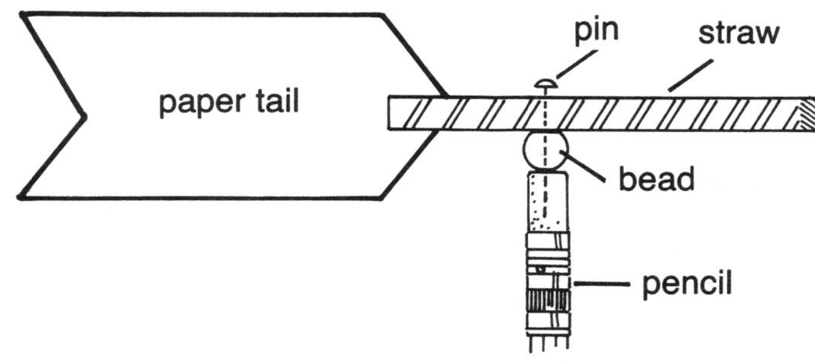

Directions: Paint the tip of the drinking straw red. This will be the pointer. Push the straight pin through the straw (about 1/4 distance from the tail end), through the bead and then into the pencil eraser. Make a paper tail using the pattern and tape it to the end of the straw. For a period of a month, use this weather vane each day to determine the direction of the wind. Students can use the chart you made to record this data. Also, have students record the weather which follows the next day.

Ask students if they notice any patterns. Have them try this experiment in different seasons. Let students see if patterns change or if they are the same.

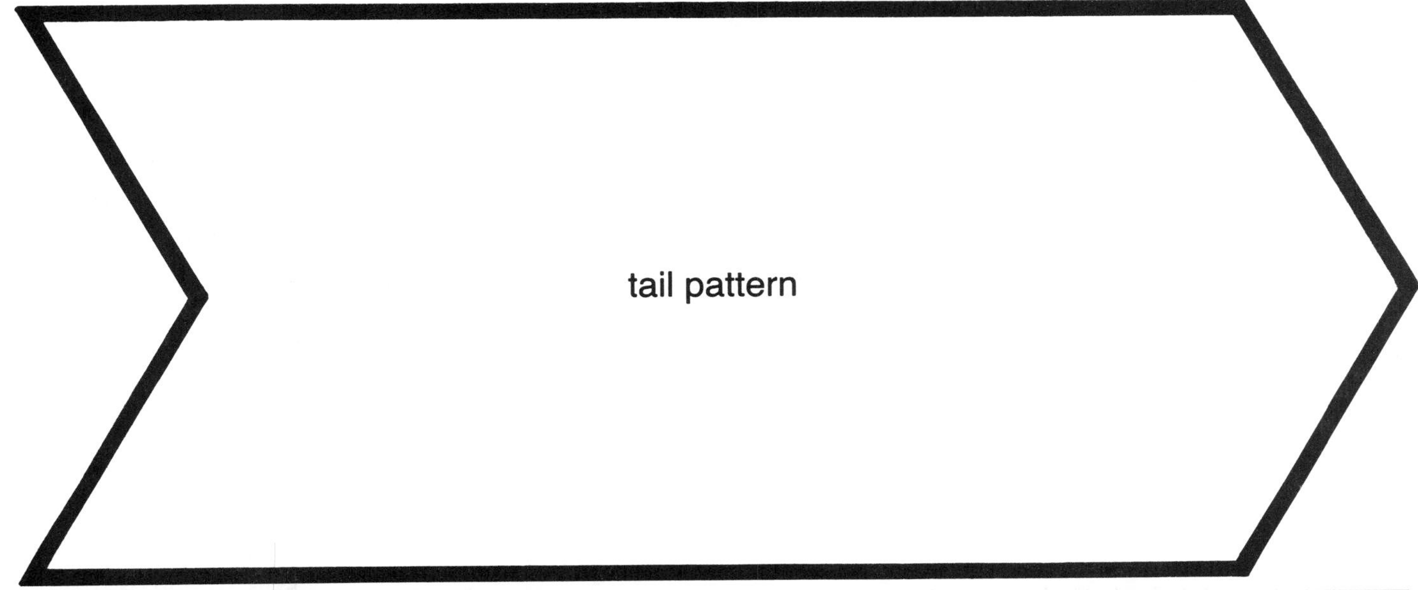

Can You Pour Air?

Weather—Experiment

Objectives: To show that air is a substance that takes up space and that can be moved

Materials: a deep basin of water such as an aquarium, 2 water glasses

Directions: Lower a water glass mouth downward into the aquarium filled with water. Next, lower another glass of exactly the same size into the container of water. Tilt the second glass until it fills up with water. Still holding both glasses under water, turn the glass filled with water up so that the mouths of both glasses are together. Now, turn the first glass upward and watch the air pour from the first glass into the second. Holding both glasses under water all the time, continue to pour the air from one glass into the other. Ask students if either glass was empty at any time.

Experiments With Air

Air—Experiment

Objective: To show that air takes up space and is a real substance

Materials: a deep container such as an aquarium, a water glass, a sheet of paper towel or a paper napkin, paper, pencils

Directions: On the board, write the questions for observation #1 and #2 from page 169 for the students to copy. Then, do the demonstration below. Fold the sheet of paper towel or paper napkin so that you can force it into the bottom of the glass. Make sure that it will not fall out when the glass is inverted. Next, lower the glass, mouth downward into the container of water. Lower it until the glass is completely submerged making sure that the mouth of the glass remains downward. Hold the glass in this position for several seconds. Withdraw the glass from the container keeping the mouth downward. After the glass has been completely removed from the water, remove the paper and examine it. Have the students answer observation #1 questions.

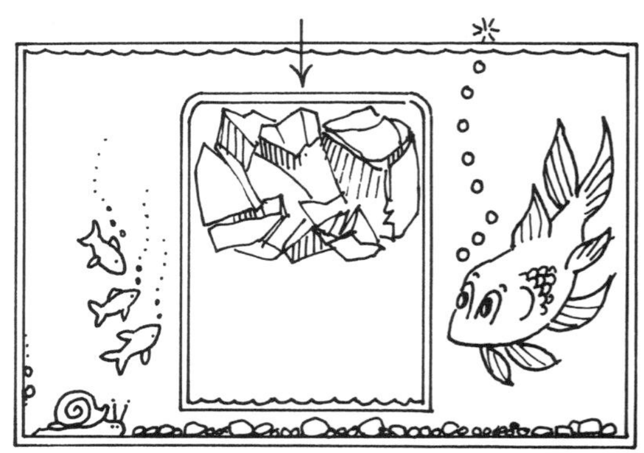

Repeat the experiment. This time, tilt the glass a little at a time. Then, remove the glass and examine the paper. Have students answer observation #2 questions.

continued on page 169

Experiments With Air continued

Air—Experiment

Observation #1

1. Was the paper wet or dry?
2. Why do you think the paper was in that condition?
3. What was in the glass besides the paper?
4. How do you know?

Observation #2

1. What do you see in the container of water when you tilt the glass?
2. Was the paper wet or dry?
3. Why?
4. How do you know?

Water Works

Water—Experiment

Objective: To discuss the properties of water

Materials: several objects that will react differently when put into a basin of water (i.e. a block of wood, paper clip, pencil, sugar, salt, sponge, piece of fabric, rubber band, eraser, baking soda, nylon netting, paper towel, nail, pair of scissors, etc.), large basin of water, one copy of a chart similar to the one below per student

Object/Item	Predictions of what will happen	Results of what happened

Directions: Have the students predict what will happen to each object when it is put into the basin of water. They should record this information on a chart you make and give to the students. Let students conduct the experiments and record what actually happened. Let students compare their predictions with their actual results.

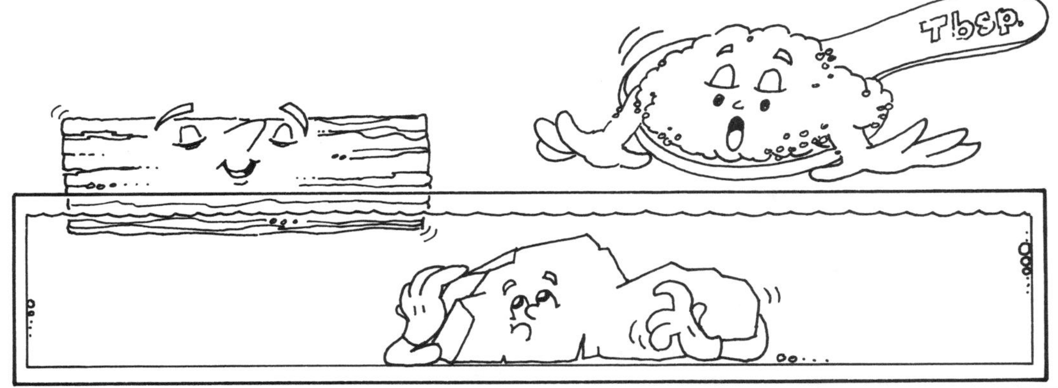

Moon Logs

Moon—Observation/ Recording Information

Objective: To log and order the phases of the moon for one month

Materials: 8" x 12" sheets of black construction paper (four sheets per student), stapler, white crayons, large classroom calendar

Directions: As students observe the moon phases firsthand, they will better understand the order of the phases and why they occur. Before you begin, students should create moon logs by folding four sheets of black construction paper in half and stapling them together. Using a white crayon, tell students to create a title and decorate the cover.

Explain to the students that it is best to begin the moon observations with the "new moon." Tell students that they will be observing the moon twice a week (or every three days) weather permitting. If clouds interfere with your planned dates to observe the moon, you will be forced to postpone it.

In their logs, the students should record the date of observation, and use half of a page on which to draw the shape of the moon that they observe. Be sure to emphasize to the students that they must pay careful attention as to which side of the moon is illuminated. Tell them to be sure to draw it exactly as they see it. As the month progresses, discuss the log entries and record the students' findings on a classroom calendar as they are shared. As the concepts arise, introduce vocabulary such as waxing, waning, new, crescent, full, first quarter, etc. Other possible questions and concepts to discuss include: "Why does the moon shine? Why does its shape seem to change? Why do we see one side of the moon? What does the surface of the moon look like from Earth? What has NASA discovered regarding the moon?"

When the logs are complete and you're observing another "new moon," discuss the amount of time that has passed since you began logging the moon. Relate the cycle of moon phases to the calendar. Ask students to make predictions regarding specific phases of the upcoming month (i.e. How much time will pass between the new moon and the full moon? Predict the date we will see the next full moon, etc.). Students can add the final touch to their log by writing a haiku poem about the moon (or another form of poetry of your choice) and writing the final draft on the inside cover of their moon log.

Stained Glass Windows

Colors—Art

Objectives: To reinforce the concepts that different colors transmit different amounts of light and that colors can be combined to create other colors

Materials: one 9" x 11" sheet of black paper per student, rolls of various colors of cellophane, tape, scissors, rulers, white crayons

Directions: In order to prepare for this activity, cut the cellophane into 2" squares (7-9 per student). The squares may vary in size and certainly do not need to be perfect. Give each student a sheet of black paper. Using the white crayons, direct students to create a one-inch border around the perimeter of the sheet of paper. Demonstrate to students how to fold the paper in order to cut a circle, oval, rectangle, etc. Explain that they should avoid making a fold near the border. Students should then make a fold in their paper and then cut out any shape. They should repeat the process by folding the paper again and snipping out another shape.

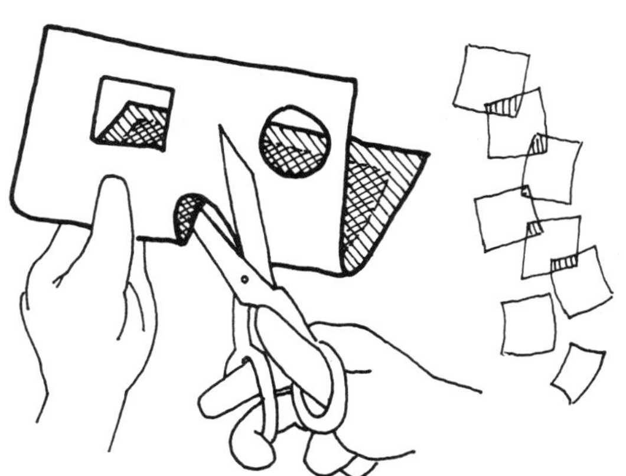

When students have cut out several shapes, demonstrate how to tape various colors of cellophane to the back of the black paper to cover the holes. (The back is the side with the white crayon markings on it.) When students have completed taping the cellophane, ask them which colors appear to be the brightest. Ask them which colors they can see through the best. If they look through the yellow pieces of cellophane, ask if they can see as clearly through them as they can through the blue. Ask which color would make the best lens for a pair of sunglasses and why. Ask which color allows the most light through and which allows the least. When you are finished examining the colors, hang the "stained glass" on your windows!

Shadow Pictures

Shadows—Art

Objective: To work with shadows

Materials: projector, 12" x 18" sheets of white and black construction paper, pencil, scissors, tape, chair

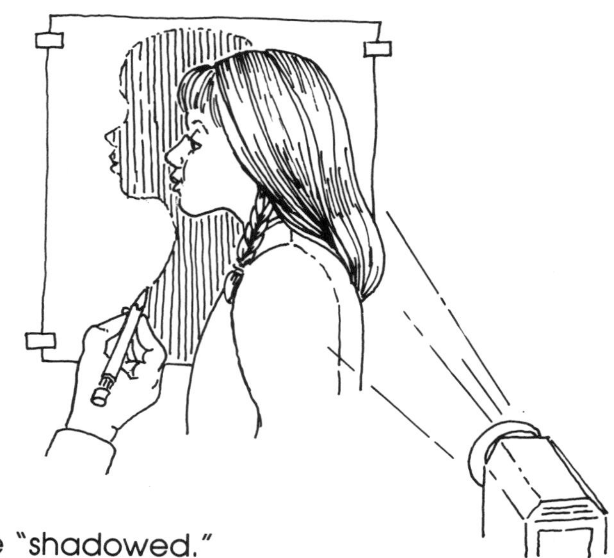

Directions: Explain to students that light creates shadows. To experiment with this, tape the 12" x 18" sheet of white construction paper to a chalkboard or a wall. Place it on the board at a height so that a student sitting in a chair in front of it will have his/her head on the same level as the paper. The student will sit on the chair facing the side so that his/her profile will be "shadowed."

Turn the projector light on and position it at a distance so that the head profile will fit on the paper. To make it smaller, move the projector closer. To make the shadow bigger, move the projector farther away. Using a pencil, trace the shadow being projected on the white paper. Tell students that it is important that the "model" sit very still while his/her shadow is being traced. Cut out the shadows and mount them on the black construction paper. See if the students can recognize their own profile shadows and those of the other students in the class.

Shine for Shadows

Shadows—Experiment

Objective: To create a three-dimensional picture in order to cast a shadow

Materials: one sheet of 9" x 12" white construction paper per student, assorted colors of construction paper, scissors, glue, markers, crayons, oaktag, masking tape, flashlights

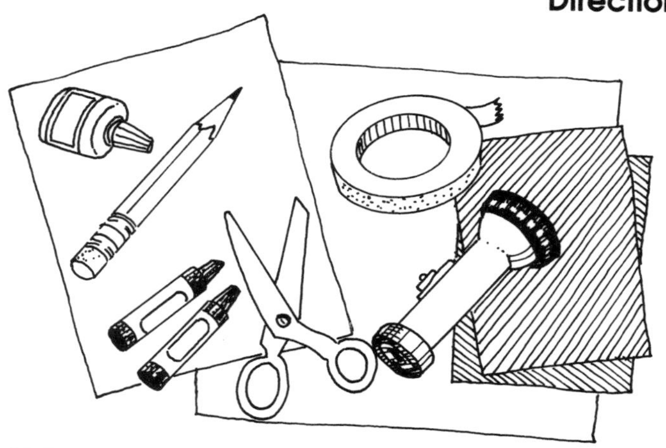

Directions: Explain to students that they will be creating a three-dimensional picture. Students must first decide on an object to create (i.e. cat, house, flower, person, etc.). Students should use the entire sheet of white paper to create the background for their chosen object. If the students decide to create scenery, remind them that they should keep the size of their object in mind. (If desired, they could simply use the side of crayons to create a colorful background rather than draw scenery.)

continued on page 173

Shine for Shadows continued

Shadows—Experiment

Next, students should create their chosen object by cutting out shapes from construction paper and gluing them together. Again, discuss scaling with the students. The object should be at least half the size of the white construction paper (as the goal is to create a white shadow on the paper when the object is finished).

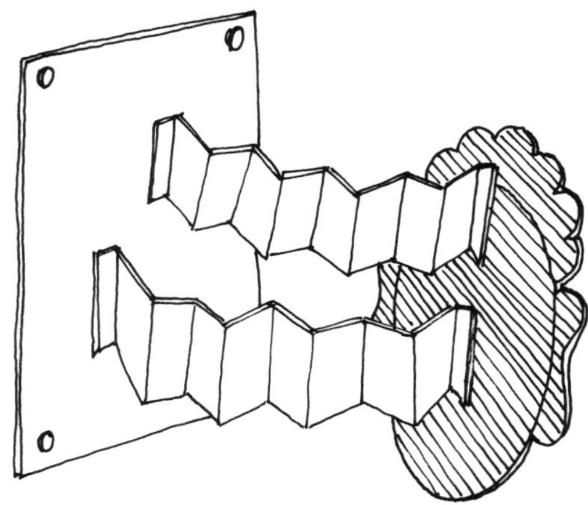

To create the three-dimensional effect and a shadow, students should cut strips from the oaktag and fold them in a fanlike, or accordion-style fashion. (See illustration.)

One end of these accordion-style strips should be glued to the back of the objects made earlier. The other end will be glued to the sheet of construction paper the students decorated earlier. The number of strips will vary according to the size of the objects created. Explain to students that the length of the accordion strips may vary as well.

When the pictures are complete, hang them on the board. Turn off the lights and allow students to shine flashlights on the pictures and observe the shadows. To structure the observation, use masking tape to mark spots on the floor at equal distances from where the pictures are hung. (For example, if you make a spot that is five meters from Caleb's picture, mark another spot that is five meters from Alexandra's picture. Be sure to keep the angle consistent.) Pair up students. Have one student hold the flashlight one meter from the ground, shining it on a particular picture, while the second student measures the length of the shadow. Ask students if all the shadows are the same for each picture. Why not?

Extension: Allow students to examine shadows of one picture from the same distance, but from different angles.

Check Out My Shadow!

Shadows—Experiment

Objectives: To observe and measure shadows and to understand why the length of shadows change

Materials: chart paper, pens, chalk, measuring tapes (several if available), sidewalk or paved area (i.e. an outside basketball court), student-made copies of the data sheet below, flashlight, graph paper (optional)

Directions: On a sunny day, explain to students that they will be going outside to measure their shadows. They will do this three times—in the morning, at noon and in the afternoon. Students should prepare a data sheet similar to the one below. Divide students into pairs.

Title

Location of the Sun	Time	Prediction	Actual
Trial 1			
Trial 2			
Trial 3			

The First Measurement: AM

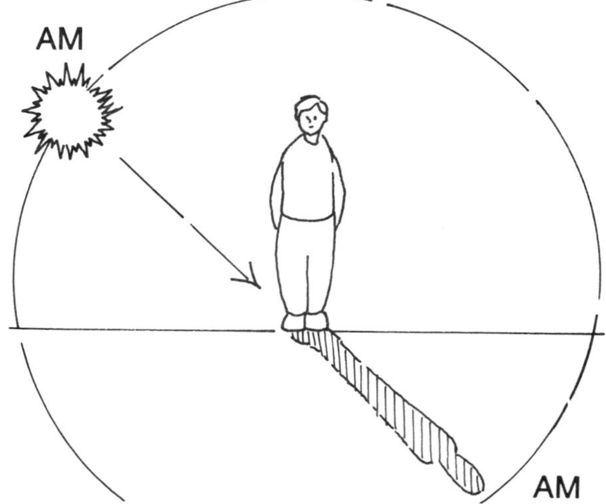

Before going outside, ask students to complete a KWL chart about shadows. On chart paper, students should write what they **Know** about shadows and what they **Want** to know about shadows. Ask students to share their information, allowing students to embellish their own KWL charts.

Next, explain to students that they will be going outside for their first measurement. Ask students to predict how long they think their shadow may be and write it on their data sheet. Once you are outside, ask students to notice the position of their light source, the sun. Ask students to write a brief description of it on their data sheet. Next, students should choose a spot to stand in. Using chalk, the other student should mark this spot with the student's initials. (The student should stand on this exact spot for all three measurements.) Next, one student should mark where the other student's shadow begins and ends. The student should record the time, measure the marked shadow and record the measurement on the data sheet as well. The second student should then choose a spot, and the whole process should be repeated.

continued on page 175

Check Out My Shadow! continued

When you return to the classroom, ask students if their shadows were the same length as their partner's. Why or why not? Ask students to share their shadow lengths. Why are some longer than others? How did their predictions compare with the actual lengths? Last, ask students to go back to the KWL charts to make any necessary changes.

The Second Measurement: Noon

Before going outside for the second measurement, ask students if they know where the sun is located in the sky at lunchtime, or noon. Next, ask students to predict the length of their shadows and record this. Go outside and repeat the process for the first measurement. Remind students to:

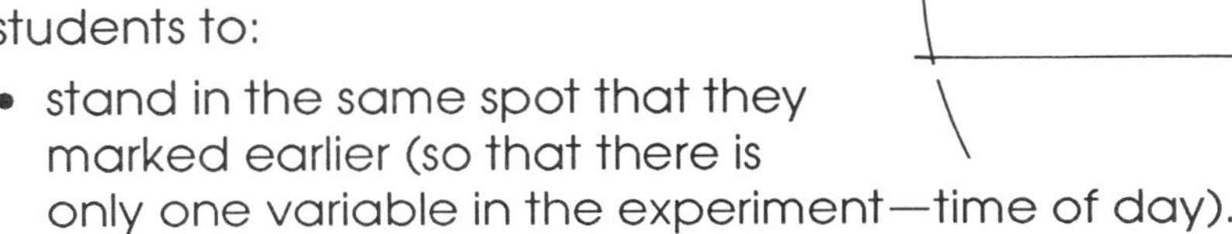

- stand in the same spot that they marked earlier (so that there is only one variable in the experiment—time of day).
- write a brief description of the position of the light source (the sun)
- record the time the measurement was taken
- record the measurement

Once you have returned to the classroom, ask students to compare/contrast lengths of shadows among classmates. Next, have students compare and contrast their first measurement with the second. Did their shadow get longer? shorter? Why do they think so? Last, students can go back to their KWL charts for revisions and/or additions.

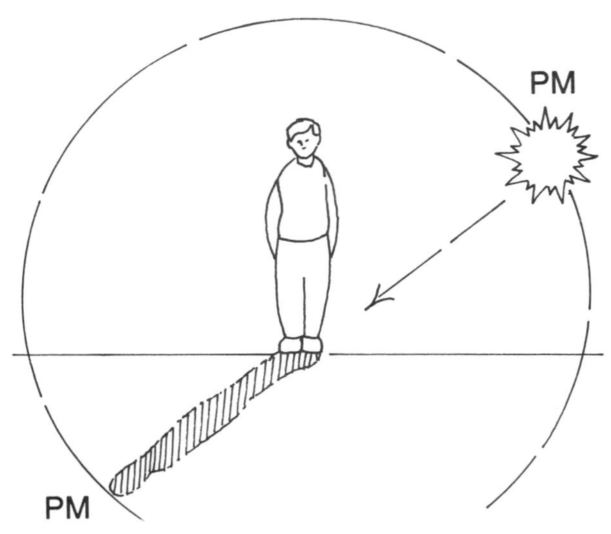

The Third Measurement: PM

Take the same steps for this measurement as you did for the first two. After the results have been discussed, simulate the experiment using a flashlight. Discuss how and why the shadow lengths change. Last, ask students to complete L, or what they **Learned** about shadows on their KWL charts.

Extension: Have students complete a double line graph with their partner. Both students should record their three measurements on one graph.

Feel the Sound Waves (Vibration)

Sound—Experiment

Objective: To demonstrate that sound is produced by vibrations

Materials: tuning fork, triangle (musical instrument), cymbals, drum

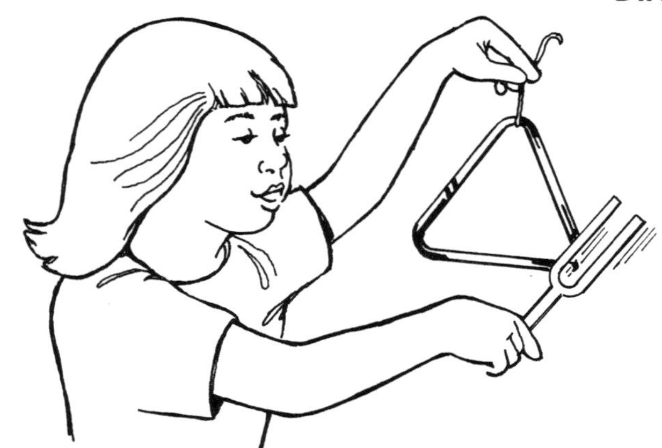

Directions: Holding the triangle by the string, strike it with the tuning fork. Instruct the students to listen to the sound. Demonstrate how you can stop the sound by holding the metal part tightly.

Next, show the students how they can feel the vibrations if they touch the triangle very lightly with their fingertips. They will feel it "tingle." When they grab it forcefully, the vibrations and the sound will stop. Repeat this procedure with other instruments.

Electricity—Light the Bulb

Electricity—Experiment

Objective: To reinforce the concept of a complete circuit

Materials: 2 flashlight batteries, a flashlight bulb, a bulb holder, 2 wires, aluminum foil

Directions:

1. Scrape off the covering of both ends of the two wires. Screw the bulb into the bulb holder. Attach the end of one wire around the screw of the bulb holder. Attach the end of the other wire around the other screw of the bulb holder. Compete the circuit using the two loose wire ends. Hold one on the bottom of the battery and the other wire on the top of the battery. Watch the light go on.

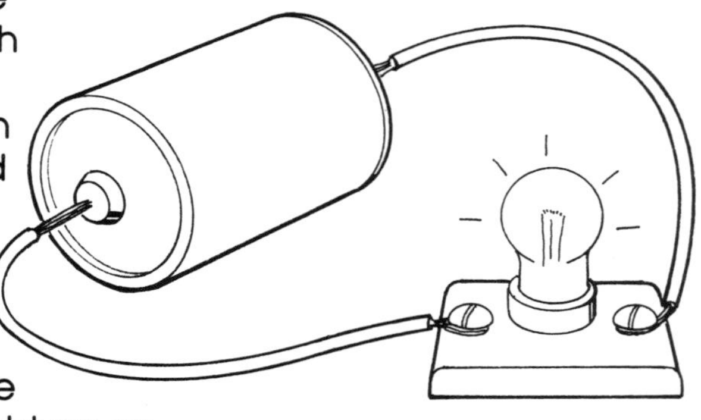

2. Put the second battery on top of the first battery so that the bottom of the second one is touching the top of the first one. Complete the circuit in the same manner. What happens to the light? (It is brighter.) Why? (more power)
3. Now use aluminum foil instead of the wires. Does the bulb light? What does this tell you about aluminum foil?

Find a Match

Electricity—Experiment

Objective: To make a game using the concept of a complete circuit

Materials: a 9" x 12" piece of cardboard, 8 pieces of wire (Cut back approximately $^{3}/_{4}$" of insulation from each end.), a dry cell, a flashlight bulb in a bulb holder, 10 short screws and 10 nuts, 2 coffee stirrers (wood), 2 paper clips, tape, two stick probes

Directions: Put 10 screws through the piece of cardboard as shown in illustration A. Put the nuts on the back of the board as shown in illustration B. Number and initial the nuts as indicated. Attach the wires firmly between points by twisting the ends around the screws and tightening the bolts to connect the wires as follows:

Point 1 to Point C

Point 2 to Point A

Point 3 to Point E

Point 4 to Point D

Point 5 to Point B

A. FRONT

1. WHAT DIRECTION DOES THE POINT OF A COMPASS POINT ? — A CORK
2. WHAT WILL FLOAT IN WATER ? — B WEST
3. WHAT WILL A MAGNET PICK UP ? — C NORTH
4. IN WHAT DIRECTION DO YOU TRAVEL TO GO FROM CANADA TO MEXICO ? — D SOUTH
5. ON WHICH COAST OF THE U.S. IS CALIFORNIA ? — E PAPER CLIP

B. BACK

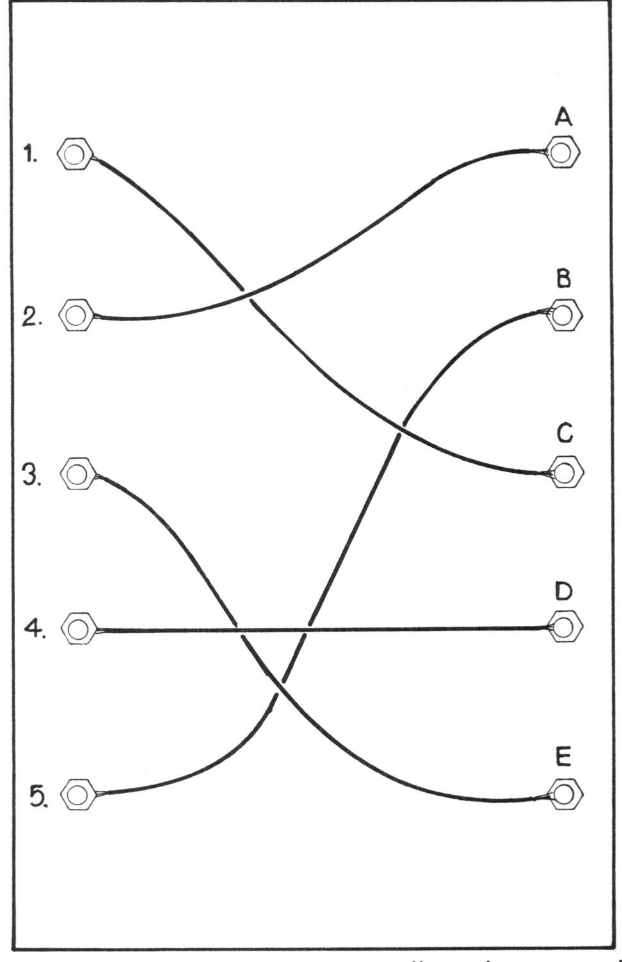

continued on page 178

Find a Match continued

Electricity— Experiment

Connect a wire from one pole of the dry cell to one screw of the bulb holder. Prepare two stick probes for use in playing the game by attaching a paper clip to each wood stirrer. Connect a wire from the other end of the bulb holder to the paper clip of one stick probe and secure with tape. Make sure the wire is long enough to cover the entire gameboard. Connect the last wire from the other end of the dry cell to the paper clip of the second probe and secure with tape. Again, make sure the wire is long enough to cover the entire gameboard. (See diagram.)

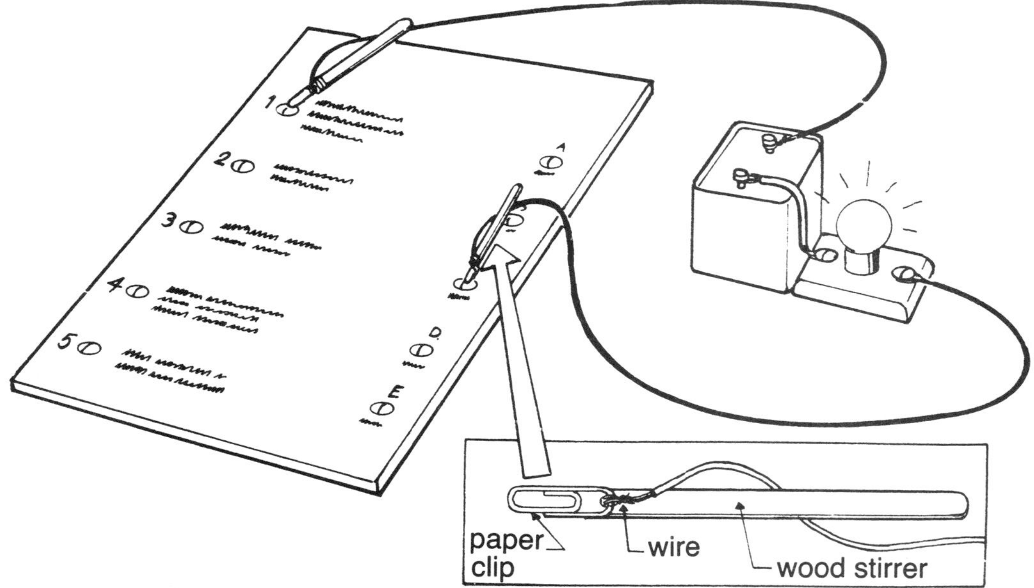

Prepare a list of five questions and write them at points 1 to 5. Put the answers on the lettered spots as follows:

Answer to #1 will be at Point C

Answer to #2 will be at Point A

Answer to #3 will be at Point E

Answer to #4 will be at Point D

Answer to #5 will be at Point B

Now the game is ready to be played. Place the clip end of one stick probe on the screw head for Question 1. Use the other stick probe to find the correct answer. The bulb will light up at the correct answer. (In this case, it will be answer C.)

Sample Questions and Answers:

1. In which direction will the point of a compass point? C. north
2. What will float in water? A. cork
3. What will a magnet pick up? E. paper clips
4. In which direction do you have to go to travel from Canada to Mexico? D. south
5. On which coast of the U.S. is California? B. west

Magnets

Magnets—Experiment

Objective: To make use of past experiences with magnets

Materials: magnet, several objects made of various materials (i.e. paper clips, staples, rubber bands, paper fasteners, coins, aluminum foil, a gold ring, a silver ring, a piece of copper wire—Just be sure to include several non-magnetic metals.), chart paper, marker

Object	Magnetic	Non-Magnetic

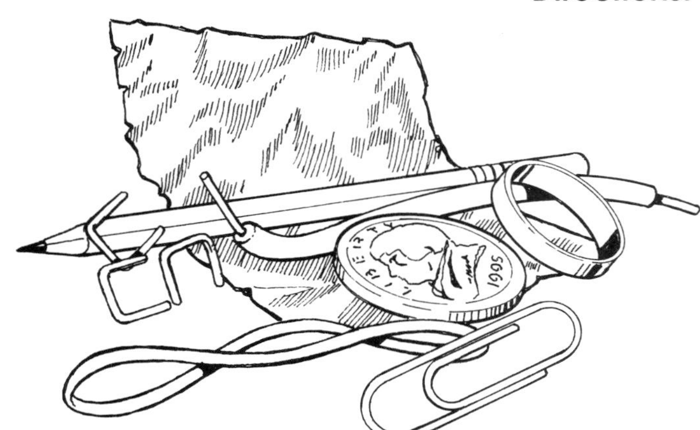

Directions: Discuss the various objects listed above. Ask students if they think these objects would be attracted to a magnet. Create a simple chart to classify the predictions of the class. (See above.) Place the objects for which the predictions have been made in the correct column on the chart. After all the objects have been classified, let students test them with a magnet. Have students rearrange misclassified objects. Discuss why these objects may have been misclassified. Reinforce the importance of scientific experiments over guessing.

Magnetic Magician

Objective: To discover what materials magnets can pass through

Materials: one strong magnet, paper clips, a sheet of paper, a piece of cardboard, a plate, a glass, a thin piece of wood, a piece of fabric, an old phonograph record, aluminum foil, a sheet of plastic, the lid of large tin can, a plastic lid

Directions: Have students place some paper clips on the top of each of the materials listed above. Tell them to move a magnet under the materials. Ask students if the magnet moves the clips through the paper, the wood, the glass, etc. If the clips can be moved, explain that magnetism is passing through. Through experimentation, the students will discover that magnetism will not pass through materials which are themselves magnetic. Ask them why they think this is so.

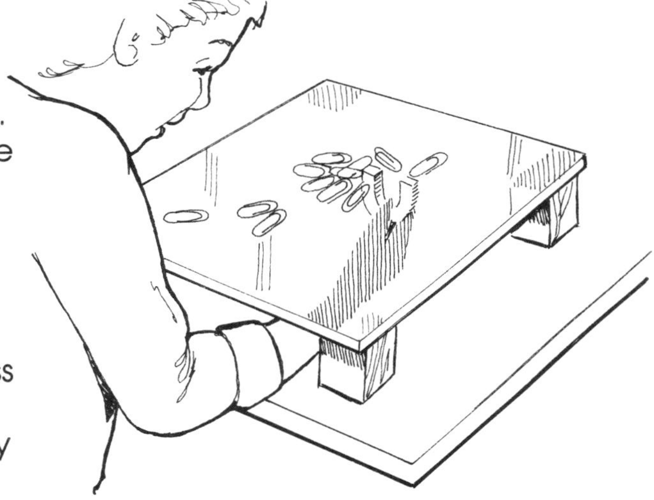

Maggie the Magnet

Magnets

Objectives: To reinforce the concept that magnets can exert a force through materials and to illustrate and complete a story

Materials: iron rod, a horseshoe magnet, two pipe cleaners, several pieces of yarn, construction paper, paper, tape, shoe box, one copy of the story on pages 181-182 per student, crayons, scissors

Directions: Before you begin, help the story come to life by creating the two characters in the story—Maggie Magnet and Iggie Iron. To do this, tape a few pieces of yarn onto a horseshoe magnet to create Maggie, and wrap pipe cleaners around the iron rod to create short hands and legs for Iggie. Next, create a setting for the story. To do this, stand a shoe box on its side. Cut off three sides of the box so that a wall is created. Tape the wall to a table or desk. Next, read the story, Maggie the Magnet (on pages 181-182) without using the characters, setting and illustrations.

After the students have heard the story, ask them if they can tell you what happened to Iggie and why. (When Maggie leaned against the wall, she pulled Iggie to the wall, exerting a force right through it!) When the possibilities have been explored, issue copies of the story to the students. With the help of the illustrations, again ask students if they can tell you what happened to Iggie. Reread the partial story to the students again, this time using the characters and setting you created earlier to create a reenactment of the story. When all students have an understanding of what happened to Iggie, have them illustrate each scene. Ask them to complete the story by solving the problem using their knowledge of magnets, and unite Maggie and Iggie. Direct them to cut apart and assemble the pages to create book. Students can create a cover using construction paper. Allow students to use the "stage" you created to perform their completed story with a friend.

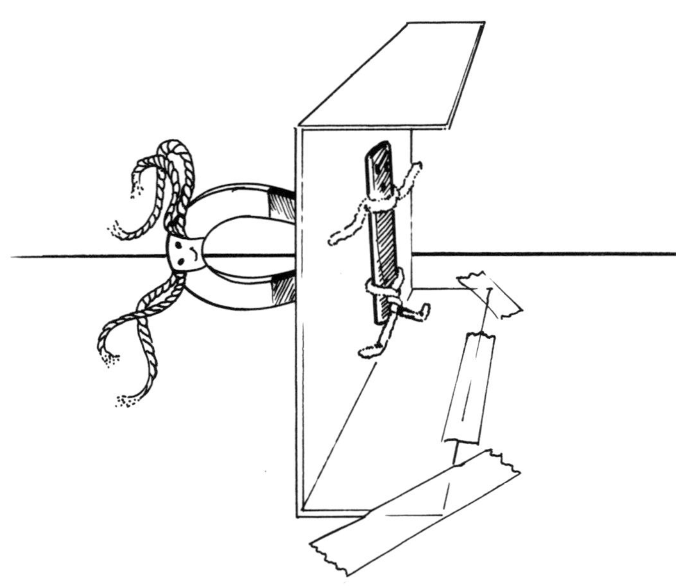

Maggie the Magnet continued

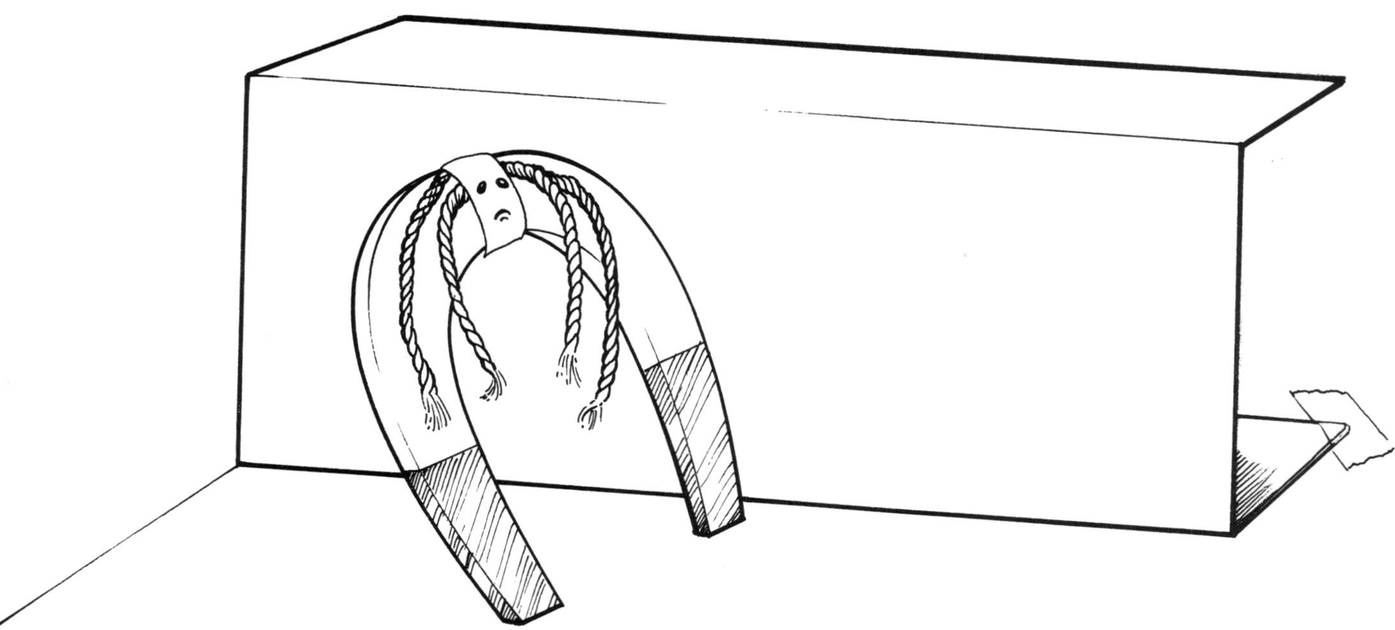

Once upon a time, in a faraway land, lived Maggie the Magnet. Maggie the Magnet was extremely upset. She wanted to see her friend Iggie Iron who lived on the other side of the wall.

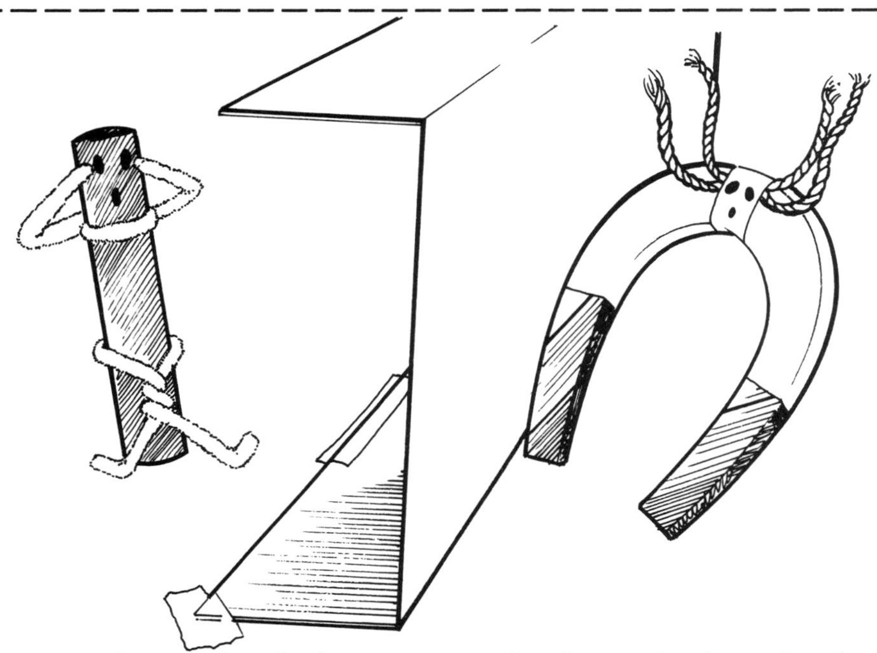

The wall is much too high for me to climb," cried Iggie the Iron.

"Oh Iggie!" exclaimed Maggie the Magnet, "I wish so much to see you! If only we could think of a way to get you over this wall."

Maggie the Magnet continued

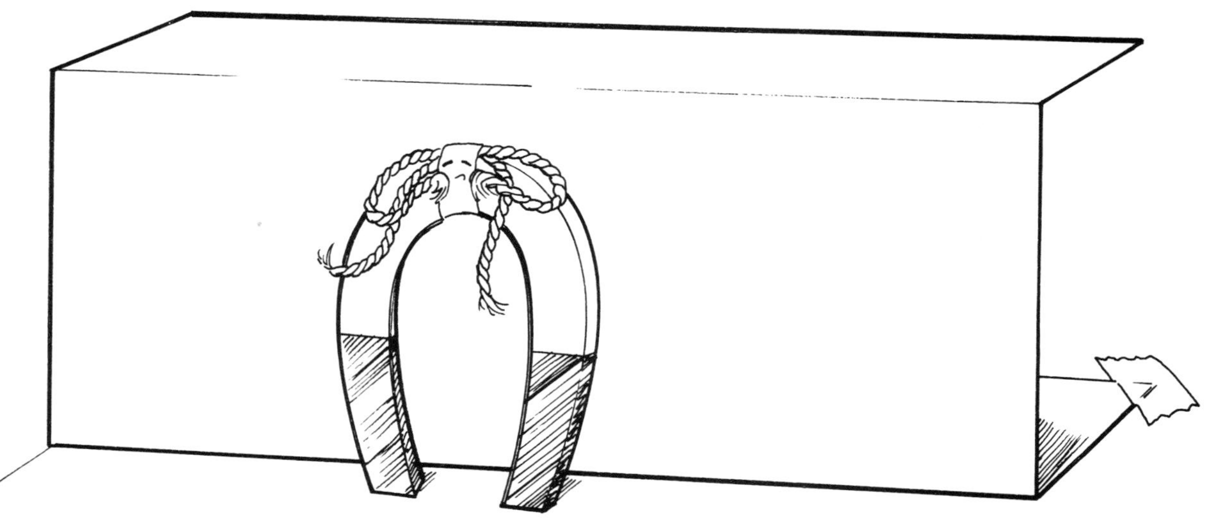

Maggie leaned against the wall and began to cry in despair. Suddenly, she heard Iggie give a yell! "Whoooooaa!" cried Iggie with surprise. Then, there was loud "thump" followed by silence.

"Iggie, are you alright?" shouted Maggie with fear.

"I think so Maggie . . . . but I'm stuck to the wall!" Iggie responded in a high-pitched voice, unsure of what had happened.

Make a Magnet

Magnets—Experiment

Objective: To reinforce learning about magnetic force

Materials: 4" nails, bar magnets, paper clips

Directions: Give each student a nail, a bar magnet and some paper clips. Using a bar magnet, have the students pick up the paper clips. Next, have them try to pick up the paper clips using the nail. Does it work? Explain to students that they will try to turn the nail into a magnet. Tell them to stroke the nail in one direction (not back and forth) with one end of the magnet about 25-30 times. Now, tell them to try to use the nail to pick up the paper clips. The nail has been magnetized. Ask students the following questions: "How many clips will it pick up? Is it as strong as the bar magnet?" Then, have them drop the nail on the floor a few times. Ask students the following questions: "Will it still pick up as many clips? What does this tell you about the effect of dropping a magnet?"

Which Way Is North?

Objective: To make a compass

Materials: magnet, pan of water, long sewing needle (Test it first with a magnet to make sure it is made of iron.), slice of cork, candle wax, standard compass

Directions: Have students magnetize the needle by stroking it in one direction with a strong magnet about 25-30 times. They then place the magnetized needle on a slice of cork and keep it in place using a drop of candle wax. This "pointer" should next be floated in a pan of water. Tell students that it is important to remember to keep all objects made of iron away from the compass as iron objects in close proximity will cause deviation in the compass.

The needle of the compass should be pointing north. Have students check this with a standard compass. Ask students if both compasses are pointing in the same direction? (yes) Ask them why. (A magnetic needle compass always points in the north-south direction towards the magnetic north and south poles.)

Which Magnet Is Stronger?

Magnet—Experimenting/Comparing

Objective: To compare the relative strengths of two magnets

Materials: 2 horseshoe magnets, paper clips, nail, 2 bar magnets, rulers, copy of the activities below

Directions: Let students try the activities below to see for themselves the strength of two magnets. The answers are: 1. The stronger magnet will pick up more paper clips. 2. The strongest magnet is the one containing the nail. 3. The stronger magnet will start to attract the nail from a greater distance.

Which Magnet Is Stronger?

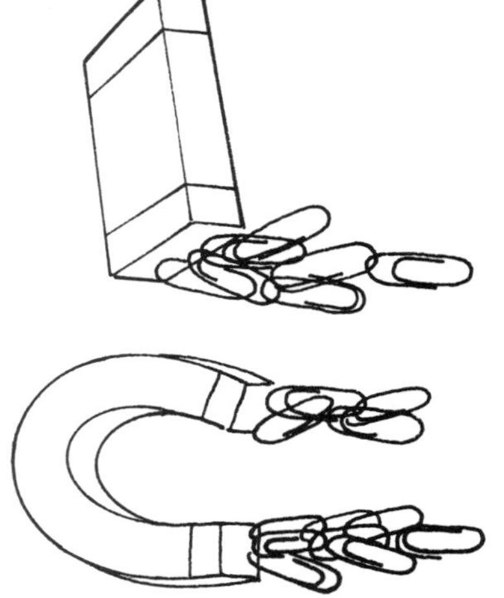

Name ______________________

1. Use the two horseshoe magnets to pick up paper clips. Record how many paper clips each magnet picks up. Repeat this with the two bar magnets and record the results. Does each magnet pick up the same number of clips each time? __________ Does one magnet pick up more clips than the other at each try? _________ Which one appears to be stronger? __________ Why? ______________________
____

2. Use two horseshoe magnets. Put a nail between the poles of the two magnets. Pull the magnets apart slowly. The nail will remain with one magnet. Which magnet do you think is stronger? ____________________ Why do you think so? ____________________________________
____

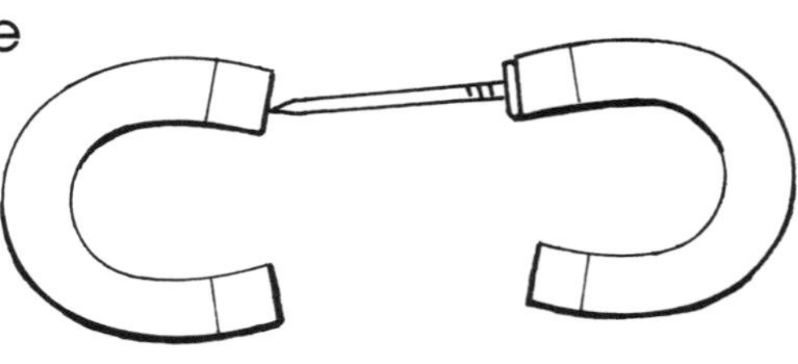

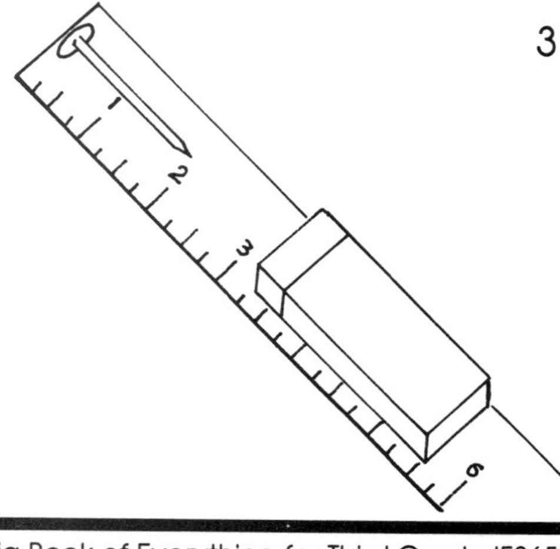

3. Use the two bar magnets. Place a nail on top of a ruler near its end. Move the magnet very slowly toward the nail. Note the point at which the nail will start to move toward the magnet. (What makes the nail move toward the magnet?) Now, repeat this with the second magnet. Note the distance at which the nail starts to move toward this magnet. Which magnet do you think is stronger? ____________________ Why do you think so? _________
____

The objectives for the activities below and on pages 186-189 are for students to explore the everyday use of machines and to manipulate gears, screws, wheels, levers, wedges, pulleys and inclined planes.

Machines—Art

Mild-Mannered Machines

Materials: books about machines, drawing paper, crayons, markers, magazines, newspapers, scissors

Directions: Explain to students that machines help to make work like pushing, pulling and lifting easier. Tell students that a machine is often made up of different parts that move, is sometimes big and complicated, and is other times small and simple.

Share with students the following examples and definitions of some simple machines:

Lever—A hammer can be used as a kind of lever. This type of machine helps to move things with less force.

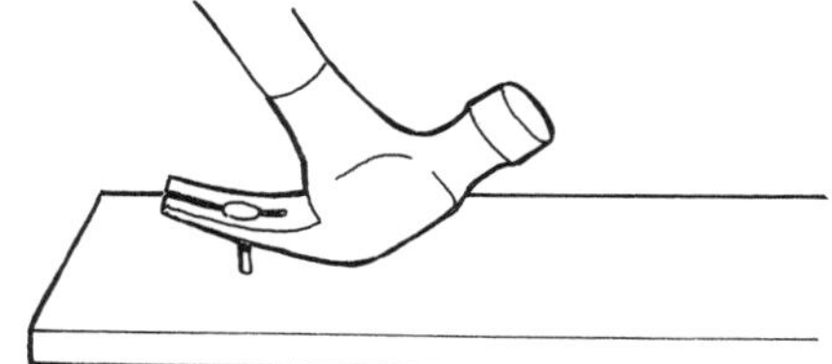

Pulley—A pulley can be used to hoist a flag or sail. Pulleys can be used to lift loads more easily.

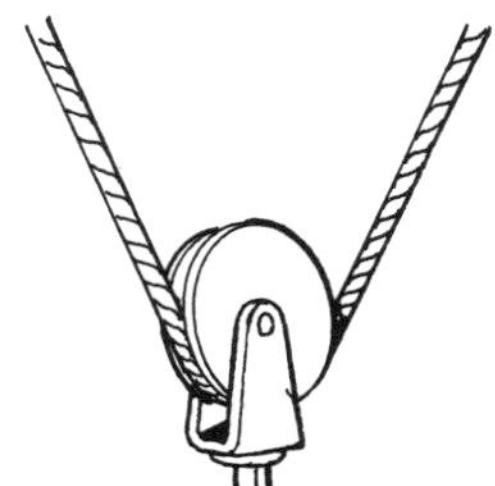

Wedge—An axe is an example of a kind of wedge. Wedges help cut or split things.

Wheel—(such as those on a wagon or car) Wheels can be used to move things more easily from one place to another.

Screw—Screws are typically used to hold things together. Sometimes screws are used to lift hinges such as the seat of a chair.

Inclined plane—A ramp up to a building is an example of an inclined plane. This type of simple machine can be used to move things from a lower place to a higher place and vice versa.

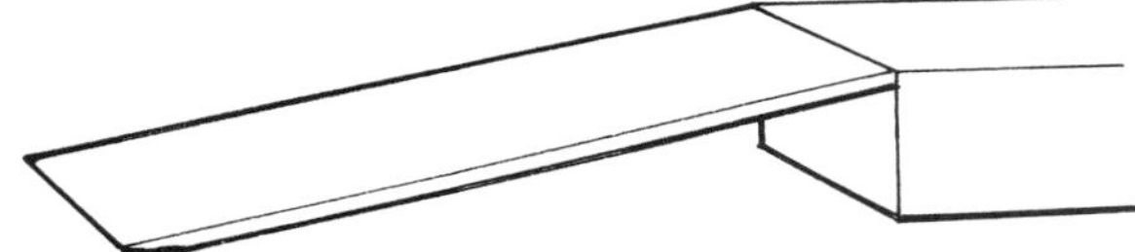

Have students make a collage of machines they use or see every day using the materials listed above.

"Inventing" the Wheel

Machines—Experiment

Experiment #1

Materials: (per group of students) textbook, string, rubber band, 3 pencils

Directions: This is a great activity to begin with to introduce students to the concept of *friction*. Divide students into groups. Have the students put a piece of string through a thin rubber band. Then, have them tie the string around a chosen textbook. Putting one finger into the rubber band, ask the students to pull the book along any flat surface. Have them observe the following: the book is hard to pull because it rubs or drags on the surface of the table, desk or floor; the rubber band stretches very far as the book is pulled. The rubbing is called friction. Explain that friction makes things hard to move.

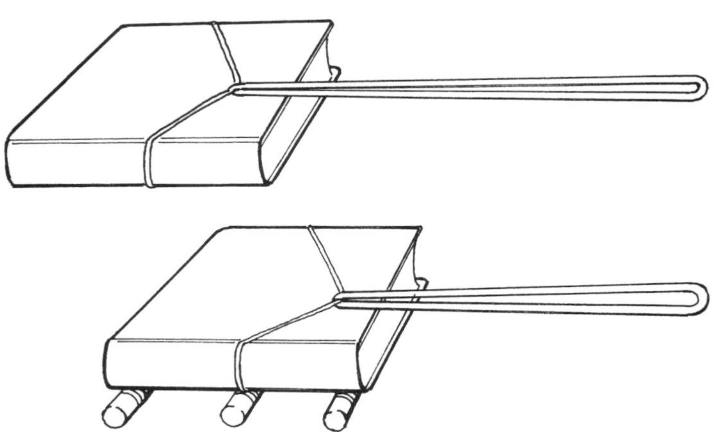

Tell students that a simple machine can be used to help reduce friction and make the work easier. Allow time for the students to hypothesize which simple machine introduced earlier could be used. Tell students that they will use three pencils as wheels. Again, allow time for the students to experiment. Finally, demonstrate how putting "wheels" under the book reduces friction and makes it easier to pull the book along the surface using the rubber band and one finger.

Put It in Gear!

Experiment #2

Materials: one copy of the gears on page 188, construction paper, markers, crayons, scissors, brads, bicycle (if possible)

Directions: Explain to students that gears are special kinds of wheels that have teeth. If possible, have the students examine the gears of a bicycle. The students should note how the large pedal is connected with the small back gear by a chain. Demonstrate by pushing the pedal to show students how the chain makes the small gear in the back work.

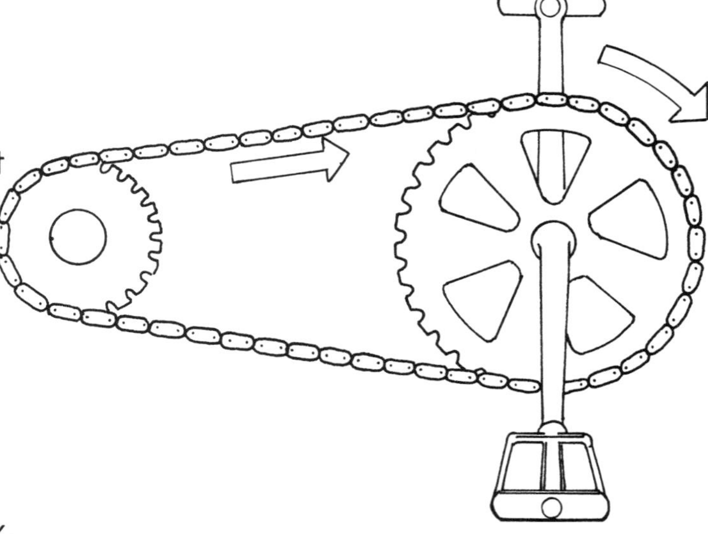

continued on page 187

Put It in Gear! continued

Machines—Experiment

To extend students' understanding, give them each a copy of the gears. Have them cut them out. Then, students fold up the points of Gear B. Have students attach the gears to the construction paper with brads so that the teeth of Gear A interlock with the folded up teeth of Gear B. When Gear A is turned, Gear B should also turn.

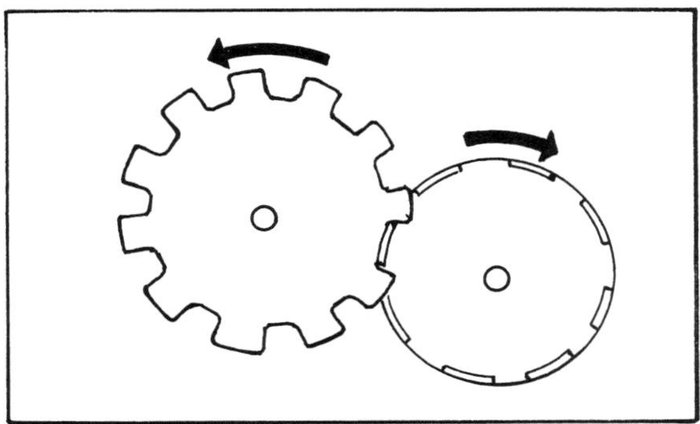

Finally, have the students draw a toy or machine that will move around on the gears they have attached to the construction paper. Encourage them to create a name for their invention and be sure the students are using the gears correctly.

Extension: Create a bulletin board to display the **Great Gears at Work!**

Pulley Power

Experiment #3

Materials: flagpole, American flag

Directions: Have your students perform a service for their school while learning about the power of pulleys. Volunteer the students in your class to help raise and lower the American flag in front of your building. (Make sure you teach the students how to handle the flag.) Demonstrate, model and practice the procedure. Then, set up a schedule for the students to assist the person normally in charge of this task. Encourage them to note that a pulley is a small wheel with a groove. The rope fits into the groove of the wheel. As the rope is pulled, the wheel turns and helps to lift an object (in this case, the flag).

This is a great way for students to see a simple machine being used in everyday life and to perform a service to their school.

Gear Patterns

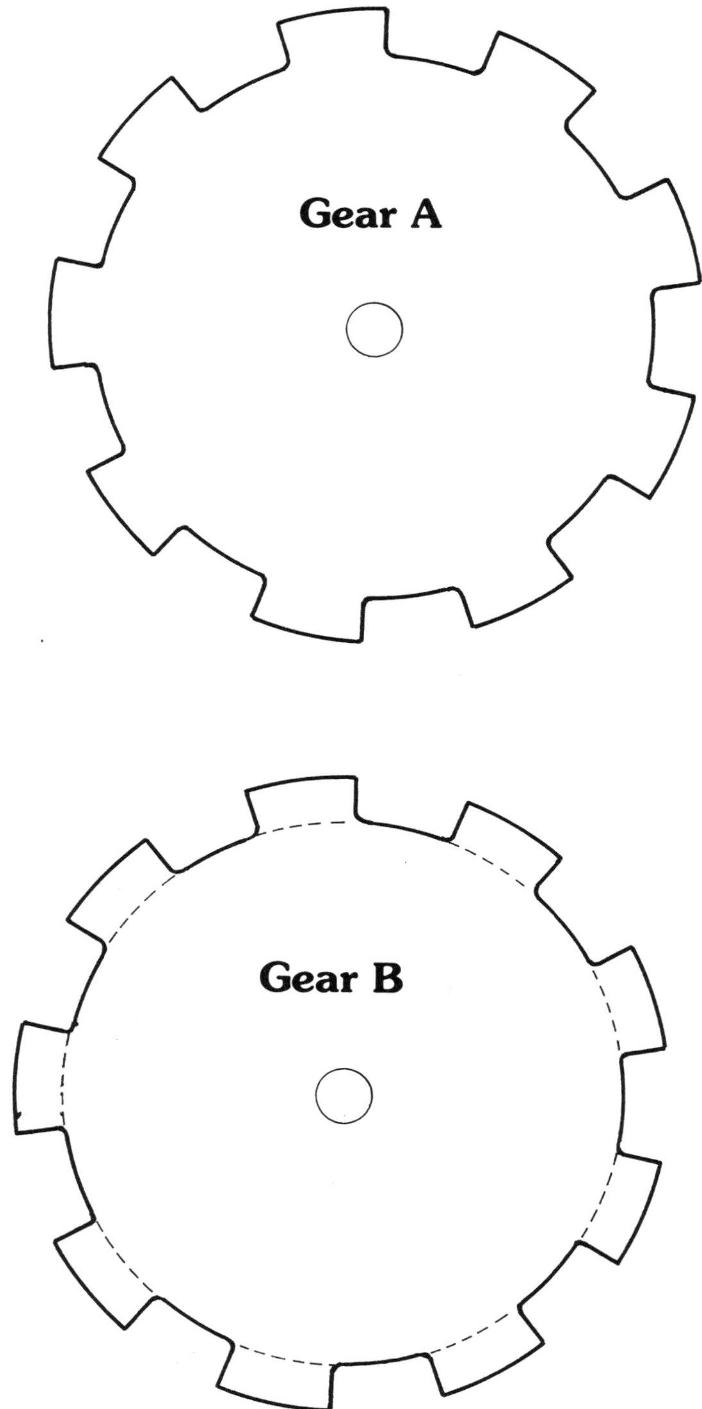

Let a Little Lever Do the Work

Machines—Experiment

Experiment #4

Materials: scissors, tongs, nutcracker, shovel, ruler, block or eraser, toy wheelbarrow

Directions: Explain to students that when a person uses a lever, they can lift a heavy load without pushing very hard. Tell them that a lever is a bar which may be made out of metal, wood or other hard material. Next, introduce the following terms to students:

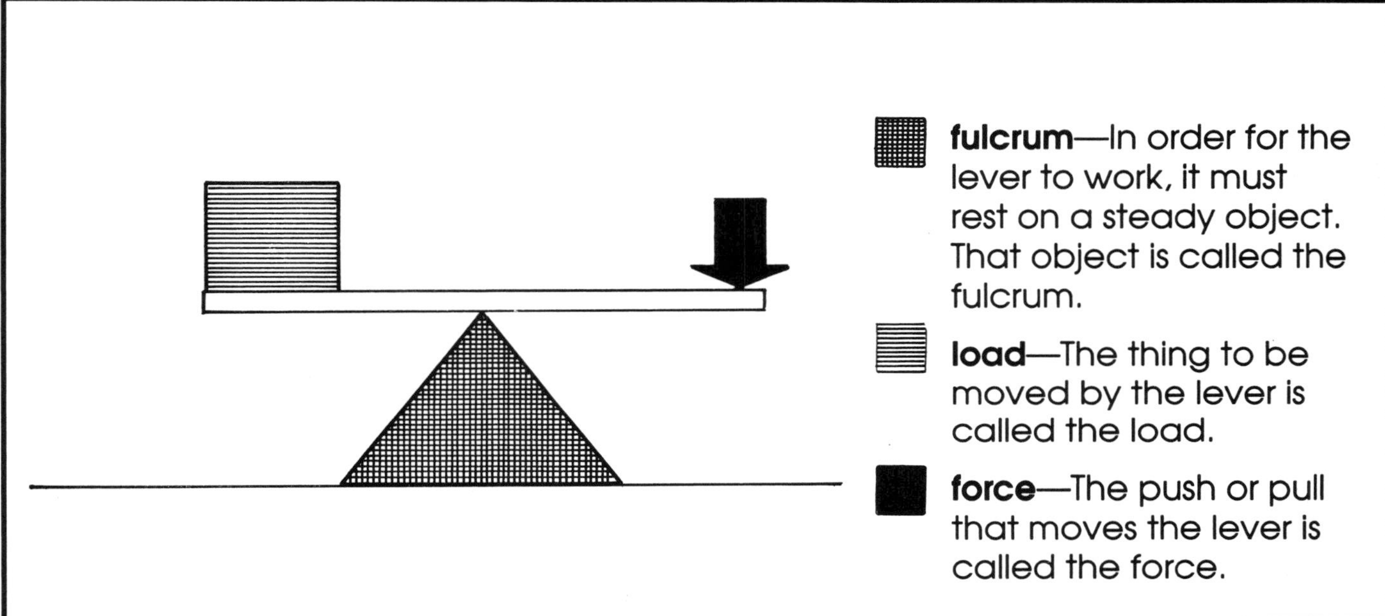

Show the students some everyday examples of levers such as scissors, tongs, nutcrackers, shovels and even their arms. Then, ask the students to create a lever using their rulers. Have them use a block, eraser or any object as the load. Allow time for the students to experiment with their levers. Pair up students that have different lengths of levers. Ask them to experiment with the two levers and to compare the amount each lever can lift. Also, suggest that the students vary the position of the fulcrum. Guide students to determine that the longer the lever, the more that can be lifted, and the closer the fulcrum is to the load, the easier it is to lift.

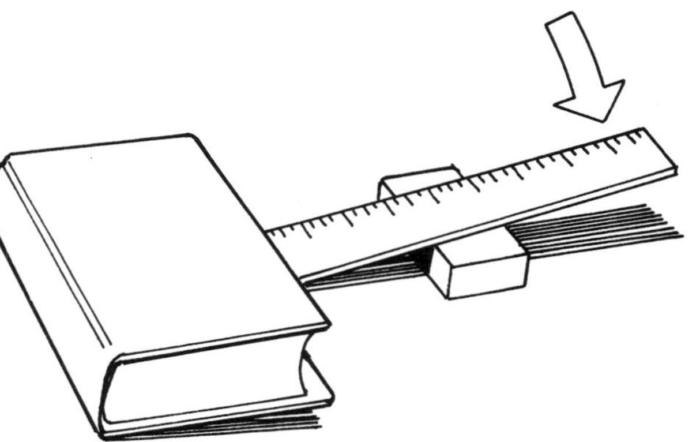

Extension: Challenge the students to find and list as many simple machines as they can in their homes. Have students compare lists.

Tall Ramps, Short Ramps

Machines—Experiment/ Recording Information

Objectives: To experiment with heights of ramps and correlate the heights with the distance an object can roll and to use a ruler

Materials: long blocks or long pieces of cardboard (to create a ramp), rectangular blocks or books (to rest the ramp upon), matchbox cars or anything else that will roll (i.e. can, pencil, marble, etc.), a student-created copy of the data sheet below for each student

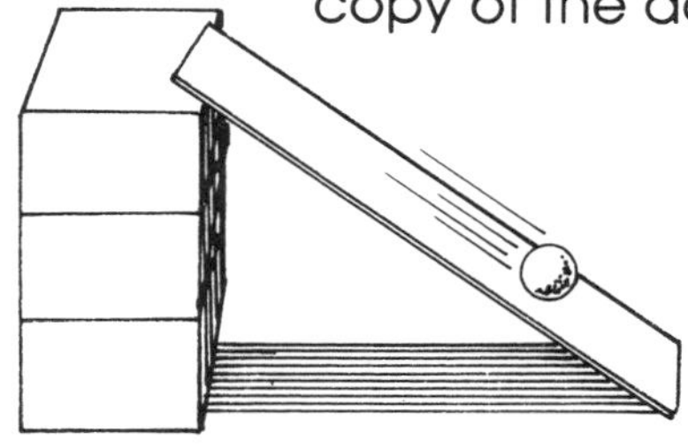

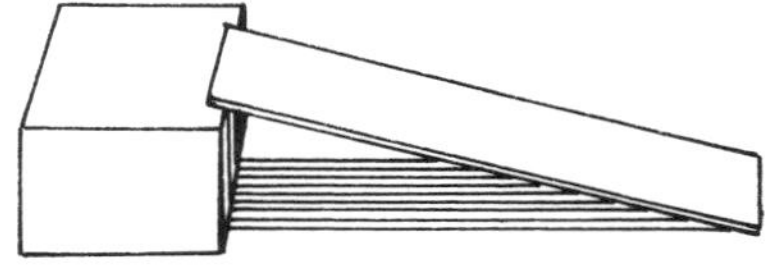

Directions: Before you begin this lesson, discuss with students the scientific process or method. (See page 132.) This lesson is designed to emphasize the concepts of "variables" and "constants." Divide students into pairs. Direct students to create a data sheet. (See example below.) Guide students through the completion of the data sheet by discussing what would be appropriate for each of the headings. The variable in this experiment will be the height of the ramp (or the angle of incline).

TITLE: (Let students choose a title.)

PROBLEM: (to find out what ramp height allows an object to roll the furthest)

MATERIALS: (whichever materials you choose to use)

PROCEDURE: (I will create two ramps of different heights by using a different number of blocks to lay each ramp on. Then, I will roll an object down each ramp three times and measure how far the object rolled each time.)

VARIABLE: (the height of the ramp)

OBSERVATIONS:

	Height of Ramp	Object Rolled
Trial One		
Trial Two		
Trial Three		
	Height of Ramp	**Object Rolled**
Trial One		
Trial Two		
Trial Three		

CONCLUSION(S): I think ________________________________

because ________________________________

continued on page 191

Tall Ramps, Short Ramps continued

The students should create a ramp, measure the height of the ramp, and then roll one object down the ramp. Next, the students should measure the distance the object rolled. Direct students to record their findings on their data sheets. The same object should be rolled two more times at this height. Students should change the variable, or the height, of the ramp, roll the object down it and measure it. The same object should be rolled again two more times, with the observer taking and recording measurements. Discuss the students' findings as a class.

"Scientific" Idiomatic Expressions

Writing

Objectives: To create a Venn diagram and to write explanations for some idiomatic expressions that relate to science

Materials: the list of idiomatic expressions (below), paper, pencils

Directions: This activity is perfect for the end of the year when students have been exposed to a variety of scientific topics. Begin by discussing what an idiom is (a peculiar expression that is familiar to a community of people). Then, explain to students that many idioms exist that relate to weather, motion, plant life, insects, mammals, etc. Ask students if they have ever heard the expression, "sweating like a pig . . ." If they have, ask the students to explain why they think this expression exists. Next, ask them if they know that pigs do not sweat! So, ask students where they think this expression came from. Ask them how they think it came about.

Ask students if they are familiar with any science-related expressions. Create a student-generated list on the board and add any of the expressions below if desired. Have each student choose an expression. Ask students to write a short paragraph evaluating or criticizing the expression. Encourage students to research, if necessary, and create new expressions (i.e. eats like a bird).

Extension: Have students illustrate these expressions to create a hilarious class book.

Scientific Idiomatic Expressions

She was sweating like a pig!
Get it in gear!
Her head was in the clouds.
Her face was as red as a beet.
Once in a blue moon . . .
When pigs fly . . .
She has ants in her pants!
He was as quiet as a mouse.
She eats like a bird.
Your room is a pigsty!
Birds of a feather flock together.
He's as skinny as a beanpole.
He was chewing like a cow.

Ecology

Students will become more aware of environmental issues as they study ecosystems and their components in cooperative learning groups and individually. They will examine the habitats and lifestyles of animals and will investigate the conditions in which they exist.

Concepts in this chapter include: environmental logs, changes in the community, erosion, oil spills, sedimentation, study of biomes, endangered species, food webs, extinction and awareness of pollution.

Students will also take an in-depth look at the rainforest, its layers and the population density and diversity of species that inhabit it. Plenty of ideas are given to make the rainforest come alive in your classroom.

A play examining the various aspects of the destruction and preservation of the rainforest is also part of this chapter. Students can participate not only in the costuming and staging, but also in the research and in the writing of some of the dialogue.

Recycling Reflections

Objective: To recognize the importance of cleaning up the environment

Materials: writing journal, book *Just a Dream* by Chris Van Allsburg

Directions: This lesson provides an opportunity for your students to reflect on how litter and neglect negatively impact our environment and, indeed, our future. Begin by reading aloud to the class the story *Just a Dream*. In this book, a little boy, who does not care much about preserving Earth, dreams about what his future will be like. To his surprise, litter and smog appear where he had envisioned robots and spaceships to be. He awakens as an enlightened and environmentally aware individual.

When you are finished reading the story, ask the students to write down what they think is the most important sentence, phrase or event from the story. Have them also write a short explanation of why they chose it. With the journal entry complete, tell the students to "square" (move into groups of four) and "share" their selections. Ask them to discuss which of the four selections they think is the most important. Encourage the "squares" to reach consensus on their choice. Gather all the groups together to share and discuss their reflections.

Ecology Password

ACID RAIN
RAINFOREST
LANDFILL

Objective: To use adjectives to describe an ecological noun

Materials: small slips of paper, chart paper, paper bag, marker

Directions: This activity is a fun way for you to review terms and vocabulary. On a separate slip of paper, have each student write a noun relating to the environment (i.e. rainforest, acid rain, landfill, etc.). Place all strips in a bag and shake them up. Have each of five students select a strip from the bag. Give them five minutes to think of ten words to describe their word. Then, one at a time, have them share those clues with the class, giving the class three guesses. The student who correctly guesses the word goes to the chart paper and writes the word. At this point, review what the students know about this environmental noun. Continue until all students have had the opportunity to describe a noun.

Soil, Oil, Toil!

Objectives: To experiment to find out why oil spills in our oceans are such a problem to clean up and to find out which material works best in picking up oil

Materials: an aquarium or other similar container; several deep pans filled with water; several cups of soil; several cups of cooking oil; sponges, nylon material, paper towels, cotton balls, cups, strainers and any other available objects that may pick up soil and oil

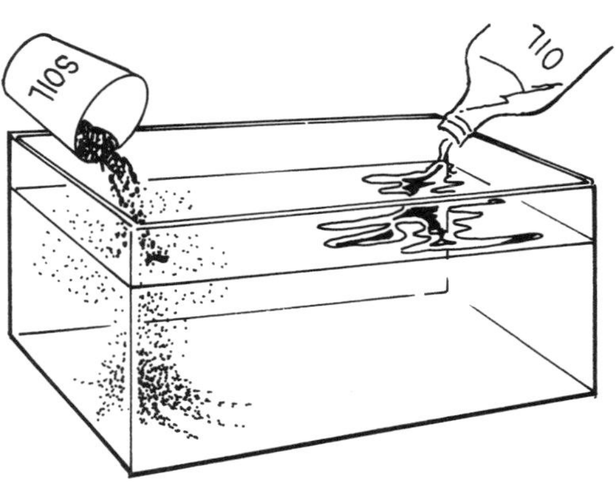

Directions: Fill the aquarium or container with water and gather the students around it. Ask the students if the water is clean. (Yes, you may not want to drink it, but a living creature would find it suitable.) Next, ask students if the water would still be clean or suitable for an animal to live in if you were to pour the soil into the container. Put a small amount of the soil in. Observe how it clouds the water and then settles to the bottom. Discuss what effect this may have on living organisms. Next, ask students to imagine that the cooking oil is crude oil and repeat the procedure above. Where does the oil settle? Explain to the students that we have the soil at the bottom of the container and oil floating at the top. Now it's time for the toil! Divide students into small groups. Tell students that they are going to repeat the procedures that were just demonstrated. Then, have students try to restore the water to its original state using any or all of the materials listed above. Before students begin, they should create a data table to record the cleaning methods and all observations made.

Name ______________

Cleaning Method	Observation
sponge	
nylon material	
paper towel	
cotton ball	
cup	
strainer	

Each small group of students should work around the pan of water. The students should "contaminate" the water with the oil and the soil and begin clean-up attempts. When students have completed the task, pose some or all of the following questions:

1. Which was easier to clean, the soil or the oil?
2. Why do you think so?
3. Of the cleaning methods you used, which method worked best in cleaning the soil? the oil? Why?
4. Why do you think oil spills are harmful?
5. Why do you think that soil is not a problem?

continued on page 195

Soil, Oil, Toil! continued

Extension: To create a better awareness of how oil spills harm the environment, place a bird feather in clean water so that the students may observe how the feather can repel water. Next, place the feather in water with cooking oil in it, and demonstrate to students how the feather becomes "soppy," no longer possessing the full ability to repel water. Ask students how this could be a problem to a bird. Ask them what they think would happen to the fur of a mammal.

Sedimentation

Objective: To observe sedimentation

Materials: 1/3 cup of one of the following: sand, silt or clay; 1/3 cup of soil; a couple of teaspoons of baking soda; several pebbles; a large, clear container with a lid (approximately one pint or larger); several cups of water

Directions: Rainwater, rivers and oceans move materials such as sand, silt, clay and soil. These materials combine with the water to form layers. This is called sedimentation. Demonstrate this process for your students. Before you begin, explain the experiment and create a chart with the students on which to record data. You will need to give attention to the layers formed and the time. When the table is completed, gather the students around you. Mix the soil and the sand, silt or clay with a couple teaspoons of baking soda. Fill the jar two-thirds of the way full with water. Place the cap on and shake. Set the jar on a table for all to observe and record the time. Next, have students record their observations on the chart you created previously.

Time of Observation	Materials	Time Passed

Erosion Before Our Eyes

Objectives: To demonstrate erosion and how plant roots prevent erosion; to draw a diagram

Materials: soil, large piece of cardboard, water, a bucket or watering can, paper towels, white construction paper, rulers, crayons

Directions: This activity works best outdoors. If this is not possible, place newspaper several sheets thick on the floor. Fill the watering can or bucket with water. Lay the cardboard down and pile soil on it, approximately 1/2" thick. Gather students around you. Discuss what erosion is, how it occurs and why it is harmful. Explain to students that you are going to demonstrate erosion.

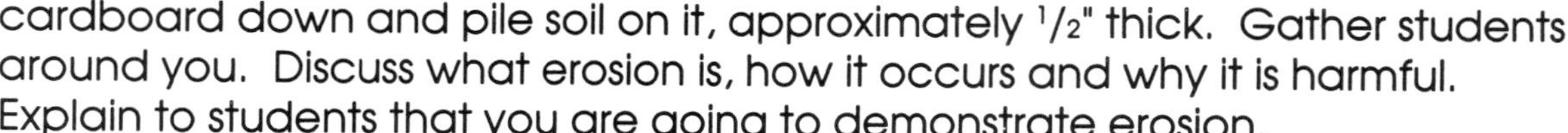

Ask for a couple of volunteers to hold the cardboard with the soil on it at a 45° angle. Slowly pour some water at the top of the incline and observe how the soil is carried down the incline. Repeat the process and examine the amount of soil at the bottom of the incline. Next, ask for some volunteers to become plants. The students who become plants will use their hands to act like roots. Ask these students to grasp some soil, and repeat the water pouring process. Discuss how the roots of the plants hold on to the soil, just as these students' hands did, and help prevent erosion. Discuss how real plant roots would also absorb the water so that there would be less of it running down the incline.

Last, ask students to create a diagram depicting the demonstration. Distribute the white construction paper and direct students to divide their papers in half. On the left side, students should illustrate erosion, on the right side, they should illustrate plant roots grasping the soil and absorbing the water.

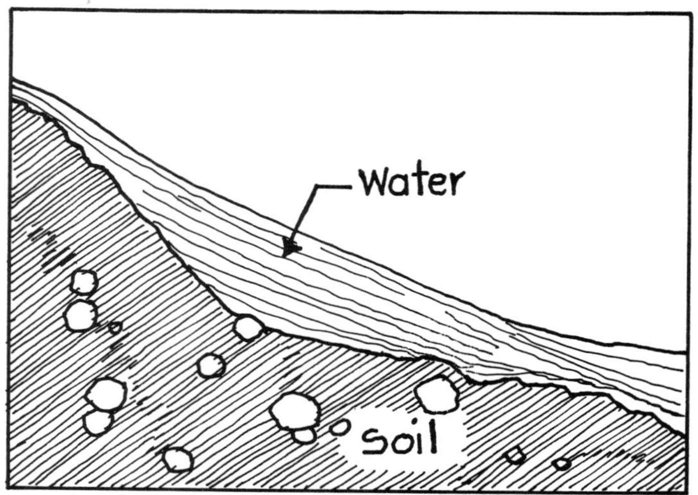

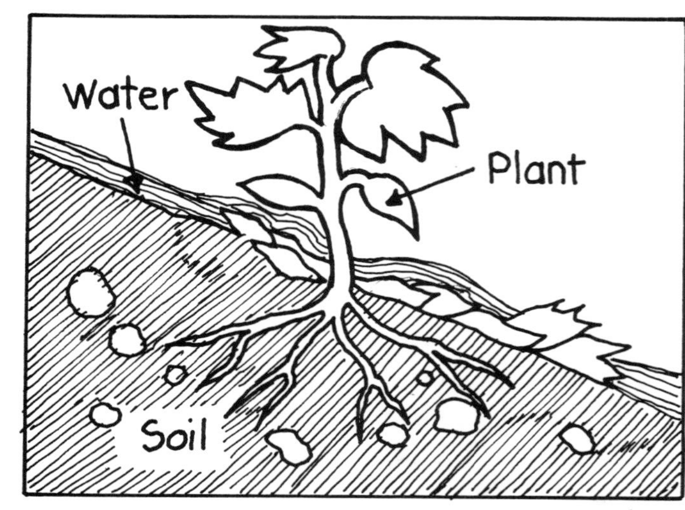

City or Country

Objectives: To have students consider ecology and progress and to decide if these two concepts can coexist

Materials: book *The Little House* by Virginia Lee Burton

Directions: Have the students read *The Little House*. Have them think about and answer the following questions:

1. What new inventions were discovered from the time the little house was built to the time it was moved?
2. What are the advantages of these inventions?
3. What are the disadvantages of these inventions? (smog, depletion of power, etc.)
4. Why did the city grow?
5. What happened to the countryside?
6. Where would you rather live? Why?
7. Do we need cities? Why?
8. Do we need countrysides? Why?

Have the students share their answers with the class. Then, divide the class into two groups. One group will be advocates of preserving the ecology and the other will present the case for the importance of the growth of cities.

Have each group select two or three persons to be the spokespeople for their group. Have the spokespeople present their statements in support of either maintaining the ecology or the growth of cities. The speakers should then be prepared to answer questions.

At the end of the debate/discussion, have the students write a paragraph suggesting at least one way that we can have growth of cities and still preserve our ecology.

A Change in Time

Objectives: To expose students to how a community can change slowly over time, taking away habitats from other living creatures and to write a creative story as a class

Materials: book *Window* by Jeannie Baker, index cards, pencils, crayons, shoe box, one copy of directions (page 198) for each student

Directions: Explain to students that you are going to read a wordless book together. As you "read," ask students to pay attention to the changes that take place in the story.

continued on page 198

A Change in Time continued

Ask them to think about why and how these changes take place. Also ask students to think about the amount of time that passes with each change. After discussing the story in length, tell students that they are going to write words to the story. Begin by choosing a name for the character. Next, explain to students that they will work with a partner to write text for two pages of the story in sequence. Explain the directions below to students and give each student a copy of them as some students may not get to write on the same day that the activity is introduced. When all students have completed their portion of the book, read it again, this time reading the text your students created!

Directions

1. You will work with a partner.
2. Read the whole book again with your partner.
3. Before you write anything, read what your classmates have written on the pages before yours. Your part of the story must match, or fit, with what your classmates have already written.
4. Brainstorm ideas with your partner. Write your ideas on scrap paper.
5. Revise and edit your work.
6. Write a final copy on an index card. On the back of the card, write the page numbers that you wrote text for and write down your names.
7. Place your card in the shoe box.

Extension: Ask students to write their own version of a window story. Ask students to look out a window in your school. Have them imagine that a change is going to take place. (The change they choose could be either an improvement or deterioration of the natural environment.) Brainstorm some possible changes that could take place, good and/or bad, and the causes of the change. Ask students to write a four-page book showing the change over time—perhaps over the length of the four seasons. Once the students are ready to make a final copy, direct them to draw a window around the perimeter of their construction paper. They can then illustrate the change inside the window and write the text underneath it. Have them create a cover and staple it all together.

Extra! Extra! Environmental Events

Objective: To create a scrapbook or bulletin board of articles, ads, labels and other materials relating to the environment

Materials: a scrapbook or bulletin board, news articles, tacks, tape or glue

Directions: Dedicate a bulletin board or even a door to ecological stories in the news. Instruct your students to be on the lookout daily for any articles, ads, labels, cartoons or headlines concerning the environment. Ask them to cut out the items and bring them into school. If enough materials are available, have students further categorize the items before hanging them. For example, all articles concerning living things might go in one area, news regarding environmental issues in another, and print about specific environments in yet another area.

Environment Logs

Objective: To increase students' awareness of their environment

Materials: lined writing paper, construction paper, pencils, stapler, crayons/markers

Directions: Explain to the students that an environment includes all things that affect an organism (a living thing). To heighten students' awareness of their environment, have them keep an environment log for two weeks. Give each student approximately 14 sheets of lined writing paper. Then, have them fold a 12" x 18" sheet of construction paper in half and place the lined paper in between the folded paper. Students then staple along the fold to secure the paper and to create a "book." With the fold on the left, have the students color and decorate the cover for their environment logs. You might have your students make two entries per day, one in the school setting and one at home. In their entries, have the students describe what they see, smell and hear in their environment and how it makes them feel. Provide an opportunity for the students to also sit on the playground for an entry.

As a culminating activity, have the students write a composition about their ideal environment. Encourage the students to read their environment log entries as they imagine the environment that they would like to live in. Suggest that students focus on their senses when writing including such phrases as: "My ideal environment sounds like _____, looks like _____," etc.

Population Posters

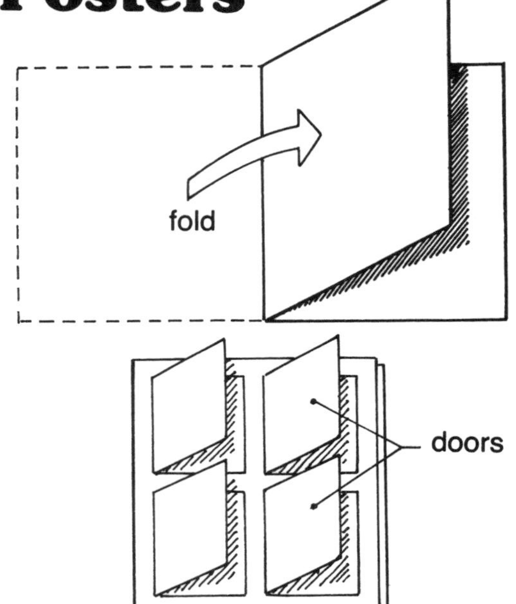

Objective: To become familiar with ecological terms that address species' populations

Materials: a piece of large construction paper or poster paper for each student

Directions: Students should be familiar with vocabulary that addresses species' populations (i.e. endangered vs. threatened, etc.). After introducing the words listed in the box below and their meanings, inform students that they will create a "door poster" to provide an example of each. Instruct students to fold their paper in half the long way and then divide it into four equal sections. Students should then cut the sections marked to create four doors.

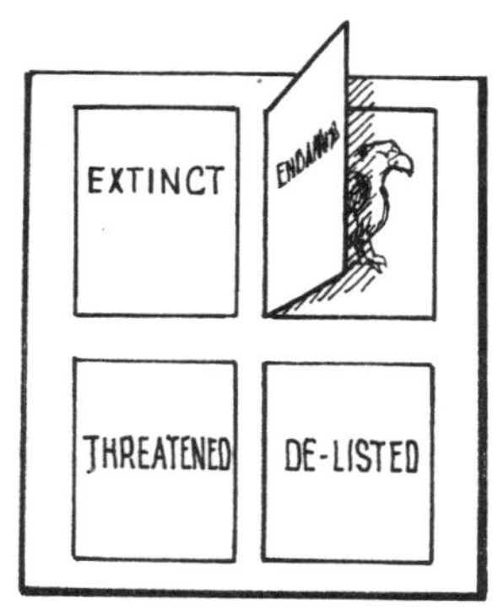

Direct students to write one of the four words listed in the box on each "door." Next, students should draw or write about a species on the inside of each door that is exemplary of the word on the outside. For example, the California condor is endangered. A student may want to write about or draw the condor underneath the door labeled "endangered." Students continue in this fashion for the three remaining doors.

Extension: Let students use their posters to play a guessing game. To play, a student supplies clues about the species behind one of the doors he/she created. After each clue, one student is called upon to guess the species. The student to identify the correct species then takes a turn, and the process is repeated.

Terms

extinct—the species no longer exists

endangered—species is in immediate danger of extinction

threatened—species with low or declining populations; species that are likely to become endangered if they are not protected

de-listed—the species' population has increased and is continuing to increase; it is no longer threatened or endangered

Endangered—Why?

Objective: To become aware of why various species are endangered

Materials: a copy of the worksheet below for each student

Directions: Many students have the misconception that pollution is the only cause for decreased animal populations. Plants and animals are disappearing at a rapid rate! After discussing possible causes of extinction, give each student a copy of the worksheet below. Divide your students into cooperative groups and ask them to research endangered or threatened animals to fit in each category. Emphasize to students that these are not the only reasons for the endangerment of species. See if they can come up with other causes and examples. Share the information on a wall chart.

Endangered—Why?

Name ____________________

DECREASED POPULATION OF PLANTS AND ANIMALS

Causes	Species
POLLUTION	
DESTRUCTION OF HABITAT	
DECREASED FOOD SUPPLY	
INSECTICIDES HARMING OFFSPRING	
POACHING	

Biome Dioramas

Objective: To create a representation of a particular ecological community

Materials: shoe box, construction paper, paint, paintbrushes, markers, scissors, various "creative" art supplies

Directions: Have students build shoe box dioramas to depict the variety of plant and animal populations that inhabit each specific ecological community. Begin by introducing the students to the word biome. A biome is a large land community with a particular climate and specific plants and animals.

Desert Biome—extremely dry

Tropical Biome—having much rainfall and warm temperatures; near equator

Tundra Biome—having permanently frozen subsoil and little vegetation; near North Pole

Temperate Deciduous Forest Biome—Having definite seasons and wet and dry periods; Central and Eastern U.S.

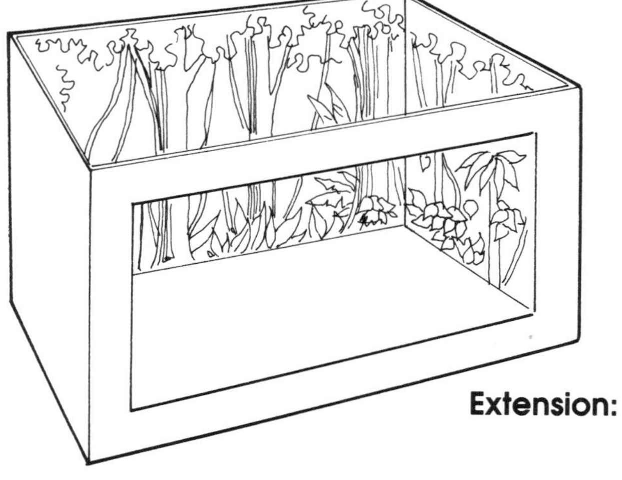

Assign each student a biome to research. Have the students gather information about the typical vegetation and the typical wildlife that inhabit each region. Ask them to also include general temperatures for the area and annual precipitation amounts. Then, allow students to be creative in representing the biome facts in their dioramas. Provide as many different materials as possible and encourage students to develop their own ideas as they "make a tree" or "build a coniferous forest."

Extension: Challenge the students to develop a food web for their biome from their vegetation and wildlife lists.

A Biome Vacation

Objective: To create a trip guide for a vacation to a selected ecological biome

Materials: reference materials, maps, travel brochures, lined writing paper, construction paper, markers

Directions: This is a great activity to use to extend a study of biomes. When the students are familiar with the various ecological regions, tell them to pretend that they are going on vacation to visit a biome. Have each student select a destination. Encourage the students to specify the biome as well as the exact location. By using a world atlas, the students may also determine the number of miles to be traveled from home and the mode of transportation needed to get there. Teach the students how to read a time zone map and to indicate any time changes they will experience as they travel to their biome destination. If travel brochures are available, have the students research the cost of any travel tickets that may be needed.

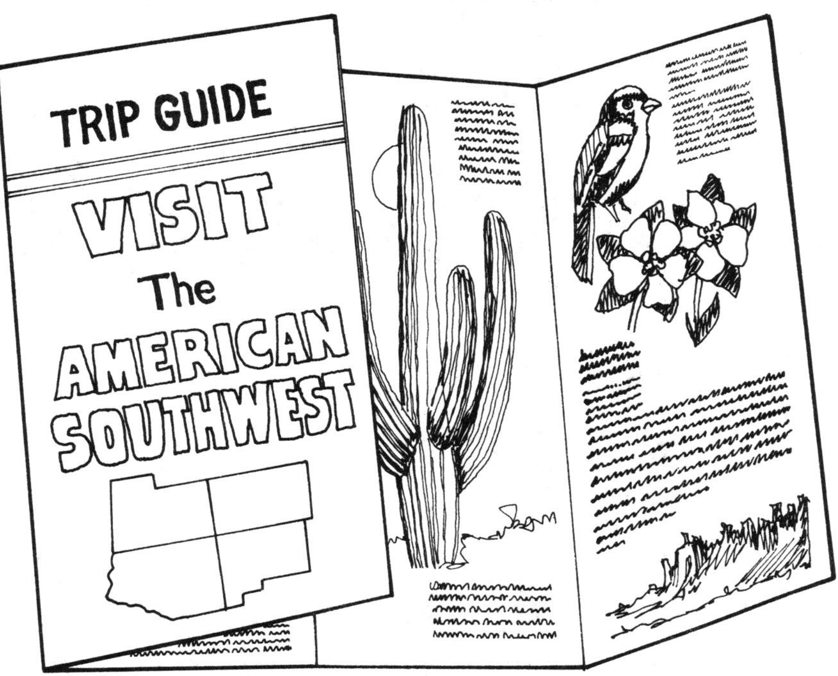

Have the students also address the following: the living accommodations, clothing needed, points of interests in the area, amount of money needed.

Have the students create a trip guide in which they organize their ideas. Students should discuss the various important planning items in short, descriptive paragraphs. Remind students to keep the climate, physical features, vegetation and animal life in mind as they plan their vacations.

Extension: Have the students design a travel poster of the biome they would like to visit to go along with their trip guide.

Food Webs

Objective: To illustrate a food web for a particular ecosystem or biome

Materials: index cards, yarn, assorted colors of construction paper (including plenty of "Earth" colors), scissors, glue, books containing pictures of a biome of your choice, masking tape

Directions: Discuss what a biome is (a community of plants and animals that live in a large geographical area having a similar climate). Choose a particular biome to study. If possible, gather books that include pictures of the biome that you have chosen. Have students create a list of as many living things in the biome as they can. (Try to list as many different living things as there are students in your classroom.) When the list is completed, classify each item on the list as a plant, insect, reptile, etc.

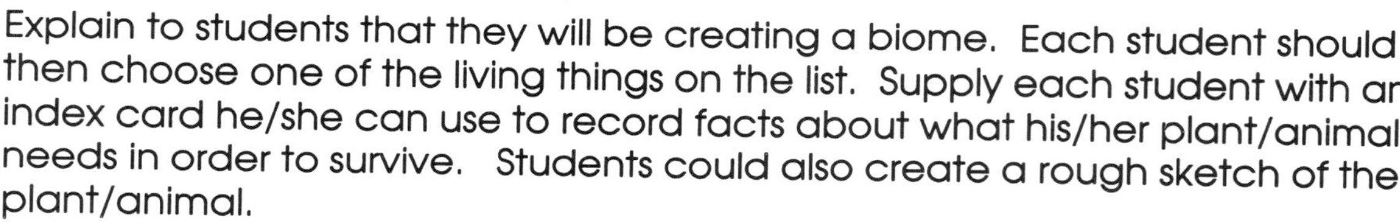

Explain to students that they will be creating a biome. Each student should then choose one of the living things on the list. Supply each student with an index card he/she can use to record facts about what his/her plant/animal needs in order to survive. Students could also create a rough sketch of the plant/animal.

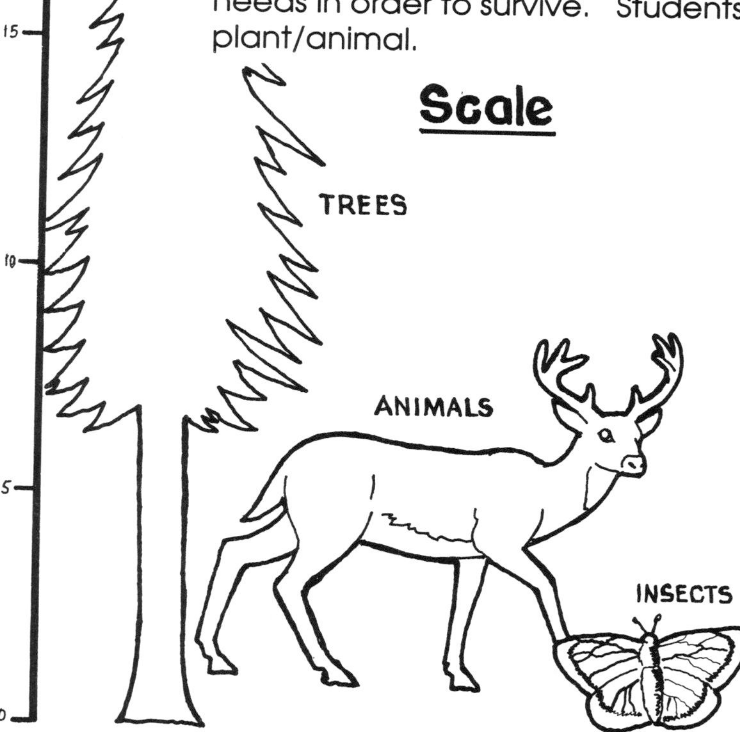

Next, direct students to create their animal or plant using construction paper. Before the students begin, create an informal scale students should follow when creating their plant/animal. (For example, insects should be no larger than two inches in height, small mammals should be approximately eight inches in height, trees should be approximately twenty inches in height, etc.) You or a student who finishes his/her work quickly should create a large sun. When all the animals/plants have been created, gather students together near a bulletin board or empty wall space. You are now ready to create the web!

continued on page 205

Food Webs continued

To create the web, you will need yarn, scissors and tape at your side. Distribute the animals/ plants the students created so that each student is holding his/her own. Begin by taping the sun to the wall in the highest spot possible. Ask students which living things in the biome get their energy directly from the sun. (plants) All students who created a plant should then come up to the board or wall to hang them up.

Next, taking the ball of yarn, run the yarn from the sun to one plant and cut it. Fasten the yarn in place with tape hiding the ends behind the pictures. Repeat this procedure for each plant. All the students who have created an animal that uses the plants for food/shelter come up next. Hang these animals up in the appropriate spot. Use the yarn to show the relationship between the plants and animals. Last, ask students who are holding an animal who eats another animal already on the board to come up. Tape these animals up and string the yarn from these new animals to the ones they eat. When all the living creatures have been placed, discuss what interdependency is and ask students for examples of it in this biome.

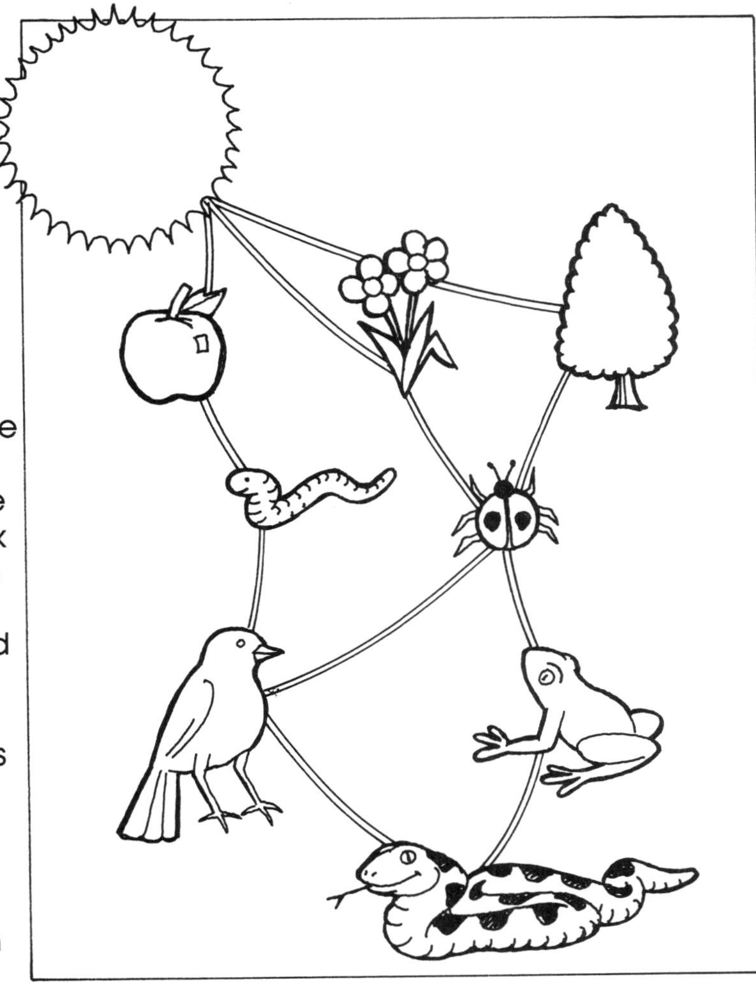

Extension: Write the word *extinct* on several index cards. With students gathered around your web, ask them how many animals or plants they feel could become extinct before the entire biome could not possibly exist. Cover one of the animals or plants with the extinct sign. Discuss the effect this would have on the rest of the biome. Ask students which populations would increase or decrease. Cover a second plant or animal and repeat the procedure. Continue the process until the students feel the biome could not exist.

Rainforest Diorama/Research Report

Objective: To learn about the inhabitants of the rainforest

Materials: shoe box or similar type of box, various materials to use to create individual dioramas (i.e. paint, paintbrushes, crayons, markers, construction paper, scissors, glue, etc.)

Directions: Have each student select one animal, bird or insect that lives in the rainforest. This will be his/her selection for further research and study. Have the students work with the following outline.

A. **Questions to Research and Answer**

1. Habitat
   a. In what part of the rainforest does your animal live?
   b. Describe its environment. How does it use the environment for survival?
2. Food
   a. What does it eat?
   b. How does it get its food?
   c. Is it in danger of being eaten?
3. Social behavior
   a. How does it protect itself?
   b. Does it attack other animals?
   c. How does it protect its young?
   d. Does it move in groups?
   e. How does it care for its young?

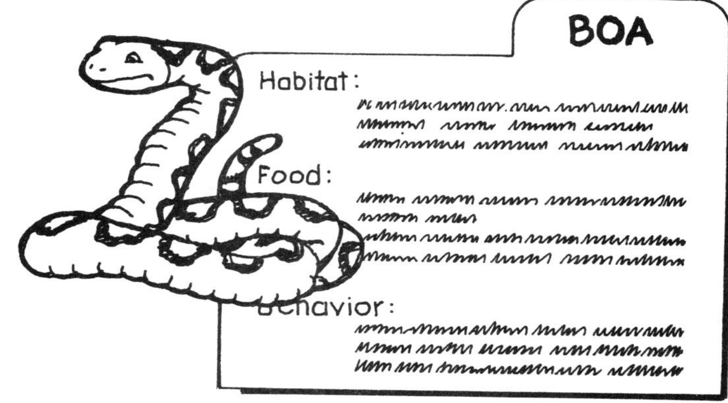

B. **Diorama**

1. Using a shoe box or something similar, create a rainforest background. The bottom of the box can be painted brown. Trees can be created from construction paper, clay or actual twigs of trees.
2. Place your animal selection where it would normally be in the rainforest. (For example, an eagle would be on top of the canopy; a sloth would be hanging from a branch of the tree.)

C. **Bibliography**

1. List the sources of your information
   a. Books—Title and author
   b. Magazines—Name of magazine, name of article, page number
   c. Other sources

Rainforest Mural

Objective: To create a classroom bulletin board displaying the rainforest ecosystem

Materials: butcher paper, paint, paintbrushes, construction paper, scissors, reference materials on rainforests, index cards, brown paper bags, tissue paper

Directions: Creating a mural can be a great theme motivator. The end result also provides a colorful backdrop upon which research and theme-related work can be displayed. To reproduce the layers of the rainforest on a bulletin board, you must begin by gathering an abundance of reference materials, especially those with colorful photographs of the rainforest. Try to also collect materials describing the various plant and animal species that are indigenous to each layer of the rainforest. Allow time for the students to browse through the reference materials. Encourage them to take special note of the plant and animal life at each layer.

Once students have an idea of the type of vegetation that grows in each area, they are ready to begin creating their mural. First, cover an entire bulletin board with butcher paper. Then, extend this paper to the floor so that the paper covers the wall to the height of approximately 6'. At this point, you might want to enlist your school's art teacher to help you and the students sketch the rainforest layers. In general, you will need several very tall trees extending above the mural paper to create the top layer, a thick covering of treetops to create the canopy, dark tree trunks, lush ferns and vines to make the understory, and moist, dark brown soil and moss to fill the forest floor.

Students can use construction paper to extend the tallest treetops high above the canopy. This will really set them apart from the other layers. When the sections are sketched out, put the painters to work. Be sure students consult the reference materials so that the colors are as realistic as possible.

continued on page 208

Rainforest Mural continued

Keep everyone busy during the mural production phase by having those not painting the backdrop draw specific plant and animal life. Encourage the students to make their sketches to fit the scale of the mural. Then, have each student color, paint and cut out a chosen rainforest plant or animal.

Staple all the different species in their appropriate layer of the rainforest. A sloth, for example, would likely be found hanging upside-down from a tree in the canopy while a tapir would likely be found foraging on the forest floor. Provide each student with a large index card on which to write a paragraph about his/her species. Then, mount these cards around the side borders of the mural and connect them with yarn.

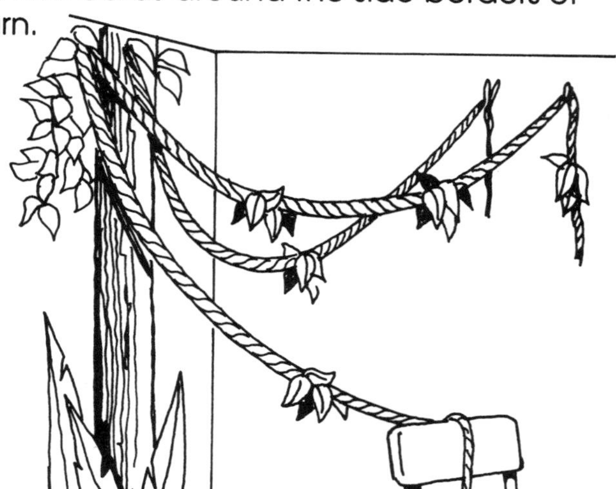

To add realism to your backdrop, create and hang vines from the mural and extending out into the classroom. Make the vines from thick twine or twisted pieces of brown paper bags. Cut out and glue leaves along the paper. Attach small strips of tissue paper as well. Staple the ends together to create a long vine. Hang these from the mural down to the students' desks.

Researching the Rainforest

Below is a collection of books that may help your students research the rainforest.

Baker, L. (1990). *Life in the Rainforests.* New York: Scholastic.

Caduto, M. (1988). *Keepers of the Earth.* Golden, CO: Fulcrum.

Cherry, L. (1990). *The Great Kapok Tree.* San Diego, CA: Harcourt Brace Jovanovich.

Dorros, A. (1990). *Rain Forest Secrets.* New York: Scholastic.

Dudley, W. (1990). *The Environment—Distinguishing Between Fact and Opinion.* San Diego, CA: Greenhaven Press.

Flackman, M. (1990). *And Then There Was One.* Boston, MA: Little, Brown.

Peet, B. (1970). *The Wump World.* Boston, MA: Houghton Mifflin.

Silver, D. (1993). *Why Save the Rainforest?* New York: Messner.

continued on page 209

Researching the Rainforest continued

For more information, have your students write to the addresses below. Let them share their information with the class.

Rainforest Action Network
450 Sansome St. Suite 700
San Francisco, CA 94111

Defenders of Wildlife
1244 19th Street NW
Washington, DC 20036

Rainforest Alliance
270 Lafayette Street Suite 512
New York, NY 10012

Rainforest Census

Objective: To understand how much life there is in the rainforest

Materials: pieces of yarn approximately 3 feet long, note pad, pencil

Directions: About half of the world's species of plants and animals reside in our rainforests. To help your students recognize just how many reside in the rainforest, give each student a three-foot piece of yarn. Have the students tie the ends together to form a circle. Then, move outside to the schoolyard. Tell the students to find a space of their own and to spread out their circles on the ground. Next, have them sit just outside the area and look carefully for as many different types of plants and animals that reside within their loops. Have them count and record their observations on a small note pad. Allow the students five or ten minutes to note the plants and animals. Then, gather the class together and have the students share their results. Finally, tell them that the same amount of space in a rainforest would have ten times as many kinds of plants and animals and some of them have not even been discovered yet.

Extension: Send the length of string home with the students and have them conduct the experiment in their own back yards.

Create a Rainforest in Your Classroom

Objective: To reinforce learning about a rainforest environment

Materials: corrugated paper, paper towel and toilet paper tubes, paint, paintbrushes, markers, tape, string, green construction paper, scissors, green tissue or crêpe paper, patterns on pages 212-213

Directions: Use the corrugated paper to form tree trunks by shaping it into a cylinder and taping the overlapping ends. Make tree trunks of varying heights and widths. The very high ones will form the upper canopy of the rainforest. Make several short ones to be the tree stumps at the edge of your rainforest to represent trees that have been cut down.

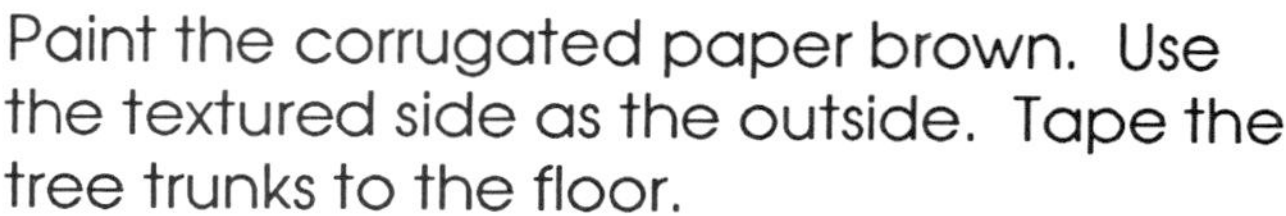

Paint the corrugated paper brown. Use the textured side as the outside. Tape the tree trunks to the floor.

Attach branches to the tree trunks using corrugated paper or construction paper to form the branches. Staple them to the tree trunk and attach them to the ceiling using string. You could also use actual twigs for branches. Have the students draw and cut out leaves using green construction paper. Attach the leaves to the branches. Make a thick top layer of leaves to form the upper canopy.

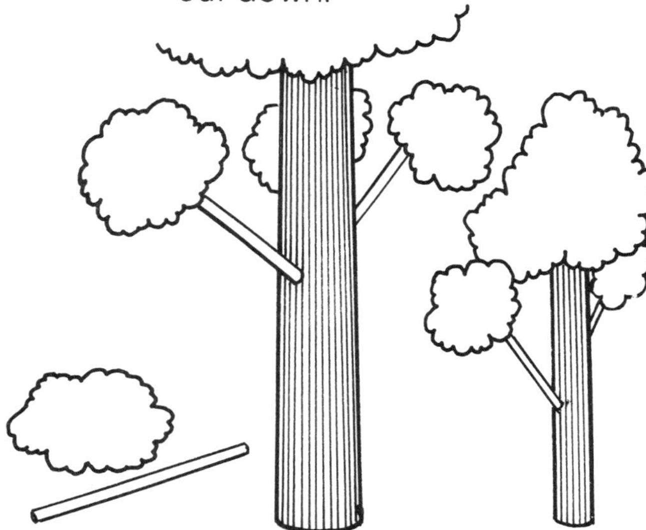

To create vines and lianas, cut the paper tubes in a spiral fashion. Paint some green and some brown and attach them to the branches. They should be placed below the canopy in the understory.

Cut green tissue or crêpe paper into strips and crumple it to create the air plants. Drape them over the branches.

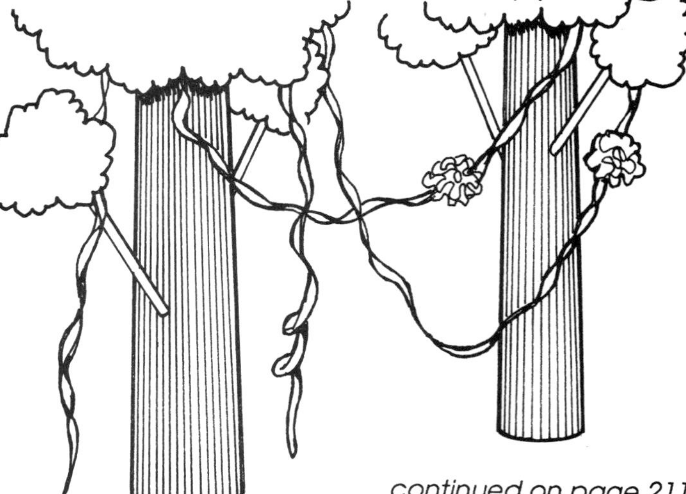

continued on page 211

Create a Rainforest...continued

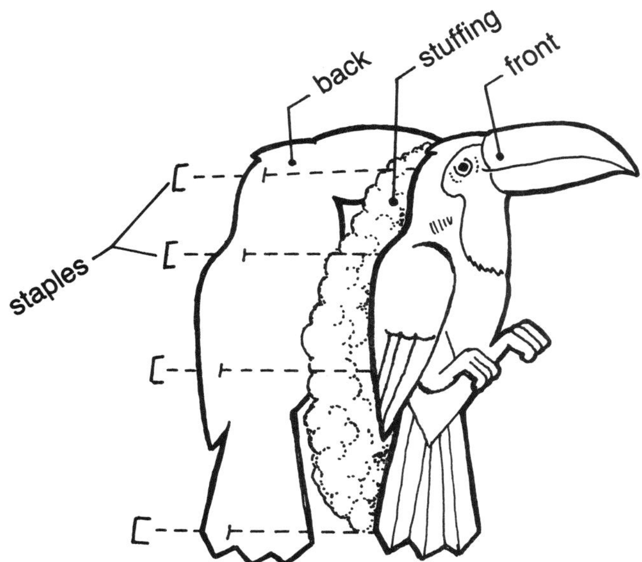

The students may create various kinds of ferns, palms and other plants to add to the rainforest.

To create the wildlife in the rainforest, use the patterns on pages 212-213. Use two patterns for each bird/insect/animal, etc. Have the students research to get the proper coloring for each of the types of wildlife. When both patterns are completed, staple them together leaving an opening at one end. Stuff the animal, insect and/or bird with tissues or cotton batting and then staple it closed. This will create a three-dimensional effect.

Place the animals, birds and insects in the appropriate places. Either use string to place them or you can use staples and/or tape. Bats, gibbons, monkeys, squirrels and parrots live in the upper and lower canopies. Antelope, deer, hogs, tapirs and rodents roam the forest floor.

Encourage the students to bring appropriate stuffed animals to school to place in the rainforest.

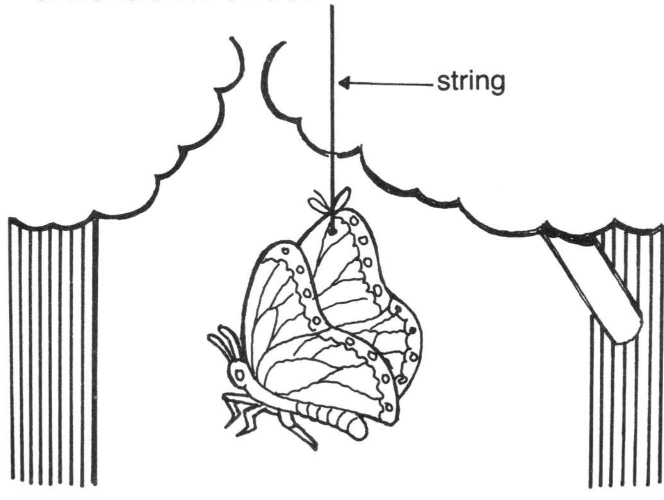

Create a river using either aluminum foil or paper painted a blue-green color.

Flowers, fruits, nuts and other edible plants can also be added.

At all times during the creation of your rainforest, the students should be doing the proper research to discover what kinds of plant and animal life exist in the rainforest. Where do they live? What do they look like? How do they blend into the environment?

The part of the rainforest that has stumps or tree trunks left will probably not have much vegetation or animal life.

Rainforest Animal Patterns

Rainforest Animal Patterns

"Voices of the Rainforest"

A Play

This play has been designed to involve your students in reading, writing and researching about the people and creatures living in the rainforest and the issues that surround them. The play is a framework, allowing students to take ownership of the production. For example, the cast of characters is flexible. Some of them may vary according to student interest. The characters' lines are flexible as well, and in some cases, only suggestions are given. (As the play progresses, explanations are provided.)

CAST OF CHARACTERS: narrators
- tapir
- mother tapir
- macaw
- blue morpho butterflies (several)
- boa constrictor
- arrow-poison frog
- driver ant
- sloth
- anteater
- local farmers
- environmental researchers (several)
- loggers (several)

Voices of the Rainforest
Presented by
Mrs. Simmons
3rd Grade Class

Scenery: See "Create a Rainforest in Your Classroom" (page 210).

Costumes: These can be simple. For example, students portraying the blue morpho butterflies can wear blue clothing and blue wings. If desired, summon the help of your art teacher to renovate baseball caps into headpieces to represent each character.

SCENE 1

Setting: the rainforest, early morning

Characters: The characters in this scene represent animals from each of the layers of the rainforest. In order to depict this, you may want to place the student who is playing the role of the animal (sloth) from the understory on a chair. Then, hide the chair with scenery. (Tree trunks could be fastened to chairs.) Short ladders could be used as well.

continued on page 215

"Voices of the Rainforest" continued

NARRATOR: Have students research the rainforest to create an introduction of the play. Some suggested ideas include:

- climate of the rainforest
- description of the layers of the rainforest
- where rainforests are found
- examples of some of the animals/insects that live in a rainforest, particularly the ones that are included in the play (At the performance of the play, characters in the play could come out on stage as the narrators speak about their habits and lifestyle.)
- the percentage of the Earth's surface that is covered by the rainforest
- an approximate number of species, or the percentage of species living in the rainforest

The narrator's introduction of the play could be enhanced by slides, use of the overhead projector, and/or as mentioned earlier, by placing the spotlight on the student portraying the animals/insects as the narrator tells about them.

The narrator could end the introduction and focus the audience with the following statement:

Today, we're going to take you to a rainforest. There seems to be a problem. Let's listen in!

(The tapir and the mother tapir are stage front. The driver ant is stage left. The blue morpho butterflies are socializing quietly stage right. The sloth should be positioned in the understory along with the arrow-poison frog. The boa constrictor should be positioned center stage behind and between the tapirs. The anteater is looking for food downstage, stage left.)

TAPIR: **Gee, mom! It seems brighter today down here!**

MOTHER: **Yes my son (daughter), you must remain by my side...I can hear the sound again today.**

DRIVER ANT: **I have heard 36 fall today!**

BUTTERFLIES: (fluttering about in confusion, speaking almost simultaneously) **What? When? How? How many? Why?**

BOA: (in a strong voice) **Settle down you fluttering flakes!** (loudly) **Yesterday it was 82. That's right! 82 big ones!** (becoming annoyed) **28 Kapoks...51 rubber trees...and 3 banana trees. All down!**

continued on page 216

"Voices of the Rainforest" continued

SLOTH: (just waking up from a doze, speaking slowly, elongating words) **Did somebody say down? I just got up here.**

(Butterflies giggle.)

(The macaw enters stage right, as if it were swooping down from the canopy. All the animals from the forest floor quickly gather around the macaw in anticipation of his news.)

MACAW: (in a grave voice) **It has been five days since our last meeting. I have sad news. Wherever the humans are, the trees fall. The family of macaws living only three rubber trees away have lost their home. The babies are crying.**

ANTEATER: **What are we going to do?**

FROG: (from the understory) **Who will help us?**

TAPIR: **What are we going to do?**

SLOTH: (again, just awakening) **Are we going to do something? If you're planning a party down there, better give me a few weeks' notice. I want to be there on time.** (He continues his nap.)

BUTTERFLIES: (simultaneously) **This sounds serious. Oh, the poor macaws! How can it be? What shall we do?**

MOTHER: **How can we stop this?**

BOA: (firmly) **We must stop this.**

End Scene 1. Curtain closes.

SCENE TWO

At this time, the narrators return to the stage. If desired, the narrators or animal characters can supply more information about what the destruction of the rainforest means to the population living there.

NARRATOR: **As the animals discuss how to help the family of macaws and how to stop the destruction, they receive a surprise.**

(All the local animals are center stage in a circle when a group of local farmers enters stage left. All the animals exit rapidly stage right, excluding the sloth who is snoozing.)

FARMER 1: **This looks like a fine piece of land!**

FARMER 2: **Yes! The land is flat.**

FARMER 3: **We could plant a crop here.**

FARMER 4: **Let's get started!**

FARMER 1: **What are we waiting for!**

FARMER 2: **OK!**

continued on page 217

"Voices of the Rainforest" continued

(The farmers move downstage to prepare to clear the land as the narrator(s) speaks.)

NARRATOR: At this point, the narrator could supply the audience with facts about the local farmer and why these farmers are clearing their land.

(A group of environmental researchers enter stage left. They are pondering, rubbing their chins, marking data on clipboards, etc. They are unaware of the farmers. The researchers move to center stage. The farmers are unaware of the researchers and continue to prepare for tree removal.)

RESEARCHER 1: **My...oh my.** (looking all about)

RESEARCHER 2: **I have spotted 50 less macaws than my last visit.**

RESEARCHER 1: **My...oh my.**

RESEARCHER 3: **The density of the forest has decreased.**

RESEARCHER 1: **My...oh my.**

SLOTH: (Stretching and yawning) **My...oh my. Hey guys, you should have told me it was a costume party. Tapir? Is that you?** (He continues his nap.)

(The researchers exit stage right).

NARRATOR: **Many groups of people have an interest in the rainforest. So far, you have met two—the local farmers and researchers. You are about to meet another.**

(As the narrator speaks, the farmers move center stage.)

(Loggers enter noisily and lightheartedly stage right. They head directly for the area where the local farmers are working.)

LOGGER 1: **HEY, what are you folks doing here?**

(The local farmers stop working.)

FARMER 1: **We are creating homes and a place to grow food for our families.**

LOGGER 2: **You can't do that!**

LOGGER 3: **We just bought this area. It belongs to us!**

LOGGER 4: **We're from the Jiffy Furniture Company.**

LOGGER 3: (rubbing the tree bark) **This tree will make a fine entertainment center!**

FARMER 1: **But we need this land! Our families are depending on us!**

LOGGER 2: **Tell that to our boss!**

(At this point, the farmers and loggers begin to argue.)

continued on page 218

"Voices of the Rainforest" continued

SLOTH: **Hey! What's all the racket?** (All on stage freeze.) **I'm trying to get some rest. I've had a busy day. I deserve some rest. Can't you solve this peacefully?** (The sloth continues his nap.)

End Scene 2. The curtain closes.

SCENE THREE

NARRATOR: **The humans decide to take the sloth's advice. They hold a summit. All are invited, the animals, the local farmers, the environmental researchers and the loggers from Jiffy Furniture. And guess who's running the meeting? You guessed it! The sloth!**

The rainforest is being used by people in many ways. After this next scene, we are going to ask you to make a decision. What do you think is the best solution?

In order to represent the interest of each of the four groups—the animals, the local farmers, the environmental researchers, and the loggers—the students in our class have written the speaking parts in this next scene. What should be done with the rainforest? Listen carefully!

(The stage is set as an auditorium, with all chairs facing the audience. At least one representative from each of the three groups is present. The stage is decorated with a flag of the rainforest (which your students can design). All are seated, awaiting the arrival of the mediator. A chair is placed stage left for the mediator. All are getting impatient awaiting his arrival, particularly the boa.)

(The sloth enters stage right, moving very slowly.)

SLOTH: **I'm sorry. I know I'm late. I was still digesting last week's meal. I told you I needed more notice.**

LOGGER 4: **We can't wait that long!**

MACAW: **It's costing lives. Wake up sloth.**

SLOTH: **Alright, alright, I'm here.** (The sloth finally makes it to the empty chair.) **Who would like to begin?**

At this point, students should read persuasive narratives they have written representing a rainforest group. (See page 219.) The narratives should include information about how each group is utilizing the rainforest and why. Between narratives, the sloth could thank the representative and introduce the next rainforest representative. When the last representative has spoken, the sloth will speak. (See "The Persuasive Narrative: A Framework" on page 219. Give one to each group.)

continued on page 219

"Voices of the Rainforest" continued

SLOTH: Now that all have shared their views, we need to think about a solution. Does anyone have any good ideas at this time? (no response) Good, because I'm all tuckered out. We will meet again. In order to show our good intentions, let's end our meeting with the rainforest summit chant:

ALL: In the interest of the people, or in the interests of the rainforest? Can there be a balance? We must try. We must try.

At the conclusion of the summit, the narrator should pose the problem to the audience and supply the directions as to how the audience should respond to your students. (You may want to use a formal ballot and set up a mailbox where students can send their responses.)

End of Scene Three. Curtain closes.

After the curtain closes, have the entire cast or a selection of students come forward to read the poem on page 220.

Create a newsletter sharing some of the facts supplied during the play. Also include the results of the audience survey!

The Persuasive Narrative: A Framework

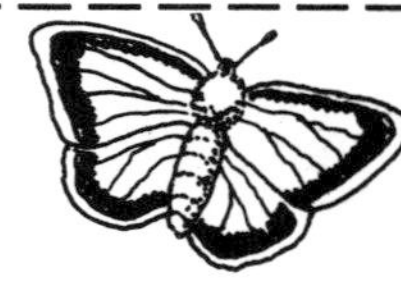

We feel that the rainforest should be used for ______________________________.

We need the rainforest! Without (the land), (trees), etc. we would __________

____ because

____.

My family depends on ____.

Furthermore, ____.

The rainforest is most important to us because _____________________________

____.

continued on page 220

"Voices of the Rainforest" continued

After the curtain closes, have the entire cast or a selection of students come forward to read the following poem:

The eagle looked down
from his perch on high.
"Where are the trees?"
he said with a sigh.
"The canopy's thinner,
In some spots, it's bare.
It's really so sad.
Doesn't anyone care?
We'll have no place to live,
no food to eat,
No fruits, no vegetables,
not even meat."

The loggers entered
the rainforest green.
There were more trees than
they ever had seen.
The trees were so dense,
so strong and so good.
"What wonderful furniture
they'll make out of wood.
The pulp will be paper
for newspapers, books
For children, adults,
for recipes for cooks."

The researchers were roaming
the forest floor,
Hunting berries and plants
never seen before.
They're researching plants
for diseases to cure.
"We're bound to find something,
that's very sure.
We've found cures before.
We know we'll find more.
There's so much to use on the
forest floor."

The farmers arrived
with their cows in tow.
Looking for more lands.
"We've seeds to sow.
The land is so fertile,
a good place to farm.
Surely we won't do any harm."

The butterflies, bees
and birds galore.
Go from understory
to the floor.
The monkeys, the sloths,
other animals as well,
All have the same story to tell.
"The rainforest is going,
We're losing our home.
Soon we'll have
no more forest to roam."

What is the answer?
How do we share?
All different species.
Have a different care.

Can we preserve the rainforest
And still have wood?
Can researchers continue
to do more good?
Can the animals continue
to live in their places
It's all up to us to
cover all bases.

Do we care?
You bet we do!
It's up to me
And it's up to you!
We'll all do our part
to serve all needs,
And we'll spare the rainforest
from many bad deeds.

Healthy Mind, Healthy Body

This chapter encompasses the areas of physical health, mental health and the social aspects of well-being. These areas are interrelated in such a way as to support the goal of developing in each student a healthy mind and a healthy body.

Students who have a positive attitude about themselves and about school, who relate well to both peers and adults, who are able to create viable solutions to social problems, who can accept and handle their emotions, and who are physically fit are probably also motivated to learn.

Keeping the above concepts in mind, the activities in this chapter have been designed to promote self-esteem as well as to encourage decision-making and positive relationships with fellow students. In addition, there are activities designed to make students aware of physical fitness (i.e. nutrition, growth, body systems and personal safety).

Keep in mind that a healthy mind and body are both part of a happy human being.

Look Who's in the Spotlight!

Objective: To increase student awareness of their classmates

Materials: a small bulletin board

Directions: Every week, pick one student in your class to be in the "Spotlight." Select a special bulletin board in your class to dedicate to this student. Allow this student to design the bulletin board to include several photos from his/her earliest days to present. The student can include pictures of himself/herself with other family members, special pets, on special occasions or on trips.

Encourage students to also bring in a special treasure. This might include a collection, a favorite book, a game or a hobby. On a special day of the week, reserve time for the student in the spotlight to share and discuss the photos he/she brought in and his/her "treasure". Encourage the rest of the class to ask questions such as:

How many brothers and sisters do you have?
What was your favorite vacation?
How do you spend your free time?
What was your funniest moment? proudest?

When each student has completed his/her presentation, have the rest of the students write a friendly letter to that person. Remarks might include an area of interest that they might have in common with the student in the spotlight or just a positive comment to make that person feel good. This activity helps the students get to know one another and also provides an opportunity for each student to share some personal experiences.

Suggestion: Provide mailboxes for the students in your classroom. Students will enjoy delivering and picking up their "mail."

Celebrate Friendship Month

Below and on page 224 are some great ideas to use for a Celebrate Friendship Month. The following objectives apply to all of the activities dedicated to this celebration:

Objectives: To encourage self-esteem in students and friendship between classmates; to help students become aware of their strengths; to help students develop a positive attitude about themselves.

Budding Friendship

Materials: brown and green mural paper, school-wide participation, one 8 1/2" x 11" sheet of white construction paper per participating class, string

Directions: To bring the students in your building together, initiate a school-wide campaign for friendliness. Ask each classroom teacher to talk about friends and the characteristics that make a person a friend. Include ideas such as kindness, support, respect, consideration, concern, love, etc. Encourage students to share stories about friends who show these qualities. From the discussion, have each class at every grade level submit two suggestions for friendly behavior. Have each class write its ideas on construction paper and colorfully decorate the poster. If morning announcements are made in your building, read several of the class' suggestions for being a good friend. Be sure to give credit to the authors.

To remind students of the various "be a good friend" suggestions, create a large tree out of mural paper and hang it in a central location of the building. Label it "Our Friendship Tree." After the ideas are shared, post the creative posters on the tree for the students to read as they pass through the hall during the school day. Friendly actions are sure to take place.

Listen to This!

Materials: blank paper, pencils, tape

Directions: Tape a blank sheet of paper to each student's back. Instruct students to mingle with each other and write a positive comment about the person they meet on that person's sheet. Be sure to stress to the students that the comments should be something good about that person. When all the students have finished, sit down in a circle and let each student read his/her own list of positive attributes. This is a great way to demonstrate the power of a compliment to increase one's self esteem.

Friends Are...

Materials: one copy of the form below per student, pencils

Directions: Encourage your students to think about what a friend is. After they have brainstormed a list of adjectives, give each of them a copy of the Friends poem form below to complete to create a poem about friends.

Friends

Friends

Friends

Friends

____________________ friends,

____________________ friends,

____________, ____________ ,

____________________ friends,

____________, ____________ ,

____________________ friends.

Those are just a few.

____________________ friends,

____________________ friends,

____________, ____________ ,

____________________ friends,

____________, ____________ ,

____________________ friends

____________________friends, too.

____________________ friends

____________________ friends

Don't forget____________________ friends.

Last of all, best of all, I like friends.

Let's Be Positive!

Objective: To help students look for the "good" or positive attributes in themselves and their classmates

Materials: an 8½" x 11" sheet of paper for each student with his/her name on it, one 9" x 12" sheet of paper per student, crayons/markers, one copy of the letter to parents (page 227) per student

Directions: Discuss with the class how each student would describe himself/herself. The obvious answers would usually include height, hair coloring and length, eye color and similar physical attributes.

Explain to the class that this only describes what each student looks like. Ask if there are other ways to describe someone. Ask students their likes and dislikes. Ask students how they interact with other people. Are they helpful, kind, friendly, considerate, understanding, sympathetic, trustworthy, sincere, honest, curious, inquisitive, and so on.

Provide students with examples of giving descriptions using famous people or fictitious characters. For example, Christopher Columbus was probably inquisitive and curious. Abraham Lincoln was honest and trustworthy. Cinderella was kind and considerate. Johnny Appleseed was helpful and friendly. Let students describe someone. Then, encourage expansion of the descriptions. (For example: John is trustworthy. If I tell him a secret, he won't tell anyone. Mary is understanding and sympathetic. If someone has a problem, she will never laugh at them. Fred is inquisitive. He always asks good questions about things. Jean is interesting. She tells great stories and she's fun to be with.)

Remind the students that people can be described in negative terms too. However, for the purpose of this exercise, tell students that they will only talk about positive attributes and characteristics. Stress the fact that there is always something positive to say about someone.

continued on page 226

Let's Be Positive! continued

Have students write two positive things about the student whose name is on the paper they receive. Students should not use physical attributes in their description. Check the papers to make sure that there are only positive attributes describing the students on the paper. If you feel the attributes are not complimentary, work individually with students writing the attributes in private until satisfactory ones are written.

Before sharing the papers with the class, have students make their own folders by folding a piece of 12" x 18" construction paper in half. Each student will draw a picture of himself/herself on the cover and select an appropriate title for the folder. Some suggestions might be—What I Like About Me!, Here I Am! or I Am Special!

Let students share their writing with the class. Be sure all remarks are appropriate and positive, keeping in mind that the purpose of this exercise is to build students' self-esteem and to focus on positive attributes. It is not to correct specific behaviors.

Give out the papers so that students can put the two positive things about themselves in their folder.

On another day, give out the same assignment only this time, have each student write two positive things about himself/herself. Tell the class that these will not be shared with the class. However, tell students that you will go over them in private conference with each student. These papers will be added to the individual folders.

The next addition to the folder will be from the parents. Send home the letter on page 227 to the parents. When they are returned, review them privately with each student and add them to students' individual folders.

Next, write two positive comments about each student. Add these to the individual folders as well. Now each student has a folder with positive comments about himself/herself written by his/her peers, parents, teacher and by himself/herself. What an important personal message this can send to a student!

continued on page 227

Letter to Parents

Date ______________________

Dear Parents,

This month in our class, we are stressing our positive characteristics. We have written positive things about ourselves and about our classmates. Some of the words we used are helpful, kind, friendly, considerate, understanding, sympathetic, trustworthy, sincere, honest, curious, inquisitive, interesting, hard-working, industrious, cheerful. We also expanded on these words giving examples of how we portray these characteristics.

Now, it's your turn. Please write down two positive characteristics your son/daughter possesses. If you would like to, you may also briefly describe these two characteristics.

Please use the form below and return it to school by ______________.

This will be added to your child's folder. Your child will then have eight positive characteristics in a folder which he/she can bring home. Your child can reread the comments telling how he/she is special!

____

- -

My child's name is ___________________________.

These are two positive characteristics of my son/daughter:

____

____

____

____

Signature ______________________

Date ______________________

I.D. Me

Objectives: To create a personal record and to discuss one's height and weight; to write about individual characteristics

Materials: one copy of the I.D. Me pattern on page 229 per student, ink pad, photograph of each student, scale and wall growth chart, hand-held magnifying glass, writing paper, pens

Directions: Begin by discussing with the students that while bodies are all basically the same on the inside, there are many other physical features that make people unique. Ask the students to stand. Then, call for all the students with blonde hair to move to the front of the room. Then, call for all the students with brown hair to move to the back of the room. Continue to categorize until all students are in a group. Explain to students that while their hair color does help to distinguish them, they are still part of a group of people. (For example, perhaps there is only one student in your class with red hair. Tell students that while there may be only one student with red hair in their class, there are many other students within the whole school with red hair.) To further distinguish the students, have each group separate by eye color within their hair color sections (i.e. brown hair, brown eyes; brown hair, green eyes, etc.). Do this until all hair colors have been distinguished by their eye color as well. Tell students that though they may be identified easily by those two physical features, they are still part of a larger group. Then, tell students that there is one physical feature that is truly unique to every person—fingerprints. Have students examine their own fingerprints by reproducing them using an ink pad and the I.D. Me pattern. Explain to the students that fingerprints can be used by the police to locate criminals or missing persons. Tell them that there are scientists who specialize in examining fingerprints and that there are four basic patterns for all fingerprints. They are:

Whorl

Loop

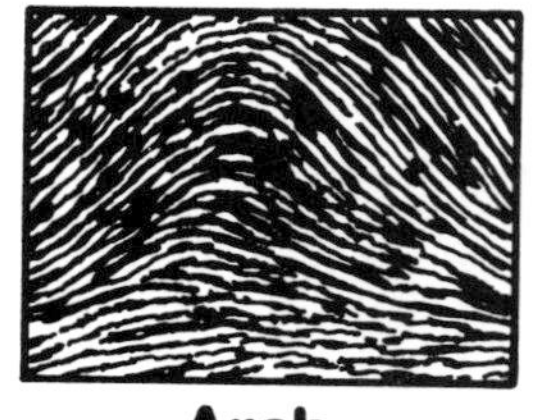

Arch

Composite

Allow time for the students to examine their own fingerprints using a hand-held magnifying glass. Help the students identify which category their fingerprint falls under. (Tell the students to use the forefinger to determine their category.) To further the study, have the students complete all the information on the I.D. Me Pattern. Have students bring in a current picture from home or provide a picture for the students to attach to the pattern. When the information has been documented, ask each student to create a short composition about his/her unique features.

I.D. Me

Photo
of
Student

Full Name: ______________________________

Address: ______________________________

____

Height: __________ Weight: __________

Characteristics: (i.e. hair color, eye color)

____

____

____

Fingerprints

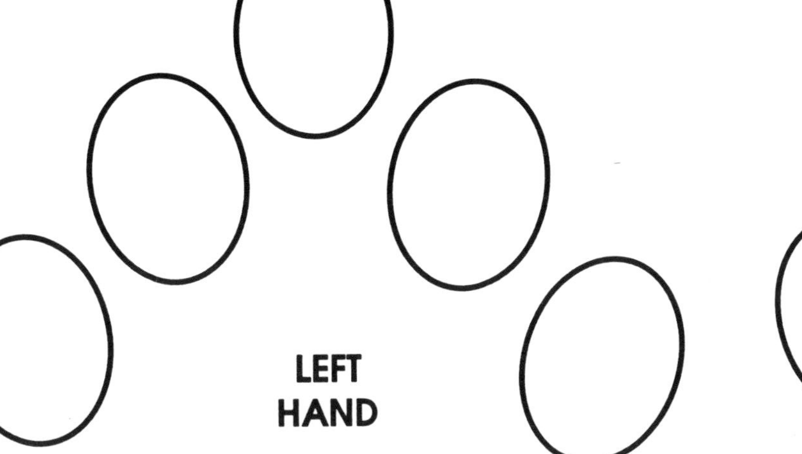

"Beleafing" in a New Year

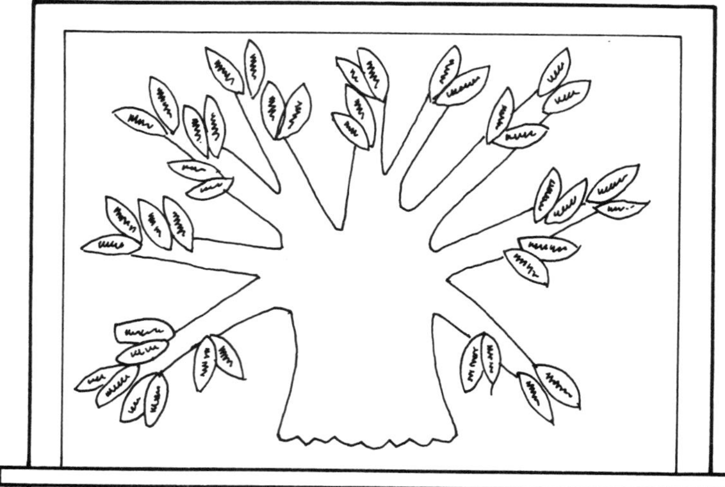

Objectives: To set goals; to become more familiar with a new group of students

Materials: two copies of the leaf pattern below per student, brown construction paper, crayons/markers, stapler

Directions: At the start of the new school year, ask students to discuss what a personal goal is and why some people set goals. Provide examples of some long-term and short-term goals. Ask students to provide you with some ways a person may achieve a goal. (For example, a long-term goal may be to become a better math student. That student may need to be sure to complete his/her math homework every night. He/she should be sure to ask questions in class, and he/she should practice his/her composition skills twice a week.) Next, ask your students to set a goal for themselves. Ask them what they can do to achieve that goal. Instruct students to color and cut out two leaves. They should record their goal on one leaf and the ideas they have for obtaining that goal on the other. Direct students to staple the two together. Create a tree from the brown construction paper to fit your bulletin board. Staple the leaves to the tree. Save the leaves until June. At that time, ask students if they were able to achieve their goal. Why or why not? Ask them what their goal is for fourth grade.

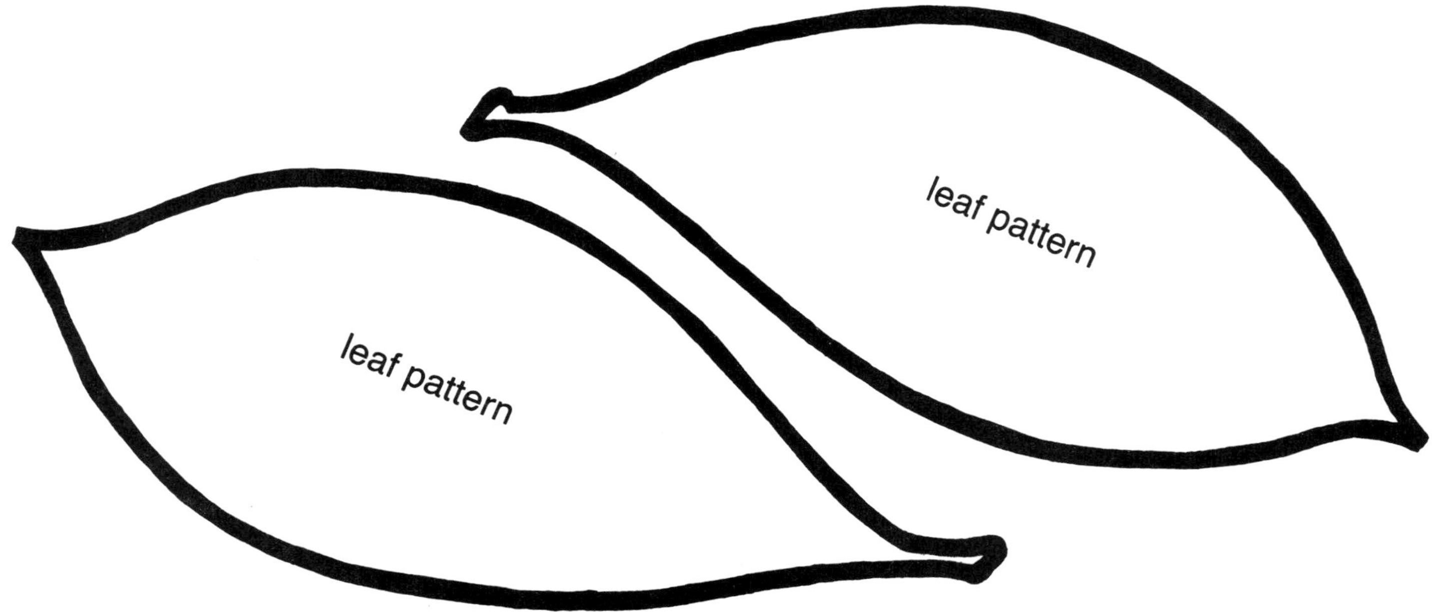

Watch Them Grow!

Objectives: To differentiate between a body's physical and maturational growth; to compare both the physical growth and maturational growth that occurs between the start of the school year and the end

Materials: measuring tape, construction paper, scissors, glue, tape

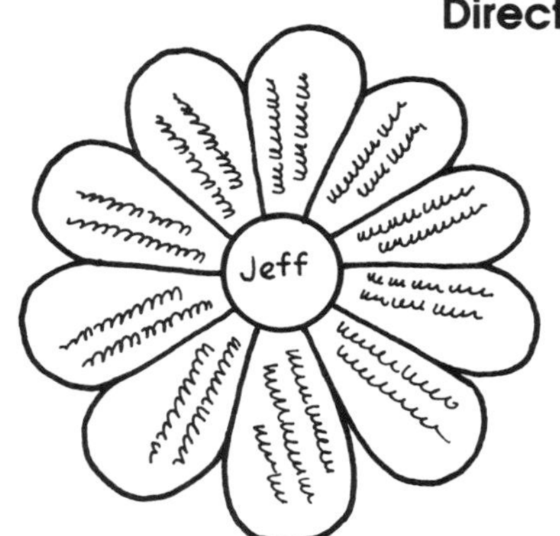

Directions: Instruct students to create the pieces of a flower from construction paper. (The basic flower with a center and petals works best. See the illustration.) Before having students assemble and glue the flower together, ask them to record some personal information on each petal such as the title of their favorite book, what they feel will be the hardest about third grade, what they fear the most, what they want to be when they grow up, what they enjoy doing most, the person they admire most, etc.

When the information has been recorded, direct students to glue the petal pieces together. Discuss how some of the feelings and desires students recorded may change as they grow intellectually. (You may want to share some personal feelings. For example: "I used to be afraid to try new foods. Now that I've grown up, I love to try strange and exotic dishes!") If desired, discuss ways in which our minds grow.

Next, discuss with students ways in which our bodies grow. Explain to students that on the back of their flowers, they should record their height and weight.

Prepare an oversized flower stem on the wall in your classroom. (Fold several sheets of green paper and cut a stemlike shape. Tape the stem to the wall.) After you measure the height of each student and after the student records his/her height on the back of his/her flower, tape the flower to a spot on the stem. Label the display with the sentence, "Watch Them Grow!" You can add a picture of a watering can and droplets of water as well as a sun if you like. When you take the display down, keep the flowers in a safe spot until June. In June, repeat the activity, and then ask the students to compare and contrast the similarities and differences between September and June. Ask students to write a paragraph indicating the way(s) they have changed or grown the most. Send the flowers home as a third-grade keepsake!

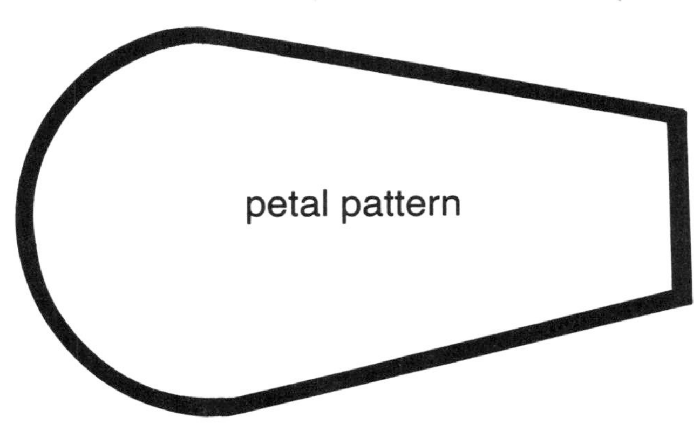

Heart Smart

Objective: To demonstrate the strength the heart needs to pump blood throughout the body

Materials: several tennis balls

Directions: Explain to students that the heart is the strongest muscle in the human body. It has the awesome responsibility of pumping blood to the brain and all other parts of the body. The heart never rests. It pumps blood night and day for a person's whole life. To help your students get an idea of the heart's power, have them hold a tennis ball in their hand. Then, tell them to squeeze the ball several times as hard as they can, using only the muscles in their arm, giving it all they've got! Your students will be amazed to learn that they have just experienced how much strength the heart needs to pump blood throughout the body 24 hours a day!

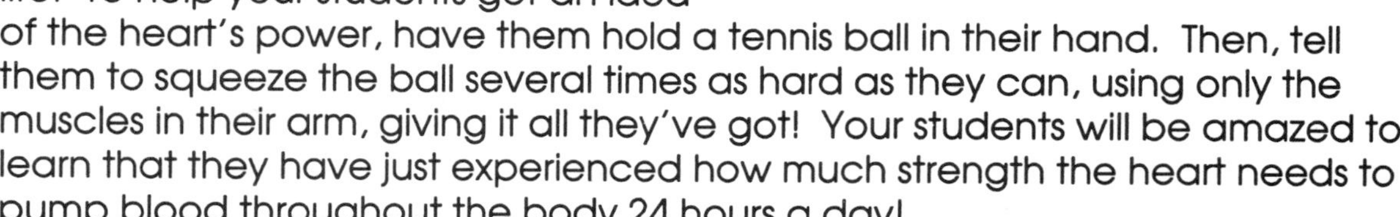

Extension: For such a strong muscle with such a big job to do, the heart is remarkably small. Have your students make a fist to simulate the size of their heart. Tell them that as they grow, so does their heart.

Pick Up the Beat!

Objective: To develop an awareness of how exercise increases one's pulse rate

Materials: timepiece with a second hand, chart paper, marker, one copy of the pulse rate chart on page 233 per student

Directions: Just like any muscle, the heart becomes stronger with regular exercise. When the heart is strong, it does not need to work as hard to pump the blood through the body. Heart-healthy exercise improves blood circulation and helps all the other organs work together more efficiently.

To teach your students about aerobic and anaerobic exercise, begin by having your students participate in a pulse-raising activity. Ask students to locate their pulse on either their wrist or neck using the tips of their fingers. Once they have felt their pulse, have them count the number of heartbeats they feel in a twenty-second time frame. Pause and ask students how many times their heart beats in 20 seconds. Then, help the students multiply this number by three to find out how many times their heart beats in a minute.

continued on page 233

Pick Up the Beat! continued

Next, ask students to jog in place for two minutes to speed up their heart rates. Instruct the students to stop, locate their pulse again and count the number of beats in a twenty-second period. Pause and repeat the above question to the students. Have them jot down the two figures and compare.

For more healthy fun, use the pulse rate chart below to have the students record changes in their pulse rate at four different intervals—at rest and after 2, 4, and 6 minutes of sustained exercise. Between each period of exercise, be sure that the students return back to their resting rate before exercising again. Instruct the students to record their pulse on the chart using a dot and then to connect the dots to see how their pulse rate changed. Ask students how body size affects pulse rate. Have them compare the pulse rates for students of different sizes to find out.

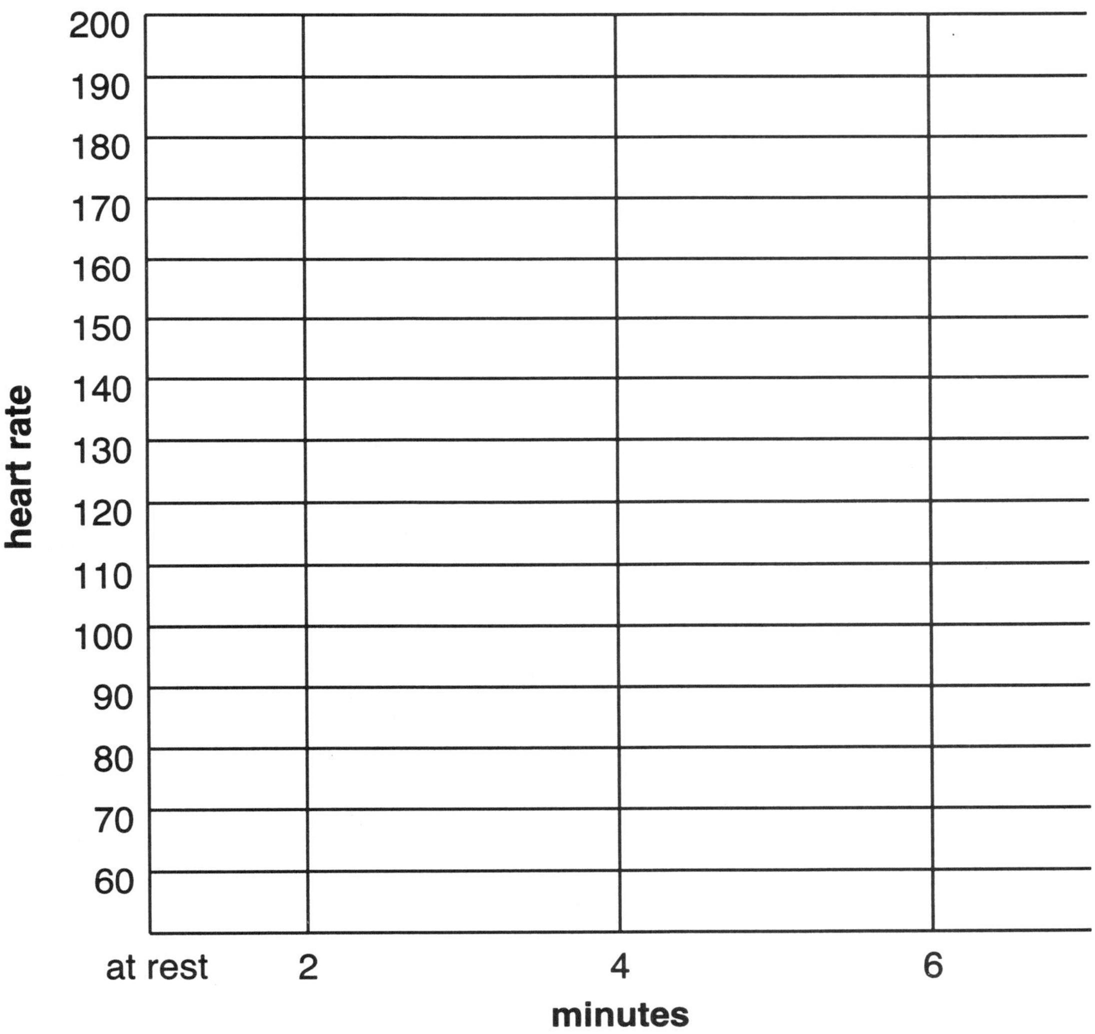

heart rate

200
190
180
170
160
150
140
130
120
110
100
90
80
70
60

at rest 2 4 6

minutes

Highways for Blood Cells

Objective: To examine the function of veins, arteries and capillaries as the vessels that carry blood throughout the body

Materials: hand-held mirror, flashlight, reference materials, diagrams of the circulatory system

Directions: Explain to students that our blood is the vehicle that transports oxygen, food and waste to and from the cells of our bodies. It travels to such exotic destinations as the liver, the muscles and the brain by the way of the circulatory system. Examine a diagram of the circulatory system, especially focusing on the heart. Tell the students that there are three basic kinds of vessels that carry blood, and that each has a special job.

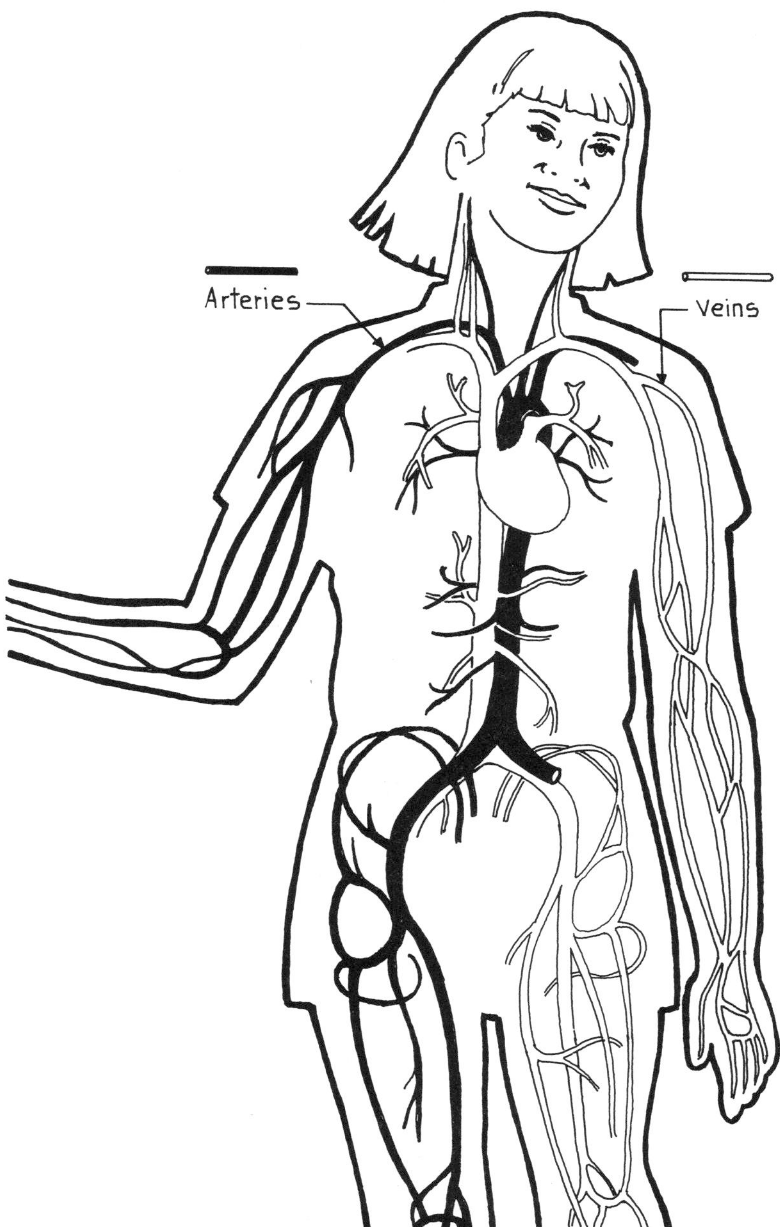

1. Arteries—carry blood away from the heart. These are the vessels that are pressed when the pulse is taken.
2. Veins—carry blood back to the heart. These are the blue lines that appear under the skin.
3. Capillaries—the tiniest blood vessels that are almost hairlike in size; these tubes filter nutrients into the body's tissues.

To move from diagrammatic discussion to real life, let students view these vessels using a hand-held mirror and a flashlight. Instruct students to look at the underside of their tongue. Looking closely, they should be able to spot thick pink lines which are oxygen-rich arteries and thick blue lines which are veins. The capillaries, though, may be more difficult to observe.

Extension:

Thousands of people suffer from heart attacks each year. Have your students use reference materials to research the following questions:

- What is a heart attack?
- What factors cause heart attacks?
- What are some steps people can take to decrease the chances of having a heart attack?

Heart Smart Exercise

Objective: To develop an awareness of the types of exercise that benefit the heart and lungs

Materials: chart paper, markers, one copy of the Personal Exercise Log on page 236 per student

Directions: Help your students create an "Exercise Chart for the Heart" to highlight activities that benefit the heart. To do this, divide a piece of chart paper into two columns. Label one side aerobic and the other anaerobic. Tell the students that aerobic exercises cause the body to use more oxygen (aerobic means "using oxygen") and that they are better at strengthening the heart. Some important tips to keep in mind when doing aerobic exercise are:

1. They increase your heart and breathing rates.
2. They are usually done for 20 or 30 minutes without stopping.
3. They should be done at least three times per week.

Using this criteria, have the students brainstorm a list of aerobic activities. For example:

AEROBIC	ANAEROBIC
Cross Country Skiing	Baseball
Jogging	Bowling
Rowing	Golf
Roller Skating	Softball
Aerobic Dancing	
Bicycling	
Running	
Fast Walking	
Swimming	

Evaluate other types of exercise that might be fun but do not really exercise the heart and lungs such as those listed above. Explain to students that these are anaerobic exercises.

Finally, to heighten your students' awareness of their own exercise habits, have them record the kinds of exercise they engage in often using the personal exercise log. After one week, have the students evaluate the types of activities that they participated in. Were they heart smart?

Be sure to stress to the students that all types of exercise are healthy for their body. Students should be encouraged to engage in these activities to improve motor coordination as well.

Exercise Chart for the Heart

Name of the Exercise	Aerobic or Anaerobic?	When? Date and Time of Day	Where?

The Food Guide Pyramid

Objective: To become aware of the components of the Food Guide Pyramid designed by the Food and Drug Administration

Materials: an enlarged copy of the Food Guide Pyramid below that will fit your bulletin board, magazines, scissors

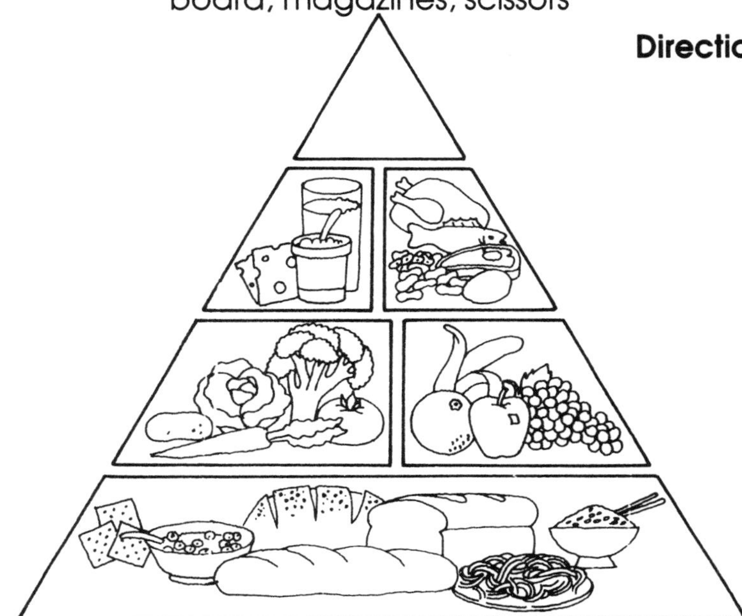

Directions: Discuss with students the components of the Food Guide Pyramid. Ask students to cut out pictures of foods from magazines to fit each category. Staple the guide to the center of your bulletin board. As students supply pictures, staple them to the left of the pyramid, adjacent to the section of the pyramid where they belong. When all the pictures have been placed, discuss the number of servings recommended for each group. Remind students to limit consumption of foods from the top of the pyramid.

Good for You

Try the activities below to foster good nutrition and good eating habits among students.

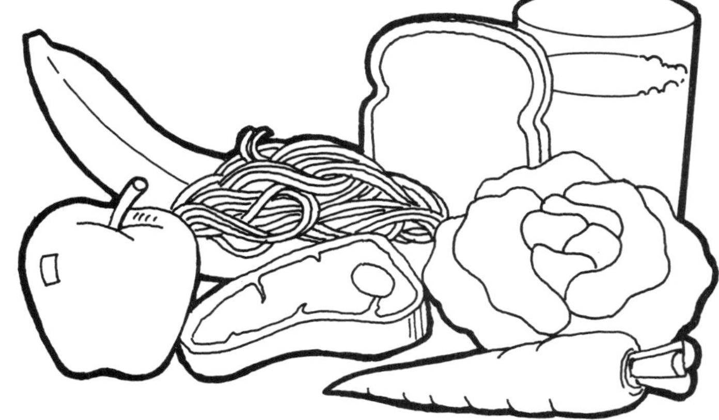

Materials: See each activity.

Directions:

1. Pretend you are the school nutritionist. It is your job to prepare school lunch menus that are tasty to eat and healthy. Make up a menu for one week. Be sure that each lunch contains at least one food from each basic food group. Also, since you should eat five servings of fruits and vegetables every day, be sure that lunch has at least two servings.
2. Prepare a menu for a day including breakfast, lunch and dinner. Include food from the basic food groups and include five servings of fruits and vegetables.
3. Have each student bring a vegetable to school. Make a salad.
4. Have each student bring a fruit to school. Make a fruit salad.

Good Sense With Your Senses

Below and on pages 239-245 are lots of fun activities for students to do to become aware of their five senses.

Sense of Hearing

Objectives: To stress the importance of the ears and to better understand the handicapping condition of the loss of hearing

Materials: paper, pencils

Directions: Discuss with the students the sense of hearing. See if they know how the ear works. Discuss with the students some parts of the ear—the outer ear, the middle ear, the inner ear, the ear canal, the eardrum and the ear lobe. Ask students why hearing is an important sense. Elicit answers from the class and write them on the chalkboard. Be sure to include responses such as:

- You can receive directions.
- You can enjoy music, radio, TV, etc.
- You can receive danger signals such as a horn, RR whistle, fire signal, etc.

Discuss rules to protect the sense of hearing. Put these on the board as well. Examples:

- Don't scream in someone's ears.
- Don't play music or TV too loud.
- Don't stick things in your ears.
- Keep your ears clean.

Try this experiment with your class. Have each student be prepared with a sheet of paper and pencil. Tell the students you are going to say a sentence in a normal voice to the class. Tell students to write down what they hear. Next, have each student cover his/her ears. Tell students to watch you very carefully while you say another sentence in the same normal voice. Again, have the students write down what they heard. Next, have the students cover their ears and this time, turn around so that the students cannot see your face. Again, say another sentence in a normal voice and have the students write down what they heard. Graph the results. How many students heard the first sentence. How many heard the second? How many heard the third? If there are more students who heard the second sentence than the third, discuss why. (The sound traveled in the opposite direction away from the class.) Many students may have used their sense of sight to "hear". They lip-read as well as listened. This is a good opportunity to discuss how deaf people may use their sense of sight to lip-read and to use signing.

continued on page 239

Good Sense...continued

Match the Sound

Materials: 2 toilet paper tubes, 4 squares of paper to cover the open ends of the tubes, 4 rubber bands, several paper clips

Directions:

1. Cover one end of each tube by placing a square of construction paper over it and securing it with a rubber band.

2. When paper clips are put in the tube, secure the other end in the same manner. Before you close the shaker, model for the class how one clip would sound in the shaker. Repeat this for 2, 3, 4 and 5 clips.

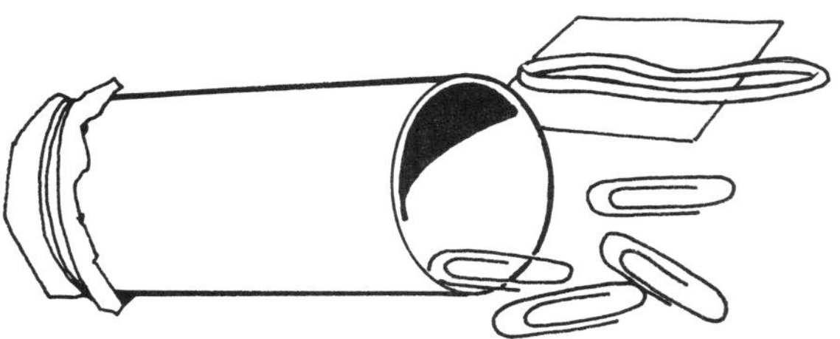

3. Next, invite one student to take one shaker and secretly put clips in it, any amount from one to five. Invite another student to try to duplicate that sound by selecting the same number of paper clips.

4. Have the class make a determination if the duplication is correct by listening to each shaker separately. In addition to paper clips, you can use erasers, paper fasteners, wooden beads or any combination of materials.

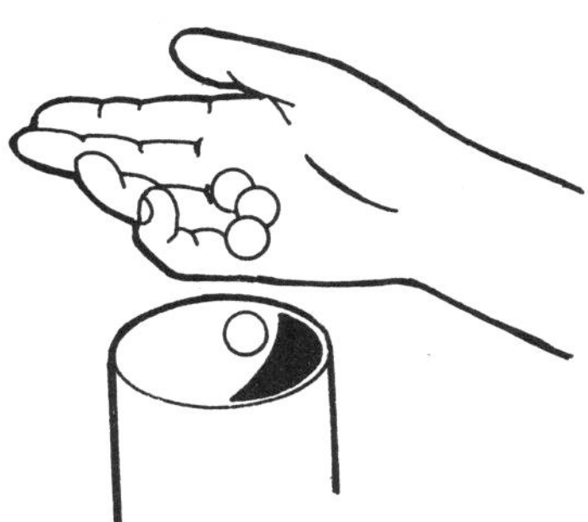

Extension: Discuss the possibility of anyone in the class having a friend or relative who has a hearing problem. Ask students what some things are that they can do to help that person (i.e. face them when they speak, speak clearly, speak a little louder, etc.). Ask students how they can be careful not to hurt that person's feelings. Ask students to pretend that they asked the person where a coat was. Tell the students that the person with the hearing problem answered, "It must be in the water". Ask students what they think he/she heard. (Probably, "Where is the boat?") It seems like a funny answer, but it would be very hurtful to laugh. Ask students what they should do. What should they not do?

Good Sense...continued

Sense of Sight

Objectives: To stress the importance of eye care and to better understand the handicapping condition of loss of sight

Materials: chart paper, markers

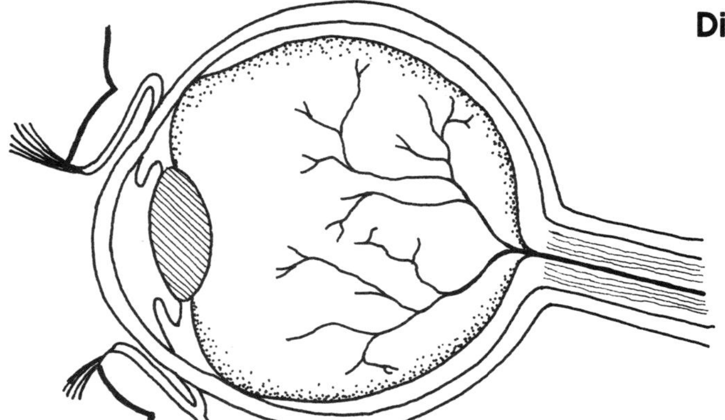

Directions: Discuss with the students the sense of sight. Ask the students the following questions:

- How does the eye receive an image?
- What are some parts of the eye? (eyeball, iris, cornea, retina, eyelashes, eyelid)
- Why is sight an important sense?

Elicit answers from the students and write them on the board. Some answers could be as follows:

- You can see where you are going. (Safety)
- You can watch TV, movies, shows, concerts, operas, etc.
- You can learn to drive a car, boat or even a plane.
- You can look at scenery.
- You can read. (This might be a good time to discuss Braille.)

Discuss rules to protect the eyes. Have students write a set of rules and then share them with the class. Make up one class chart using the rules the students have written. Some examples of rules could be as follows:

- Don't rub your eyes.
- Don't throw rocks, sticks, pebbles, sand, snowballs, etc. at someone.
- Don't run with pencils or sticks in your hand.
- Always hold your hand over the cutting blades of a pair of closed scissors when walking with them.
- Don't hold a book too close to your eyes.
- Use proper lighting when working.

continued on page 241

Good Sense...continued

I Spy

Objective: To use descriptive words and the sense of sight to describe an object

Materials: one sheet of paper per group of students, pencils

Directions: Divide the class into two, three or four groups depending upon the size of the class. Each group selects a leader who starts the game with one sheet of paper. He/she selects an object in the room without telling anyone what it is and writes down one thing about it. (For example, I spy something white.) The paper is then passed to the next student who looks for something white in the room and adds another characteristic (i.e. I spy something white and black.). Continue this way throughout the group (i.e. I spy something white and black and round. I spy something white, black and round with numbers, etc.). After the group has completed the description, have each student name what he/she had in mind when he/she wrote "I Spy". Ask how it changed when more characteristics were added. (In the process, it may have changed from a sheet of paper to a book, to a puzzle piece, to a clock, etc.)

Experiment

Objective: To help students realize the importance of the sense of sight

Materials: blindfold, "Pin the Tail on the Donkey" or other similar game

Directions: Most of the students will know the game "Pin the Tail on the Donkey", but few have related it to the importance of sight or the problems of the blind. Set up an area in your room where you can illustrate this. (To make it a simple game, you can pin the hands on the clock.) Have a few students walk up to pin the hands in the center of a clock. Without their eyes covered, it is an easy task. Then, tell the students to pretend that they have lost their sense of sight. Put a blindfold on students one at a time, and have them try to pin the hands on the clock. Be sure to have an area cleared for safety and watch carefully to protect the blindfolded student from getting hurt. After the "game", ask students how it felt to be without sight. Did they use their ears and/or hands to help them "see"?

continued on page 242

Good Sense...continued

Topics for Discussion:

- How do blind people "read"? (Braille; talking books; Some people volunteer to read books to be taped for the blind.)
- How do Blind people move about? (seeing eyes dogs, special canes)
- How can you help? (understanding)

A good research topic would be the special training of seeing eye dogs. Below are questions students could include answers to:

- What kind of dogs are used?
- Where are they trained?
- How long is the training?
- How are they used?
- How trustworthy are they?
- How expensive is it to train a seeing eye dog?
- How expensive is it to own a seeing eye dog?

Sense of Touch

Touch and Tell

Objective: To make students more aware of what they can discover using their sense of touch

Materials: cardboard box, scissors, glue, one copy of page 243 per student, items to put in the box for the students to touch (See below.)

Directions: Turn an open box upside-down. Cut a hole in one side of it. Cut the toe off of a sock. Glue the sock to the outside of the box around the hole. Push the sock sleeve into the hole in the box. Gather several things to put inside the box such as a bowl of cooked spaghetti, piece of clay, box of marbles, rock, piece of fur, absorbent cotton, jacks, bar of soap, ice cube, wet sponge, dry sponge and sandpaper. Number the items on a sheet of paper so that each student gets a chance to feel them in the same order. Discuss descriptive adjectives with the students. Elicit some from the class and write them on the chalkboard. Place one of the items you gathered under the box. Give each student a copy of page 243. Have each student put his/her hand in the box. He/she should then write in some appropriate adjectives that describe what the first object felt like. Then, have each student guess what the object is. After you have used all the objects with all the students, have them share their descriptive adjectives and the noun guesses with the class.

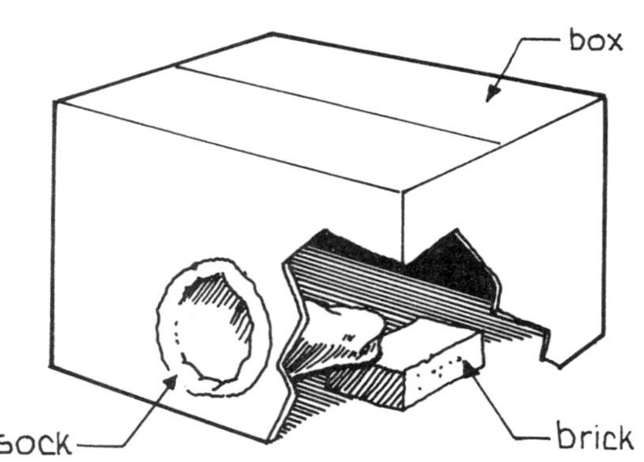

continued on page 243

Touch and Tell Chart

Item #1	Item #2	Item #3
It felt ________________. ________________. ________________. ________________. I think it is ____________.	It felt ________________. ________________. ________________. ________________. I think it is ____________.	It felt ________________. ________________. ________________. ________________. I think it is ____________.
Item #4	**Item #5**	**Item #6**
It felt ________________. ________________. ________________. ________________. I think it is ____________.	It felt ________________. ________________. ________________. ________________. I think it is ____________.	It felt ________________. ________________. ________________. ________________. I think it is ____________.
Item #7	**Item #8**	**Item #9**
It felt ________________. ________________. ________________. ________________. I think it is ____________.	It felt ________________. ________________. ________________. ________________. I think it is ____________.	It felt ________________. ________________. ________________. ________________. I think it is ____________.
Item #10	**Item #11**	**Item #12**
It felt ________________. ________________. ________________. ________________. I think it is ____________.	It felt ________________. ________________. ________________. ________________. I think it is ____________.	It felt ________________. ________________. ________________. ________________. I think it is ____________.

Good Sense...continued

Sense of Smell

Objective: To help students understand that some things can be identified just by their aroma

Materials: small containers such as frozen juice containers covered with aluminum foil that has holes punched in it, markers, trays, paper, pencils

Directions: Put a small amount of the following in separate containers:

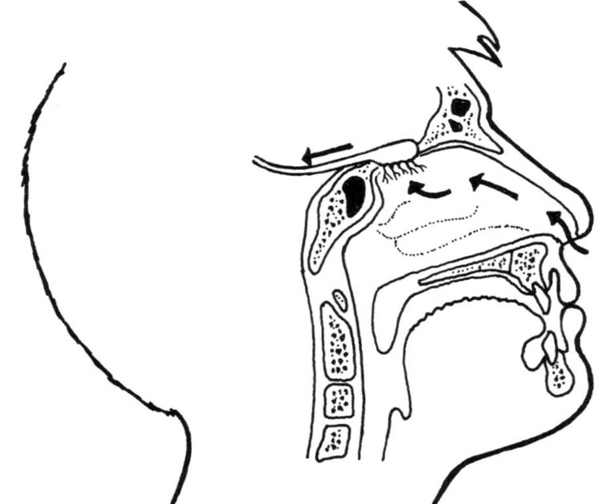

1. cotton ball saturated with vinegar
2. cotton ball saturated with cologne
3. cotton ball saturated with vanilla extract
4. cotton ball saturated with mint extract
5. cut onion
6. clove of garlic
7. cinnamon
8. ground pepper
9. ground coffee beans
10. orange slices
11. piece of chocolate

Number the containers and place them on trays in various parts of the room. (Don't set them too close together. You don't want the aromas to mix.) Instruct the students to number 1-11 on their paper. After smelling each container, students are to write down what they think they are smelling next to the appropriate number. It is important at this point to stress to students that they do not stick their nose too close and do not take a deep sniff. This is a controlled school experiment. They should not do this experiment at home. Some things may be harmful to smell such as ammonia, bleach, other cleaning fluids or powders. After all the students have entered their aroma selections on their papers, have them share them with the class. Make a bar graph to record students' guesses. Ask students what the most and least recognizable aromas were.

continued on page 245

Good Sense...continued

Sense of Taste

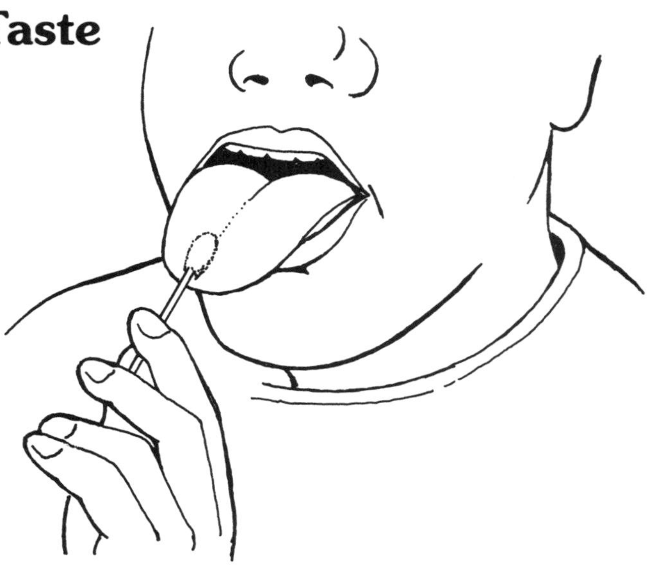

Taste Will Tell

Objective: To explore the sense of taste

Materials: paper, pencils

Directions: Discuss with the class how different foods taste (i.e. salty, sweet, sour, tart, spicy, bland, bitter, peppery, etc.). Tell students that people may have different descriptions for the same foods. Our taste buds determine the sensation we get when we eat foods. Smokers, for example, have their taste buds dulled by smoke, and they will not get the same taste sensation as nonsmokers. People who are not used to eating spicy foods will find a little bit of spice very "hot" while those used to eating highly spiced foods will find the same little bit of spice very bland.

Make a list of various types of foods (i.e. chocolate, lemon, pretzel, potato chips, orange juice, cranberry juice, lemonade, milk, coffee, catsup, ice cream, salad dressing, chili, etc.). Your list may vary depending upon the students in your class and the types of foods that are popular in your area.

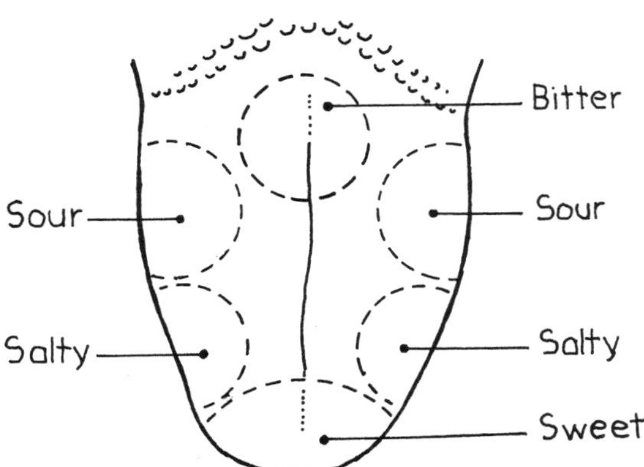

Have the students write a brief description of the taste, the texture and the taste sensation of the foods listed. Then, have the students write a description of the combination of tastes that they had for lunch. Ask them which were pleasing tastes and which were not. While a particular food may look the same to all and feel the same to all, ask students if it tastes the same to all. Why or why not?

Safety Makes Sense

Objectives: To become aware of the rules of pedestrian safety, bicycle safety, automobile and bus safety and to help the kindergarten and first-grade students understand the importance of safety rules

Materials: paper, pencils, crayons, markers

Directions: Discuss with the class the various safety rules they should be aware of as a pedestrian, a car passenger and a bicycle rider. See examples on page 246.

continued on page 246

Safety Makes Sense continued

Pedestrian safety:

Cross at the corner.

Look both ways and then look again for turning cars. Be sure to listen as well.

Cross on a green light if there is a light.

Do not walk between parked cars.

Do not run into the street after a ball.

Always pay attention to the traffic.

Look and listen.

Bus safety:

Remember the 3S rules: sit down, sit back, stay sitting.

Use seat belts if available.

Keep hands, feet and head in the bus—not out the window.

Keep feet out of the aisle.

Use soft voices so you don't distract the driver.

If crossing the street after you leave the bus, cross 10 feet in front of the bus only after the driver waves you on.

Automobile safety:

Always use a seat belt.

Keep head, feet and hands in the car at all times.

Be aware of traffic signs (i.e. traffic lights, stop sign, R.R. crossing, one way, pedestrian crossing, etc.)

Bicycle safety:

Always wear a helmet.

Watch for pedestrians and cars.

Obey all traffic signs and traffic signals.

Ride on the right side of the road or sidewalk.

Use hand signals.

After you have discussed the many safety rules, divide the class into four groups. Assign each group one of the four safety areas. Have each student in the group select one safety rule in his/her assigned area. Then, model for the class how to turn the safety rule into a rhyme—either a couplet or a quatrain.

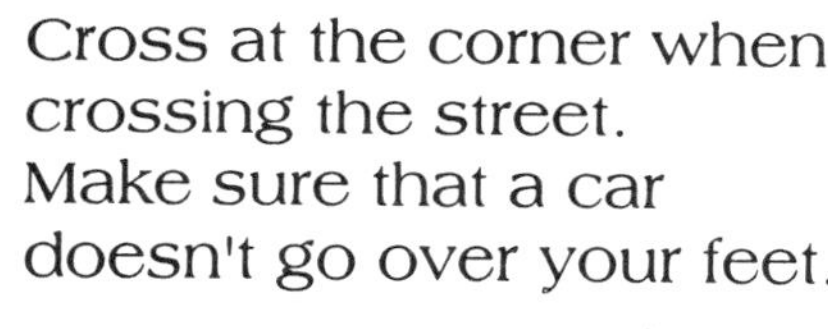

Cross at the corner when
crossing the street.
Make sure that a car
doesn't go over your feet.

Always wear your helmet
when riding your bicycle.
You even need a helmet
if you're riding on a tricycle.
In case you fall
against a wall,
it will keep your brain
from a great big pain.

Then, let students try writing their own poems. Have the students illustrate their poems. Then, assemble each group's work into a book. You will have four books. Have a representative of each group read its book to the kindergarten and/or first grade in your school. Circulate the four books so that each kindergarten and/or first-grade class in your school has had a chance to read and discuss each one.

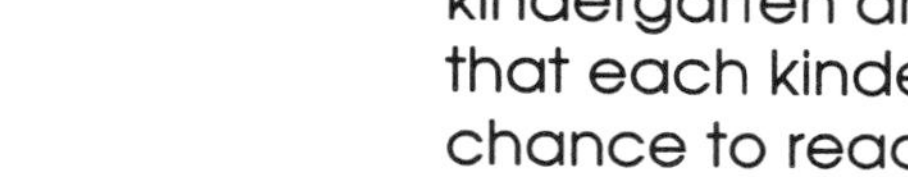

Social Studies

In the third grade, social studies draws upon and expands students' interest in their communities, the country and the world. It encourages students to reflect upon their individual responsibilities as integral parts of their family, their school community, their city or town, their state, their country and the world. The relevant and viable activities in this chapter provide students with the basis for growth in social awareness as they are prompted to gather, evaluate and analyze information. The nature of the activities provides for an experiential approach through research, cooperative groups, role-playing and simulations. Students should have an awareness of current events and knowledge of the basic processes of government. Emphasis is placed on self-awareness and the interdependence of people within their communities. Some of the objectives included in this chapter are:

1. to promote awareness of our national heritage
2. to research historical figures
3. to foster multicultural awareness in order to celebrate pride in one's heritage
4. to study the history, geography and customs of one particular country or community
5. to define the concept of family and its various structures
6. to investigate the lawmaking process and taxation
7. to understand the mechanics of a campaign and an election
8. to learn about and conduct polls
9. to identify ways to become better school citizens
10. to learn about the Bill of Rights
11. to develop map reading skills and knowledge of a map's components
12. to read and create time lines
13. to develop an awareness of the relationship between geography, economy, climate and one's lifestyle
14. to develop a sense of geographical location
15. to investigate various careers

Celebration of National Holidays

Below and on pages 249-262 are activities which promote student awareness of our national heritage and help them understand the celebration of patriotic holidays in relation to their own culture.

Thanksgiving • Thanksgiving • Thanksgiving • Thanksgiving • Thanksgiving • Thanksgiving

Discussions and celebrations of Thanksgiving provide a good opportunity for you to stress citizenship and multicultural awareness in your classroom. It is also a good time to involve parents in a classroom or grade level celebration. (See letter to parents on page 254.) Read the class *The Thanksgiving Story* by Alice Dalgliesh to introduce students to the origin of this holiday.

Suggested Reading: *The First Thanksgiving* by Lena Barksdale
The Plymouth Thanksgiving by Leonard Weisgard
The Coming of the Pilgrims told from Governor Bradford's Firsthand Account by E. Brooks Smith and Robert Meredith

I Am Thankful for . . . (Activity 1)

Objective: To create a bulletin board to help students realize what they have to be thankful for

Materials: oaktag, brown tissue paper or crêpe paper, assorted colors of construction paper, pencils, white glue, scissors, paper for sentence strips, stapler, one copy of the turkey pattern (page 250) for each student

Directions: Cut out a large circle from oaktag. This will be the body of the turkey. (The size will depend upon the size of your bulletin board. You may want to piece together the oaktag to make a large enough circle.) Cut the crêpe paper or tissue paper into 2" squares. Using an unsharpened pencil or the back, flat end of a pencil, have students take turns placing the pencil in the center of each square. Then, they fold the sides of each paper down so that it wraps around the pencil. Show students how to dip the paper lightly into the white glue so that just the flat end gets glue on it. Students place the glue end on the circle and remove the pencil. The paper will stand up from the oaktag circle. This circle should be covered completely, the fuller the better! It would be a good idea to leave it in a designated spot in the classroom so that the students can add to it during spare moments. When completed, mount the turkey's body in the center of the bulletin board.

continued on page 249

Celebration . . . continued

Thanksgiving • Thanksgiving • Thanksgiving • Thanksgiving • Thanksgiving • Thanksgiving

"I Am Thankful for . . ." continued

Next, have the students draw and cut out feathers from the different colors of construction paper. These can vary in size to create greater interest. Attach the feathers to the bulletin board as shown on page 248. Cut them out and attach the legs as shown.

The head should stand away from the body. To do this, cut two 1" x 3" strips of oaktag. Staple them in the center. Fold out tabs at both ends. The tabs on one end will be attached to the bulletin board.

The title of the bulletin board, **I Am Thankful For . . .**, will be the sentence starter. Discuss with the class what the Pilgrims were thankful for. Then, discuss what people today might be thankful for. Finally, bring it to a more personal level. Ask the students what they are thankful for. After brainstorming several thoughts, give each student a sentence strip. Have him/her write something for which he/she is thankful completing the sentence heading on the bulletin board. Mount these sentence strips on the board as illustrated above.

A day or two later, give each student a copy of page 250 and have the students elaborate on their sentence. They might want to add why they are thankful or describe further what they are thankful for. Save this paper for the Thanksgiving book (page 253).

The First Thanksgiving (Activity 2)

Objective: To write a story about the first Thanksgiving

Materials: paper, pens, markers or crayons

Directions: Have students write a story about the first Thanksgiving after reading and discussing the books listed on page 248. The stories should include answers to the following questions:

- Who were the Pilgrims?
- Why did they come to America?
- How did they come to America?
- When did they travel to America?
- How did the Native Americans help the Pilgrims?
- Who planned the special feast?
- Why was the special feast planned?

Have the students illustrate their stories. Save their stories to put in individual Thanksgiving books (page 253).

Turkey Pattern

I am thankful for __________

Celebration . . . continued

Thanksgiving • Thanksgiving • Thanksgiving • Thanksgiving • Thanksgiving • Thanksgiving

All Aboard! (Activity 3)

Objective: To write essays about a pretend trip aboard the *Mayflower*

Materials: paper, pens, markers or crayons

Directions: Have students imagine that they are aboard the *Mayflower* coming to America. They should write an essay explaining what their life is like. Students may want to include things like their family life, recreation, education, food, games, sleeping quarters, etc. Have them also include something about their feelings (i.e. what they think about this trip, what their fears are, what their hopes are, etc.). Have the students illustrate their essay and save it for the Thanksgiving book (page 253).

Write a Compact! (Activity 4)

Objectives: To understand what a compact is and to write one

Materials: paper, pens

Background: Explain to the class that Plymouth, now part of Massachusetts, was the second English colony in the New World. It was set up by the Pilgrims who arrived there in 1620. They had left England to be able to practice their religion in peace.

The Mayflower Compact was written by William Bradford, the second governor of Plymouth Colony. It was the first agreement for self-government enacted in America. It established rules and laws the people of the colony had to follow.

Directions: Discuss with the class what laws and rules the Pilgrims might have written down in the Mayflower Compact. Ask students why they think the Pilgrims needed a compact and why they think they wanted a compact.

After students have an understanding of the purpose of a compact, discuss with them the ideas of writing a compact. Brainstorm with the students the kind of compact they might want and/or need. Some examples might be: a cafeteria compact, a recess compact, a class compact, a school compact, a family compact, a community compact, etc.

Write a class compact together. Then, let each student write his/her own compact. Before the compact is written down, the students should write a statement as to the necessity for his/her particular compact. Share the students' compacts with the class.

Celebration . . . continued

Thanksgiving • Thanksgiving • Thanksgiving • Thanksgiving • Thanksgiving • Thanksgiving

Let's Pretend! (Activity 5)

Objective: To have students write essays pretending to be a Native American

Materials: paper, pens

Directions: Tell students to pretend that they are Native Americans and that some strangely dressed people who speak a strange language live near them. Have students write an essay explaining how they feel about these people and how they will act with them. This can also be reversed. Students could pretend they are Pilgrims.

How Corny! (Activity 6)

Objective: To realize the importance of corn and its variety of uses

Materials: paper, pens, dictionaries

Directions: Discuss with the class how the Native Americans introduced corn to the Pilgrims and taught them how to plant, grow, harvest and use the corn.

Have the students present their ideas as to why corn was so important. Ask them how it affected the lives of the Pilgrims. Then, have the students make a list of the various ways corn can be used. (See list below.) After they make the list, have students categorize it to show the great versatility of this crop. The students might want to look in the dictionary under corn to help expand their lists.

- corn on the cob—vegetable
- creamed corn—vegetable
- corn chowder—soup
- cornmeal—grain
- corn bread—bread
- corn muffin—bread
- cornmeal cereal—hot cereal
- cornmeal mush—hot cereal
- Indian pudding—cereal/dessert
- corn pone—bread
- popcorn—snack
- corn flakes—cold cereal
- corn oil—food oil
- cornstarch—a thickener for food
- corn sugar—a sweetener
- corn syrup—a sweetener

Celebration . . . continued

Thanksgiving • Thanksgiving • Thanksgiving • Thanksgiving • Thanksgiving • Thanksgiving

It's OK to Act Out! (Activity 7)

Objective: To dramatize situations which were familiar to the Pilgrims and the Native Americans involving people who lived during this time

Materials: paper, pens

Directions: After the students are familiar with the Pilgrims and the part the Native Americans played in their lives, set up some situations the students can act out. Some characters you could include are Governor Bradford, other Pilgrims, Massasoit (chief of Wampanoag tribe), Samoset, Squanto, other Native Americans.

Some situations you could set up could be a first meeting, Native Americans teaching the Pilgrims something, Pilgrims teaching the Native Americans something, a Thanksgiving celebration, etc. The students could also give you some ideas for other situations.

A Thanksgiving Book (Activity 8)

Objective: To assemble work students have made throughout the study of Thanksgiving

Materials: students' work they have made during their study of Thanksgiving, construction paper, markers, notebook rings or other materials to use to bind pages together

Directions: Each student will assemble his/her own book. It should include the following:

1. a story about the First Thanksgiving (page 249)
2. an essay about how a child on the *Mayflower* would feel (page 251)
3. an "I Am Thankful for . . ." essay (page 248)
4. a "Let's Pretend!" story (page 252)
5. any recipes (if the students did the cooking in the "Thanksgiving Celebration" page 254)

Have each student select a title for his/her book, prepare a cover page with an illustration and illustrate the other writings in the book when appropriate. Students can bind, staple or put the pages together with notebook rings.

Celebration . . . continued

Thanksgiving • Thanksgiving • Thanksgiving • Thanksgiving • Thanksgiving • Thanksgiving

Thanksgiving Celebration (Activity 9)

Objective: To celebrate the end of the study of Thanksgiving

Materials: letter to parents, food items, paper products to serve food on and with

Directions: Plan a Thanksgiving Celebration with your students. This can be either a class activity or a grade level activity. Decide what foods would be appropriate to serve, what foods the students can prepare in school, how you would like the parents to help, etc. Some suggestions of food to serve are turkey (whole turkey, turkey breasts or deli sliced turkey), sweet potato pudding, applesauce, cranberry sauce, corn bread, butter, popcorn.

There are several ways you can go about getting the food for your celebration. You can have the parents prepare all or some of it, or the students can prepare it. If the students do the preparing, each class could be responsible for making enough of a certain food for the entire grade level.

Concerning the accumulation of ingredients, you can have the parents buy the ingredients and send them to school with their students, or the students can make a shopping list from reading the recipes, and the class can take a trip to a local market to buy the ingredients. You might also want to enlist the financial assistance of your school PTA if that is available to you.

If you have a handy parent and/or teacher, it would be fun to make Pilgrim and Native American costumes for the students to wear at the celebration.

Send a letter to parents similar to the one shown to let them help you execute your celebration.

Dear Parents,

This month we are studying about the Pilgrims, the Native Americans and the First Thanksgiving. The culmination of our study will be the recreation of the First Thanksgiving. The celebration will take place on __(date)__ , at __(time)__ , in __(place)__ . We will need your help. Please indicate below in which areas you will be able to help and return this to school.

- ❑ cook
- ❑ provide food items
- ❑ sew
- ❑ set up, serve, clean up

Thank you for your assistance and cooperation.

Sincerely,

____

Celebration . . . continued

Columbus Day • Columbus Day • Columbus Day • Columbus Day • Columbus Day • Columbus Day

Columbus Day Dynamics!

Objective: To keep a log about a journey on one of Christopher Columbus' ships

Materials: paper, pens

Directions: Discuss the celebration of Columbus Day with the class. (It honors Christopher Columbus' first voyage to America in 1492.) Stress the difficulties Columbus encountered in funding his expedition and in the trip. Also discuss his discoveries. (He had a hard time getting anyone to back him because he wasn't very accurate on his idea of the size of the world and because of the expense involved in his request. Concerning difficulties in his trip, Columbus had trouble with his crew, the weather, the Portuguese, etc.)

Have each student pretend that he/she is a sailor aboard the *Niña, Pinta* or *Santa Maria*. Students should keep a log—a nautical record of a ship's voyages— similar to a diary. The log should include sightings, weather conditions, jobs done, relationships among the crew members, feelings and emotions, problems aboard the ship, solutions of problems, food, entertainment, etc. It would be interesting if students noted the actual age of the real crew.

Presidents' Day • Presidents' Day • Presidents' Day • Presidents' Day • Presidents' Day

Wonderful George Washington (Activity 1)

Objectives: To draw George Washington and to write three facts about him

Materials: drawing paper, crayons, books about George Washington

Directions: Have the students draw a sketch of George Washington. Have them start with an oval face and then add hair, eyes, mouth (always closed so as not to show the wooden teeth) and nose. (No matter what variations the students have, these always wind up resembling George Washington.) Under the picture, students should write three facts about George Washington.

Celebration . . . continued

Presidents' Day • Presidents' Day • Presidents' Day • Presidents' Day • Presidents' Day

Vote for George! (Activity 2)

Objective: To make posters and write speeches containing a persuasive message

Materials: posterboard, markers

Directions: Have students bring in any campaign material they can find. Discuss it with them and the role it plays in a campaign. Then, tell students that George Washington is running for President of the new United States and that they are his campaign manager. Students then make posters urging people to vote for George Washington. Each student's poster should be different. Have them use catchy campaign slogans. Students should also make a list of reasons why people should vote for George Washington. Students can also write a campaign speech for him. Display students' posters around the school.

VOTE for WASHINGTON!

He led our armies. Now let him lead our COUNTRY!

Cherry Tree Fun (Activity 3)

Objective: To ponder two legendary questions relating to George Washington

Materials: paper, pens, poem (below)

Directions: Discuss the George Washington cherry tree legend with the class. Then, read the poem below to them:

After reading the poem, pose these two questions to the class:

1. Do you think the cherry tree incident really happened?
2. Do you think that George Washington never told a lie?

Have the students write an answer to both questions. Have them explain why they feel that way.

When George Washington was very young,
He took his little hatchet.
He chopped his Father's cherry tree.
He only meant to scratch it.
"Who chopped my cherry tree?"
His Father asked.
"T'was I Sir.
I'm really very sorry, but
I cannot tell a lie, Sir."

Celebration . . . continued

Presidents' Day • Presidents' Day • Presidents' Day • Presidents' Day • Presidents' Day

Say It Again, George! (Activity 4)

Objective: To write a speech

Materials: paper, pens, camcorder (optional)

Directions: Have students pretend that they are George Washington at Valley Forge and that their soldiers are cold and hungry. Ask students to write a speech to boost their soldiers' morale. Or, students can pretend that they are George Washington and were just elected President of the new country. Tell students to write a speech they would give to the people on television. Let students give the speeches to the class. Videotape them if possible.

Lincoln Log Cabins (Activity 5)

Objective: To create log cabins

Materials: tongue depressors, white glue, paint, paintbrushes, construction paper, oaktag, books about Abraham Lincoln, scissors, pens

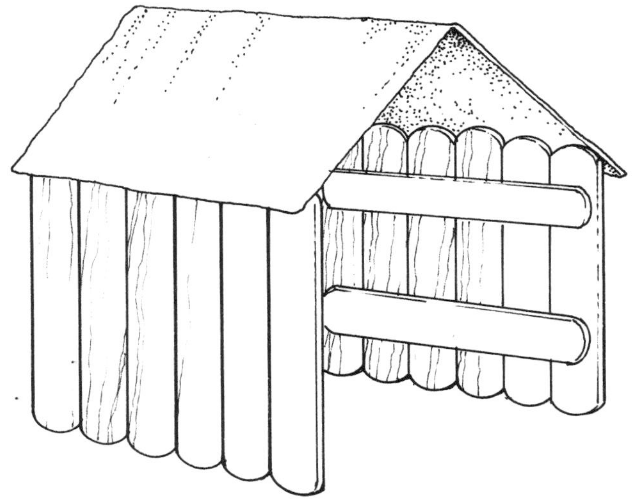

Directions: Have students arrange tongue depressors in an overlapping fashion to form a square. Students should continue in this fashion gluing the sticks in place until the log cabin is as high as students want it. Let students paint on the doors and windows. Then, they can make a roof either from tongue depressors or construction paper. Students then glue the log cabin to a piece of oaktag and write three facts about Abraham Lincoln on the oaktag.

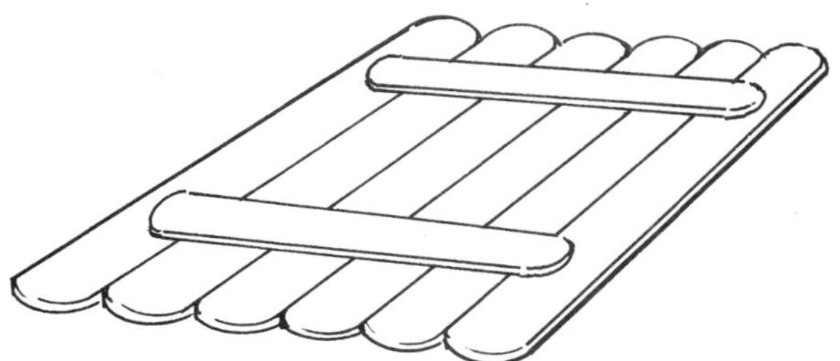

Celebration . . . continued

Presidents' Day • Presidents' Day • Presidents' Day • Presidents' Day • Presidents' Day

Lincoln's Big Decision (Activity 6)

Objective: To write a story involving a response to a situation centered on slavery

Materials: paper, pens

Directions: Have students pretend that they are Abraham Lincoln and that slavery has not yet been abolished. Tell them that a runaway slave has come to them for help. If the slave is caught, he/she will be sent back to his/her master and probably beaten. If the students help him/her, they will be breaking the law and while they do not like the law, they are the President of the United States. Have students write about what they will say to the slave and what they will do.

Debate Time (Activity 7)

Objective: To debate issues

Directions: Explain to students that Lincoln ran against a man named Stephen Douglas for President. These men were involved in a series of debates. These debates centered on slavery. Divide students into teams. Have the teams debate certain issues. They can be classroom, school, city or national issues.

Martin Luther King, Jr. Day • Martin Luther King, Jr. Day • Martin Luther King, Jr. Day

We All Join Hands! (Activity 1)

Objective: To promote understanding, tolerance and friendship

Materials: construction paper, markers, scissors, stapler

Directions: Have the students draw self-portraits on construction paper using markers. They should draw a full body portrait. Then, have them cut out their self-portrait. Mount them in an arc pattern on a bulletin board covered with paper in such a manner so that they are all joining hands.

Celebration . . . continued

Martin Luther King, Jr. Day • Martin Luther King, Jr. Day • Martin Luther King, Jr. Day

Dr. King Quatrain (Activity 2)

Objective: To use quatrain poetry to describe the life and peacemaking efforts of Dr. Martin Luther King, Jr.

Materials: large alphabet stencils, markers, ruler, writing paper, pencils

Directions: After reading about and discussing the life of civil rights leader Dr. Martin Luther King, Jr., use this lesson to see how students apply their knowledge of this man. Assign each student a letter in his full name:

D R. M A R T I N L U T H E R K I N G, J R.

(Several students may need to pair up, depending upon the size of the class.) Have each student or pair of students create a four-line poem integrating their knowledge of Dr. King. Explain to students that they will begin their quatrain (ABCB rhyming scheme) poem with their assigned letter and a word that relates to Dr. King. For example:

D is for dream. Or, M is for minister.

The remaining lines might sound as follows:

D is for dream
of the peace for the land
that all men are created equal
and together we should stand.

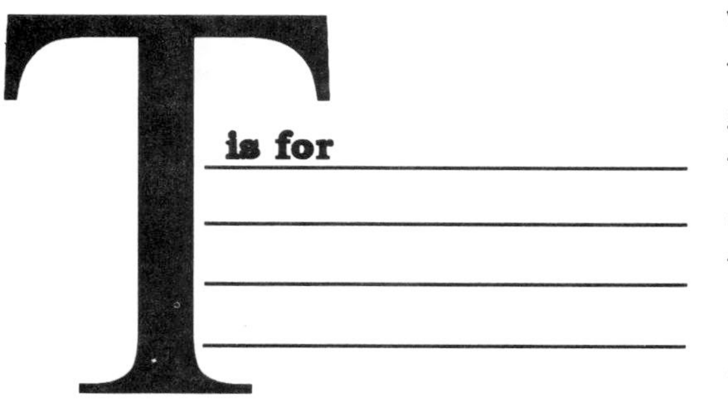

When students have completed their poems, have them trace their assigned letter using a large alphabet stencil and color the letter using markers. To the right of the letter, have students draw four lines using a ruler and write the remaining lines of the poem.

The finished products should be lined up like an acrostic poem on a bulletin board. Read the entire poem with each student/pair reciting his/her/its own verse.

Keeping the Peace! (Activity 3)

Use this activity in the writing center to supplement a classroom discussion of Dr. Martin Luther King, Jr.'s peacemaking efforts.

Objective: To create a book describing peaceful solutions to a variety of situations

Materials: copies of the dove pattern (page 261), copies of the activity cards (page 262), 10 sheets of white construction paper per student, ruler, pencil, scissors, markers, crayons, hole punch, yarn

Directions: From the white construction paper, have each student trace and cut out ten doves.

continued on page 260

Celebration . . . continued

Keeping the Peace! (Activity 3) continued

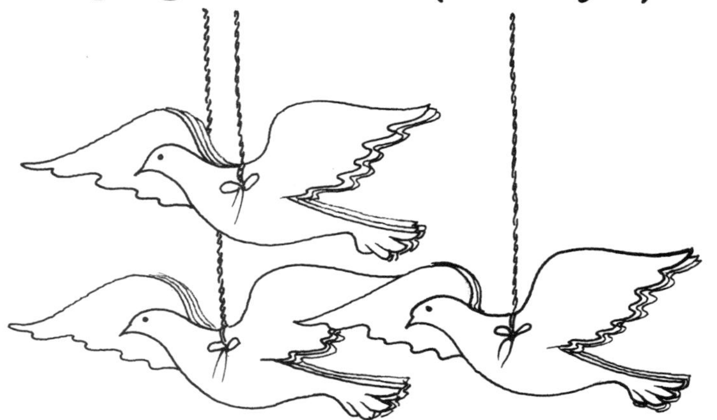

Then, instruct students to punch a hole in the center of the first dove's back. Students can use this hole as a pattern to guide the placement of the remaining holes. Students then thread a piece of yarn through the holes and tie to assemble the pages together.

With the exception of the cover and one other page, have students create lines using a ruler on the front of each dove page to help them keep their answers neat.

When all this is complete, students are ready to select an activity card and follow its directions. Students may also add borders or illustrations to the back side of each page if they like.

When students have finished all of the activities presented on the cards, have them decorate the cover producing a title such as "Ideas for Peace." Share students' books and discuss their various suggestions for keeping peace. Hang the doves from the ceiling as peaceful, soaring reminders to students to solve problems sensibly.

Peaceful Solutions (Activity 4)

Objective: To come up with peaceful solutions to problems

Materials: pencils, paper

Directions: Discuss Martin Luther King, Jr. with students (his philosophy regarding peaceful solutions, why we honor him, the bus boycotts, the marches, etc.).

Next, have each student select a problem and work out a peaceful solution to it. The problem could relate to the classroom, school, city, nation or world. The problem and its solution should be presented orally to the class. After the presentation, the class may ask questions and come up with other solutions to the problem. The solutions brought up should be peaceful ones. (Sample problems: fight on the playground, bully in the class, unkind actions/words of classmates)

Suggested Reading:

Meet Martin Luther King, Jr. by James T. Dekay

The Picture Life of Martin Luther King, Jr. by Margaret B. Young

Martin Luther King Day by Linda Lowry

Dove Pattern

Celebration . . . continued

Martin Luther King, Jr. Day • Martin Luther King, Jr. Day • Martin Luther King, Jr. Day

A Peaceful Plan

List five things that kids can do to make their community more peaceful.

Making Dreams Come True

Write your dream for the future. List three things you can do to make your dream come true.

Working Together

Write about a time that you and a classmate worked together. Have your classmate illustrate it for you.

Solving Problems

Write a problem-solving plan. Tell how to settle differences on the playground without fighting.

Making Changes

Draw and color a picture of something you would like to change.

Write how you would make this change happen.

All Alike

Draw and color a picture of someone who looks different from you.

Write three ways in which you and this person are alike.

A Special Gift

Draw and color a picture of a birthday gift you think Dr. King would have liked.

A Happy Event

Patriotism, kindness and brotherhood made Dr. King happy.

Write about something that has happened in our community that would have made Dr. King happy.

Biographical Charts

Objectives: To research a historical figure and organize the biographical information on a chart

Materials: one large sheet of paper per student, pencils, crayons, markers, glue, scissors

Directions: Create or generate a list of historical figures students may want to learn more about. Each student should then research a person of his/her choice. Students should research in order to find the following information about their person:

1. where he/she was born
2. who the members in his/her family were
3. what this person is/was famous for; what his/her accomplishments are/were
4. what influenced this person to accomplish what he/she did
5. why they chose this person to research

Inform the students that they will be creating a biographical chart on which to display the above information. Tell them that they may use pictures, symbols, sentences, outlines, photographs, etc. on their charts.

In order to create the chart, each student should divide his/her paper into six equal sections creating six boxes. Each box should contain a piece of the above information. The top left box may contain a sketch, or picture, of the subject accompanied by the name of the person and will serve as a title for the chart. The second top right box may contain information regarding the birthplace (i.e. it may be a sketch of the home, a city name with a symbol to represent that city such as, "San Francisco and the Golden Gate Bridge," etc.). The middle boxes should contain information about the subject's family and famous achievements. If the subject was an inventor, for example, a student may cut out pictures of the inventions. Family members could be represented by stick figures. The bottom left box should tell of anyone or anything that may have influenced this person to do what he/she did. The last box should explain why the student chose this particular person to research. Let students present their charts. Display them.

Who Am I?

ELIZABETH BLACKWELL
First Woman Doctor

Objective: To learn about famous people in the history of our country

Materials: list of famous people, box, encyclopedias, books about the famous people on the list

Directions: Make a list of famous people in the history of our country. Put a variety of people on the list including political and historical personalities, athletes, etc. Some examples include:

- George Washington
- Thomas Jefferson
- Abraham Lincoln
- Christopher Columbus
- Governor William Bradford
- Gloria Steinem
- Pocahontas
- Jane Addams
- Martin Luther King, Jr.
- Jackie Robinson
- George Washington Carver
- Mary McLeod Bethune
- Susan B. Anthony
- Bill Clinton
- Hillary Clinton
- Paul Revere
- Scott Joplin
- Betsy Ross
- Mark Twain
- Michael Jordan
- Jackie Joyner-Kersee

Have enough names so that everyone in the class gets a different name. It would also be a good idea to select names of people that are at least somewhat familiar to the children. Put all the names in a box and have each child draw one name.

Have the children research their selections. Give each one an assigned date on which he/she will present his/her person to the class. Explain that the presentation will be oral (it may be read) and will not include the name of the famous person. The class will then try to figure out who the person is from the information given. Below is an outline you may want students to use for the presentation.

— Name of person being described
— Male or Female
— Living or Dead (If dead, when did this person live?)
— What is this person famous for?
— What field did this person work in?
— Where did this person live or work?
— Other important information

Women's Rights

Complete the activity below and on page 266 to heighten students' awareness to the many contributions women have made.

Grandma Moses and Rural America (Activity 1)

Objective: To create a mural depicting typical American life

Materials: mural paper, bright tempera paint, paintbrushes, pencils, encyclopedias and books on American folk art, scratch paper

Directions: Tell students that Anna Mary Robertson, or Grandma Moses, was over 70 years old when she seriously began to pursue painting. She was a self-taught artist who based her colorful realistic scenes of 19th century rural life on her childhood memories.

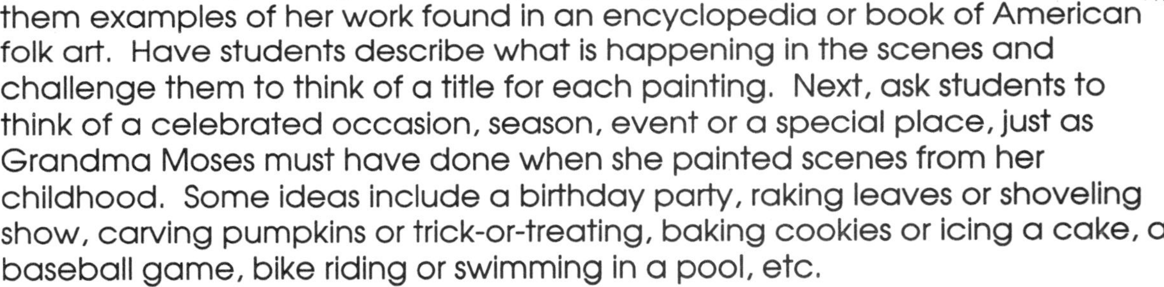

Familiarize students with Grandma Moses' style of painting by showing them examples of her work found in an encyclopedia or book of American folk art. Have students describe what is happening in the scenes and challenge them to think of a title for each painting. Next, ask students to think of a celebrated occasion, season, event or a special place, just as Grandma Moses must have done when she painted scenes from her childhood. Some ideas include a birthday party, raking leaves or shoveling show, carving pumpkins or trick-or-treating, baking cookies or icing a cake, a baseball game, bike riding or swimming in a pool, etc.

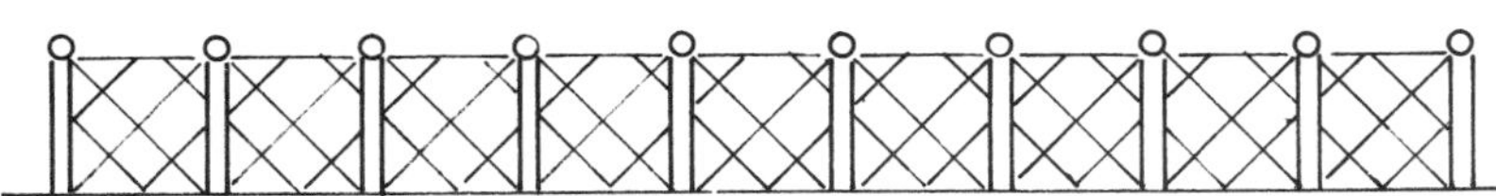

Let students plan their own scenes by first sketching them on scratch paper using a pencil. On mural paper, group the sketched scenes where possible to create a layout of American scenes. Let students draw their scenes on mural paper. Then, they can paint them. Encourage students to add small figures and to use a fine paintbrush to add detail.

Since color was an essential feature of Grandma Moses' work, supply the students with an array of dazzling paint colors. Allow students to create new shades of paint by mixing colors. The students will enjoy bringing their scenes to life.

Women's Rights continued

Women's Suffrage (Activity 2)

Objective: To conduct interviews relating to women's rights

Materials: paper, pens, map of United States

Background: The first women's rights convention was held in Seneca Falls, NY in 1848. The speaker, Elizabeth Cady Stanton, read the Declaration of Sentiments, modeled after the Declaration of Independence, at the convention. The sentiments were debated by the crowd, and at the end of the second day, a vote was taken on whether to adopt them. When the final count was in, 68 women and 32 men had voted to adopt the Seneca Falls Declaration. Elizabeth Cady Stanton, Lucretia Mott and others had awakened the people of the United States to the rights of women. They laid the foundation for the women's suffrage movement in the United States.

Directions: Use a map of the United States to locate Seneca Falls, NY, the site of the first women's rights convention. (If you have taught the Bill of Rights, point out to students that the convention exercised our First Amendment rights to free speech and assembly.) Also, point out to students that the women of 1848 had very few rights. They often could not work or further their education or vote for anything! Discuss how the daily life of women in the 19th century differed from women of today.

After the discussion, pair up the students and have them imagine that they are a TV news anchor of today interviewing a 19th century person, male or female, who is opposed to women's rights. Have the pair work together to create a set of interview questions and the responses. Tell them to think about what a person might have said about the Seneca Falls Convention and about the women attending the convention. Then, have the pair select roles and act out the scene for the class.

Extension: Several newspapers back in the 1800's reported on the Seneca Falls event. Have students write news stories considering what those papers and others might have printed and why.

International Day Celebration

An International Day is a great way to foster multicultural awareness, celebrate the heritage of the children in your class and emphasize pride in one's heritage. Try some of the activities below and on pages 268-279 to let your students have fun celebrating their heritage!

Presentation Pride (Activity 1)

Objective: To learn about one's country of origin

Materials: encyclopedias and other books about countries, paper, pens, graph paper

Directions: Have the children in your class find out the country, or countries, that their parents, grandparents or great grandparents, etc. came from before they came to this country. Have the children select one of these countries to make a presentation on to give to the class. The presentation may include any or all of the following suggestions or any other suggestions the students may have:

1. location of the country
2. the city or town
3. when relative left
4. why relative left that country and why he/she came to the United States
5. an artifact, article of clothing, etc. from that country
6. a particular food indigenous to the country
7. a folktale from the country
8. holiday and special holiday customs of the country

It would be special if some of this information could come from the parents, grandparents, etc. However, other resources can also be used. For instance, the library, the tourist bureau and the embassy of each country are good sources of information. The tourist bureau and the embassy usually respond very well to requests for information written by students. Below is a sample letter students could write.

> Address of Sender
>
> Date
>
> Address of Recipient
>
> Dear __________ ,
>
> My name is __________ . I am in third grade at __________ school in __________ . I am studying about __________ because my __________ was born there. I would appreciate it if you would send me any information about my _________ 's native country ___________ .
>
> Thank you very much.
>
> Sincerely,
>
> ____________________

continued on page 268

International Day Celebration continued

Presentation Pride continued

Assign each child a date on which he/she will make the presentation to the class. Keep a chart noting all the countries that have been presented. When the presentations are completed, compare the students to a tossed salad. Count how many "ingredients" are in the salad. Indicate to students how healthy a salad is and explain that a good salad has more than one ingredient, and all the ingredients go well together.

Make a bar graph indicating each country presented and how many children presented the same country.

Let's Get to Know . . . (Activity 2)

Objective: To study the history, geography, customs, etc. of one particular country

Materials: paper; pens; encyclopedias, books, travel brochures and other sources of information about the country you choose to study

Directions: Select a country that may have special relevance to your class. Contact a local travel agency, the tourist bureau for that country (if available) and/or the embassy for that country to ask for travel brochures, pamphlets and any other information that they have available.

Set up an area in your room where you can put books about the country and information from other sources.

Divide the class into groups to research specific areas about the country. Some of the areas could include the **Geography of the Country** (location, mountains, rivers, lakes, major cities, climate, etc.), **Government/Political Information** (population, flag, national anthem, type of government, political subdivisions, etc.), **Manners and Customs** (language, holiday celebrations, foods, dress, etc.), **Art/Music** (famous artists, famous musicians, architecture, museums, etc.), **History** (famous people, origins, rulers, wars—political alliances, etc.), **Economics** (principal industries, agriculture, imports and exports, etc.), **Miscellaneous Facts** (religions, sports, problems of the country, education, etc.).

continued on page 269

International Day Celebration continued

Let's Get to Know . . . continued

Nepál

Give each group an outline to follow. Have each group prepare a report on its specific area. Have the class learn songs in the language of the country and a dance that might be indigenous to the country. Invite guests to the International Day Celebration. The guest list can include parents, grandparents, a "special person," a local senior citizen group or another class. To invite guests to the party, send home the letter below or write one of your own.

continued on page 270

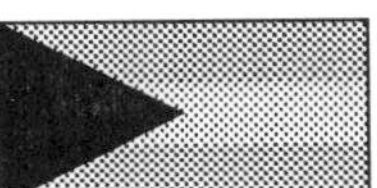      

Date ____________________

Dear ____________________,

On ____________________, our class is having an International Day Celebration. The country we are studying for this celebration is ____________________. We would like to invite you to share this occasion with us. The festivities will take place in our classroom, #__________, from __________ to __________.

Sincerely,

____

Please RSVP and return the slip below to school by ______________.

__________ will attend.

number of people __________

__________ I cannot attend.

Signature ____________________

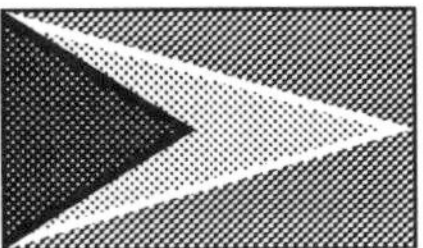 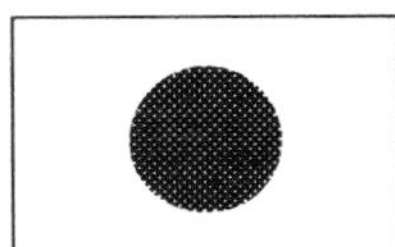    

International Day Celebration continued

Let's Get to Know . . . continued

If it is necessary to limit attendance because of limited space, you could indicate in your letter that this is a Special Person Day, and each student can invite one special person.

For the celebration, divide the class into groups. Each group will prepare a special food of the country. Research the foods and provide recipe books from which the children can select recipes. When each group has selected a recipe, send the letter below home to parents.

On the special day, decorate the room with flags of the country, illustrations and maps. If possible, have the children wear costumes of the country.

For the program, have the groups present their reports, sing songs and perform any dances they may have learned. Display books, pamphlets and any artifacts made in that country that the students may have brought to school. Have the children serve the foods they made to the guests.

This International Day Celebration can take place once during the year or as often as once a month depending on how many countries you want to study.

Date ____________________

Dear Parents,

We need your help for our International Day Celebration. Each child in the class has selected a recipe to prepare for the special day. Please help your child with the preparation of the food.

Your child's recipe is attached. Please make sure that he/she brings this food to school on ____________________.

Thank you for your cooperation.

Sincerely,

____

International Day Celebration continued

A Cultural Mosaic (Activity 3)

Objective: To create a list of new experiences people who immigrate to the United States must face

Materials: one sheet of large watercolor poster paper per student, watercolors, paintbrushes, book *Making a New Home in America* by Maxine B. Rosenberg, variety of multicultural books, chart paper, marker

Directions: You and the students will work together in a large group to develop a pictorial representation of the world's multicultural composition. To achieve this, read *Making a New Home in America* or a similar immigrant story. In this book, the four children described are newcomers to the United States having immigrated with their families. They all experience some fear, confusion, wonderment and surprise with their new lives in the United States. Upon completion of the story, have the students discuss the changes that each child experienced and document their ideas on chart paper. Explain to students that the differences the children faced were due to their cultural upbringing. Their life with their family taught them special values and traditions.

Have each student use watercolors to paint a rainbow on a poster-size sheet of paper. Point out to the students that while each color is distinct (red, orange, yellow, green, blue and violet) and adds beauty to the whole, the colors also blend at the edges. Tell the students that in the weeks to come, the class will be exploring how this rainbow is just like the "Cultural Mosaic" of the United States of America.

Explain to students that they will be studying about different cultures. Display both the rainbow and the chart to be referred to throughout the study. Also, have the book *Making a New Home in America* available to the students as well as a variety of children's literature that represents the multitude of cultures that will be experienced within the unit.

International Day Celebration continued

Meet My Family Bulletin Board (Activity 4)

Objectives: To define the concept of family as a group of people who live together and share many experiences and to realize that each family is unique in its structure (members and size)

Materials: drawing paper, crayons, markers, pencils, scissors

Directions: Have each student draw pictures of the members in his/her family using a separate piece of paper for each person. Provide various sizes of cut paper, encouraging the children to choose the size they believe is appropriate for each member.

After all members of the students' families have been created, have each child cut them out and display them as a group on a large bulletin board entitled **Meet My Family**. It is important to develop the concept that all families will not have a mother and father, and some will have neither a mother nor a father. Children should be aware of the fact that family groups differ.

Use the bulletin board as a springboard for discussions centering around the purpose of family. Discuss with the students questions like: "What living things live in families? Why do some animals live in families? Why do people live in families? What are some things that your family does as a group? What are some things that members of your family do individually?"

My Family Is Special! (Activity 5)

Objectives: To describe similarities and differences in family structures and to realize that families are both similar and different

Materials: one copy of the student activity sheet per student (page 274), pencil

Directions: Using the family members that each child created in the previous lesson, begin a discussion on how families are similar in their needs.

Then, discuss how families are different. Ask students to name one way that their family is unique. (Each family is unique in that it is the only family made up of each student and the unique members of his/her family.) Allow time for many student responses and encourage wide participation.

continued on page 273

International Day Celebration continued

My Family Is Special! (Activity 5) continued

Have the children move into small cooperative groups and pass out the activity sheets. This sheet will help students to see their own families as special. Depending on time constraints, the activity can be completed in class or taken home and filled out with the help of each student's family.

As the sheets are completed and returned, have the students share them with the class or their small groups. Help the students identify families that are like their own. Ask them questions such as, "In what way are other families like your own? Is there a particular family group different from yours? In what way?"

Where Did My Family Come From? (Activity 6)

Objective: To learn about and fill out a family tree

Materials: one copy of the family tree per student (page 275), map or globe

Directions: Tell the students that they are going to try and find out the countries in which their parents and grandparents (and perhaps great grandparents) were born. Explain that these people, or relatives, are also called ancestors, or the people from whom we are descended.

Introduce the following concept: "Most of us were born in the United States but not all of us. Most of our parents were born in the United States, but not all of them. We are almost all alike because some of us are citizens of the United States. But almost all of us are different, too, because our families came from another country, or many different countries."

Tell students that they have been talking about their family groups to which they belong. Sometimes how a person looks, what he/she does and his/her name tells what groups he/she belongs to. But sometimes, these do not give us much information. So, to find out many more things about a person, you must ask that person.

Give each student a copy of page 275. Ask the students to go home and fill it out with the help of their parents.

When the charts are returned, sum up the exercise by encouraging the students to tell about where their families came from by reading their charts.

Help the students locate the countries on the map or globe. Have the students design little family flags that could be attached to the map or globe to indicate their family's country of origin. The completed charts should be kept in a special "family" folder along with the activity from Activity 5.

Name ____________________ Date ______________

My Family Is Special!

We are ____

____ .

We have ____

and ____ .

and ____

We do special things like ______________________________

and ____

and ____

and ____ .

We like these special things because ____________________

____ .

We know special people like ____________________________

____ .

We want ____ .

We can ____ .

We eat ____

______________________________ for favorite meals.

We help each other ____________________________________

and ____ .

You may also wish to include a photograph of your family!

Where Did My Family Come From?

Name ____________________

Please write in only the country of birth for each relative listed below.

________	________	________	________	________	________	________	________
Great-Grandmother	Great-Grandfather	Great-Grandmother	Great-Grandfather	Great-Grandmother	Great-Grandfather	Great-Grandmother	Great-Grandfather

________ Grandmother

________ Grandfather

________ Grandmother

________ Grandfather

________ Mother

________ Father

________ me

International Day Celebration continued

Family Teachers (Activity 7)

Objective: To describe how families function as transmitters of information

Directions: To build on what makes families unique, this lesson involves the things that children learn from their own family. Parents and siblings are a child's first teacher, and children learn many things at home before they begin school.

Have the students think for a few minutes about the most important thing they have learned from someone in their family. Ask for volunteers to give their responses. Make two columns on the board—one entitled "I learned to . . ." and one entitled "From . . ." Record the students' responses in the two columns. Have students tell the class who taught them the special skill or activity and record this in the first column. Record who taught them in the second column. For example:

"I learned to . . ."	"From . . ."
ride a bike	dad
bake cookies	grandmother
catch a baseball	big brother
fish	uncle
play chess	grandfather
skate	mom

After the class has completed the list, study it to find similarities and differences. Lead the students in a discussion of the importance of these things learned at home as compared with the things they learn in school. Talk about the family as teachers.

Extension: Have the students list things they learned from their own families (with words or pictures) and things they would like to learn more about. Have the students put a star around the things they could teach someone else.

Hopi Planting Chant (Activity 8)

Objective: To generalize about the variety of ways in which the values of cultures are communicated over the years

Materials: copies of the Hopi Indian Chant (right), chart paper, markers, picture of Arizona's desert land

Preparation: On a large sheet of chart paper, print the chant. Attach several pictures of the desert land of Arizona around it.

NEVER PLANT JUST ONE SEED.
ALWAYS PLANT FOUR—
THE FIRST FOR YOUR ENEMY,
THE SECOND FOR THE POOR,
THE THIRD FOR THE PESTS WHICH
PREY UPON THE FIELD.
TAKE FOR YOURSELF
THE FOURTH SEED'S YIELD.

continued on page 277

International Day Celebration continued

Hopi Planting Chant (Activity 8) continued

Description: Begin the lesson by explaining to the students that the Hopi Indians have lived for hundreds of years in a part of the United States (Arizona) where there is little water. Tell students that these Native Americans have learned to grow their food in these conditions. Ask for a volunteer to locate Arizona on the map.

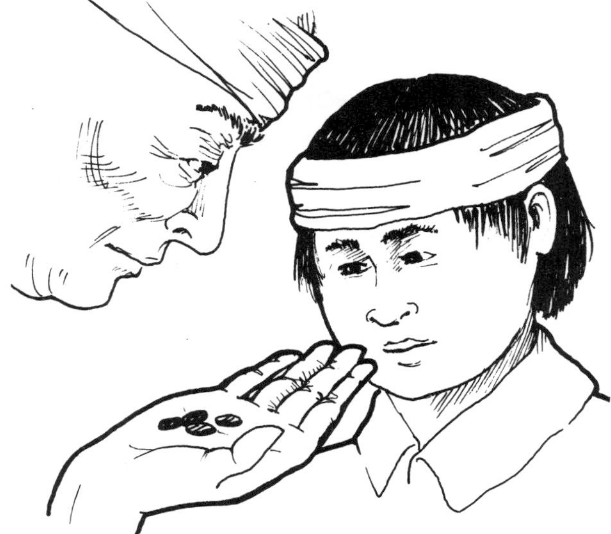

Explain to students that the Hopi Indians pass their wisdom on to their children in many ways. One way is through the Hopi Planting Chant. Read the chant with the students. Then, generate discussion with students by asking some of the following questions: "What do you think the Hopi parents were teaching their children with the chant? Why do you think they used a chant to teach this lesson? How do you think the children learned the chant? How do you think the chant was passed down from generation to generation?"

The students should conclude that parents teach their children the things that are important to them. These values are taught in a variety of ways.

Radio Days and the Games People Play

The main objective for activities 9-11 is for students to experience a variety of ways in which the family serves as a transmitter of cultural heritage. The basic idea the children should grasp from the activities is that families have passed down skills, values and traditions in many ways, and all of these things contribute to one's cultural heritage.

Lei It On Me (Activity 9)

Objective: To make gifts with love

Materials: book *The Gift of Hawaii* by Laura Bannon, colored paper, flower pattern/stencil, straws cut to 1", string approximately 40" long, masking tape, scissors

Directions: Prepare the students for this lesson several days prior to it by having students choose a song and a game that they enjoy together with their family and that they learned at home from their parents, grandparents, brothers or sisters. Have students bring these in and share them with the class.

continued on page 278

International Day Celebration continued

Lei It On Me! (Activity 9) continued

Encourage the students to bring in samples of things that are traditional within their family—songs, games, holiday and other traditions, etc. that have been passed down from generation to generation. Also, you might have students bring in a bag lunch for a "picnic" in the classroom.

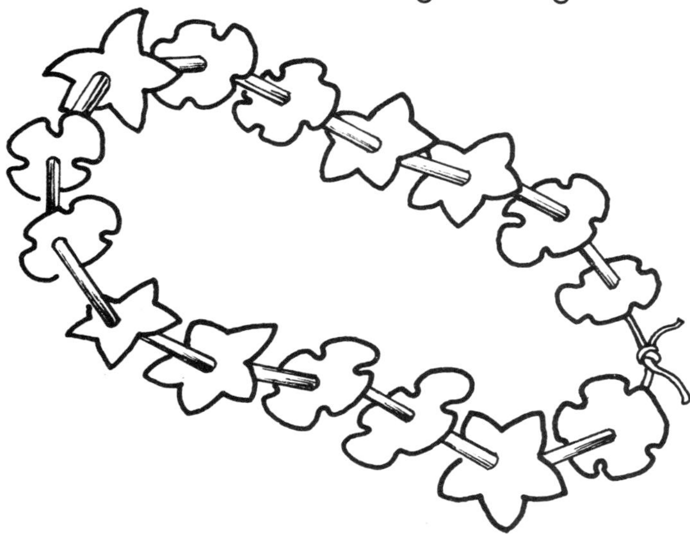

Read *The Gift of Hawaii* to your students. It is about a boy who wants to buy his mother a muumuu for her birthday, but he has no money. Instead, he decides to make his gift one of love—a lei. Discuss with the children the concept of gift-giving. Ask them what they could do if they wanted to give someone a gift of love.

Using colored paper, have each student cut out 15 flowers. Then, students should take turns stringing first a flower, then a straw spacer, then a flower again, etc. Put the materials listed at a table with enough chairs so that several students can work together.

Eye See It! (Activity 10)

Objective: To learn about a legend and make a god's eye

Materials: two Popsicle sticks, several different colors of yarn, scissors

Directions: Share with students the legend of Ojo de Dios, or god's eye.

This legend tells of a beautiful Aztec (Mexican) princess who was born blind. The gods promised to restore her sight if anyone could show what a god's eye looked like. Many attempts were made, but none pleased the gods. One day, the rays of the sun shining on one of the princess' tears reflected a brilliant array of colors. The girl's mother saw them. She chose yarn in the colors, and wove them around crossed sticks. As soon as she had finished, the princess was able to see.

Today, the Ojo de Dios may be found in homes of people from many different cultures throughout the world. They are used as decorative art as well as to bring blessings to the home. It is believed that the cross formed by the sticks symbolizes the four forces of nature: earth, fire, water and air. The eye in the center is to ward off evil.

continued on page 279

International Day Celebration continued

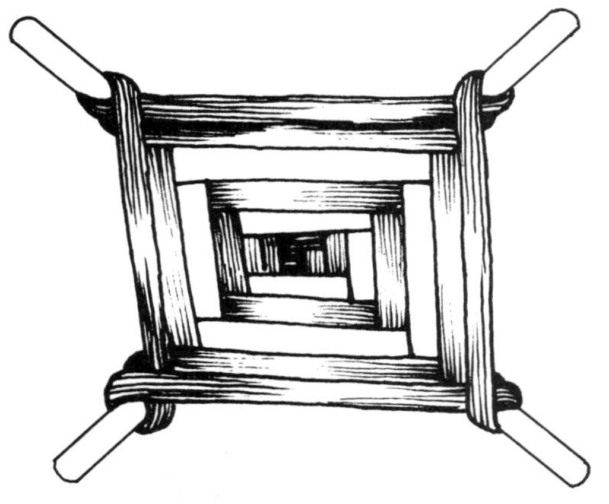

Eye See It! (Activity 10) continued

Have students make a god's eye. To do this, they must tie two sticks together at a 90° angle. Show them how to go around the sticks once, rotating as they go. To change colors, students just tie new yarn to the end of the original color on the sticks and keep going. You may want to have a sample students can use as a guide.

Native American Pottery (Activity 11)

Objective: To help students become aware of and appreciate pottery

Materials: book *When Clay Sings* by Taylor Bury, clay, books depicting a variety of Native American art forms

Directions: Tell students that pottery-making is an ancient art which many Native Americans have practiced for centuries. The skill of pottery-making is passed down from generation to generation. It is part of many Native Americans' cultural heritage.

Read *When Clay Sings.* Take the time to study the illustrations and discuss the story. Help the students appreciate the importance of the pottery and the inscribed designs which reflect the feeling these early people had for animals.

In cooperation with the art teacher, have the students begin working with clay in art class, making various shapes using only their hands as tools.

To enrich what the children are experiencing in art class, make available to them books depicting a variety of Native American art forms.

Discuss and expand on the following questions: "How did people get the things they need for cooking and eating long ago? What did they use to make bowls? Where did the clay come from? How did they make clay bowls? How are most bowls made today? Do some people still make bowls by hand? Why did people decorate the bowls?"

How a Bill Becomes a Law

Objective: To create a flow chart and dramatize the lawmaking process

Materials: four 5" x 8" index cards, four 5" arrows cut from construction paper

Directions: Introduce students to the steps involved in the lawmaking process. (See below.) Break your class up into four groups and assign each group one of the following roles: creators of the bill, House of Representatives, Senators and President.

Next, give each group an index card. Each group should brainstorm what its particular responsibilities are in regards to the lawmaking process and write them on the index card. Under this, the groups should write their responsibilities concerning the lawmaking process. Review this process again, but this time, create a flow chart as the process progresses. Collect the cards from the groups as each group's responsibilities are discussed and tape them to the board. Use the arrows to show the flow and changing directions of the process.

Now, you are ready to have students dramatize the lawmaking process. Begin by deciding on a problem that may be alleviated with a new law. (Some possible issues include bicycle helmet law, homelessness, endangered species, the right to bear arms, a longer school day with longer recess periods, etc.) You may want the entire class to discuss possibilities and then have the "Bill Creators" group decide upon the bill and put it into writing. Encourage students to be practical and concise. When the bill is complete, have students role-play the process with each group acting on it. Students can use the flow chart as a guide.

How a Bill Becomes a Law

1. Someone, or a group of people, sees a need for a law. It may be a member of Congress, or it may be you.
2. A member of Congress, the President and other government officials may propose a law to Congress.
3. Usually, Congress must pass the bill by a majority vote or else the bill dies.
4. If the bill is approved, it is sent to the President.
5. If the President signs it, it becomes law.
6. If the President does not sign it within ten days, it becomes a law. If he/she vetoes it, it goes back to Congress.
7. Congress votes again. Now, the bill must receive 2/3 vote in both houses. If it does, it becomes law without the President's signature. If it does not get 2/3 vote, the bill dies.

Classroom Tax?

Objective: To personalize the tax system for third graders

Directions: After defining tax (money paid to finance government services and activities) and discussing why students' parents pay an income tax, discuss with students the possibility of a classroom tax. Pose the following questions to students: "Would collecting taxes help our classroom? If so, how? If taxes were to be collected, how would the amount of money collected from each student be determined? What would the money, or tax, be used for? Should the teacher pay a tax?" As you discuss the questions, encourage students to be aware of and examine the United States tax system before arriving at their own answers.

Extension: Determine what the classroom needs are (tissues, paper, pencils, etc.) and create a budget. Hold a debate concerning the idea of a classroom tax. Allow students to vote for or against implementing a classroom tax. (In order to keep the budget reasonable, you may want to implement the tax for a month, or if the budget is elaborate, even a week!) Before the vote, be sure to discuss how students will earn their tax money, if the idea should be approved by your third graders.

TV Tax?

Objective: To understand the purpose of a tax

Directions: Discuss with students the idea of a tax imposed on watching television or for playing a video game. With the class, create a reason for the tax, and set the tax rate per show/game. Ask the students to answer the following questions: "How would you feel? Would you watch/play the same amount of time as you do now? If you could only watch one program/play one game each week because of a high tax, which one would it be? Do you feel a tax like this would be a good idea?"

Election Day Activities

November elections every year provide an excellent opportunity to involve students in current events. This is also a great way for students to become aware of the candidates, the campaign issues and the mechanics of a campaign and an election. The elections can be federal, state and/or local. Another wonderful thing about the elections is that they, and the activities on pages 283-285, provide students and their parents with the opportunity to spend time together. Send home the letter below before beginning these activities.

Following are some additional activities that you may want the students to complete:

- Have the students write news articles reporting on the debate, the polls and/or the election.
- The students can make posters reminding people to vote.
- Have the students make up campaign slogans for the candidates.
- The students can write news articles about the candidates.

Dear Parents,

This month, your child will be studying the following election: ______________________________ . The children will become familiar with the candidates, the election issues, the mechanics of a campaign, a debate and an election.

Your child will have various assignments including finding and discussing articles from newspapers and news magazines. Please be prepared to help your child find articles and discuss them at home with him/her.

We will also be conducting a debate in our class. At this time, children will be asked to formulate questions they would like to put before the candidates. Discussions about the candidates at home will be helpful to your child. Encourage him/her to follow the debates in the media and to be aware of the campaign issues.

We hope that these activities in school will make the children more aware of the democratic procedure by which we elect our officials. We also hope that it will make them more interested in current events and more interested in reading about them in newspapers and news magazines.

Thank you for your interest and cooperation.

Sincerely,

Election Day Activities continued

Getting to Know You (Activity 1)

Objective: To follow a campaign and the involved candidates

Materials: newspaper, magazines, scissors, pictures of candidates in an election you choose to follow, boxes or envelopes

Directions: Discuss elections with students and choose one to follow. Set up a bulletin board for the duration of the campaign. Divide the bulletin board into a number of sections corresponding to the number of candidates to whom you are devoting this lesson. Put a picture of each candidate in his/her own section.

On a rotating basis, assign students to bring in newspaper or magazine articles relating to a particular candidate. The students can present their articles to the class. This should not be a reading of the article, but rather an explanation of it. It should be relative to the candidate's views on issues, and it can be either positive or negative. Put these articles on the board in the appropriate section.

At the end of each week, have an election update discussing all the articles brought in during the week. Remove the newspaper clippings and place them in a special envelope or box set aside for each candidate. Save these for future reference.

Start the next week with a new group of news items. They may be about the same or entirely different issues.

Debate Time (Activity 2)

Objective: To learn about and hold a debate

Materials: newspapers and magazines about candidates in a chosen election

Directions: About one month before the election, start to prepare for the candidates' big debate. Discuss with the class the format of a debate and the rules of a debate. You might want to have some practice debates at this time involving some school-related issues (i.e. number grades vs. letter grades or pass/fail grades; school lunch vs. lunch from home; etc.). A social issue of interest to third graders would also be good for a practice debate.

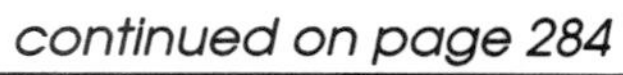

continued on page 284

Election Day Activities continued

Debate Time (Activity 2) continued

Three weeks before the candidates' debate, have students help you select several students to represent the candidates and several students to act as a panel posing questions. The remainder of the class should be divided into reporters and the general public. A moderator should also be selected.

Candidates should prepare the opening and closing statements of the debate. The panel, the reporters and the general public should prepare questions on all of the issues involved in the campaign. This can either be a homework assignment or it can be done in class. To ensure that all issues are covered, specific assignments can be made. Questions should be discussed in the classroom and duplicate questions can be combined. Candidates should be informed of questions prior to the debate so that they can prepare appropriate answers. It would be a good idea for you to work with each representative group separately as well as with the entire class.

Establish a time frame and be certain that it is strictly adhered to. Hold the big debate in the classroom or in front of parents.

Predictions, Polls and Voting (Activity 3)

Objective: To learn about and conduct polls

Materials: chart paper, marker

Directions: Explain to students that polls can be used to predict the winner, or they can be used to calculate the percentages of people voting for each candidate.

HOW WOULD YOU VOTE?		
	Today	After Debate
Andrew		
Bart		
Cassy		
Dean		
Eleanor		
Frank		
Greg		
Helen		
Jack		
Lauren		

Before the debate, described in Activity 2, poll the class to predict the outcome of a class vote and graph the results. After the debate but before the general election, conduct a class election and graph the results. Compare the vote after the debate with the poll before the debate. Have students discuss why the debate changed any votes if it did. At this point, poll the class to predict the outcome of the general election and graph the results. After the general election, compare the poll with the actual outcome.

Election Day Activities continued

An All-School Vote (Activity 4)

Objectives: To learn about the voting process and to set one up

Materials: paper; shoe box with lid; red, white and blue paint; paintbrushes; chart paper

Directions: Have the students prepare ballots for the whole school or for the entire third-grade level. A sample ballot is shown. Prepare a ballot box using a shoe box painted red, white and blue for the occasion. Put a list in the top of the box.

GENERAL ELECTION

For President
Alexander ☐
Mohammed ☐

For Vice-President
Tanya ☐
Logan ☐

For Treasurer
Theresa ☐
Keshandra ☐

For Secretary
Jamal ☐
Tom ☐
Sigrid ☐

Two days before the election, hand out the ballots. Have a representative from your class go to each class that is going to participate in the election to distribute the ballots. The representative should also explain to students how to mark the ballots. Tell the representative to remind the voters that the ballots must be returned on election day.

Poll your class to predict the number of students in the school who will remember to vote. On the day of the general election, take the ballot box to each participating class so that students can cast their ballots. Tabulate the results and publish them across school. Have students record and publish the following information: the winner, the number of students who voted, the number of students who forgot to vote, the percentage of students who voted. Students can graph the results. On the day after the election, compare the actual vote of the people with the school vote.

Super Citizens

Objective: To identify ways to become better school citizens

Materials: chart paper, marker, journals, pencils

Directions: This activity is designed to develop students' awareness of their own personal contributions and responsibilities to the school community.

To begin, explain to the class that students have rights, rules and responsibilities to the school community. The rules help maintain order, promote health and safety and protect individual rights. With the students, discuss and make a chart of the various classroom and school rules (i.e. please raise your hand; be prepared; no hats; no running in the halls; etc.). Encourage students to share their thoughts as to why these rules are important.

continued on page 286

Super Citizens continued

Next, ask students what they can do to maintain and promote order, health and safety within the school. Ask students the following questions to help guide them:

What can I do in school . . .

that will make me proud of myself?

that will make the class a better group?

to help another classmate?

to be a better member of the class?

Have students write their responses in their journals.

Learning About the Bill of Rights

As citizens of the United States, we enjoy some important freedoms which affect every aspect of our lives. At times, we view these freedoms as basic, and they are often taken for granted. In many other countries, such fundamental freedoms as the right to practice one's own religion or express one's thoughts in speech or writing are precarious or nonexistent. The activities below and on pages 287-293 are designed to teach students about those blessings of liberty that Americans have long enjoyed.

That's Right! (Activity 1)

Objective: To understand what rights and amendments are

Materials: word web pattern, pencil

Directions: Discuss with students the meaning of the word *rights*. Encourage students to share their ideas in small groups and to create a mind map or word web to illustrate their thoughts on the concept. To do this, give time for each group to discuss and list its ideas and examples of the word *rights* onto one word web. Bring the groups together and have each one share the items it listed on its word web. You might select several students' suggestions to label on a "master" word web drawn on the board. Then, guide students to compose an understandable definition of *rights* such as: Rights—something that one may properly claim as due, including a power or a privilege. Discuss this definition in students' terms by relating it to your classroom. Explain to students that they have a right to learn in an environment that is safe. Each student also has the right to take a test in a quiet atmosphere. Elicit responses from students to evaluate their understanding of this concept.

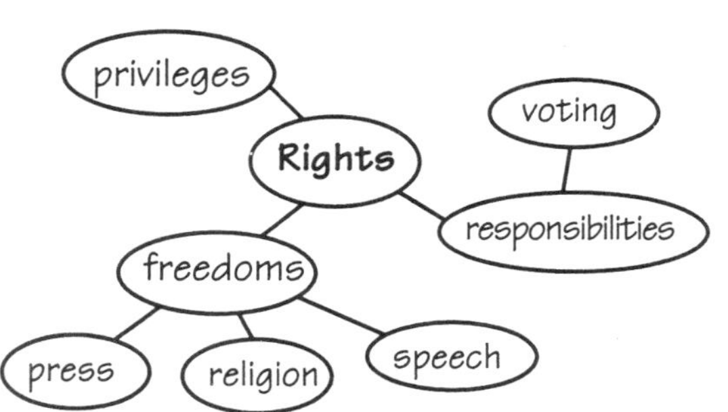

At the end of this discussion, introduce the word *amendment* to students. Explain that it is the act of changing or modifying something. Tell students, for example, that when they revise a piece of writing, they will often make an amendment to their original ideas by adding or changing sentences or words to make the writing sound better.

Bill of Rights continued

Making It Right! (Activity 2)

Objective: To learn about the Bill of Rights

Materials: copy of the summary cards (pages 288-289), copies of the Bill of Rights, magazines, scissors, glue, posterboard, crayons, markers

Directions: Tell students that the original Constitution was first signed in 1787. However, many people agreed to support it only if basic rights were added. This was done in 1791. The first ten amendments to the Constitution are called the Bill of Rights. (Review the meaning of amendments if necessary.) Provide each student with a copy of the Bill of Rights. Lead the class in reading the document aloud. Return to each of the first ten amendments and reread them to the students. Stop after each one and read its summary card (pages 288-289) to summarize its meaning for the students. Encourage students to discuss what the amendment means in their own words before moving on to the next one.

Afterwards, divide the class into ten groups. Have each group take one amendment and illustrate its meaning in collage form on a piece of posterboard. Students may write their assigned amendment in the center of the posterboard and then use magazine pictures or drawings to represent the right ensured in that amendment.

Extension: Since 1791, there have only been 16 amendments added to the Constitution. Some of these amendments have extended our rights as citizens of the United States. (See summary cards on pages 288-289.) Assign groups of students one of the last 16 amendments to research and report on to the class.

Students might also write reports on some of the people who worked to have the amendments added to our Constitution. Some of these people include George Mason, James Madison, Patrick Henry and Elbridge Gerry.

Bill of Rights Summary Cards

1.

Freedom of Religion

Freedom of Speech

Freedom of the Press

Rights of Assembly and Petition

2.

The right to bear arms

3.

Limits the quartering of soldiers

4.

Limits searches and seizures

5.

The right to due process of law, including protection against self-incrimination

6.

Rights of a person accused of a crime, including the right to be represented by a lawyer

7.

Right of trial by jury in civil cases

8.

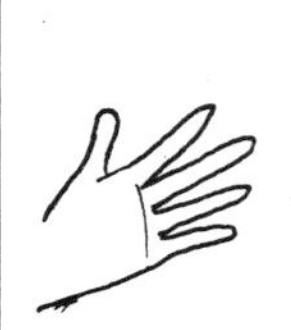

Unfair bail, fines, and punishment forbidden

9.

Citizens entitled to rights not listed in the Constitution

10.

Some powers reserved to the states or the people

16 Additional Amendments

11.

It's impossible for a citizen of one state to sue another state in federal court. (1795)

12.

New way of electing President and Vice President (1804)

13.

Abolished slavery (1865)

14.

Made former slaves citizens of the U.S. and of the state in which they lived (1868)

15.

No one could be denied the right to vote because of race, color or because of having been a slave. (1870)

16.
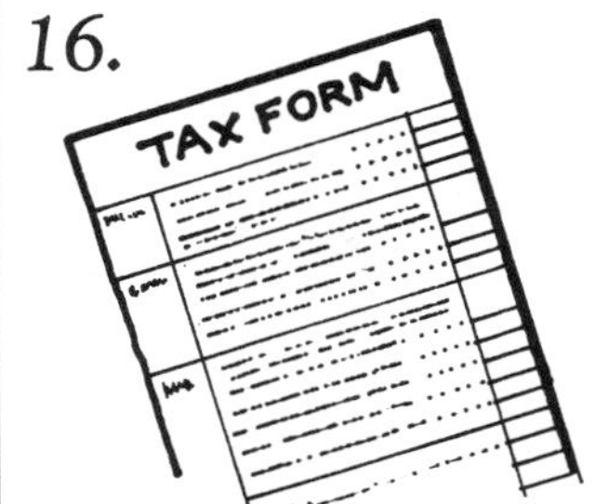

Power of federal government to collect income tax (1913)

17.

Election of senators by the people (1913)

18.

Banned the sale of alcohol (1919)

19.

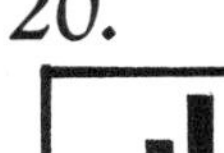

Gives women the right to vote (1920)

20.

Sets the date when the President's and Congress' terms begin

21.

Repeals the 18th Amendment

22.
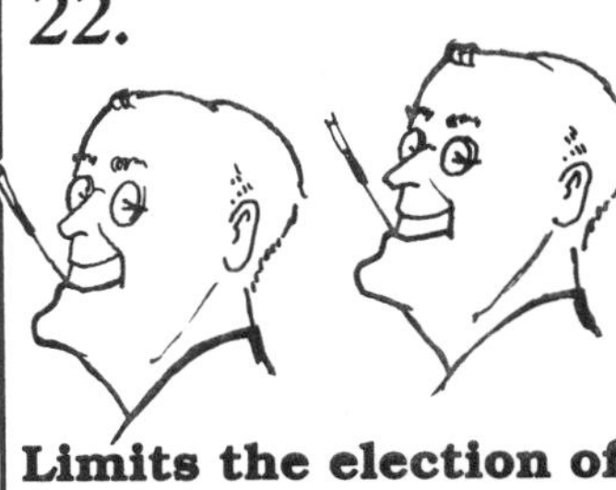
Limits the election of the same person as President to two times (1951)

23.

Gives people in Washington, D.C. the right to vote for President (1961)

24.
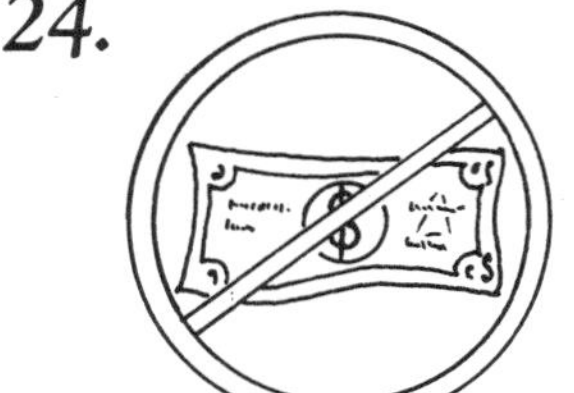
Forbids having to pay a tax to vote in a national election (1964)

25.

Says who is next in line if something happens to the President (1967)

26.

Sets 18 as the voting age (1971)

Bill of Rights continued

Categorization Gone Crazy (Activity 3)

Objective: To categorize amendments and other situations according to four given terms

Materials: dictionaries, one copy of the word wheel pattern (page 291) for each student, summary cards (pages 288-289), pens, pencils

Preparation: Display the summary cards of the first 10 amendments (or all 26 if you wish) to the Constitution so students can see them.

Directions: Divide the class into four groups and give each group a topic such as Liberty, Justice, Equality or Property. Give each student a copy of the word wheel pattern. Begin by asking students to look up the definition of their topic in the dictionary. Have students summarize the meaning of the word and then write both the term and its definition in the center of the word wheel pattern.

When students have done this, turn their attention to the summary cards of the first 10 Constitutional Amendments that you have posted. Ask the students to examine the cards and select which of the amendments would be included under their assigned topic. Encourage students to discuss their choice and to reach a consensus before listing an amendment on the word wheel. When the students have completed their evaluations, have each group present its categories to one another with explanations of its rationales for categorization.

Lead students in a discussion of common daily examples of those rights contained within the amendments like the reading of Miranda rights when a person is arrested or belonging to a church youth group.

To further the activity, display students' word wheels around the summary cards on a Bill of Rights bulletin board. Ask students to find examples representing each topic from biographies, stories they have read, movies they have seen, or people (famous or fictitious) they have observed.

Word Wheel Pattern

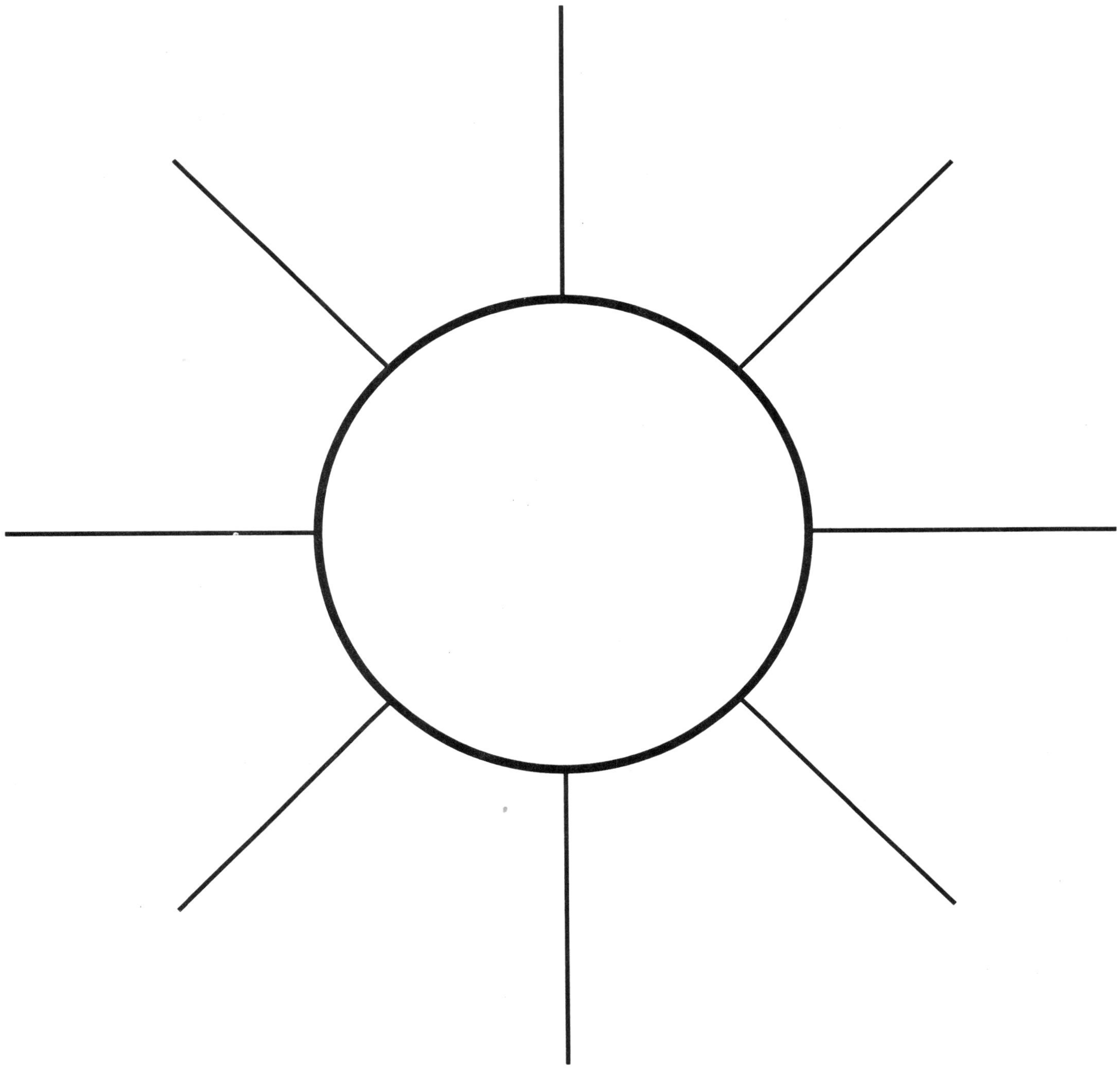

Bill of Rights continued

These Are Our Rights! (Activity 4)

Objective: To heighten student awareness on the presence of the Bill of Rights in current events

Materials: periodicals, newspapers, scissors, glue stick, construction paper

Directions: Create a "Current Bill of Rights News" bulletin board. Begin by asking students to read and clip any newspaper or periodical articles pertaining to issues involving freedoms secured in the Bill of Rights. Have the students mount the articles onto construction paper and attach them to the bulletin board. Share the articles weekly or biweekly with the class. Have students discuss and analyze the issues. You could also have students prepare a class magazine focusing on any Bill of Rights issues especially relevant to children.

Anticipating Amendments (Activity 5)

Objective: To advance students' critical thinking and creative writing skills

Materials: summary cards of all 26 amendments (pages 288-289), dates of amendments, writing paper, pencils

Directions: Have students examine the types of liberty cases that were common in the 18th, 19th and 20th centuries. (Examples: 18th century—first 11 amendments; 19th century—12-15 amendments; 20th century—16-26 amendments.) Then, ask students to predict what issues they anticipate will be common in the 21st century. Students may draw conclusions as to those issues that are currently in the spotlight from the current news articles posted on the bulletin board. Lead the students in a discussion of what rights they would like to see added as amendments to the Constitution in the next 50 years.

Bill of Rights continued

Other Ideas for Teaching the Bill of Rights

1. Assign writing projects such as essay, research or opinion papers to students about topics of historical, current or personal interest related to the Bill of Rights.
2. Obtain copies of written bills of rights of states or of other nations and compare and contrast them with the United States Bill of Rights.
3. Organize a celebration of the anniversary of the Bill of Rights—December 15, 1791. Encourage students to use historical facts in creative ways.
4. Discuss the meaning of the Bill of Rights for people who are journalists, authors, judges, police officers, citizens, lawyers, business leaders, religious leaders, politicians, etc.

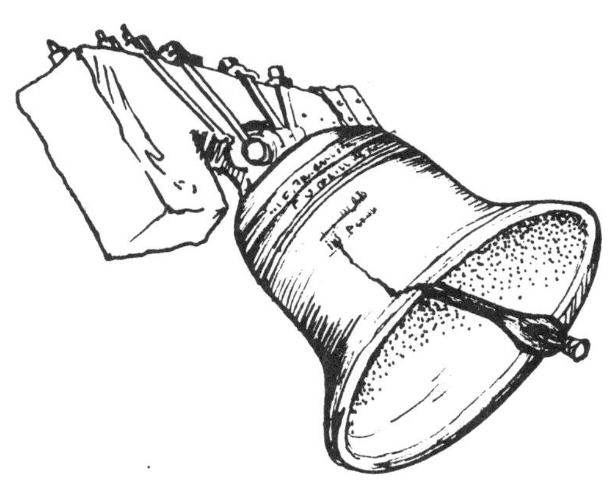

5. Organize a concert and feature music associated with liberty. Involve your school's chorus, band and/or orchestra. Sing songs such as "God Bless America," "We Shall Overcome," "America the Beautiful," etc.
6. Ask the art teacher to share famous paintings, sculptures, etc. whose themes involve human rights and liberty.
7. Help students create a papier-mâché replica of the Liberty Bell. Have students research its origin and history.
8. When an individual is native to the United States, he/she is automatically a citizen of the U.S. by birth. However, many people come to the U.S. and make a deliberate decision to become citizens of this country. Discuss the naturalization process with your students.
9. Have groups of students write plays demonstrating the rights and responsibilities of being a U.S. citizen.
10. Citizenship requires involvement, and one of the strongest ways of fulfilling our responsibilities is exercising our right to vote. Discuss this issue and hold a vote in your classroom.

Citizenship Windsock

Objective: To heighten students' awareness of our national heritage

Materials: scissors, 9" x 12" sheets of blue construction paper, glue, string or yarn, markers, red and white crêpe paper (the kind used for streamers), foil stars, pictures of the U.S. flags from the original one to the one flown today, hole punch

Directions: Citizenship includes being aware of the patriotic celebrations of our nation. Flag Day on June 14 is among these celebrations. Ask students what freedom in America means to them. Ask them how they feel about being free. Tell students that one symbol of freedom in our country is the American flag. Have students examine the flag in your classroom and list those observable facts about it (i.e. it is red, white and blue, has seven red stripes, six white stripes, 50 white stars and a field of blue). Ask the students if they know of any nicknames for the flag (i.e. "Old Glory," "Stars and Stripes"). Then, tell students that our first flag had only 13 stars. Share pictures of the flag and its changes throughout the years.

To create a windsock, give each student a 9" x 12" sheet of blue construction paper. Then, give each student seven red and six white strips of crêpe paper streamers about 18" long.

Students should then glue the strips to one 12" side of the blue construction paper, alternating colors.

While the streamers dry, have students glue foil stars or stars they cut out onto the blue construction paper.

continued on page 295

Citizen Windsock continued

Students should carefully bring the short ends of the blue construction paper together to form a cylinder and glue them together.

Students punch three holes at the top of the blue paper in a triangular formation so that the windsock will be balanced.

Three pieces of string about 12" long are cut by students. Then, students tie them in the holes that have been punched.

Tie the three pieces of string together at the top in a big knot.

Extension: Read *I Pledge Allegiance* by June Gwanson which breaks down the various parts of the pledge and defines each part. Discuss the importance of the "promise." Brainstorm with students places where they have seen the American flag and times when they have recited the Pledge of Allegiance.

Share the flag rules (below) with the class. If there are Boy Scouts or Girl Scouts in your class, ask them to demonstrate how to fold and care for an American flag.

Flag Rules

1. Fly the flag at every school and official place.
2. Take the flag down in bad weather.
3. Keep the flag from touching the ground.
4. Fold the flag to put it away.
5. Lower the flag to half mast to honor the dead.
6. Take the flag down at dusk unless it is illuminated.

A Floor Map Story

The objectives of the four activities below and on page 297 are to create a class story in which the setting involves a floor plan of your school and to map the story.

Map It Out! (Activity 1)

Objective: To compare a sketch with a floor plan

Materials: drawing paper, pencils, book *Mouse Views* by Bruce McMillan

Directions: Read *Mouse Views* to students. Be sure to discuss the map at the end of the book. The following activity is a variation of this story.

Discuss with students what a floor plan is. Provide examples if possible. Then, explain to students that they are going to create a floor plan of one of the floors in their school.

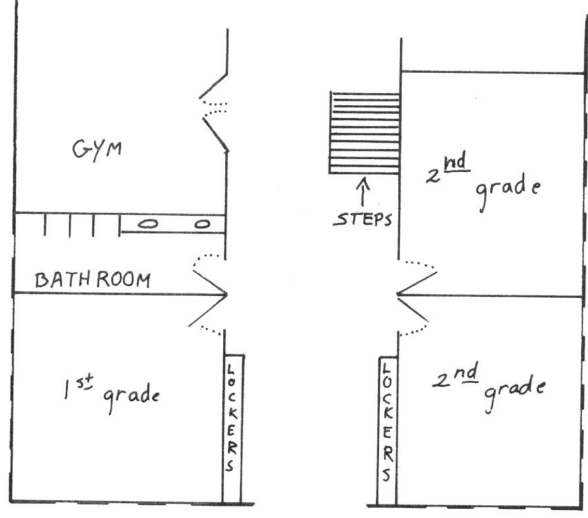

Ask students to sketch the floor they will be mapping. They should begin by drawing a hallway. Next, ask students to try and visualize what rooms they would see if they were to walk down that hallway. Ask students questions such as: "Are the rooms all the same size? How many rooms are on the left side? How many are on the right? Should the gym look the same as the nurse's office?"

Next, take a walk down the hallway students sketched with their sketches in hand. Move slowly so that students can take "notes" to correct any errors on their rough sketch. Go back to the classroom and discuss what students saw and what was drawn.

What We Saw! (Activity 2)

Objective: To illustrate part of an object

Materials: paper, pencils, crayons, markers

Directions: Now that students have an idea and a "feel" for their floor plan, they can create a wordless book entitled, "What Our Class Saw." Have students take another walk. This time, their job will be to choose one item from a room you assign them and illustrate it to create one page of the book. Divide students into groups and assign each group a room on the floor plan. For example, three students may be assigned to the gym, three students to a custodial closet, three students to Mrs. Decker's third-grade classroom, etc.

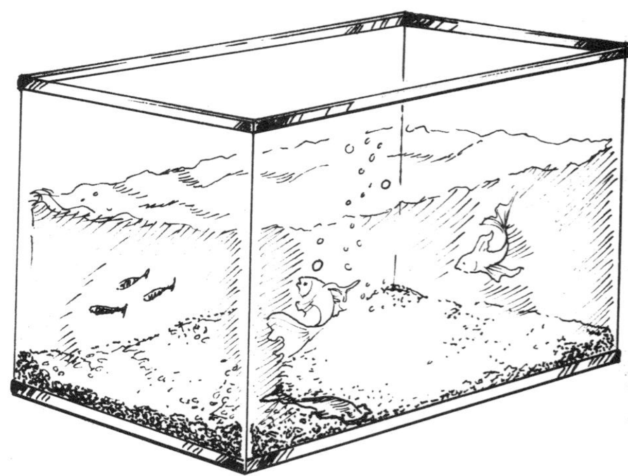

continued on page 297

A Floor Map Story continued

What We Saw! (Activity 2) continued

Encourage students to choose items to draw that are unique to their particular room (i.e. Only Mrs. Decker's room has a class pet, only the music room contains a drum, etc.). When the walk is completed and you have returned to the classroom, instruct students to draw only a portion of their chosen item. If a student chose to draw the rabbit from Mrs. Decker's third-grade classroom, that student could then illustrate the pet's ear or tail. When all students have completed their illustrations, assemble them in the order they would appear on the floor plan.

Chart It! (Activity 3)

Objective: To draw rooms to scale

Materials: graph paper, tape, pencils, pens, measuring tape

Directions: If large graph paper isn't available, tape several sheets of 8 1/2" x 11" graph paper together so that you can create a chart-size floor plan. Groups of students will need to make a trip to their assigned room to take measurements. When students have completed this task, create a scale for the floor plan.

Next, students should calculate the size of their room as it will appear on the floor plan, according to the scale you have selected. You can draw the rooms on the graph paper for students and complete the floor plan by including the scale, labeling the rooms and creating a title.

Guess! (Activity 4)

Objectives: To guess what an object is by looking at only part of it and to locate where it belongs on a map

Materials: illustrations from Activity 3

Directions: With the assembled illustrations in hand, share the pictures with the class. As you and the class guess what the illustrations are a part of, ask students to locate the origins of the objects on the floor plan. Mark the route of your walk on the floor plan. Last, have students give themselves a hand for a job well done!

Write, Hide, Read and Go Seek!

Objective: To write and read directions

Materials: paper, pencils, a small prize supplied by students (i.e. a small treat, a pencil, a note, etc.)

Directions: To play, students must write directions for another classmate to read and follow. The directions should lead to a small prize supplied by the student who wrote the directions.

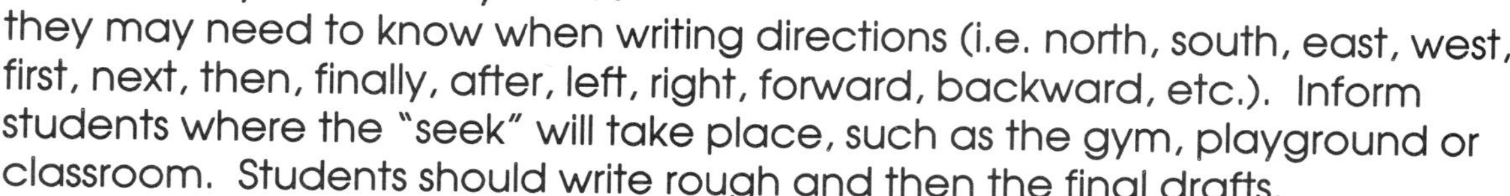

Begin by brainstorming with students any vocabulary words they may need to know when writing directions (i.e. north, south, east, west, first, next, then, finally, after, left, right, forward, backward, etc.). Inform students where the "seek" will take place, such as the gym, playground or classroom. Students should write rough and then the final drafts.

When all students have finished writing, they should hide the secret prizes according to their written directions. Next, pair up students. Have them exchange papers and "Read and Seek!" When all students have located their prize, discuss the successes and problems of the activity. Did students include all the necessary information? Were the directions clear? To conclude the activity, ask students to evaluate it by recording one problem and one success.

Symbol Survey

Objectives: To familiarize students with the purpose of symbols and to understand the purpose of standardized symbols

Materials: one copy of the survey form (page 299) for every two students, book *I Read Symbols* by Tana Hoban, crayons, four large sheets of construction or chart paper

Directions: Pair up students. The pairs take turns asking each other the questions outlined on the form. One student uses the left side of the form and the other uses the right side. Each student records his/her partner's responses without using any words, only symbols.

When all students have finished interviewing, have students share their findings and the symbols they used. Ask students to explain why they chose the symbols they did.

continued on page 299

Symbol Survey continued

After all students have had a chance to share, discuss the data by asking questions such as, "What were the similarities and differences in the responses? What were the similarities and differences in the symbols?"

Ask students why it was difficult to understand someone else's response recordings. (Because they were all different i.e. pizza could have been represented by a triangle, a circle or a "p", etc.).

If possible, share Tana Hoban's book *I Read Symbols* with the class. Discuss with students why we use symbols. Next, record all the different responses from the questionnaires on the board. Tally each one. Break students into four groups. Assign each of the groups the job of unifying, or standardizing, the symbols so that each response is represented by one symbol.

Extension: Have students create a pictograph using the information and symbols. Students should create a separate pictograph for each question on the survey.

Symbol Survey

Interviewer ____________________ | Interviewer ____________________

Interviewee ____________________ | Interviewee ____________________

FAVORITE FOOD	FAVORITE MOVIE	FAVORITE FOOD	FAVORITE SUBJECT
FAVORITE SUBJECT	FAVORITE PASTIME	FAVORITE MOVIE	FAVORITE PASTIME

Coordinated Housing

F G H I
6 7 8 9
STEP
DUKE
KNIGHTS AVE
SPHERE CIRCLE
CIRCLE DR
North Park
ROYAL OAKS
QUEENSWAY BLVD
OPAL DR
MATISSE
AZURE
VERDI
MIRO
CERISE
SMART
DUFY
MOZART
ARGENT
BACH
Park

Objectives: To locate home addresses on a map and to identify the corresponding coordinates

Materials: a map of your town/city which includes coordinates (phone book maps often do), index cards cut in half (one half of a card for each student), coffee can or similar, large piece of paper, crayons, markers

Directions: Hang the map of your city/town on the bulletin board or wall. Before beginning the activity, assign students to find out what streets are located near their home.

Next, discuss what coordinates are and what they are used for. (The game "Battleship" provides experience with coordinates.) Display the map and ask students to describe where something is located without citing coordinates. This will help students realize the use and value of coordinates. You may also want to use an imaginary map including coordinates on an overhead projector to help students understand. Independently, have students examine the map and write down their name and the coordinates of their home on an index card.

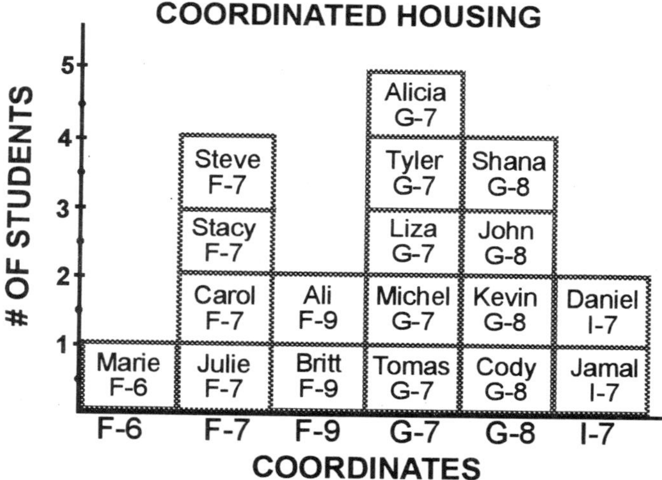

Set up a bar graph. Label the vertical axis **# of students** and the horizontal axis **Coordinates**. Survey the class to find out the variation of coordinates (i.e. How many students live in the coordinate area of G-7?). Next, call out a set of coordinates and have all students with those coordinates bring their card up to you. Glue the cards to the graph to create a bar. (See illustration.) Continue with this procedure until all coordinates have been exhausted. Title the graph and summarize the outcome.

Cookie Pictograph

Objective: To introduce or review the concept of pictographs by creating one as a class

Materials: large sheets of paper, crayons, one sandwich cookie per student, milk, cups, napkins

continued on page 301

Cookie Pictograph continued

Directions: Hang the large sheet of paper in students' view. Give each student a cookie and a cup of milk. Tell them that they are to begin eating the cookie, but before they are finished with it, you are going to stop them to discuss the cookie. Have students begin eating the cookie without discussion. After 30 seconds or so, stop the students from eating their cookies. Ask them what their method was in eating the cookie. Did they eat the inside cream first, or the outside cookie? Did they simply bite into it without taking it apart?

Record their responses and the number of responses on the board. Let students finish their cookies while discussing how the information can be set up in a pictograph. Divide the large paper into sections, writing a few words to describe the cookie-eating methods in each one of the sections. Decide on symbols to represent each of the cookie-eating methods and determine the value of each symbol. Place the symbols on the graph. Create a title and a key. Discuss what the purpose of presenting information in this manner may be. Discuss with students the other kinds of information which could be presented in a pictograph.

City, Suburb or Town? Where Would You Choose to Live?

Objective: To master the vocabulary and properties of cities, suburbs and towns

Materials: paper, pencils, books, pamphlets

Directions: With students, list the attributes of each of the three types of communities. Collect information about one specific city, suburb and small town, preferably all located in the same state. (The job is easier if you choose three communities from your own state. This way, you can gather information by conducting personal or phone interviews. Perhaps even a phone book would help a student learn something about the community.) Students will work in cooperative groups to determine which of the three communities they feel is best for them. Students need to determine from the information they collect where they would choose to live and why.

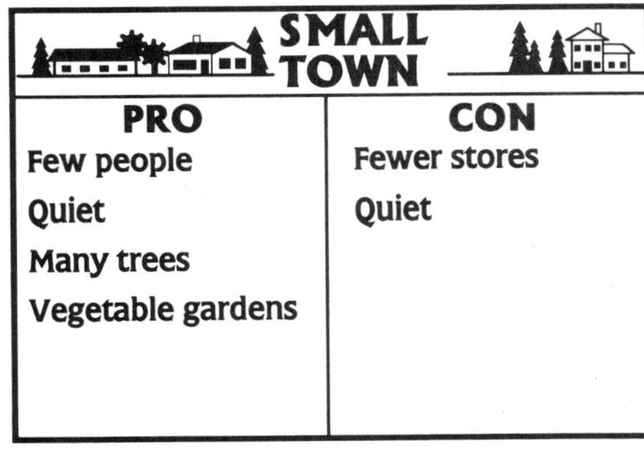

SMALL TOWN

PRO	CON
Few people	Fewer stores
Quiet	Quiet
Many trees	
Vegetable gardens	

continued on page 302

City, Suburb or Town? . . . continued

CITY	
PROS	CONS
Museums Exciting Many Stores	Noisy Few trees Traffic Lots of People

Across the top of their paper, students should write the names of the three types of communities and then brainstorm what they already know to be the pros and cons of living in each of these communities. (A student may list "lots of stores" as a pro under city, and they may list "lots of traffic" as a con.) Students should then work with their group to share and continue the pro/con list for each type of community. (A pro listed on one student's paper may be listed as a con on another student's paper.)

When the group work is finished, discuss the lists as a class. Direct students to draw a star next to each item on their list that appeals to them the most. Next, they should draw a sad face next to each item on the list they that find the most unappealing.

Finally, students should evaluate the likes and dislikes they marked, and make a choice— city, suburb or town. Finish the activity by having students write about their choice and why and how they made their decision.

School Year Time Line

Students will understand the concept of time lines with this activity. Since it is introduced in September, it can be quickly and easily reinforced each and every month.

Objective: To create a time line of school/classroom activities as the year progresses

Materials: paper for the time line, paper, ruler, markers

Directions: To create the time line, hang your paper (you may want to use the entire wall) and evenly space each of the school months on it. Number each of these sections from 1-30 (or 31). These will represent the days of the month. You may want to begin the time line by marking some or all of the activities already posted on the school calendar (i.e. the science fair, a fund-raising project, issuing of report cards, etc.). Then, the time line can also serve as a reminder of events for you and the students.

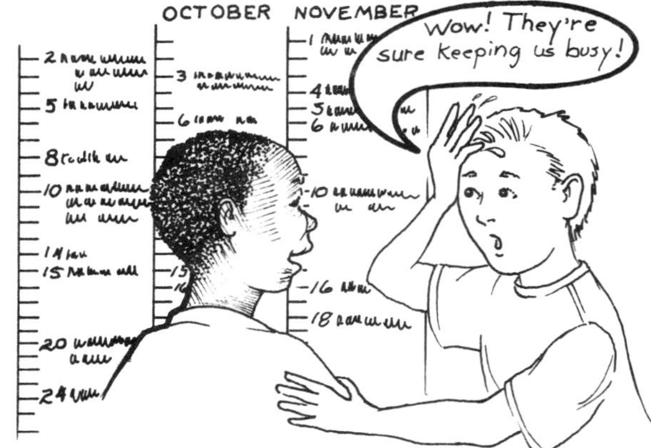

As the year progresses, add important events to the time line as they occur. You could put groups of students in charge of recording the events for each of the months. You may want to have students vote for the events that should be included. At the end of each month and at the end of the year, students will be able to recall and admire all they have accomplished.

Land Forms in 3-D

Objective: To create a model of land forms

Materials: a large piece of cardboard to act as a base for the land form (about the size of a table in your room), natural colors of paint, paintbrushes, newspaper, flour, water, glue, shoe boxes, oaktag, powdered detergent (white), paper plate, books depicting all types of land forms

Directions: Have students help you create a list of land forms (mountains, plateaus, hills, islands, prairies, plains, rivers, lakes, oceans, coasts, etc.). Explain to students that they will work together to create a model of various land forms. Groups of students can work together on specific land forms, or students can work individually. (For directions on how to create various land forms, see below.) When models are complete, assemble them on the cardboard base and have students paint them. Be sure to discuss where, how and why the land forms are to be placed on the cardboard base. (For example, water flows down ice-capped mountains to form rivers. Water collects from rivers to form lakes. etc.) Students can label the land forms and add construction paper or twigs to act as trees if desired. Snow can be added using the white detergent and glue.

Have students follow the directions below to create:

- **Mountains/Hills**—Create cones of various heights out of oaktag. Cover the cones with papier-mâché to give them an authentic look.
- **Plateaus**—Cut shoe boxes to the size you would like your plateau to be. Turn the box upside-down and papier-mâché the top.
- **Rivers, Lakes, Oceans**—Paint these directly onto the cardboard base.
- **Island(s)**—Turn a paper plate upside-down and papier-mâché it.

Community Features

Objective: To recognize and compare the influences of geographic or economic features upon communities

Materials: sentence strips, markers, world map

Directions: After studying a variety of communities, create this interactive bulletin board to reinforce student learning and to allow them to look at the same information in a variety of ways. Select one of the following geographic or environmental factors: mountains, water, deserts, islands, tropics, farmland, manufacturing, forests, coastline. Post the selection as a heading on the bulletin board.

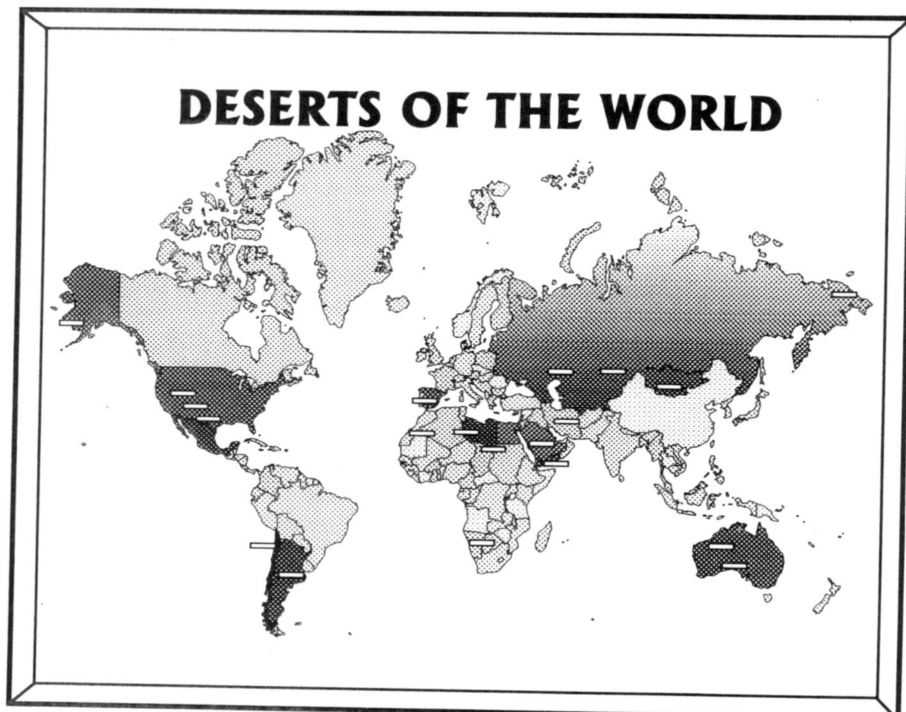

Throughout the day, have students brainstorm a list of communities that possess or are near that feature. Go over the list at the end the day and compare/contrast the cities that the students posted. Change the heading the next day and ask students to think about how the new topic relates to the cities already posted. Throughout the day, have the students remove any communities that do not fit the new category and add any that do. Continue changing and reorganizing the data. Allow students to change the headings, too.

Community Experiences

Objective: To develop an awareness of the relationship between geography, climate and one's lifestyle

Materials: posterboard, markers, reference books

Directions: Select urban communities from different geographic areas for students to study. As students study the areas, compare and contrast each community's lifestyle. Students might work on this throughout the year, as a culminating activity, independently, in groups or in pairs. Explain to students that climate, topography, soil and vegetation will influence the way in which people live within the community. Then, have the students create a variety of Venn diagrams to compare and contrast the specific communities. (See example shown.)

continued on page 305

Community Experiences continued

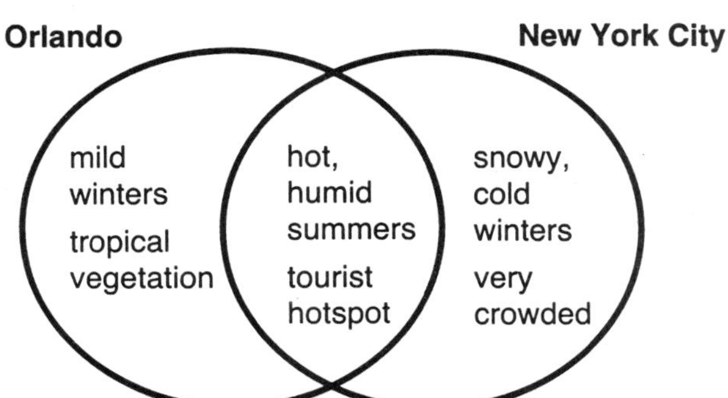

The topics for the diagrams may range from community types to occupations, food, shelter, clothing, recreation, climate, physical features, soil and vegetation, transportation, etc. The students may elect to do research in the library or refer to their text or classroom discussions to find their data. When the Venn diagrams are complete, have students share their findings with the class.

Extension: Ask the students to listen carefully to their classmates' descriptions of the various world communities studied. Then, have them select the community they would most like to visit and write a paragraph explaining their choice. Ask students to make at least three specific references learned from the Venn diagram for that community. Have them tell what is special about this city and what they would see and do there.

Vacation Destinations

Objectives: To locate cities on a state, country or world map and to develop a sense of geographical location

Materials: maps of world, country, your state and your county (if available), yarn or string, scissors, 3" x 3" square pieces of construction paper, markers, tacks, atlases and brochures

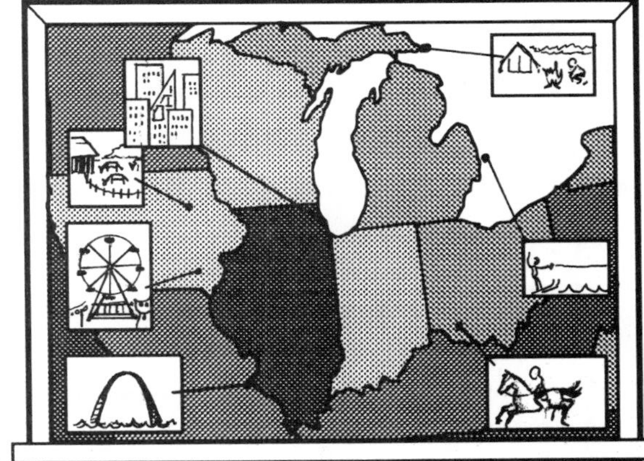

Directions: Prepare a bulletin board by posting maps of the world, country, your state and/or your county. Introduce the activity by asking the students to draw a picture of a vacation destination they have already visited, are planning to visit, or would like to visit in the future on a 3" x 3" piece of construction paper. Explain to students that they will be asked to locate the place on the appropriate map. Encourage students to consult an atlas, textbook, brochures, or their parents to obtain general directions for locating their vacation spot. When the students have completed their drawings, have them post the picture on the bulletin board next to the appropriate map. Have the students attach a piece of string/yarn from the picture to the actual location on the map. Secure the string/yarn with a tack. Allow time for students to share their experiences or dreams about these places.

Note: This is a fun activity to do before school vacations but be sure to use a local map for those students who will not be leaving town. Do not be surprised if you begin planning some new vacation destinations for your own family!

We Are the World!

Objectives: To construct a globe and to be aware of the land and water masses on Earth

Materials: a large beach ball or round balloon, newspaper, newsprint, paper towels, wheat paste or flour and water, white glue, container to mix in, paint, paintbrushes, paper, markers, globe, world map, large spoon

Directions: Have the children look at a globe and a flat representation of the globe. Point out to students the ocean and the continents, the equator, the Tropics of Cancer and Capricorn, the Arctic Circle and the Antarctic Circle, the North Pole and the South Pole.

Tell the children that the class is going to make a globe. In preparation, discuss with the class what you will put on the globe. Have each child make a list of what he/she thinks should go on the globe. The four categories below should form a basis for the globe.

Continents	Oceans	Lines of Latitude	Seas	
North America	Pacific Ocean	Arctic Circle	Mediterranean Sea	Yellow Sea (Asia)
South America	Atlantic Ocean	Tropic of Cancer	South China Sea	Sea of Japan
Europe	Indian Ocean	Equator	Bering Sea	North Sea
Asia	Arctic Ocean	Tropic of Capricorn	Caribbean Sea	Red Sea
Africa		Antarctic Circle	Sea of Okhotsk	Black Sea
Australia			East China Sea	Baltic Sea
Antarctica				

To prepare the globe, make one of the papier-mâché recipes as described below. Use a plastic container, a pie tin or waxed carton to mix the paste mixture in.

- **Wheat Paste** (like paper hangers use)
Add water to wheat paste making it into a fairly thin mixture.
- **Flour and Water**
Mix together flour and water into a fairly loose paste. Add a little white glue to make it stronger.

continued on page 307

We Are the World continued

Tear the newspaper into strips. Dip the strips of newspaper into the paste mixture. Scrape off the paste with your fingers until it stops dripping. When the paper feels slippery, it is ready to be used. Place it on the beach ball and smooth it down. Continue this until the beach ball is covered. When it is thoroughly dry, apply another layer. Continue in this manner for five or six layers. Make the last layer plain newsprint paper or white paper towels torn into strips.

After the globe is completely dry, have students paint it blue. Then, have the children draw or trace the continents on construction paper. Each continent should be a different color. Be sure to have the relative sizes correct. Each continent should be labeled and cut out. Place them on the globe in their correct location. Be sure to add the following major islands: Japan, New Zealand, Madagascar, Hawaii, Philippines, Indonesia, Iceland, Greenland and the Caribbean Islands.

Using markers, label the oceans, the seas and the lines of latitude listed on page 306. This will be the basic globe. Below are other extension activities that can be used depending upon your objectives.

1. Using symbols, you can place other land features and/or political subdivisions (i.e. mountains, rivers, lakes, political subdivisions, cities, etc.) on the globe.
2. To make a topographical globe, tear newspaper into small pieces. Soak the paper in warm water for 24 hours. Drain off the water and squeeze the paper in your hand until you have a pulpy mass. Mix it with the paste until it will hold together. It should be soft and pliable and you should be able to shape it like clay. Put some on the globe in the appropriate places to form mountain ranges (i.e. Rockies, Appalachian, Pyrenees, Alps, Himalaya, Ural, Adirondack, Andes, Great Smoky, Green Mountains, White Mountains, etc.).

3. Draw in lines of latitude and longitude.
4. Label the countries within the continents as well as any other seas students come up with.
5. Draw in or paste on other islands such as Solomon, Marshall, Falkland, etc.

Let's Make a Match!

Objective: To reinforce the states and their capitals

Materials: 2 boxes, small pieces of paper, basket

Directions: Write the name of each state on a small piece of paper. Do the same for the capitals. Put the names of the states in one box. Put the names of the capitals in another box. Have the students take turns making a selection from one or the other box. Do this until all 100 are selected (50 states and 50 capitals).

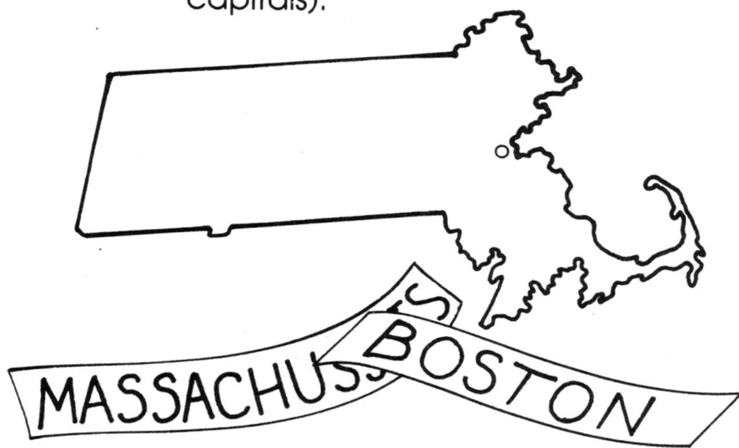

Give each student a turn to read one of his/her selections. The student who has his/her "match" (state/capital) puts the pair in a separate basket.

Students continue taking turns in this manner making pairs matching state to capital. If the student who has the match to the name called does not recognize it, move on to the next turn. Eventually, as there are fewer names left, the more difficult ones may become more evident.

Capital Locations

Objective: To reinforce states and their capitals

Materials: outline of map of 50 states, box, small pieces of paper, push pins

Directions: Attach a large outline of the map on the bulletin board. Each state should have only the state name and a dot for the location of the capital city on it. Write each of the capital city names on a small piece of paper. Put them in a box and have the students draw the names.

Have the students take turns reading the names of the cities. If they know the correct placement on the map, they may attach their city to the correct state. If they don't know the correct state, move on to the next student. Eventually, as fewer choices are left, the correct placement will become more evident.

A Model Community

Objective: To plan a model community

Materials: book *The Living City* by Frank Lloyd Wright, 9" x 12" sheets of paper, pencils, kraft or mural paper, tape, boxes or Legos™ or other construction toys, twigs, paint, paintbrushes, small toy vehicles, writing paper

Directions: Discuss with the students the community in which you live. If you are in a large city, you might want to confine your discussion to the neighborhood.

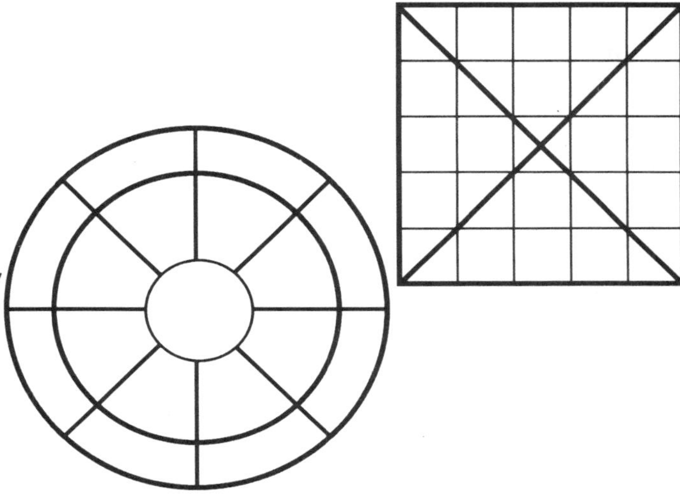

On the board, list some of the things in the community that are important for the health, welfare and well-being of the people living there. Some examples include schools, hospitals, post office, parks, recreational areas (i.e. tennis courts, baseball fields), playgrounds, swimming facilities, stores, transportation facilities (i.e. train station, bus station, airport), houses (i.e. private and/or apartment houses), library, fire stations, police stations, government buildings (i.e. town hall), churches, synagogues, etc. At this point, you might want to introduce students to the architecture of Frank Lloyd Wright and the multi-axial plan upon which Washington, D.C. was planned by Pierre L'Enfant beginning in 1791. Spaces between radiating avenues are divided either geometrically or on a gridiron pattern in Washington, D.C.

To begin the city, plan the layout of the streets. Have each student make a small scale plan on a 9" x 12" sheet of paper. Decide with the class which street plan you will adopt. (See examples shown.) Tape kraft or mural paper onto a large board or table top. Have the students draw in the street plan you have selected. Discuss with students the placement of the various facilities. Have the students justify why they might place a particular building or park, for example, in the center of town or in the outskirts. Ask students why they think the community should be built around a park or a town hall and why. Ask them where the stores should be, where the airport should be, etc.

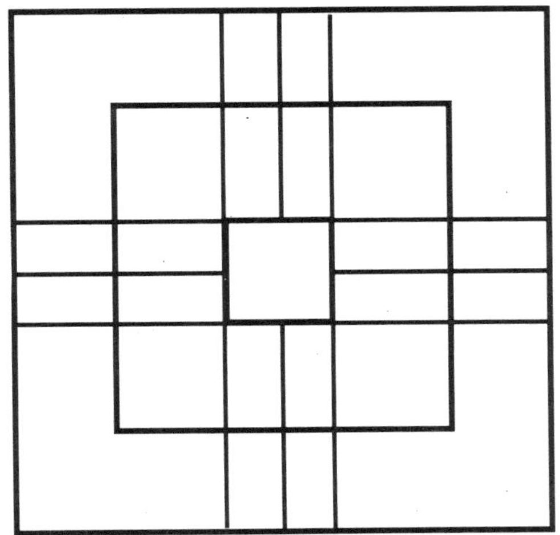

When building the community, buildings can be constructed from various size boxes, from Legos™ or students can use buildings from various construction toys (if available).

continued on page 310

A Model Community continued

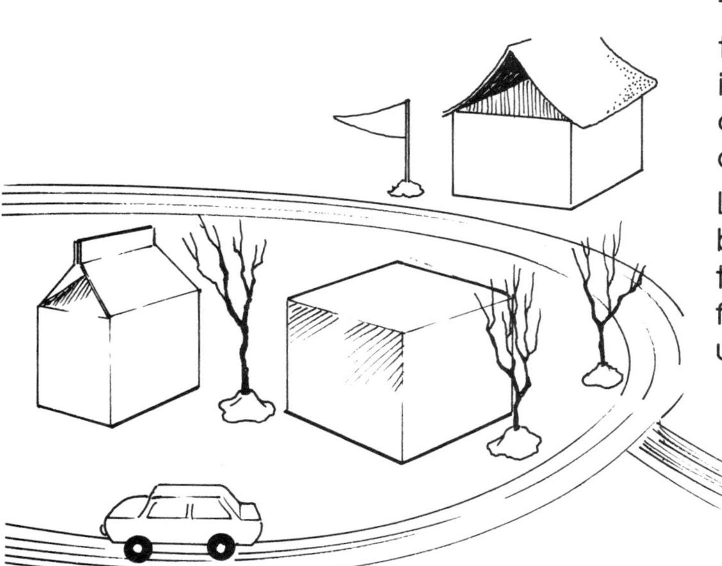

Twigs from trees or bushes can be used for the trees, and grassy areas can be painted in; toy airplanes can be placed at the airport and small toy cars, trucks and buses can be placed on the streets and roads.

Let students make flags to fly for the public buildings such as the post office, school, town hall, etc. When your community is finished, have each student write an essay using the following outline.

A. A name for this community
B. Would I like to live here now?
   1. Why or why not?
   2. What do I like or not like about this community?
C. Would I like to live here after I am grown up?
   1. Why or why not?
D. Is there something I would like to change?
   1. What?
   2. How?
   3. Why?
   4. To what?

Infomercials

Objective: To have students review and reteach content material to the rest of the class

Materials: video camera and tape (if possible); Other materials will depend on each infomercial.

Directions: Discuss the concept of "infomercials" with students Explain to them that they will be creating infomercials. Assign small groups of students a section of material to be taught. Students should include this information into a type of play. Inform students that they must create and use at least one visual (i.e. a chart, graph or table) in their infomercial. When students are ready, have them perform their infomercials. If possible, videotape them and watch them together.

Native Inhabitants—A Community Profile

Objectives: To learn about people native to specific communities

Materials: encyclopedias and other references about communities, paper, pens, copy of the outline (below)

Directions: Discuss with the students how people around the country and/or around the world live in different kinds of homes, wear different kinds of clothing, eat different kinds of foods, enjoy different types of recreation, etc.

Have each student select a community. It can be local, national or international. It can be a large city or a small town. Each student should then research the community of his/her choice and take notes following the outline. When the outline is completed, have each student write a report translating his/her notes into paragraphs using complete sentences.

Remind students that the outline is for taking notes only. They don't have to use complete sentences on it. However, when using this information for their report, tell students that they must write in complete sentences in paragraphs and use correct punctuation.

A. Name and brief description of the community
   1. Location—what state or country? Is it in the mountains, at the shore, inland, in the desert?
   2. Size

B. Language(s) spoken
   1. If more than one language is commonly spoken here, why do you think this is so?

C. Shelter
   1. Type of housing (apartments, private homes, igloos, huts, etc.)
   2. What are the houses built with (brick, wood, stucco, mud, clay, adobe, etc.)?

D. Food
   1. What ethnic foods are prevalent?
   2. What ingredients are prevalent?

E. Holidays
   1. Patriotic
   2. Religious
   3. When and why are they celebrated?
   4. How are they celebrated?

F. Local Customs
   1. Festivals
   2. Local celebrations

G. Local Government
   1. Officials
   2. Elections
   3. Local laws

H. Recreation
   1. Special sports
   2. Recreation related to location (cold climate, hot climate, seashore, mountains, etc.)

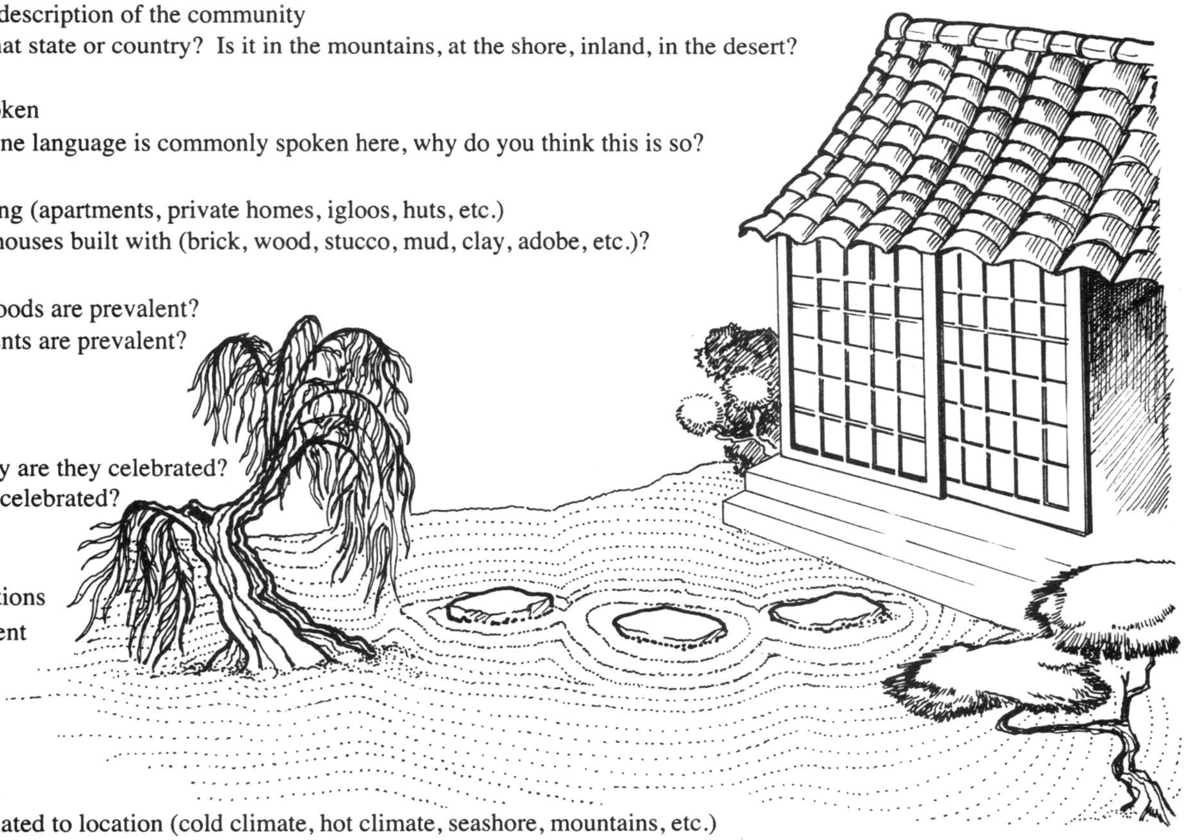

Careers

Objective: To learn about various careers

Directions: Discuss with students different careers that people have. Talk about professions, skills, careers in art, music, transportation, service fields, etc.

Have each student select a career to research. It can be a field he/she might be interested in or an area he/she might want to find out about. There will be three areas for the students to research and to give their reactions to. The areas are included in the outline below which should be given to the students to follow.

An **ENTOMOLOGIST** studies insects.

The students can research this topic in different ways. The library is always a good source for research. They may also interview someone in their field, or they may visit a place of business which encompasses the career choice.

Extension: Have each student make a collage depicting the career he/she chose. Students can include pictures and words in their collages.

A. Requirements for Career
   1. What education is needed?
   2. What training is needed?
   3. What skill(s) is needed?
   4. What preparation must take place?
   5. Is there a licensing requirement? a test requirement?
   6. How do you start to work in this field? job? apprentice? on your own?

B. On the Job
   1. What kind of work does this career entail?
   2. What do you envision the work day to be like?
   3. Is the job always the same or does it change from time to time?
   4. What is the time factor? Does the work involve regular hours or can you set your own time?

C. Why should someone want to go into this field?
   1. Interesting
   2. Exciting/fun
   3. Helpful
   4. Money
   5. Family's interests
   6. Skill that one may have

Bulletin Boards

Bulletin boards can be used in a variety of ways. They are great to use to introduce a new theme, concept or idea, and they also provide a wonderful place to let students show off good work.

Interactive bulletin boards should be a vital part of every classroom. As reinforcement tools, these bulletin boards provide a fun way to keep concepts and ideas fresh in students' minds. The boards also become more meaningful to students when they take an active part in creating and/or using them.

In addition to the bulletin boards presented in this chapter, there are other bulletin board ideas found throughout the book that are relevant to specific activities.

Here's the Scoop!

Objective: To welcome students to your class

Materials: all different colors of construction paper, scissors, glue, marker

Directions: One way to welcome students to your class is to create a fresh and friendly display of ice cream cones. Place each student's name on a scoop of ice cream. Add the title: **Here's the Scoop!**

In order to become more familiar with one another, students can conduct class surveys. The surveys can include questions about family, pets, hobbies, favorite foods, etc. The surveys can be displayed around the bulletin board to let the rest of the school in on the "scoop." As a class, write a story compiling the survey information. Write the story on chart paper and hang it below your "cool" new group!

We've Got Personality!

Objective: To communicate likes, dislikes, personalities, plans for the future, and hobbies using pictures and slogans

Materials: shoe boxes, wrapping paper, magazines, scissors, glue

Directions: Have each student cover a shoe box with wrapping paper. Instruct students to decorate their shoe box with pictures and slogans cut from old magazines. Tell them that their choices could reflect things they like and dislike. Have them think about the following: things that make them happy, things that they are good at, adjectives that best describe them, things that make them feel the best about themselves, careers that might interest them.

When the boxes are completed, display them all together on a classroom shelf. Make a sign that reads: **We've Got Personality!** Place each individual personality box near the "Look Who's in the Spotlight!" (page 222) bulletin board. Make a special time for each student to share his/her pictures, strengths, interests and dreams.

Fall Is in the Air!

Objectives: To record observations of the autumn season using the five senses

Materials: one copy of the oak leaf pattern below per student, crayons, pencils, scissors, brown mural paper, note pads, pencils, writing paper

Directions: After a lesson about the five senses, take your students outside to experience autumn. Remind students how our fives senses are used to help us observe and gather information.

To begin the activity, instruct students to find a quiet spot to look at, listen to, smell, touch and taste (or at least think about tasting) the sights, sounds, scents and sensations of autumn. Let students record their ideas on a small note pad if you like. After about 15 minutes, return to the classroom. Have each student begin to compose a short paragraph incorporating his/her observations. When the students have edited their writings for spelling and punctuation, have the students write their final drafts on their oak leaf pattern. Then, using the side of a crayon, have the students add some fall color on top of their writing. Meanwhile, create a simple tree trunk and branches out of brown mural paper and attach them to a bulletin board. Attach the students' autumn observations to the branches of the tree. Remember to place some leaves on the ground, falling through the air, or in fun piles to jump in!

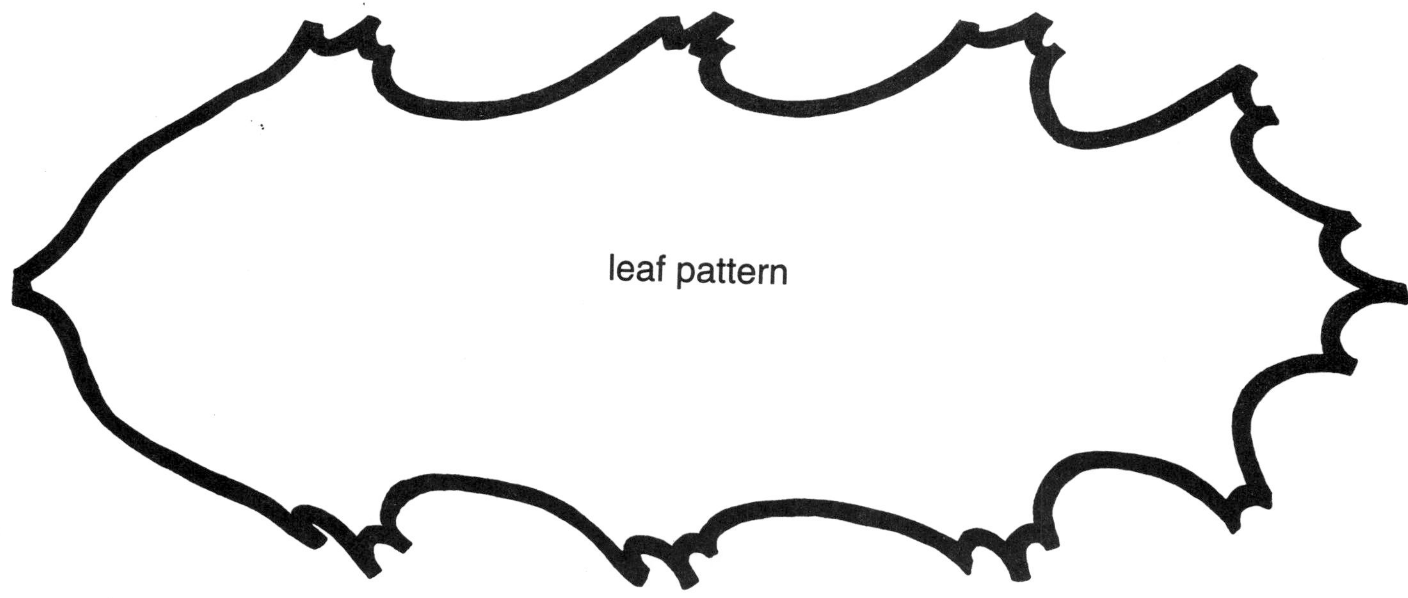

It Figures!

Objective: To recognize and illustrate figures of speech

Materials: drawing paper, crayons, markers, scissors

Directions: Ask students to brainstorm figures of speech. (See examples below.) Direct students to choose one phrase representative of figurative language and illustrate its literal meaning. Have students cut out their illustration. Put the illustrations on the bulletin board in a collage fashion. This creates a humorous bulletin board and helps students remember the concept.

Examples of Figures of Speech

Let's hit the road.
Hit the lights!
The setting sun sank into the ocean.
My heart sank.
She exploded with laughter.
You could hear the words for miles.
She left with a heavy heart.
The cat got her tongue.
He put his food in his mouth.
The song ran through his mind.
Love is in the air!
Don't let the cat out of the bag.

Safety in Sports

Objectives: To emphasize the rules for safety in sports games and to emphasize the proper equipment to use or wear

Materials: drawing paper, crayons, markers, sentence strips

Directions: Have each student select his/her favorite sport or activity. Include such things as baseball, soccer, swimming, hiking, gardening, bicycling, camping, boating, horseback riding, etc.

Each student will draw a picture of himself/herself observing at least one rule of safety while participating in the selected activity. Cut out the picture and mount it on the bulletin board. Have each student then write a sentence on a sentence strip stating the safety rule illustrated. Mount this on the board under the appropriate picture.

Extension: Have students make charts listing the safety rules and safety equipment necessary for the activities selected.

Shape City

Objective: To reinforce geometry concepts

Materials: scissors, colored construction paper, stapler, markers

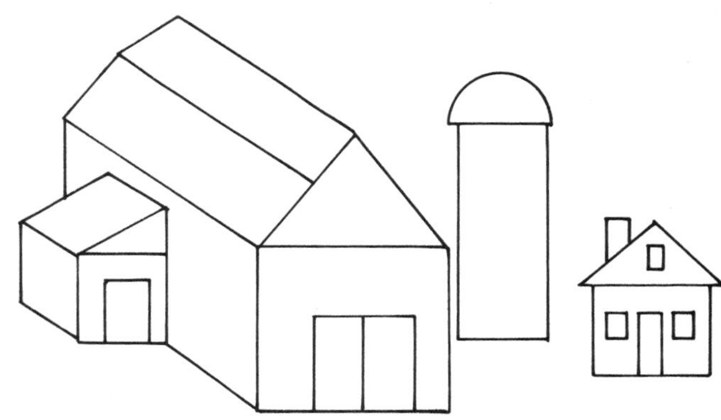

Directions: Divide a large bulletin board into three sections using a colorful border. Label each section one of the following, **In the City**, **In the Country**, and **In the Suburbs**. Then, divide the class into three groups and assign each group one of the community types. Have each group cut out a variety of geometric shapes in various colors and sizes. Discuss with each group how the shapes could be made into vehicles and buildings that would be characteristic of its assigned community. Allow the students to work together to create a scene using the geometric shapes, adding details such as people for interest.

Extension: This activity can also accommodate other classroom themes. For example, if your are studying the ocean, have students use the shapes to create an underwater scene or a beach scene. If you are learning about space, have the students create a space station, vehicles, planets, etc.

Pick a Pair of Pears

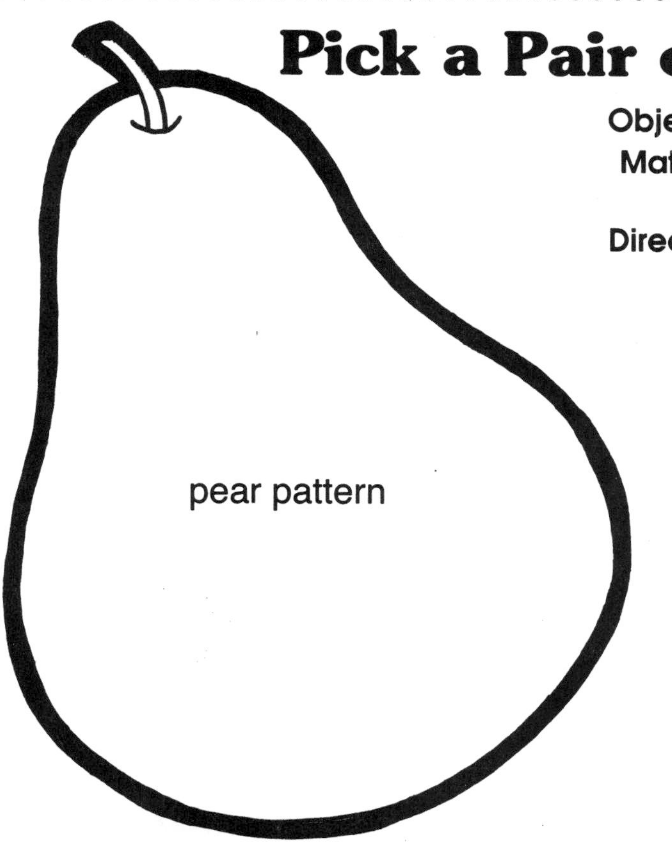

Objective: To practice matching concepts

Materials: two copies of the pear per student, scissors

Directions: Use the pairs of pears in any of the following ways: for two words that are synonyms, homonyms or antonyms, for vocabulary words and their definitions; for math facts, etc. Ask students to record the information of your choice and display them randomly on the board. Students can work in pairs to match pears. To make this interactive board self-correcting, code the backs of the pears that are pairs with matching numbers, letters or colors.

Hook Book Lending Library

Objective: To encourage writing and sharing of written work

Materials: several hooks and several loops (as used for weaving)

Directions: Set this up as either a bulletin board, a row of hooks around the room or on one wall. In any case, the hooks should be at a level students can conveniently reach but high enough to ensure student safety. Encourage students to put their creative writing work into book form to share with the class. Have students illustrate their books. They can then be stapled together, bound or assembled, with notebook rings.

Attach a loop (as used for weaving) to the upper left-hand corner of each book. Then, hang up the books on the hooks. Students may take a book off a hook to read, enjoy and return to the hook. After about two weeks, change the books, adding new ones. The Hook Book Lending Library can be rotated throughout the school year.

Suggestion: Velcro™ can also be used instead of hooks. If using Velcro™, add a blank page to the back of the book for the Velcro™. When the student author takes the book home to keep, the Velcro™ page can be removed without damage to the book.

My Gift to the World...

Objective: To have students think of ways they can contribute to their family, school, world, etc.

Materials: wrapping paper, one copy of the gift tag below per student, scissors

Directions: Cover a bulletin board with gift wrap. (You could ask each student to bring in a small, unusable piece and create a collage of gift wrap.) On the gift tag, ask students to record what they feel could be their biggest contribution to their family/school/community/world. (For example, I can recycle, I can help my community by..., I want to become a... so that I can..., I can help save energy by..., I can help senior citizens by..., I can help my family by..., I can help my school by..., I can become a better student by..., etc.) Display the gift tags randomly on the board.

gift tag pattern

Literature Selections

Language Arts

Adler, D. (1985). *My Dog and the Knock Knock Mystery.* New York: Holiday House.

Baker, B. (1983). *The Turkey Girl.* New York: Macmillan.

Base, G. (1988). *The Eleventh Hour.* New York: Abrams.

Bonsall, C. (1962). *Who's a Pest?* New York: Harper & Row.

Bunting, E. (1980). *The Robot Birthday.* New York: Dutton.

Christian, M. (1981). *April Fool.* New York: Macmillan.

Holland, M. (1958). *A Big Ball of String.* New York: Random House.

Howe, D. (1979). *Bunnicula.* New York: Atheneum.

Howe, J. (1982). *Howliday Inn.* New York: Atheneum.

Lobel, A. (1978). *Grasshopper on the Road.* New York: Harper.

Parish, P. (1972). *Play Ball Amelia Bedelia.* New York: Harper & Row.

Pearson, S. (1979). *Molly Moves Out.* New York: Dial.

Roop, P. (1985). *Keep the Lights Burning.* Minneapolis, MN: Carolrhoda Books.

Ross, P. (1985). *M & M and the Mummy Mess.* New York: Viking.

Taylor, M. (1984). *Mr. Pepper Stories.* New York: Atheneum.

Math

Hoban, T. (1986). *Shapes, Shapes and Shapes.* New York: Greenwillow.

Jonas, A. (1987). *Reflections.* New York: Greenwillow.

Mahy, M. (1987). *17 Kings and 42 Elephants.* New York: Dial.

Mathews, L. (1975). *Bunches and Bunches of Bunnies.* New York: Scholastic.

Winthrop, E. (1986). *Shoes.* New York: HarperTrophy.

Science

Allison, L. (1976). *Blood and Guts: A Working Guide to Your Own Insides.* Boston, MA: Little, Brown.

Branley, F. (1967). *Floating and Sinking.* New York: Crowell.

Bruun, R. (1982). *The Human Body.* New York: Random House.

Bulla, C. (1962). *What Makes a Shadow?* New York: Crowell.

Carle, E. (1969). *The Very Hungry Caterpillar.* New York: Philomel Books.

Carle, E. (1990). *The Very Quiet Cricket.* New York: Philomel Books.

De Paola, T. (1975). *The Cloud Book.* New York: Holiday House.

Gibbons, G. (1991). *The Puffins Are Back!* New York: HarperCollins.

continued on page 320

Literature Selections continued

Hooper, P. (1987). *A Bundle of Beasts.* Boston, MA: Houghton Mifflin.

Livingston, M.· (1984). *Sky Songs.* New York: Holiday House.

Marchesi, S. (1988). *The Glow in the Dark Night Sky Book.* New York: Random.

Martin, C. (1987). *I Can Be a Weather Forecaster.* Chicago, IL: Chicago Press.

Pringle, L. (1975). *Chains, Webs and Pyramids.* New York: Crowell.

Ryder, J. (1985). *Inside Turtle Shells, and Other Poems of the Field.* New York: Macmillan.

Shaw, C. (1947). *It Looked Like Spilt Milk.* New York: Harper.

Simon, S. (1984). *The Moon.* New York: Four Winds.

Tresselt, A. (1946). *Rain Drop Splash.* New York: Lothrop.

Whitney, C. (1985). *Whitney's Star Finder.* New York: Knopf.

Ziefert, H. (1988). *Egg Drop Day.* Boston, MA: Little, Brown.

Ziefert, H. (1987). *Trip Day.* Boston, MA: Little, Brown.

Ecology

Baker, J. (1991). *Window.* New York: Greenwillow.

Burton, V. (1942). *The Little House.* Boston, MA: Houghton Mifflin.

Caudill, R. (1976). *Wind, Sand and Sky.* New York: Dutton.

Fleischman, P. (1988). *Joyful Noise, Poems for Two Voices.* New York: Harper.

Lasky, K. (1985). *Home Free.* New York: Four Winds.

Lobel, A. (1983). *The Book of Pigericks: Pig Limericks.* New York: Harper & Row.

Peet, B. (1970). *The Wump World.* Boston, MA: Houghton Mifflin.

Seuss. (1971). *The Lorax.* New York: Random House.

Showers, P. (1994). *Where Does the Garbage Go?* New York: HarperCollins.

Udry, J. (1956). *A Tree Is Nice.* New York: Harper.

Yolen, J. (1986). *Ring of Earth.* San Diego, CA: Harcourt.

Van Allsburg, C. (1990). *Just a Dream.* Boston, MA: Houghton Mifflin.

Social Studies

Hoban, T. (1983). *I Read Signs.* New York: Greenwillow Books.

Hoban, T. (1983). *I Read Symbols.* New York: Greenwillow Books.

Fritz, J. (1987). *Shhh! We're Writing the Constitution!* New York: Putnam.

Leedy, L. (1990). *The Furry News: How to Make a Newspaper.* New York: Holiday House.

Maestro, B. (1987). *A More Perfect Union.* New York: Lothrop.

McMillan, B. (1983). *Mouse Views.* New York: Holiday House.

